# INSIGHT ⊙ GUIDES

# CARIBBEAN
## THE LESSER ANTILLES

WITHDRAWN

www.insightguides.com/Caribbean

# ◉ Walking Eye App

Your Insight Guide now includes a free app and eBook, dedicated to your chosen destination, all included for the same great price as before. They are available to download from the free Walking Eye container app in the App Store and Google Play. Simply download the Walking Eye container app to access the eBook and app dedicated to your purchased book. The app features an up-to-date A to Z of travel tips, information on events, activities and destination highlights, as well as hotel, restaurant and bar listings. See below for more information and how to download.

## MULTIPLE DESTINATIONS AVAILABLE

Now that you've bought this book you can download the accompanying destination app and eBook for free. Inside the Walking Eye container app, you'll also find a whole range of other Insight Guides destination apps and eBooks, all available for purchase.

## DEDICATED SEARCH OPTIONS

Use the different sections to browse the places of interest by category or region, or simply use the 'Around me' function to find places of interest nearby. You can then save your selected restaurants, bars and activities to your Favourites or share them with friends using email, Twitter and Facebook.

## FREQUENTLY UPDATED LISTINGS

Restaurants, bars and hotels change all the time. To ensure you get the most out of your guide, the app features all of our favourites, as well as the latest openings, and is updated regularly. Simply update your app when you receive a notification to access the most current listings available.

Shopping in Oman still revolves around the traditional souks that can be found in every town in the country – most famously at Mutrah in Muscat, Salalah and Nizwa, which serve as showcases of traditional Omani craftsmanship and produce ranging from antique khanjars and Bedu jewellery to halwa, rose-water and frankincense. Muscat also boasts a number of modern malls, although these are rare elsewhere in the country.

## TRAVEL TIPS & DESTINATION OVERVIEWS

The app also includes a complete A to Z of handy travel tips on everything from visa regulations to local etiquette. Plus, you'll find destination overviews on shopping, sport, the arts, local events, health, activities and more.

## HOW TO DOWNLOAD THE WALKING EYE

Available on purchase of this guide only.
1. Visit our website: www.insightguides.com/walkingeye
2. Download the Walking Eye container app to your smartphone (this will give you access to both the destination app and the eBook)
3. Select the scanning module in the Walking Eye container app
4. Scan the QR code on this page – you will be asked to enter a verification word from the book as proof of purchase
5. Download your free destination app* and eBook for travel information on the go

* Other destination apps and eBooks are available for purchase separately or are free with the purchase of the Insight Guide book

# Contents

# THE BEST OF THE LESSER ANTILLES: TOP ATTRACTIONS

From the breathtaking scenery – which extends far beyond beaches of powdery white sand – to marine parks, turtle-watching, dockyards and dramatic forts.

△ **Pitons, St Lucia**. The ultimate Caribbean landmark is spectacular from every angle. Twin volcanic peaks rise sheer out of the sea clad in a green mantle of forest with sparkling bays at their feet. See page 225.

▽ **Harrison's Cave, Barbados**. A huge, crystalized limestone cavern with passages, tunnels and massive chambers, filled with stalagmites and stalactites, pools, and streams, lit up for a spectacular tour on a little electric train. See page 257.

▽ **Montserrat Volcano Observatory**. Allows you a first-hand glimpse of nature's devastating power, with views over the Exclusion Zone to the ash-covered former capital, Plymouth, and a fine scientific exhibition of the volcanic explosions. See page 182.

△ **Kurá Hulanda Museum, Curaçao**. The region's best museum, this private collection includes a moving permanent exhibition on the slave trade and African civilizations, housed in a courtyard where slave auctions were once held. See page 281.

◁ **Waitukubuli Trail, Dominica**. A project to integrate old trails into a network running from the south to the northern tip, touching east and west coasts, is now a shining example of community tourism. See page 202.

▽ **Brimstone Hill Fortress, St Kitts & Nevis**. This 17th-century British fort is the best preserved in the region, with stupendous views from its perch on a volcanic plug and cannon still facing out to sea. See page 165.

△ **Frigate Bird Sanctuary, Barbuda**. Thousands of frigate birds nest on the tops of emerald green mangroves on Codrington Lagoon, the red pouches of the displaying males a delightful contrast to their fluffy white chicks. See page 179.

△ **Nelson's Dockyard, Antigua**. The last surviving Georgian dockyard in the world is full of character, tucked into English Harbour, a safe haven for the British Navy in Nelson's times and still popular with today's sailors. See page 177.

▽ **Night-time turtle watching**. Many beaches attract hawksbill, Green, and giant leatherbacks in the egg-laying season, particularly on the eastern, Atlantic coasts of islands such as Dominica and St Lucia, and on the north coast of Trinidad. See page 264.

▽ **The Baths, Virgin Gorda, BVI**. Boulders the size of a house appear scattered like giants' marbles on the beach, forming grottoes and pools for good swimming and snorkeling if not crowded with day-trippers. See page 120.

# THE BEST OF THE LESSER ANTILLES: EDITOR'S CHOICE

Unique attractions, festivals and carnivals, best beaches, diving and snorkeling, food and drink, shopping… here, at a glance, are our recommendations, plus some essential tips for travelers.

## BEST BEACHES

**Englishman's Bay, Tobago.** Undeveloped, with an offshore reef, this half-moon beach is stunning and peaceful with the forest tumbling down to the sand. See page 273.

**Palm Beach, Barbuda.** Seemingly endless white sands, with stretches of shell pink, separate the ocean from the lobster-breeding area of Codrington lagoon. See page 178.

**Grand Anse, Grenada.** Over a mile (1.5km) of white sands are accompanied by fine views, shady palms, and plentiful water sports on offer. See page 245.

**Colombier, St-Barthélemy.** Empty of any trappings of human civilization – there's not even a road – this beautiful beach is still a favorite with nesting turtles. See page 147.

**Deadman's Bay, British Virgin Islands.** Turquoise waters, palm-fringed sands, and a glorious view of island-outcrops mark this romantic spot on Peter Island off Tortola. See page 123.

**Maracas Bay, Trinidad.** Surrounded by forest-covered mountains, this fine spot draws a local crowd keen to party, while Atlantic surf ensures an invigorating swim. See page 264.

*Grand Anse, Grenada.*

## EVENTS AND FESTIVALS

**Goat and crab races, Tobago.** These Easter-time events are taken very seriously indeed, with large bets placed on favored animals – and "jockeys." See page 314.

**Shakespeare Mas, Carriacou, Grenada.** Recitations of this most famous of bards' works take on Carnivalesque proportions, with elaborate masks and costumes, and prizes. See page 313.

**Mango Festival, Antigua.** July–Aug. A celebration of the region's favorite fruit, with competitions for biggest produce and best "magic mango menu." See page 312.

**Flower festivals, St Lucia.** "La Rose" in August and "La Marguerite" in October reach their climax in Micoud. See page 313.

**Easterval.** Union Island, the Grenadines, holds a weekend of music, culture and boat races at Easter. See page 314.

*Goat-racing, Buccoo village, Tobago.*

*Set your sights on whale watching in Dominica.*

## BEST OUTDOOR ADVENTURES

**Hike to the Boiling Lake, Dominica**. The six-hour round trip won't disappoint you; deep rainforest, thick tree ferns and waterfalls are all to be found en route. See page 202.

**Sailing tours in the Grenadines**. Chains of tiny volcanic islands make this the most idyllic spot for sailing; the rugged and spectacular scenery was the backdrop for *Pirates of the Caribbean*. See page 236.

**Wind- and kitesurfing**. Many of the islands have great conditions, but Bonaire, Aruba, Barbados, Tortola and St Lucia are particularly good for both sports. See page 321.

**Hiking Trinidad's northern coastline**. This is one of the few remaining undeveloped coastlines. A long trail traverses cliffs, rainforest, stunning beaches, and lagoons. See page 264.

**Canyoning, Dominica and Martinique**. Rushing mountain rivers, waterfalls, pools, gorges, and ravines overhung with rainforest create the perfect environment for climbing and abseiling in the canyons. See page 215.

**Climbing**. This is not a common activity on a small island, but Bonaire and Terre-de-Haut in Les Saintes offer heart-stopping climbing and rappeling, with breathtaking views. See page 316.

**Whale and dolphin watching**. Deep underwater trenches around the islands attract the world's largest creatures, and boat trips to get closer to them are offered on several islands including Dominica, St Lucia, and Grenada. See page 205.

*Windsurfing on Bonaire.*

## BEST CARNIVALS

The setting and the sunshine provide the perfect backdrop to the ultimate in parties. Traditionally Carnival precedes Lent, but some are held at other times of year.

**Port-of-Spain, Trinidad.** January–February/March. The best carnival in the world is a fully participatory affair with a rich history, 100,000 costumed revellers, unremitting soca, calypso, and steel pan music, and a season-long lead-up of events for every taste and age group. See page 263.

**Willemstad, Curaçao.** January–February/March. With a month-long festival culminating in the main event, this is a friendly and often wild party featuring the region's best tumba and tambu music performers. See page 278.

**Fort-de-France, Martinique.** January–February/March. Puppets, red devils, drag queens, and stringed instruments characterize the largest celebration in the French Antilles, continuing through Ash Wednesday and accompanied by zouk, salsa, soca, and reggae. See page 212.

**Crop Over, Barbados.** August. Traditionally celebrating the final sugar harvest, this festival is one of the region's most exuberant, with calypso, soca music, elaborate street parades, and dancing. See page 258.

**St Kitts and Nevis.** December–January. A smaller but still exciting carnival, engulfing both islands in calypso performances, partying, and a fantastic "j'ouvert" event on Boxing Day. See page 161.

*Carnival time, Port-of-Spain, Trinidad.*

## BEST FOOD AND DRINK

**Seafood.** From St Lucia's "fish fries" on Friday or Saturday night to fresh lobster from Anguilla to Tobago, or conch stews and curries, the region's favorite food is its most delicious. See page 83.

**Rotis, Trinidad.** Where India meets the Caribbean, this staple is a variety of vegetable, meat, or seafood curries wrapped in a large layered "skin." Try a shrimp roti with curried potato, channa dahl, and green mango. See page 86.

**Bouillon, French Antilles/region-wide.** A soupy stew served across the French-influenced islands, made with fresh fish such as dorado, with lime, tomato, and spices, or, in St Lucia, with chicken or other meats, lentils, red beans, dumplings, and plantain. See page 310.

**Oil down, Grenada.** A delicious stew of chicken, goat, or saltfish, cooked with breadfruit, and other vegetables, in coconut milk. See page 241.

**Dutch-world specialties.** The ABC Islands offer Dutch- and Indonesian-influenced dishes, such as thick *pinda saus* (peanut sauce) served with meats or fries; *keshi yena*, Edam or Gouda cheese stuffed with local meats and vegetables. See page 308.

**Ti-punch.** Drunk on half the islands but perhaps best enjoyed on Martinique, this is both sweet and sour, made with either white or dark rum, freshly-squeezed lime and sugar or cane syrup. See page 309.

**Fresh fruit juices.** From passionfruit or mango to delicious red sorrel; creamy soursop to sweet citrus, the selection of fruits on offer is second to none. See page 308

*Ti punch.*

*Musician at Barbados' Crop Over.*

## BEST DIVING AND SNORKELING

**Bonaire Marine Park.** Protected walls of coral stretching the entire length of the island's west coast, with 80-plus named sites, make this the king of Caribbean shore dives. Snorkelers close to shore will see magnificent elkhorn, staghorn, or brain coral and colorful fish. See page 292.

**Saba Marine Park.** The marine park circles the island. Pristine reefs in crystal-clear waters lie a short boat ride offshore. Highlights are pinnacles, and a labyrinth created by lava flows. See page 151.

**Tobago.** Known for drift dives, brain corals, and numerous manta rays, the sites around Speyside are exquisite. See page 272.

**Bequia and Tobago Cays, the Grenadines.** Two marine parks, superb for diving and snorkeling with a range of sites including coral reefs and walls. See page 237.

**Reserve Cousteau, Guadeloupe.** Remarkable for their warm water from hot volcanic springs, these colorful reefs are popular with both divers and snorkelers. Well-equipped dive shops with licensed instructors will organize individual dives or courses. See page 193.

**Dominica.** Steep, deep drop-offs and walls, hot volcanic springs, pinnacles, and coral gardens are all close to shore, giving opportunities for unparalleled diving. See page 204.

*In St Lucia's Diamond Botanical Gardens.*

## BEST GARDENS

**Den Paradera, Curaçao.** A beautiful herbal garden stocked with 300 species, all with medicinal properties, many saved from the spread of urbanization. See page 281.

**Andromeda Botanic Gardens, Barbados.** More than half a century of horticulture has produced this stunning hillside garden with more than 600 species of plants from around the world. See page 256.

**Papillote Wilderness Retreat, Dominica.** This is an exquisite botanic garden in a natural setting in the rainforest, intersected by a stream and hot mineral water pools. See page 201.

**Diamond Botanical Gardens, St Lucia.** An historic plantation garden brimming with color, where the steamy hot springs were made into restorative baths in the 18th century. See page 226.

**Jardins de Balata, Martinique.** These gardens with a view over Fort-de-France bay have a stunning collection of 3,000 species, full of color and life, and with hummingbirds to match. See page 214.

## BEST MARKETS

**Castries, St Lucia.** The Central Market is a pleasant mix of T-shirts and souvenirs together with fruit, vegetables, meat, fish, and flowers. See page 221.

**Marigot, St-Martin.** A delightful seafront market with vendors selling souvenirs, fruit, and vegetables in a picturesque setting. See page 137.

**Pointe-à-Pitre, Guadeloupe.** Caribbean charm with old wooden houses and lively spice and flower markets accompanies a modern European mall. See page 190.

**Fort-de-France, Martinique.** Several markets in town are a kaleidoscope of color, with fruit and vegetables and traditional clothes made of Madras cotton and worn by the vendors. See page 212.

**Kingstown, St Vincent.** A rough and ready, vibrant farmers' market by the waterfront near the fish market and banana boats. See page 233.

**St George's, Grenada.** Aromatic nutmeg, vanilla, cinnamon, cloves, and other herbs, spices, and organic cocoa perfume the air of this wonderful market. See page 242.

*Explore the deep off Bonaire.*

## MONEY-SAVING TIPS

**Travel off-season.** The climate between April and June is almost as good as January and February on most islands, with accommodations and other prices reduced by around 30 percent. See page 296.

**Use local transport.** Car rental can be prohibitively expensive, and public transport is surprisingly usable on many islands. If you don't mind unpredictable (though frequent) schedules and cozy (i.e. crowded) journeys, public buses can be a great way to meet local people. See page 297.

**Fly with a charter company.** If you are traveling transatlantic and independently, extra seats on chartered planes can sometimes go at half the price of scheduled services if you book at the right time. See page 296.

**Book an apartment.** Most islands have various self-catering options, which can save you money if you're traveling with three or more people. See page 306.

**Talk to local people.** Local restaurants usually offer bargains compared to hotels – and often serve equally good food. And you are putting money back into the local community – ask around for the top spots. See page 308.

*Coconut trees brush Turtle Beach in Barbados.*

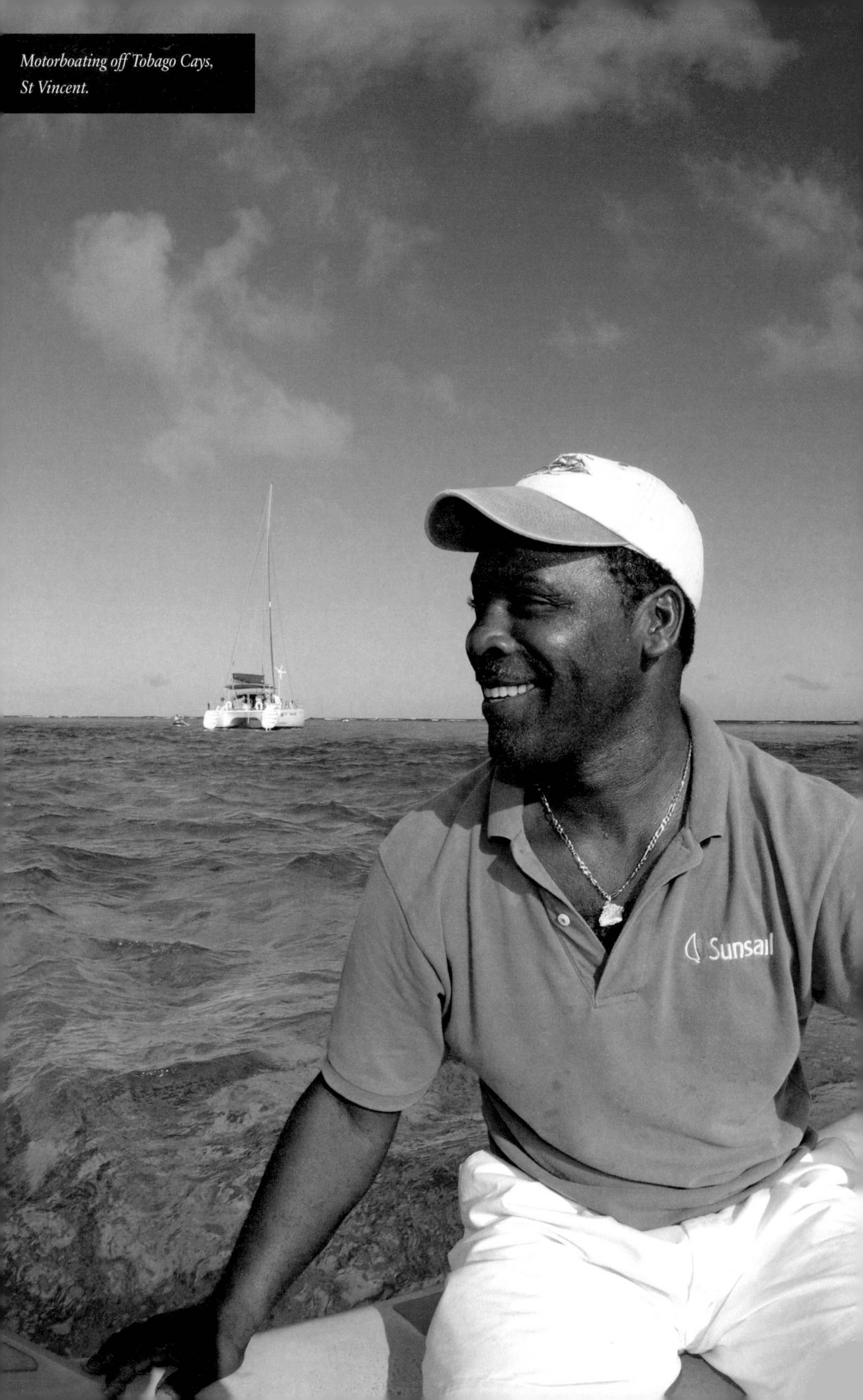


*Motorboating off Tobago Cays, St Vincent.*

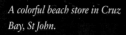
*A colorful beach store in Cruz Bay, St John.*

SLIDE TO OPEN!

*Bathing at Trinity Falls, St Vincent.*

# WELCOME

Stay a while in the sunny Caribbean and
you will discover a rainbow of cultures
and a rich and exciting history.

*A brightly painted dwelling
in Anguilla.*

The Lesser Antilles comprise some of the most beautiful landscapes on earth. Within this chain of more than 20 major islands and countless uninhabited cays and islets, there is every conceivable shade of blue in the water, every variation of flower, every brightly colored bird. Indeed, it seems as if everything is unimaginably perfect.

However, the world tends to forget that the Eastern Caribbean is not one great holiday resort but a collection of small nations and territories struggling to forge economic and political independence, with an astonishingly diverse culture – each island proud of its own. To a greater or lesser degree, the islands have been settled by migrant tribes from South America, 16th-century gold-seeking Spaniards, or their European planter rivals: the French, English, Dutch, Danes, and even the Knights Templar of Malta; add pirates, religious and political refugees, and a huge African slave culture, then add in Indians, Chinese, Syrians, Lebanese, more South Americans… and you have the dizzying concoction that makes up these islands.

*Cruise passengers disembark.*

The racial mix has produced an astonishing musical and artistic energy, which climaxes in the exuberance of Carnival. Nobel laureates, writers, singers, musicians, artists, cricketers, and Olympic athletes are the success stories and role models of West Indians today. From Rihanna to Viv Richards, Derek Walcott to the Mighty Sparrow, talent is an export with worldwide popularity.

Long gone are the days when fortunes were made from plantation agriculture; now the West Indies can barely feed their own, ever-increasing population. With limited economic options, governments now exploit their islands' beauty and natural resources, encouraging tourism to provide employment. As these hospitable islands have become more accessible, there is a danger that their soul will be submerged in the onslaught of leisure developers. But if you tread carefully you can help preserve the spirit of the Caribbean, and because the people are, in general, so open, you can easily explore all its realms: political, religious and cultural.

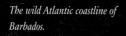
*The wild Atlantic coastline of Barbados.*

# ISLANDS IN THE SUN

### The rich diversity of these tropical islands is plain to see – from their mountain rainforests to the ocean deep.

The islands of the Lesser Antilles form a delicate necklace of coral, basalt, and limestone stretching from the Virgin Islands in the north through a 1,500-mile (2,400km) arc to the Dutch islands of Aruba, Bonaire, and Curaçao off the coast of Venezuela in the south.

Each small landmass is often within sight of another. So when Amerindians, the earliest people to colonize the Eastern Caribbean, started to move north from South America, they could stand at the northern tip of one island and see – if only as a blurry mauve outline across a truculent channel – the southern tip of the next island. It was an encouragement, perhaps, to move on, to see what new creatures, plants, landscapes, opportunities lay on the horizon.

*French West Indies, Guadaloupe.*

> *The wild Atlantic side of most Eastern Caribbean islands has more in common with a Scottish seascape than the gentle white-sand beaches of the hotter and drier Caribbean coast usually only a few miles away.*

## Each island to its own

The Eastern Caribbean islands are physically (and culturally) places of great variety. The images of sparkling white sand, clear turquoise sea, and shimmering coconut palms of the travel advertisements do the region a disservice. It is a far richer region than that, with each island's topography reflecting its story.

From the pristine rainforests of Dominica and St Lucia, where rain pounds the mountaintops with up to 300ins (760cm) of water annually, and tree ferns shimmer in a silver light, to the dry, brittle scrublands of acacia and logwood of St-Martin or Barbuda, there seems to be a vegetation for every mood. Even if you stay on only one island, there is often a remarkable range of ecology to be explored: from rainforest canopy to coastal swamp and coral reef.

The flatter islands are less varied and, in many cases, they have been more vulnerable to exploitation. Thus Antigua and Barbados lost their original forest covering to sugar-cane plantations, leaving a landscape largely of "bush," with residual areas given over to the cultivation of sugar and vegetables, or the rearing of livestock.

## The ocean and the deep blue sea

Yet wherever you arrive in the Caribbean you are greeted by a sweetness of smell and the breezes of the cooling trade winds. Its tropical climate delivers relatively constant hours of sunshine, and a temperature hovering around 86°F (30°C) in the Eastern Caribbean.

The trade winds, which guided the first Europeans to the Caribbean at the end of the 15th century, blow in from the northeast, first over the typically wilder coasts of the wetter windward sides, which are buffeted by the tempestuous Atlantic Ocean, and then across

*The ruins of an old sugar mill.*

in a more gentle fashion to the tranquil, leeward Caribbean Sea.

## Alive and kicking

With the exception of Barbados, which is perched out on its own, much of the island chain (from Saba to Grenada) was created by volcanic action when the two tectonic plates which sit beneath the "necklace" shifted. The eastward-moving American plate pushed under the westward-moving Caribbean plate and threw up what became this pattern of islands. However, Barbados, to the southeast, was formed by a wedge of sediments pushed up slowly; it is encrusted with the remnants of ancient coral reefs which developed as the

water became shallower over the sediments. To the south, Trinidad and Tobago were joined to Venezuela during the ice age when the sea levels were much lower, accounting for the similar fauna and flora on the islands.

Some islands are much older than others: those that have been worn down by erosion, subsided below sea level and then raised up again are the flatter, drier islands of Anguilla, St-Martin, Barbuda, and Antigua, on the outside of the volcanic rim.

> *Trinidad is the only island that is home to four species of venomous snake – the bushmaster, two types of coral snake, and the fer de lance.*

The geologically younger islands are physically more dramatic, with mountain ranges and steep-sided valleys. Some, such as Montserrat, Guadeloupe, St Vincent, and Martinique, have experienced volcanic activity in the 20th century – from the devastation of the town of St-Pierre in Martinique in 1902, when some 30,000 people were wiped out, to the most recent activity, which began in 1995 in the Soufrière Hills in the south of Montserrat. This crisis resulted in the "closure" of two-thirds of the island, and the evacuation of much of the population.

*Soufrière* (from the French word for sulfur) is the name given to volcanoes in the region and several neighboring villages. In St Lucia, for example, the "drive-in" volcano, with its moonscape of bubbling mud, mineral pools of boiling water, and sulfur springs, is near the southern village of Soufrière.

This dramatic landscape continues underwater where there are mountains, including a submarine volcano just north of Grenada called Kick 'Em Jenny, hot springs, caves, lava flows, overhangs, pinnacles, walls, reefs, and forests of elkhorn coral.

Volcanoes apart, the threat from hurricanes is a constant feature of life in most of the Eastern Caribbean, with really only Trinidad and Tobago and the ABC islands lying safely outside the hurricane belt. The hurricane season (June too soon, July stand by, August it must, September remember, October all over) interrupts the rainy season, from May to Christmas, often to devastating effect, endangering lives and destroying homes, businesses, and crops. The traditional dry season is from around Christmas to May, when water may be in short supply. It is then that the flowering trees and shrubs, like the red-bracted poinsettia, put on their most festive display.

## Tropical wildlife

While the flora of the Lesser Antilles is of international importance, the region is less well-endowed with fauna. Many animals, such as the agouti, opossum, and the green monkey (found in Barbados, Grenada, and St Kitts and Nevis) were introduced by man. The mongoose, a creature that resembles a large weasel, was brought over to control rats and snakes, but as rats are nocturnal and mongooses aren't, they succeeded in becoming pests too, plundering birds' nests and rummaging through garbage.

The islands in the middle of the necklace received fewer migrants of both bird and animal life. However, the relative isolation of some of them allowed for the evolution

*The aftermath of Hurricane Gonzalo, St Martin, 2014.*

## RIP-ROARING HURRICANES

A hurricane blows up when the atmosphere's pressure plunges far lower than that of the surrounding air. Usually spawned in the Atlantic, continuous winds of up to 150mph (240kph) blow around the eye, a calm central zone of several miles across, where the sky is often blue.

Hurricanes can reach up to 500 miles (800km) in width and travel at 10–30mph (16–48kph), speeding up across land before losing force and dying out. They leave massive destruction in their wake, but islanders are warned of approaching storms and official hurricane shelters are allocated (see Travel Tips). Lists of hurricane names are drawn up 6 years in advance in alphabetical order by the National Hurricane Center in Miami. The tradition started during World War II when US servicemen named the storms after their girlfriends. In 1979, male names were added to reflect equal opportunities.

Most hurricanes occur between June and November, and the average lifespan of a hurricane is 8 to 10 days.

Memorable hurricanes in recent years have included Lili (2002) and Ivan (2004), which hit Grenada and St Vincent; Tomas (2010) which brought mudslides in St Lucia; Irene (2011) which passed over the Leewards, causing widespread destruction and at least 56 deaths across the Caribbean, US and Canada; and Erika (2015) which caused at least 31 deaths, and intensive flooding and landslides in Dominica.

of endemic species: Dominica and Montserrat are the home of a large frog known as a mountain chicken, that is found nowhere else in the world. Lizards and geckos are everywhere but the poisonous fer de lance snake lives only on St Lucia, Martinique, and Trinidad. Red-bellied racer snakes are found only on Saba and Sint Eustatius; St Lucia has the only whiptail lizard in the Eastern Caribbean, living on its offshore islets; remnant populations of the endangered Lesser Antillean iguana, hunted for their meat, survive on six islands including Saba and Statia. Night-

*Sulfur springs on St Lucia.*

time can be a noisy affair on any island as frogs of all sizes tune up, with some of the loudest often being the tiniest.

The Windward Islands each have their own indigenous parrot, which have become endangered through loss of habitat caused by hurricanes and farmers, and there are other indigenous birds on many islands. While you may not always see a parrot, every day will bring a hummingbird winging its way in a million flutters "to a hibiscus near you." Indeed, birds are a constant presence, although you will have to go to Trinidad and Tobago (for their 469 species) for the most exotic.

Seabirds and other waterbirds should not be overlooked either, as their existence is closely linked to the islands. From the herons and egrets stalking through swamps and wetlands, to the magnificent frigate bird that cannot walk on land but soars for days in the sky, to the awkward brown pelican perched on a jetty or the graceful red-billed tropic bird skimming the water in search of squid or flying fish (which the frigate bird may force it to disgorge later), there is a wide range of birds to look out for.

## A money spinner

Although these small islands are largely rural in character, clinging to fishing and farming traditions and celebrating festivals linked to these activities, in the last decades of the 20th century their economies began to shift away from agriculture to tourism. It is now the region's greatest money spinner, bringing employment and dollars. Like the first colonizers, who dramatically altered the island hinterlands by clearing the forests – first for tobacco, then coffee and cocoa, and then for sugar – the tourist industry has changed the coastlines forever. The bays where fishermen once pulled in their nets, or where colonies of birds nested in mangrove stands, now provide for the very different needs of tourists.

The fragile environments of these small islands are, in some cases, in danger of sinking under the weight of visitors. Local and international environmental groups are vocal in contesting the destruction of important mangrove stands for hotel building; the destruction of habitats and wildlife corridors when roads and buildings appear; the damage done to coral reefs by careless tourists and the anchors of cruise ships; plus the cultural threat imposed on small societies by the hordes of holiday-makers, apparently with limitless funds.

"Sustainable" tourism is now the buzzword, and some islands, such as Dominica and Trinidad, which have not developed a "sand, sea, and sun" tourism have declared policies for developing along those lines, with the involvement of the communities affected. Visitors, too, are discovering that there is more to the land- and seascapes of the Caribbean than the limited view from a sunlounger; between them, environmentalists, policy-makers, and visitors may ensure that the diversity of that island necklace will survive.

# Ecosystems of the Lesser Antilles

**Although most of the primary rainforest has been destroyed there is a huge variety of ecosystems on the islands.**

The archetypal image of a Caribbean island is one of volcanic mountains clad in forest growing right down to the seashore, the Pitons of St Lucia being a prime example. There is, however, a huge variety of ecosystems on the islands, despite their small size. An island such as St Lucia or Martinique may contain rainforest, cloud forest, elfin forest, dry tropical forest, thorn scrub, coastal wetlands, swamps, and mangroves. Even the Pitons have several different vegetation zones, depending on altitude.

Little primary rainforest can be found on the islands as it has been cleared by man or destroyed by hurricanes or lava flows. However, many islands have good secondary rainforest, much of it protected, and an invaluable water catchment resource. What is often referred to as rainforest is in fact montane forest, found on the middle slopes of the mountains of the Caribbean. Trees here reach a height of 32–40ft (10–12 meters) and are covered with mosses, lichens, and epiphytes (sometimes known as air plants; they live on other plants but use them only for support, and are not parisitic). Elfin woodland is found on the highest peaks, such as on Saba's Mount Scenery, almost permanently in cloud with low temperatures and lots of wind. Trees here are dwarf versions of what grows on lower slopes, more spreading in habit and contorted by the wind. They are often covered with epiphytes, mosses, and lichens, which thrive in the moist atmosphere and high rainfall.

Areas with a more moderate rainfall have a semi-evergreen forest, where many trees shed their leaves in the dry season and burst into flower, so that their seeds are ready for the next rainy season. Dry woodland areas are less rich in species, the trees are shorter, and there are fewer lianas and epiphytes. Most trees shed their leaves in the dry season and their bark is thick, helping them to retain moisture.

Drier still are the areas of thorn scrub, usually found near the coasts, where the ground might have been cleared at some stage, followed by the grazing of goats, sheep, and cattle. The tallest plants here are usually no more than 12ft (3 meters) and they have adapted to dry conditions by growing very small leaves, or no leaves at all in the case of cactus, and the most successful have thorns or spines to ward off grazing animals. Closer to the beach are sea grape, manchineel, and coconut, which can tolerate a higher salt content in the soil.

## Protecting the mangroves

Mangroves grow on the coast in shallow bays, lagoons, estuaries, and deltas where the soil is per-

*A scarlet ibis can't help but catch the eye.*

manently waterlogged and the mud is disturbed daily by the tides. There are many different types of mangroves, but they are an important breeding ground for fish, and home to crabs, molluscs, and many birds.

In Barbuda an enormous colony of frigate birds, who are unable to walk on land, and a number of other birds have taken over a huge area of mangroves in Codrington Lagoon, while in Trinidad, the Caroni swamp is the night-time roosting place of the scarlet ibis and egrets, and both areas have become major tourist attractions. Mangroves can be cut back to make charcoal and they will regenerate within a few years, but if they are cleared completely for a marina or resort hotel, valuable nurseries are lost forever.

# WEST INDIES.

*A    T    L    A    N    T    I    C*

Tropic of Cancer

*O    C    E    A    N*

oods Kay

rench Kay

Mariguana

Cayque

que

North Cayque

Grand Cayque

Grand Kay

Cayques

Inague

r Heneage

Meuchoir Quarre

Shoal

Bajo de la Plata

Tortuga

Le Cap Francois

P.t Guarico

P.te de Plata

Bajo Navidad

Nicolas

R.t

S. Maro

Dondon

Santiago

C. Samana

Samana

Cabo Viejo Frances

C. Raphael

Bajo Navidad

C.t Arribonte

Col du

C.del Engano

St. Juan de

Porto Rico

Virgin Gorda

Anegada

Sombrero

Anguilla or Snake I.

P.t Truce

HAITI or

Aruo

St. DOMINGO

St. Domingo

P.E.spada

Zacheo

PORTO RICO

Virgin

Isles

Virgonia

C

P.te Nevia

R. Ozama

Saona

Mona

La Mona

St. Thomas

Crabs

Martins

St.

St. Bartholomew

Barbuda

A

laguemel

I. Yuma

Porto Real

C. Roxo

Saba

St. Eustatia

R

Baiente

P.te Nisao

Caso de Muertos

P.t Carredas

S. Cruz

St. Christophers

B

I. Beata

Alto Vela

Bieque or Crab I.

Nevis

Antigua

B

Montserrat

E

Guadaloupe

Grand Terre

A

Basse Terre

Basse Terre

Deseade

N

Aves I.

Sainte

Marie Galante

Dominica

N

Roseau

I

*B    E    A    N        S    E    A*

F.t St Pierre

F.t Royal

Marti

S

Gros C.

Castrie

St. Luci

L

Orua or Aruba

Oost Hook

Curacao

Buen Aire

St. Vincent

Kings Is.

Barba

A

Bequia

Bridge

N

Rocca

Horchilla

Carriacou

D

C. Coquibacoa

la Vela

R.T

B. Honda

C. San Roman

G.t or Coro

Nicacos P.t

Aves I.

Blanca

Granada Bank

S. George

Granada

S

Testigos

Dragons Mouth

Gulf of

Venezuela

Coro

Tortuga Salada

Margarita

C. Tres Puntas

L.T

To

Searb

Maracaybo

R. Tocuyo

S. Felipe

Valencia

Gulf of Triste

P.t Cabello

La Guayra

C. Codera

Coche

Cariaco

Cumana

G.t of Paria

P.to Galer

Trinidad

P.t Galgo

MARAC

AYBO

Carora

Leon de Caracas

Barcelona

Blanca

Joseph

Laguna de

Barguisimeto

Gold Mine of S. Pedro

*CUMANA*

M.ths of the Orinoco

Maracaybo Gibraltar

# DECISIVE DATES

### AD 1000–1200
Carib tribes from South America travel north through the Lesser Antilles in dug-out canoes, displacing resident Arawak-speaking people.

### 1493 and 1498
Christopher Columbus is the first European to discover the Eastern Caribbean islands.

## Colonization: 16th–17th centuries
### 1592
The Spanish are the first settlers, in Trinidad, building St Joseph. Three years later, Sir Walter Raleigh destroys it.

### 1623
The English establish a colony on St Kitts, then Barbados (1627), Antigua (1632), Anguilla (1650), and the BVI (1680).

### 1635
The French colonize Guadeloupe and Martinique.

### 1634–36
The Dutch take the ABC Islands.

### 1648
Treaty of Concordia divides St-Martin between the French (north) and Dutch (south).

## Sugar and slavery: 1638–1797
### 1638–1779
Slave trade flourishes in Curaçao; slaves are sold on to the sugar-growing islands.

### 1690
St Kitts and Nevis hit by earthquake; tidal wave wipes

*A family of Carib or Kalinago people, St Vincent, 1794.*

out Nevis's capital, Jamestown.

### 1754
St Thomas, St John, and St Croix become the Danish West Indies.

### 1775–83
American Revolution causes famine in British West Indies due to trade embargoes.

### 1779
Stock Exchange crash in Europe sends sugar industry further into decline.

### 1784
France cedes St-Barthélemy to Sweden in exchange for trading rights.

### 1797
British invade Trinidad.

## Reform and rebellion: 1802–1902
### 1802
Spanish Treaty of Amiens gives Trinidad to the British; Tobago

finally ceded to Britain by France.

### 1816
Easter Rebellion in Barbados of 5,000 slaves led by Bussa. St Kitts, Nevis, Anguilla, and BVI administered by British as a single colony.

### 1834
Emancipation Act "frees" slaves in British West Indies. French follow in 1848 and Dutch in 1863. An "apprenticeship" system is introduced.

### 1845–1917
Thousands of East Indians arrive in Trinidad for an indentured period of five years; many remain.

### 1848
Slave rebellion in St Croix precipitates their emancipation in the Danish West Indies.

### 1902
La Soufrière on St Vincent erupts, killing 2,000. Two days later, Mont Pelée on Martinique erupts, destroying St-Pierre and killing 30,000.

## Independence: 1914–83
### 1917
Danish West Indies sold to US.

### 1917–24
Oil refineries built on Curaçao and Aruba.

### 1946
French islands change status to *départements* of France,

officially becoming regions in 1974.

**1951**
Universal suffrage granted to British colonies.

**1954**
Dutch islands granted full autonomy in domestic affairs as part of the Netherlands; in 1986 Aruba is given separate autonomy.

**1958–62**
Formation of Federation of the British West Indies; fails when Jamaica and Trinidad and Tobago pursue independence.

**1966**
Barbados granted independence.

**1967**
Britain's islands become states in voluntary association with Britain, with internal self-government. Anguilla breaks away from St Kitts.

**1969**
British invasion welcomed by Anguilla; becomes a British Dependent Territory in 1980.

*Bridgetown, Barbados.*

**1973**
Foundation of CARICOM (Caribbean Community) to liberalize trade.

**1974**
Grenada is first of Associated States to gain independence.

**1976**
Trinidad and Tobago becomes a republic within the British Commonwealth.

**1978**
Dominica gains independence.

**1979**
St Vincent and the Grenadines gain independence. La Soufrière erupts. Grenada experiences a bloodless coup; St Lucia gains independence.

**1981**
Antigua and Barbuda granted independence.

**1983**
US and Caribbean forces invade Grenada after the government is overthrown. St Kitts and Nevis gain independence.

# Modern times: 1985–2010

**1985**
Exxon closes oil refinery in Aruba with disastrous effects on the island's economy.

**1990**
Arms smuggling scandal in Antigua involves PM's son Vere Bird Jr. Muslim fundamentalists attempt to overthrow government in Trinidad.

**1995–98**
Volcanic eruptions on Montserrat. The capital, Plymouth, and the south abandoned. Population moves north or abroad.

**2005**
Inauguration of Caribbean Court of Justice in Trinidad.

**2006**
Trinidad and Tobago and Barbados join Caribbean Single Market and Economy (CSME).

**2010**
Netherlands Antilles dissolved. Aruba, Curaçao, and Sint Maarten become constituent countries of the Netherlands; Bonaire, Saba, and Sint Eustatius become special municipalities.

**2011**
Barbados' historic Bridgetown and its Garrison is added to the Unesco World Heritage List.

**2015**
Bernard Whiteman becomes Curaçao's PM. BHP Bilton is granted licence to explore for oil in waters around Barbados.

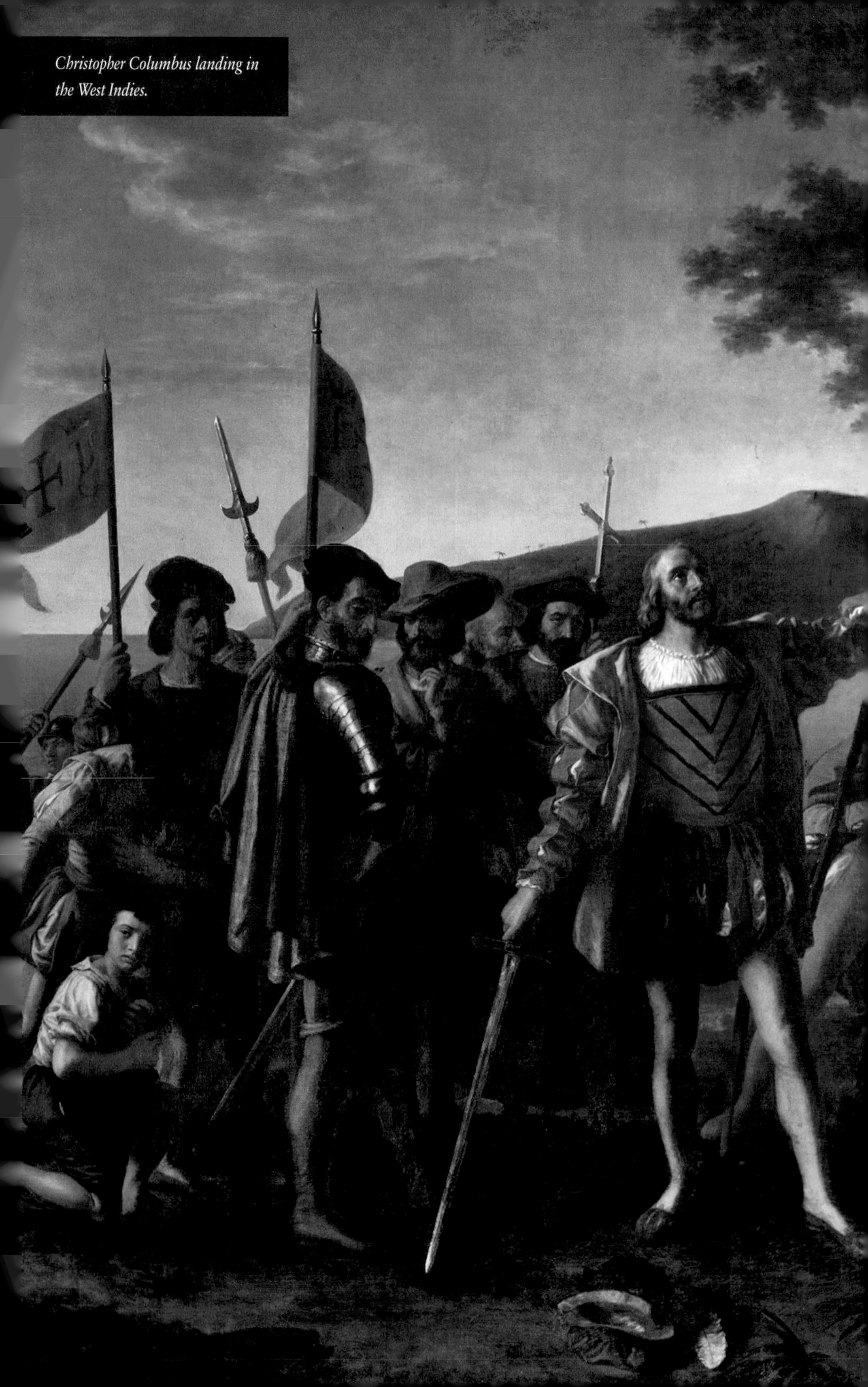

*Christopher Columbus landing in the West Indies.*

# THE COLONIAL PERIOD

When Christopher Columbus came upon the islands of the Caribbean, he threw names at many of them as he sailed past. The colonists arrived 100 years later.

Accounts by Spanish historians and other European travelers tell of a vibrant Indian civilization which existed before the arrival of Columbus at the end of the 15th century. In fact, most of what is known about the Indians comes from these accounts.

However, such observations have to be read with care because, with the single exception of the Dominican monk, Bartolomé de Las Casas (1474–1566), the defender of the Indians in the early 16th century, they were filled with the hubris of European men who saw the native inhabitants as savage children hardly fit for missionary enterprise. Alternatively, some of the accounts presented the inhabitants of this new world in Utopian terms, in contrast to the decadence of European life. Beatriz Pastor, in *Discurso narrativo de la Conquista de América*, has shown how these psychologically conditioned responses oscillated between two opposite pictures: savage cannibalism or romantic primitivism. European visitors saw what they wanted to see. More recently, archeological investigations have allowed us to fill in some of the gaps in our knowledge.

*A family of Charibbee Indians, indigenous to the Lesser Antilles, in 1802.*

## Amerindian immigrants

The earliest known settlers of the Lesser Antilles came from the Orinoco region of South America through Trinidad and up the island chain from the south (see page 40). The first period of migration was around 5000 BC. The Indians Columbus found in the Lesser Antilles were referred to as Caribs, who had absorbed the supposedly more peaceful Arawak people, killing the men and breeding with the women. They were described as warlike, aggressively conquering other islands as they expanded their fiefdoms and even sacrificing and eating their prisoners. It is from them that the words Caribbean and cannibal are derived. However, their descendents, still living on Dominica today, refer to themselves as Kalinago, not Carib, and suggest that the practice of keeping the shrunken heads or bones of their ancestors in their homes may have misled the Spaniards into thinking that they were sacrificial victims.

Much of this Indian civilization disappeared under the pressures of European conquest and colonization. English and French soldiers and settlers undertook what were in effect genocidal wars against the native populations of the islands. The rest died of the common cold or smallpox, against which they had no immunity.

They returned the favor by giving Columbus' sailors a form of syphilis, which became virulent in Europe at the end of the 15th century.

## Colonial rivalry

The 17th and 18th centuries were the major formative period of the Lesser Antilles, marked, successively, by war and rivalry between European nations, the establishment of settlements and colonies and introduction of a sugar economy, the organization of the slave trade, the implantation of chattel slavery, the rise of white superiority, and slave rebellions.

historian and politician, Dr Eric Williams, called it a condition of "in betweenity". The island of St Croix (now part of the US Virgin Islands), for example, changed sovereignty at least seven times in a period of less than 100 years, including a brief rule by the Knights Templar of Malta.

The European powers saw their new tropical possessions as an opportunity for enriching the emergent state systems of post-Reformation Europe, both Catholic and Protestant. And they wanted to weaken Spain's influence in the New World. Throughout much of the 16th century Spain had dominated the high seas, plying to and

*Battleships – a constant sight around the islands during the 1700s.*

The early Spanish claim to the Caribbean islands was not challenged by its European rivals – England, France, Denmark, and Holland – for over a century, by which time the Spanish hegemony was anchored mainly in the Greater Antilles – Cuba, Hispaniola, and Puerto Rico – where there was real treasure, although there was a brief Spanish episode in Trinidad.

Because they were the first ports of arrival for the invading European fleets, the Lesser Antilles bore the brunt of the inter-state rivalry. It was a period of almost uninterrupted insecurity for the region, when the political ownership of any island could suddenly change. The native populations could wake up on any morning to discover that they had a new set of masters. West Indian

from the Caribbean with treasure. In an attempt to break their monopoly, Sir Francis Drake had become the first official pirate, reaping the rewards for the English queen, Elizabeth I.

## Pirates and buccaneers

European chancelleries and war ministries continued to use pirates and buccaneers – fugitives from justice – to harass the Spaniards in the 17th century. Sir Henry Morgan (1635–88) started his infamous career as a British licensed privateer. Dutchman Esquemiling wrote *The Buccaneers and Marooners of America* in 1674: "...from the very beginning of their conquests in America, both English, French, Dutch, Portuguese, Swedes, Danes, Courlanders, and all other nations that navigate the ocean, have frequented the West Indies, and filled them with their robberies and assaults."

European governments eventually agreed to dispense with these motley forces when they became too much of a nuisance to their own ships. Governor Woodes Rogers' suppression of the pirate stronghold in New Providence in the Bahamas in 1722 marked the end of piracy.

## Naval warfare

By 1700, the four great powers of Caribbean economic and military aggression – France,

> "If our number is small, our hearts are great; and the fewer persons we are, the more union, and the better shares we shall have in the spoil," Henry Morgan told his men after a raid in 1668 yielded 250,000 "pieces of eight."

Some of the most decisive battles were fought here, most notably when Admiral Rodney destroyed the French fleet in the Battle of the Saints off the Windwards in 1782. He then destroyed the commercial port of St Eustatius, a

*A map showing Central America and the Antilles Islands of the Caribbean Sea, mid-to-late 1750s.*

Holland, Spain, and Britain – had established flourishing island colonies when the Atlantic seaboard colonies of Massachusetts and Virginia were hardly beyond their first stages of settlement. The colonization of the islands and Spanish Main produced cities rivaling those of Europe in size and magnificence.

Stretched like a line of watchdogs across the route between Spain and her New World empire, the islands were perfectly positioned for the establishment of naval stations, like Nelson's Dockyard in Antigua. If, as the saying goes, the Battle of Waterloo (1815) was won on the playing fields of Eton, then it is equally true to say that the Battle of Trafalgar (1805) was won in the naval stations of the Lesser Antilles.

supply center of arms for the anti-English forces in the American Revolutionary War. Even today, Statians recall Rodney's sack of their island, known as the Golden Rock, just as Southerners recall Sherman's burning of Atlanta in the American Civil War.

The governments of mother country and local colony were forced, often at ruinous expense, to build defenses, such as the Brimstone Hill fortifications on St Kitts. For the populations of the time, life must have been marginal and precarious. St Croix alone, the island center of the Danish West Indies, was occupied in 1650 by three different European war parties. Such warfare continued until the Napoleonic Wars, when the political map of the region was eventually settled by the 1815 Treaty of Vienna.

## Profits of paradise

However, the history of the New World, called the Enterprise of the Indies, was not just war. War was simply the prelude to trade. Once the European powers had more or less settled their respective "spheres of influence" – Trinidad, for example, was finally ceded to Britain in the 1802 Treaty of Amiens that ended the Seven Years' War – the Lesser Antilles settled down to its socioeconomic-cultural development as

*French soldiers in Guadeloupe, circa 1807.*

---

### THE TRIANGULAR SLAVE TRADE

As demand for slaves grew on the islands in the 17th and 18th centuries, the leading merchants in the profitable trade were mostly from Britain, Portugal, France, and Holland. Traders ensured that their ships never traveled empty, by sailing from Europe with manufactured goods, guns, and ammunition, which they sold to African rulers in return for slaves. These slaves were then transported across the Atlantic in the Middle Passage and sold in the Americas: the Caribbean islands, Brazil, and North America. The homeward leg of the journey found the holds full of sugar, rum, cotton, coffee, cocoa, and other produce from the colonies.

---

*Welsh Royalists, Dutch Jews, Cromwell's prisoners, Puritan merchants, Catholic friars – all kinds of people traveled to the Antilles. Some sought adventure, others refuge, but many were banished there for a variety of misdemeanors.*

peripheral economies of the European states. That meant the development of sugar as a staple crop and the sugar plantation economy, supported by the slave trade, which lasted some 300 years from the 16th to the 19th centuries, supplying a large, cheap labor force capable of heavy, unremitting work under brutalizing tropical conditions.

## Island patterns

From north to south these islands shared a common pattern of colonialism and slavery, deriving prosperity from the sugar economy, either producing sugar or developing as commercial trade centers. For example, in the north, St Thomas, under Danish rule, developed as an important commercial trade center as it was too hilly for sugar, while St Croix, also ruled by the Danes, developed as a sugar plantation economy. Of course, there were differences between the islands. For instance, Barbados was English and Guadeloupe French. In the south, Trinidad emerged as a Franco-Hispanic Catholic society while Tobago became an English-speaking Protestant society of small farmers and fishing folk. Antigua became a sugar colony while mountainous Dominica had little to do but develop an infant lumber industry. In the French Antilles, Martinique early on developed a small creole middle class consisting of the professional elite, while Guadeloupe remained mainly agricultural. This distinction survives to the present day.

In the Dutch Antilles, Curaçao became another commercial trade center as it was too arid for sugar, while Bonaire developed a small salt-pond industry and became a prison for rebellious slaves. Even the Lilliputian islands of Anguilla, Barbuda, and the Grenadines, as dependent wards of large sugar islands, were affected by the sugar economy.

## The slave trade

As a consequence of Europeans' seemingly insatiable taste for sugar, the islands, with few exceptions, became arrival ports and slave markets.

The triangular trade, between the European ports, African trading posts and the Antilles, laid the foundations of slavery as a domestic institution. Richard Ligon described in his book *A True and Exact History of the Island of Barbados* (1657) how the smallholdings of early lower-class white immigrants were replaced with large-scale sugar plantations manned by slaves.

Later, the British dramatist and politician Richard Sheridan's study of the rise of the colonial gentry in 18th-century Antigua showed how no entrepreneur in that society could hope to survive unless he was also a planter-merchant.

Naturally enough, it was a society of ranking status in three tiers, composed of upper-class whites, mixed-race people (known contemporaneously as mulattos) or freed persons of color – the consequence of the Antillean miscegenative habits – and then slaves at the bottom of the pile.

## White plantocracy

Each group had its own pride and prejudices. The white plantocracy was arrogant, racist, and socially gross. In fact, much of its ancestry in the islands was suspect: the 18th-century Jesuit Père Labat noted in Martinique that his

*Caribbean market in the 19th century.*

*Plantation profits were sent to the absentee owners in England, who wasted them on a lifestyle of such prodigality that it disgusted even 18th-century observers.*

The entire house of Antillean society was built over this slave basement. It became a strange melting pot of white colonists, black slaves, indentured servants, freed Indians, Catholics, Protestants, heretics, Jews, transported political prisoners, felons, "poor whites," all mingled in a fascinating exoticism under tropical skies. It was a *picaroon* world of all colors and creeds, slowly learning to co-exist with each other.

slave-owner neighbors were originally engaged as servants. These observations hardly made Labat popular in those old creole communities and explains why, after some 14 years, he was recalled by his superiors and never allowed to return. There were, however, many members of the aristocracy who traveled to the West Indies to make their fortunes out of sugar. Younger sons who didn't want to join the army or the church often opted for the colonies, and this new family money paid for the construction of many of the grand 18th-century houses with their beautiful landscaped parks that still grace the English countryside. Regency architecture in cities such as Bristol and Bath was paid for by the slave trade. Even in fiction, it was accepted

# Chains of slavery

**Slavery provided labor for the sugar plantations and allowed European colonists to prosper while their workforce suffered.**

For 300 years, slaves were transported across the Atlantic from West African ports to the Caribbean, Brazil, and North America. Estimates of the total number range from 11 million to 20 million, of

*Slaves planting sugar cane, 1826.*

whom more than half were shipped in the 18th century. They landed from ships in which they had been packed together like sardines in the hold for the months-long voyage from West Africa, each of them chained down to prevent any chance of rebellion or suicide.

## The horror of the slave ships

Conditions in the ships were just sufficient to keep the enslaved people alive, although many died on the journey. Those that became ill with diseases that rampaged through the holds, such as smallpox and dysentery, were thrown overboard. That so many survived is due to the slave traders choosing only the strongest, healthiest-looking men and women.

Once off the ships in the Caribbean, in trading islands such as Curaçao and St Thomas, the slaves were sold to plantation owners. They became property – part chattel, part real estate – that could be sold or traded against debts.

## Plantation life

On the plantations, living conditions were abysmal. Slaves were housed in floorless huts, with barely enough food to keep them working for 12 hours a day, 6 days a week. Historian Karl Watson has written that slaves in Barbados started their day at half-past five in the morning, when the plantation bell summoned them to the main estate yard to receive instructions. After being given ginger tea, they were divided up into gangs of 20 to 60 and sent out to dig cane holes, to manure, or to cut and crop mature cane under a burning sun until dark.

The work discipline was relentless, as John Luffman reported in the 1780s: "The negroes are under the inspection of white overseers…subordinate to these overseers are drivers, commonly called dog-drivers, who are mostly black or mulatto fellows of the worst dispositions; and these men are furnished with whips which, while on duty, they are obliged, on pain of severe punishment, to have with them, and are authorized to flog wherever they see the least relaxation from labor; nor is it a consideration with them, whether it proceeds from idleness or inability, paying, at the same time, little or no regard to age or sex."

The slaves were given their food weekly. A typical weekly ration consisted of 28lbs (13kg) of yams or potatoes, 10 pints (5 liters) of corn, 8oz (225g) of fish, and 1.75 pints (1 liter) of molasses. The yearly ration of clothing would have been a jacket, shirt, a pair of trousers, and cap for a man, and a jacket, gown, petticoat, and cap for a woman.

The slaves that acquired skills fared better than the field workers, sometimes becoming overseers of other slaves (many rebellions were thwarted through slaves informing on each other) cattle keepers, carpenters, blacksmiths, and tailors. Domestic slaves – maids, cooks, and butlers – were also more trusted and better treated than the field workers.

However, the white owners generally regarded their slaves as lazy, irresponsible, grossly sexualized, potentially rebellious, and intellectually and racially inferior. But often, the only way slaves could resist was through quiet, covert protest such as malingering, feigning illness, working slowly, sabotaging property, and even, in extreme cases, poisoning their masters.

that sugar plantations funded a way of life, as in *Mansfield Park*, by Jane Austen, when her patriarchal character, Sir Thomas Bertram, goes off to Antigua for a year to sort out problems on his sugar estate. But the resident wealthy, aristocratic owners were a minority; most preferred to stay at home and reap their rewards in absentia. Fortunes made in sugar and slavery were then invested in the industrial revolution, first in Britain, then in the rest of Europe.

The islands at this time were overcrowded not only with African slaves, but also with the white riffraff of Europe who hoped to escape

coloreds" or *gens de couleur* – a highly significant group who occupied a marginal position between whites and slaves. The whites saw them as social upstarts, presumptuously claiming to be "white when in fact they were black." Also, their numbers were growing rapidly while the numbers of whites was in decline. After all, it was a rare white man who did not father colored children, except for the descendents of the Scottish-Irish "poor whites" of the 17th century, known today as "Redlegs" in Barbados.

The history, then, of the Antilles during much of this period was the story of this mixed-

*Slave plantation, Antilles, circa 1667.*

their lowly origins. Their skin color gave them a new status in the islands. In this sense, the social history of the islands during this period is in part the sexual exploitation of black women by white plantation males, whether overseers, accountants, indentured servants, or even masters. Better, after all, to be a *grand seigneur* in Martinique than a lowly serf in Provence.

Few visitors failed to note the ostentatious display of wealth and the extravagant style of entertainment practiced by the planters, one of the causes of their perennial indebtedness.

## Gens de couleur

A history of interracial breeding produced the second group in Antillean society, the "free

race's group's struggle for social status and for political and civil rights. The first breakthrough in political rights occurred in the late 18th century in Antigua, when free persons of mixed race possessing the necessary property qualifications were allowed to vote at elections.

## Social respectability

This long drawn-out rise of the people of color was important for two reasons. In the first place, though hardly a revolutionary movement, it did revolutionize society. Like the whites, the "mulattoes" had important interests in slave holding. They resented their own subordination, but did not resist the social structure of which it was a part. They needed the white group as a role model in their search for social respectability, and the white populace needed them as allies against slave unrest and, even worse, slave rebellion. In the French Antilles the official Code Noir of 1785 reflected the negrophobia of the time, listing some 128 grades of color, by which every person in the colony was awarded a status. The free coloreds had to stay on good terms with the white governments, both local and abroad, in order to gain concessions for themselves.

The free coloreds responded to those concessions by developing their own extravagant

of colored persons as white citizens, on the basis of good conduct and social standing.

## The slave population

The slaves generally came from West Africa. Philip Curtin, in his definitive book, *The African Slave Trade*, estimated that from its beginnings in the early 16th century to its termination in the 19th century, some 12 million Africans were brought to the New World by means of the triangular trade. Others have estimated the total at up to 20 million. Only some 3 percent of the transatlantic trade took place in the 16th cen-

*The horrors of slavery.*

*Mulattoes enjoying a dance.*

lifestyle – wearing precious stones and silk stockings, holding masked balls, and adopting the use of ceremonial gunfire at funerals. Social snobbery thus supplanted common racial brotherhood, and the Antillean free coloreds, at least in the formative 18th-century period, became known as a group given more to lavish social display than to mental activity and academia. Lafcadio Hearn wrote in his book on Martinique, although it applied to all the islands, "Travellers of the 18th century were confounded by the luxury of dress and jewelry displayed by swarthy beauties in St Pierre. It was a public scandal to European eyes." Finally, a remarkable royal edict of 1831 in the Danish Virgin Islands permitted the legal registration

tury, mostly by the Portuguese to their colony in Brazil, but it started to pick up in the 17th century, when around a quarter of the translocation took place, and became a huge enterprise in the 18th century when more than half of all slaves were shipped to the Americas.

Whatever their social standing in Africa, whether they were princes or paupers, they arrived as unnamed chattel slaves. They were later to be renamed by their slave owners and masters, which accounts for the Europeanized names of their descendents.

The present-day reversion to African names is a phenomenon of the 20th century, since the Black Power movement began to influence black communities in the US, Europe, and the Caribbean in the 1960s and 1970s. The loss of name was, in a psychological sense, important because it was a part of the total loss of liberty that deprived the African of his right to be regarded as a human being, never mind an equal.

> As a form of rebellion, slaves retained a way of life – in dance, music, and religion – which endured alongside that of the white minority population.

## African traditions

Yet there was play as well as gruelling work. "Every people," wrote the political writer Edmund Burke (1729–97), "must have some compensation for its slavery." And so, from the very beginning, the slaves brought with them their traditions of song and dance. Music played a very large part in their lives; a music that emerged out of a blending and meeting of both the imported European musical forms and the various African song and dance formulations. These encounters gave rise to completely new, exciting forms of dance and music which became uniquely Antillean.

A similar process of creolisation took place, during this early formative period, with language. In the New World setting – planter, overseer, slave, with all of their respective duties and obligations – had to learn to understand each other. The problem was solved, ad hoc, by the invention of creole *patois*, which differed between islands.

## Slave rebellion

The habit of what was called in the French islands *petit marronage* – of running away from the estate for short periods of time to visit a woman friend, or attend a prohibited church meeting, or just simply to feel a taste of freedom – often escalated into rebellion. Such rebellious attempts, all crushed with severe cruelty, occurred regularly, but most notably in St John in the Danish West Indies in 1733, Antigua in 1736, St Croix in 1759, Grenada in 1795, and Barbados in 1816. Most of the slave-owning class lived in fear of slave rebellion. Danish Virgin Islands Governor Gardelin's slave mandate of 1733 was typical in its severity of punishments for slaves guilty of bad

behavior, not to mention those guilty of rebellious behavior.

Certainly they showed that slaves had a capacity for insurrectionary leadership. There were leaders like Tackey and Tomboy in Antigua, who planned to kill all the white people and set up an Ashanti-type black kingdom on the island. Nanny Grigg, in Barbados, told her followers, according to the official record, that the only way to get freedom was to fight for it. Then there was Daaga, who led, although after Emancipation, a brief mutiny of the 1st West India Regiment in Trinidad in 1837. He told his interrogators, on the

*A French soldier training bloodhounds to recognize the smell of a slave.*

eve of his execution, that the seeds of the mutiny had been sown on the passage from Africa.

Two other forces helped destroy the slavery system in the 19th century. First, the economic factor: slave labor was more costly and less efficient than free wage labor; an over-supply of sugar led to catastrophic drops in world prices; and the West Indian planters lost their privileged position in the British market as the world free-trade policies were established. Second, the influence of the British religious-humanitarian movement, led by William Wilberforce (1759–1833) and Thomas Clarkson (1760–1846), finally convinced public opinion of the un-Christian character of the system.

# Amerindians

**Archeologists have discovered a lot about the Amerindians, and while no great monuments remain, traces of their heritage are still evident.**

## Migration and settlement

The first inhabitants of the Lesser Antilles arrived in Trinidad about 7,900 years ago from the Orinoco region of South America. A pre-ceramic

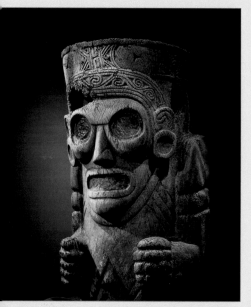

*Taino wood carving depicting an idol found in Santo Domingo.*

(Archaic) people, referred to by archeologists as Ortoroid, they were principally hunter-gatherers, and 28 sites of habitation have been identified, including Banwari Trace, believed to be the oldest archeological site in the Lesser Antilles. A human skeleton found there has been dated to about 5,400 years ago. Stone and bone tools for fishing and hunting have been uncovered, together with grinding stones and pestles for preparing vegetables. From Trinidad they moved up the chain of islands as far as the Virgin Islands and Puerto Rico, where the earliest Ortoiroid site dates from about 6,900 years ago.

The Ortoiroid were eventually displaced by the Saladoid, who followed the same route from 2,000 to 1,400 years ago, bringing horticulture (cassava,

yucca, and maize) and pottery technology. After them, it is thought that another wave of migrants, the Ostionoid culture, arrived between 1,400 and 1,200 years ago, bringing different pottery styles. They appear to have been more sophisticated, developing permanent settlements with ceremonial centers containing ball courts on some islands.

Changes in ceramic styles led to two later phases of the Ostionoid culture being termed Elenoid (1,200–850 years ago) and Chicoid (850–500 years ago). It is these people that the Spaniards called Arawak or Taino Indians. On the Greater Antilles there were large villages of some 1,000–1,500 people with a hierarchical structure, well-defined religious beliefs, and efficient horticultural techniques.

In the Lesser Antilles, however, a few hundred years earlier, a new group of Orinoco River valley migrants had begun to occupy the island arc. By the time of the Spanish arrival, they had displaced the Arawaks on all islands up to and including the Virgin Islands and were engaged in attacking the Taino of Puerto Rico. These people were referred to as Carib, but their few remaining descendents call themselves Kalinago. Within 200 years, genocidal wars, slavery, and disease had eliminated all but a few pockets of Caribs in isolated mountain areas. Today, the 3,000 Kalinago living on a reserve in Dominica maintain some of their old traditions, but only a handful are believed to be of pure blood.

## Family and social life

Men and women lived in separate dwellings on a communal basis. Their houses were of timber and thatch and they slept in hammocks. The only complete floor plan of houses in a village has been uncovered in Sint Eustatius, dating from AD 600–900. Here they are round or oval, of different sizes and capable of housing up to 30 people. The biggest houses were supported by large timbers of up to 25ft (8 meters) high, set in deep holes.

The men did the heavy labor of preparing the soil, carving canoes, hunting, fishing, and defending the village, and teaching the boy children. The women looked after the infants and the older girls, cultivated and harvested the crops, did the cooking, wove baskets, mats, ropes, fishing nets, and hammocks, and made ceramic pots, calabash bowls, and other vessels. It is believed that while the Caribs killed or enslaved the Arawak men, the women were more valuable. The resulting surplus of women led to polygamy, but also a very strong Arawak female influence on Carib culture.

Most of the Amerindian (Arawak/Carib) settlements on the Lesser Antilles were by the sea or at the mouth of rivers. They hunted for some of their food, such as agouti, iguana, birds, and land crabs, but fish and shellfish were the main source of protein. These they caught with their hands, baskets, nets, spears, poison, or lines. Cassava was a staple food, and the cassava bread still eaten today is made in the traditional way. They also grew yams, maize, cotton, arrowroot, peanuts, beans, cocoa, and spices as well as herbs for medicinal purposes or for face paint.

They had no hard metal, but fashioned stones, coral, and shells into tools such as manioc graters, who inhabited the islands. However, there are not many sites of interest to the average visitor. Houses made of timber and thatch quickly disintegrate, while piles of shells and other waste don't quite have the "wow" factor of a pyramid in Guatemala. There are pictographs dotted around the islands, in caves, or on river banks, where drawings could be made on rocks, but these are the extent of any written heritage.

Islanders have, instead, inherited skills and techniques, some vocabulary, and a way of life. Evidence of Amerindians can be seen in the English words for Caribbean, barbecue, hurricane, hammock, cassava, iguana, savannah, tobacco, and

*The cassava root, a staple food in the Caribbean.*

pestles, fish hooks, knives, and weapons. It took months to fell a tree and hollow it out by burning and gradually chipping away at it until they had carved a canoe, some of which were up to 75ft (23 meters) long and capable of carrying 50 people. Canoes can still be seen on Dominica and are used for ceremonial occasions or festival races. In 1997 a group of Kalinago set out from Dominica in their canoe, Gli Gli, and paddled 700 miles (1,125km) to reconnect with the Carib Indians in Guyana, from where their ancestors may have come.

## Legacies and lifestyles

Archeological digs, with the involvement of foreign universities, are constantly striving to uncover the gaps in our knowledge of the pre-Columbian people even more that are in regular use in Spanish. In cooking, favorite dishes are still cassava bread (*casabe*), corn bread (*funchi*), pepperpot stew, and *casareep*, while the native vegetables such as squash, sweet potato, and chilli are considered typically Caribbean.

Many of the farming and fishing techniques are showcased at Fond Latisab Creole Park on St Lucia (see page 223), where farmers cultivate their plants and trees according to practices handed down to them by their forefathers. They utilize drumming for communication, traditional bamboo pots are used for crayfishing, and cassava flour (*farine*) and bread (*casabe*) is made, and sold – the latter a practice that was unknown in pre-Columbian days.

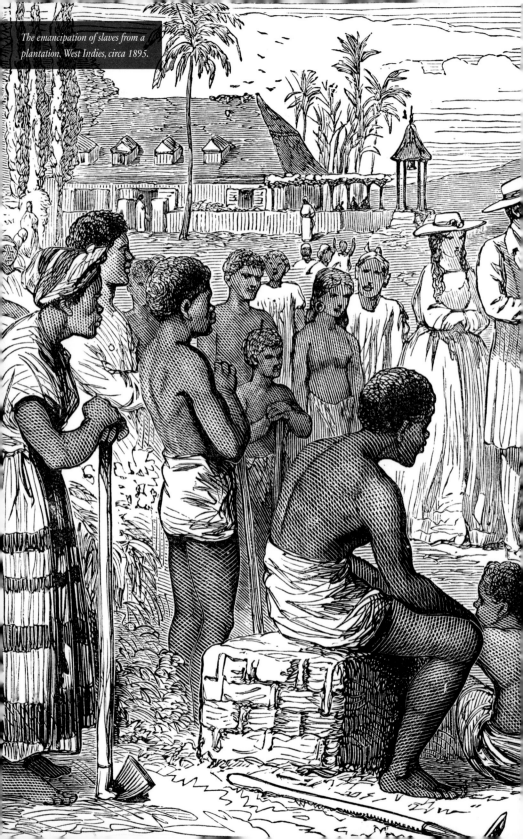

*A young indentured laborer from India who came to Trinidad in the 19th century.*

# ROADS TO INDEPENDENCE

As the freed slaves struggled for survival, an urban workforce grew up. A vocal labor movement developed into political parties with independence on their agenda.

With slavery finally abolished – in the British islands in 1834, the French islands in 1848, and the Dutch islands in 1863 – the post-emancipation period began. This lasted until the vast social and political changes unleashed by World War II (1939–45) started the ball rolling toward most of the islands being given independence.

The freed slaves were permitted for the first time to develop an independent economic life. Previously denied land of their own, those with money bought up parts of abandoned estates, fought for the use of Crown lands, and organized networks of staple crop production and sales outlets in the towns. Starved of labor, the plantations hired thousands of East Indian indentured contract workers brought to parts of the region from Asia between 1838 and 1917.

*Migrant workers cutting sugar cane in Trinidad, circa 1897.*

> *Emancipated slaves became the nutmeg farmers of Grenada, fishermen of Antigua, banana growers in St Lucia, small sugar producers on St Croix, cocoa farmers of Trinidad, and the market women, or "higglers," of all the islands.*

## Employment shortages

Much of what the new, free farmers produced were cash crops, destined for sale in the local market or even abroad. They were peasants in the sense that their lifestyle, with all its old kinship patterns of family, was rural; but their economic values were capitalist. They operated, often with shrewdness, as sellers and buyers in a free-market island economy. As a class, however, they were stratified, like all classes, for there

were at once the rich farmers and the poor farmers, as is still the case today.

The abolition of slavery was not, however, the panacea that the masses had hoped for. Their economic opportunities were limited on most islands by a lack of surplus farming land, no access to credit, and no manufacturing jobs to absorb the excess labor. Conditions for black workers did not improve and indeed plantation owners often treated them worse than under slavery when they had an interest in their health. Low wages, food shortages, poor living conditions, and crushing poverty forced many from their homes in search of work.

In the 1880s, the French began work on the Panama Canal; by 1888 20,000 men, 90 percent of them Afro-Caribbean, were engaged in excavating the channel. A second labor force was assembled when the US took over construction in 1904–14, again, mostly from the West Indies. At the peak of construction, 40,000 workers were involved. The fortunate survivors returned home with cash in their pockets and were able to start businesses or buy land.

At the same time, an urban workforce evolved in trade and commerce centers like St Thomas, Fort-de-France, Bridgetown, Port of Spain, and Willemstad. In the 1900s another workforce developed around the oil refineries

force for industry, commerce, and agriculture. Conditions that were bad enough in the 1920s were made worse by the Depression. The British colonies became known as the "slums of the empire" with a declining sugar industry supporting an estate labor force by means of an exploitative task-work system.

In St Kitts and St Vincent, the wage level had barely advanced beyond the daily shilling rate introduced after Emancipation a century earlier. There was gross malnutrition and chronic sickness; a housing situation characterized by decrepit, verminous, and unsani-

*Farm workers on strike in the 1940s.*

in Trinidad, Curaçao, and Aruba, and banana companies like the Geest group in St Lucia. With the oil companies came full-scale capitalism, resulting in technological dependency; a growing separation between European and colonial economies, with an increasing imbalance of trade; external ownership and control; the influx of foreign managerial personnel; and a system in which the colonies sold cheap and bought dear: they produced what they did not consume, and consumed what they did not produce.

## Breakdown of colonial rule

Between the two world wars, the native workers served as a dependent, low-paid, docile labor

tary conditions; and a working class, when it had work, in a state of economic servitude to a well-organized employer class. The defense mechanisms of a strong trade-union movement were stultified by the existence of punitive legislation.

Such conditions led to labor riots that swept through the English-speaking islands between 1935 and 1938 and to bloody encounters between workers and the police, especially in Barbados and Trinidad. These riots, plus the findings of the British Royal Commission of 1938, helped to further the formation of new worker movements, which led to the creation of new political parties seeking, first, internal self-government and, second, independence.

Some of the new leaders, like Grantley Adams (1898–1971) in Barbados, were black, middle-class lawyers. Most were grassroots leaders, such as Vere Bird in Antigua, Uriah Butler in Trinidad, Robert Bradshaw in St Kitts, and Eric Gairy in Grenada. As all were greatly influenced by the politics of the British Labour Party; the parties they founded were also called labour parties.

## Winding road to independence

It was not a straightforward march to independence. A movement led by Grantley Adams, favoring a federation between the islands,

culminated in the short-lived West Indies Federation (1958–62). That broke up mainly because Jamaica and Trinidad were not prepared to sacrifice their sovereignty to a central federal government. Nor did they want federal taxation.

Trinidad and Tobago were immediately granted independence within the British Commonwealth (1962) and were followed by Barbados in 1966. But the end of the Federation left the smaller Leeward and Windward islands out in the cold. As a result, in 1967, the British Government changed their constitutional status to "associated states," which gave them the right to

*Historian Dr Eric Williams, the first prime minister of Trinidad and Tobago, in 1962.*

## PRIDE AND PREJUDICES

By the start of the 20th century, the economic power of the white population had weakened, but whiteness was still regarded as the ideal image. In contrast to the USA, which classified itself by a simple black-white caste system, in the Antilles the classification system was more a subtle "shade" prejudice.

Social status depended upon fine degrees of skin color with wealth and income a factor. Whereas in US society money talked, in Antillean society money whitened. This led to evasive habits of identity, summed up by the Martinican phrase, *peau noire, masque blanc* (black skin, white mask). The white populace retained their identity by marrying only within their own group.

Today, prejudices have not disappeared, but they tend to relate more to ethnicity in as far as the "native" US Virgin Islanders look down on the immigrants from the Leeward Islands, Trinidadians regard Grenadian immigrants as "small islanders," and the East Indians and Creole black population retain stereotyped images of each other. The French islands tend to resent the influence of the metropolitan immigrant (from France) in big business or government, as they are often prone through ignorance to alienating the local people.

However, on the whole, the Antilleans, with all their differences, still manage to lead a relatively harmonious existence together.

internal self-government but left foreign affairs and defense to London. Some islands, such as St Kitts, Nevis, and Anguilla, were lumped together. Anguilla took exception, breaking away and demanding a return to British jurisdiction, which it retains today.

One by one, the British islands gained independence within the Commonwealth. Grenada was first in 1974, followed by Dominica in 1978, St Lucia and St Vincent and the Grenadines in 1979, Antigua and Barbuda in 1981, and St Kitts and Nevis in 1983. Nevis made an attempt at secession from St Kitts in August 1998, but

However, a strong separatist movement grew up in Aruba and the island broke away in 1986, forming its own parliamentary democracy with a status equal to the rest of the Netherlands Antilles. Curaçao and Sint Maarten also voted for self-government, and on the symbolic date of October 10 2010, the Netherlands Antilles was formally abolished. Aruba, Curaçao, and Sint Maarten are independent countries within the Kingdom of the Netherlands, while the smaller islands of Bonaire, Saba, and Sint Eustatius are special municipalities.

*Antigua and Barbuda celebrate independence in 1981.*

failed when only 62 percent voted in favor in a referendum. However, Anguilla, Montserrat, the Turks and Caicos, the Cayman Islands, and British Virgin Islands have clung to the Crown, and are known as Britain's Overseas Territories.

## Dutch and French loyalties

With the arrival of the oil companies, Dutch political and union leaders became more involved in their relationships with them than with The Hague. The same inequity of power between mother country and colony remained, but it was alleviated by the innovative Dutch Kingdom Statute of 1954, which gave the colonies direct representation in the Dutch cabinet and parliament as an autonomous state.

The French Antilles have a close relationship with France. The *loi cadre* passed by the Paris National Assembly in 1946 established the islands as overseas departments, *départements d'outre-mer* (DOM) – with St-Barthélemy and St-Martin joining with Guadeloupe to share equal status with Martinique. This gave islanders all the rights of French citizens, and equal representation in national politics with economic support from France, which has tempered the development of separatist movements. In 1974 their status improved when they became *régions* with more administrative power. However, in 2007, St-Martin and St-Barthélemy seceded from Guadeloupe and became *collectivités d'outre-mer*, first-order administrative divisions of France.

PARLAMENTO
DI
ARUBA

PARLAMENTO
DI
ARUBA

STA
VA
ARU

# MODERN TIMES

**The new independent nations have come of age and are hoping to put small-island corruption behind them. Tourism is the economic miracle, but the islands are now exposed to international variables.**

The new independent nation states saw the rise of a new and more modern government. Locally trained civil servants replaced the colonial "expatriate" administrative staff; and the state became increasingly involved in the economic sectors. Some industries were nationalized, and governments became majority shareholders in others. For example, in Trinidad, thanks to the oil boom of the 1970s, the government became involved in numerous different commercial enterprises. Such changes reflected and expressed wider socioeconomic and cultural changes.

With the growth of industrialization and modernization – electronics in Barbados, oil refining in St Croix – came rural depopulation, with people flocking to the towns in search of a better standard of living. Privately owned condominiums, tracts of middle-class housing, and public-housing projects were built in response. Education was promoted and the regional University of the West Indies (UWI) was founded with main campuses in Jamaica, Trinidad, and Barbados. Airlines were born – an insignia of national pride – like British West Indian Airways (BWIA) in Trinidad (now Caribbean Airlines) and Leeward Islands Air Transport (LIAT).

*Cruise ship entering port at Nassau, Bahamas, 2013.*

## Fresh challenges

The nascent independent democracies initially faced problems in adjusting to power with no colonial overseers. On some islands money and politics mixed to encourage an element of government corruption: an ex-prime minister of Dominica was convicted of a plot (backed by South Africa), to overthrow the elected government of his successor; a top cabinet minister in Trinidad had to flee to Panama after being accused of making money on a racecourse complex project; and a leading member of Antigua's former ruling family, the Birds, was embroiled in gun running and drug dealing.

The money involved in such scandals often originated from international drug rings, arms merchants, and organized crime syndicates. Thus, the small-island politician became entrapped in a world of high-stakes intrigue which he was ill-equipped to deal with.

## Private lives, public secrets

There have been political leaders of high caliber, such as Grantley Adams and Errol

Barrow in Barbados and Dr Eric Williams and A.N.R. Robinson in Trinidad and Tobago. It is possible, though, for a politician to manipulate a system in which personal charisma is sometimes more important than ideology. Power can be obtained when votes are exchanged for favors, and thus an elaborate network of family, friends, and job-holders is held together by patronage. Since government is the main employer, the juiciest plums are jobs in the local civil service.

It is a kind of market-square politics that emphasizes crowd oratory. In this kind of political arena, private lives become public secrets. In Trinidad it is called *picong, mauvais langue*, robber talk. To listen to its most skilled practitioners at a Caribbean political meeting is to understand the Caribbean gift for talk, its spirit of ribald irreverence, its street defiance of the high and mighty, which is all pulled together in the famous Trinidadian calypso form.

## The effects of big business

With economic development, an affluent middle class emerged, and the basic standards of living, in housing, education, and health, improved immeasurably. But consumerist tastes evolved through American movies, television, and tourism, which generated expectations that could not be realized.

Errol Barrow, the first prime minister of an independent Barbados, said that the high cost of living was not the problem, but the cost of high living. Absolute standards of life have improved, but the gap between rich and poor is still growing.

This is not helped by the tourist industry. From the Virgin Islands to the ABC islands, the landscape is dotted with luxury resorts owned by overseas hotel chains, offering all-inclusive vacations where everything can be paid for at home. Similarly, the growth of the cruise ship industry has led to huge demands on the infrastructure of small islands, but tours and meals are usually paid for on board, leaving passengers limited to spending their money on handicrafts and trinkets while on land. There is employment, but little tax revenue from the employers goes back into the government coffers for the benefit of all. Meanwhile, the rural population is aging and very few young people are going

into farming, preferring to work as maids and bartenders.

Worst of all, development by import capital has increased the structural dependency of the region's economy on multinational companies. Some of them seek cheap labor, others – like the pharmaceutical companies – freedom from environmental legislation at home. Others, especially in high finance, set up offshore operations for worldwide business. These situations are hazardous when a small island becomes host to a single industry. In 1984, for example, major oil companies,

*A banana farmer packing his produce.*

### GREEN GOLD

Bananas are the perfect crop for the small Caribbean farmer. They take only 6 months to grow, they are happy on steep hillsides, and they fruit all year round, providing a steady cash income. Even a hurricane is not a disaster, as bananas can be quickly replanted and harvested. So it is little wonder that they have been celebrated as the farmer's "green gold."

Nonetheless, with the decline of the industry as a result of the EU's termination of preferential trade deals, and fierce competition from US producers, farmers have been known to turn to another green gold – marijuana.

such as Exxon, evacuated Aruba and Curaçao, devastating their economies.

## Economic difficulties

The years since the 1990s have not been kind to the region's beleaguered small-island economies. Traditional export crops have been swamped by competition from other parts of the world. The end of subsidies from Britain and the European Union spelled the end of the struggling sugar industry, which is now confined to small parts of Barbados and Trinidad. "King Sugar" no longer rules.

*Sailboats ready for action on Anguilla.*

Preferential treatment for bananas grown by smallholders in St Lucia, Dominica, St Vincent, and Grenada has been halted by a World Trade Organization (WTO) ruling, in 1997, that the EU system was illegal. Small growers cannot compete without protection against the big growers of Ecuador or Costa Rica. Neither can the islands' small manufacturing sectors compete with Latin America, after the introduction of the Free Trade Area of the Americas (FTAA) in 2005, which scrapped tariffs on goods exported into the US and vice versa. Regional economic and legal integration through the Caribbean Community (CARICOM) is attempting to deal with the region's major challenges and opportunities.

## Tourism takes over

Most of the Caribbean is now firmly reliant on the tourist industry. Many islands, such as St Kitts and St Lucia, are building on their few remaining tracts of undeveloped coastline in the search for foreign exchange – much to the consternation of the region's environmentalists – but alternative incomes are few and far between. One such alternative is the transshipment of South American cocaine, which remains an (albeit illegal) recourse for many of the region's urban gangs – and reaches into business and political circles too.

> The advent of sugar substitutes in Europe and North America has meant that "King Sugar" no longer rules the Caribbean.

Tourism, however, is a fickle industry and demand can evaporate overnight, leaving hotel rooms empty and tour operators twiddling their thumbs. After the 9/11 terrorist attack on New York, travel to the Caribbean took a nose-dive. The 2009–10 international financial crisis had a similar impact, as potential travelers, worried about their livelihoods, decided to stay at home. A hurricane can leave ministers of tourism scrambling to reassure vacationers that their regions are safe, that their hotels are open for business, and that tourist custom is desperately needed.

Visitors from Europe are much sought after because, having traveled further, they stay longer than US visitors, and spread their money around more as a result. Consequently the UK's green tax increase on airline tickets caused huge consternation in 2010–11 with Caribbean destinations feeling unfairly disadvantaged.

Fortunately, the years 2014 and 2015 saw a recovery in tourism in almost all Lesser Antilles destinations and an increase in the number of visitor arrivals – stay-over European visitor arrivals in particular – and prospects for the near future of the region seem to be favorable.

Ironically, it seems that although the islands may have gained political independence from their colonial masters, they remain dependent on the state of the world economy for their income and prosperity.

# Ecotourism, sustainable, and community tourism

**Tourism is essential to the economy of the islands but the environmental consequences have to be considered.**

As man's footprint on the earth becomes ever larger and the land more downtrodden, so environmental concerns assume greater importance. Small islands, by their very nature, are fragile and need protecting, on land and under water. Large resorts bring in thousands of visitors yearly and generate much-needed employment, while cruise ships spill thousands more on to the streets of harbor towns, keeping taxi drivers and tour guides busy, but at an ever-growing cost to the environment.

Each new hotel comes under pressure from environmentalists to show its green credentials but the sheer volume of people is a concern. The US Virgin Islands, for example, receive more than 2.5 million visitors by air and sea each year, swamping the local population of 0.1 million, while Sint Maarten's 77,000 residents welcome 1.5 million cruise ship and stay-over visitors. Is this sustainable? Can islands' infrastructure and natural environment cope? There is a niche market in the Caribbean for "ecotourism," but what does that term imply?

To some, ecotourism conjures up images of rustic forest cabins along the lines of Dominica's 3 Rivers, an award-winning lodge with camping and wooden huts on stilts, solar, wind and hydro power, composting toilets, recycled gray water, and chemicals limited only to preventing termites from eating the premises. However, there is now a luxury end to the ecotourism market: Rosalie Bay, near 3 Rivers, is a new, very comfortable, elegant hotel with turtles nesting on the beach. It is also solar- and wind-powered with on-site water filtration, and uses organic produce from its kitchen garden and from local farmers.

Similar attempts to lessen the impact of tourism are being made throughout the Lesser Antilles, from solar showers and lighting at Ecolodge Rendez-Vous in Saba, to an advanced wastewater system at Captain Don's Habitat in Bonaire. Solar hot water and, increasingly, solar power are common in these sunny islands and many hotels now request that you reuse your towels to conserve scarce water. Much conservation work is going on back-of-house of which guests are oblivious.

## Committed to the community

Ecotourism, sustainable tourism and community tourism are descriptions that frequently overlap. Both 3 Rivers and Rosalie Bay take very seriously their commitment to the local community, through employment, training, investment and sponsorship of local events. It took many years to build Rosalie Bay, but once it was done, the hotel retrained the construction workers to become barmen or other hospitality personnel, while their wives, some of whom had never

*Waitress at the Rosalie Bay Resort.*

had a job before, trained as cleaners and cooks. All the furniture was made by a local craftsman and the village supplies guides and gardeners. Not one of them had ever worked in tourism before.

Dominica continues to promote community, sustainable tourism with the inauguration of the Waitukubuli Trail. Divided into 14 segments, the trail has been cleared and marked by volunteers from the local communities. In return, hikers on the trail, which runs the length and breadth of the island, will hire local guides when necessary and stay in bed-and-breakfast places or homestays at the end of each segment. Community tourism here will generate employment in rural areas and ensure that revenue stays within the community while having a very low impact on the natural environment.

Bahamian performers at the De Scotiabank Caribana Lime Festival.

*Demonstrating the art of basketry in Antigua.*

# A CARIBBEAN BLEND

**The culture of the Lesser Antilles is bursting with vitality, all due to the rich social mix of people living here that the French Antilleans call *créolité*.**

Almost everyone in the Caribbean islands is, in some sense, a stranger. Not just the tourists, of course, or the wealthy expatriate communities, the Europeans and North Americans who have opted for a tropical idyll. But also the "locals" who, although they and their ancestors may have been born in the Caribbean, are likely to have their roots in a different continent.

The modern-day Caribbean is peopled by the descendents of African slaves, Indian and Chinese laborers, European colonists, and Middle Eastern traders. Even the Caribs originated from the great rivers and deltas of the South American mainland.

Many of today's people have ancestors who arrived in chains after being crammed into suffocating ships for weeks on end. The great majority came against their will, snatched from another life and brutally transplanted into a strange new world.

And yet their descendents have stayed, and many have prospered. Slavery continues to cast a shadow over the region and is held responsible for all manner of economic and social problems, but the contemporary Caribbean wastes little time on nursing historic grudges. On the contrary, a strong and positive sense of identity, both national and regional, has grown out of past injustices, and most people in these islands look forward rather than back to a tortured history.

## Creole mix

Caribbean societies are by their very nature a mix of different people and cultures. The word "creole", originally referring to a European-descended settler born in the Americas, has come to signify this combination of cultural

*Maintaining those family ties with warmth and humor.*

### NATIONAL IDENTITY

These small islands are essentially rural in character. With a few exceptions most island capitals are like small market towns, picturesque but parochial. The younger generation is growing up with television and the internet but a sense of national identity remains linked to the land, and traditional, rural festivals are still celebrated. It is tempting to regard the islands as an earthly paradise, yet it is a distortion, for their history is of slavery and colonialism. Even now poverty forces people to migrate. This tension between the people and their history is captured in the works of many Caribbean writers, particularly, perhaps, in the poetry of Derek Walcott.

influences, blended into a distinctive whole. Languages, cooking, clothing, and architecture all carry the term, which, as in New Orleans, implies a highly spiced fusion of ingredients.

## The European factor

European influence has marked the Caribbean since the first Spanish expeditions, but in the Eastern Caribbean the dominant nations were Britain, France, and, to a lesser degree, Holland. Their imprint is still clearly to be seen in the cricket pitches of Barbados, the haute cuisine of Martinique, and the gabled warehouses of

town centers, this heritage is not so obvious, but in fishing villages or farming communities it is unmistakable.

## Asian influences

Add to this the sights, sounds, and flavors of the Indian subcontinent, characterized by Hindu temples and prayer flags, and local variants on curry, and the creole mix begins to take shape. Other ingredients are important too; more recent migrants from China, Madeira, and Africa have preserved elements of their respective cultures, and few islands are without

*A game of schoolboy cricket, Speightstown, Barbados.*

Curaçao. But with the exception of a handful of left-over colonial outposts, the days of European rule are long gone, and it would be hard to see in any Caribbean territory a miniature imitation of the old metropolises.

Europeanness has merged into Africanness, the set of languages, customs, and beliefs that came to the Caribbean with the millions of slaves across the "middle passage." Surviving the culture shock of slavery and the imposition of colonial values, African influence is stubbornly omnipresent: in rural housing, agricultural techniques, food, music, and dance, as well as belief systems such as the Yoruban Orisha or Shango faith, and the syncretic Spiritual Baptist (Shouter). In modern

*Creole culture values freedom above all else – and freedom includes the right to live life at your own pace.*

an influential group of Syrian or Lebanese-descended people. But perhaps most important is the constant contact with North America and its cultural exports.

In the French islands they have a word for it: *créolité*. It is what sets Caribbean people apart from other cultures, what makes island life distinctive and unique. It also implies a blending process, an ability to absorb influences and shape them into something different – it's a dynamic process, one that never stays still, and one that perhaps accounts for the bursting vitality of the region's culture.

## Creole tongue

Creole languages are widely spoken across the Caribbean and are a complex cocktail of linguistic elements. They all use West African grammatical structures and mostly European vocabulary. In Martinique and Guadeloupe (and to a lesser degree, St Lucia, Dominica, Grenada, and Trinidad), French provides the basis for the local creole, with traces of English and Spanish. But don't expect to understand it even if your French is fluent.

Creole was spoken among slaves from widely differing backgrounds in Africa and so combines a multitude of different linguistic sources. Guadeloupean creole, for instance, contains the English-descended *kònbif* (corned beef) and *djòb* (job) as well as such African-inspired words as *koukou-djèdjè* (hide and seek) and *zanba* (devil).

Without doubt, the most eclectic creole is papiamentu, spoken in some of the Dutch islands, but principally in Curaçao. From there

*A Creole restaurant in Mayreau, The Grenadines.*

## WORDS OF WISDOM

In Barbados, general conversation is peppered with wise old sayings especially in the rural areas. Here are a few you may hear:

*Hansome don' put in pot* – sustained effort is needed to achieve anything worthwhile.

*News don' lack a carrier* – there is always someone to pass on gossip.

*Two smart rats can' live in de same hole* – two tricksters won't get on together.

*Goat head every day better than cow head every Sunday* – it is better to be treated reasonably well all the time than have first-class treatment some of the time.

*Head en' mek fuh hat alone* – use common sense.

*Pretty-pretty things does fool li'l children* – superficial things impress superficial and naive people.

*Ole stick o' fire don' tek long to ketch back up* – old love affairs can soon be revived.

*A eyeful en' a bellyful* – just because you can see it, it doesn't mean you can have it (said by women to men).

*De higher de monkey climb, de more 'e show 'e tail* – the more you show off, the more exposed your faults become.

*De las' calf kill de cow* – taking the same risk too often can have disastrous consequences.

*Fisherman never say dat 'e fish stink* – people never give bad reports about themselves.

# Dominoes

**Dominoes is more than a social event – it is taken very seriously, and there is even a campaign for it to become an Olympic sport.**

A few sharp cracks and the group of men huddled over the small table leap to their feet with a roar of jubilation. Dominoes may appear to be a sedentary game, but it is far from quiet and peaceful. It is

*A well-worn domino table testifies to the game's popularity.*

played very fast and a game is over in minutes. The dominoes are often slammed hard down for maximum effect and the atmosphere can be tense.

Played by young and old on all the islands, it is a game for just a few players, which can be played anywhere, often out on the street in the evening or under the spreading mango tree with a tot of rum or a beer. You will rarely see women playing out on the street, but they are keen competitors too. It is a game that requires very little investment in equipment and can be played anywhere. Any sturdy, flat table will do, and all the better if you can score on it with chalk.

Dominoes is not just a social event, however. Played at club level it becomes a serious competitive sport with league matches. The World Council of Domino Federations (WCDF) is headquartered in Barbados (the word "World" is a slight misnomer, as the Caribbean dominates and Canada and the United States are the only other member countries, but the council aims to encourage wider membership). The WCDF has eight disciplines covering three-hand and four-hand dominoes: team four-hand, four hand pairs, male and female three-hand, king and queen domino, mixed pairs and female pairs. Got that?

The week-long World Domino Championship, held every other year since 1998 (it was held annually from 1991 to 1998), has been won by Barbados more times than any other country. Dominica has won a couple of times but St Lucia is Barbados' main rival, having won the title five times to Barbados' eight. Antigua hosted the 2008 Championship, St Lucia that of 2010, Florida was the venue for the tournament in 2012, and Barbados in 2014.

There is a campaign for dominoes to be an Olympic sport, but organizers face an uphill battle achieving the required standards. It could be many years yet before competitors are considered athletes, subject to strict anti-doping rules, however agile their minds are. Currently, club rules specify no eating, no drinking, and no talking once the game commences, but that's it.

Dominoes originated in China, where legend has it that a soldier invented the game to entertain troops waiting to go into battle. The tiles were made of ivory and are still affectionately called "bones." Brought to Venice in the 18th century by Chinese traders, the black and white tiles reminded Italians of the hoods of Dominican monks, and the nickname "Domini" was coined. The new parlor game of Venice and Naples soon spread across Europe to Britain and from there to the Caribbean via the sugar and slave trade.

## Helping children to get ahead

Dominoes are used in schools to help with cognitive development and improve children's mathematical skills. In the Caribbean it is a point of reference when islanders meet each other for the first time. Confident in their own abilities they are keen to challenge anybody to a game, wherever they are. Even Dr Ralph Gonsalves, Prime Minister of St Vincent and the Grenadines, is proud to be an honorary member of the WCDF, convinced that he is a better player than anyone else. And who would want to argue with the prime minister of St Vincent and the Grenadines?

it spread more widely throughout the region via the men from many different islands who worked in the oil refineries. This language has had a magpie tendency to take words from wherever it could: Dutch, English, Spanish,

> The common language of Aruba, Bonaire, and Curaçao is papiamentu – a combination of dialects with no fixed spelling – which is used for newspapers, books, and debates in parliament.

groups throughout the region is nothing short of spectacular, ranging from established Anglicans and Roman Catholics to the new generation of Pentecostals and other evangelical sects. Church-going on a Sunday morning is a serious business, as you will soon notice from the sheer activity on country roads and village streets as people in their Sunday best head for their chosen service.

Religion, like language, is a living example of creole adaptability. The slave owners may have only half-heartedly imposed Christianity on their slaves, but the people responded

*School children in St-Martin.*

Portuguese, and some African sources. The result can be baffling when heard but strangely familiar when seen in written form, especially if you know some Spanish. *Pan* means bread and *awa* means water (*pan* and *agua* in Spanish), while *kaya* is not very far from *calle* (street) or *aki* from *aqui* (here). The English speaker may recognize *motosaikel* (motorcycle).

## A choice of worship

If linguistic ingenuity is a characteristic of Caribbean societies, then so too is religious feeling. Driving through small villages in Barbados or Antigua you would be excused for thinking that churches outnumbered potential parishioners. The profusion of church

enthusiastically, soon creating an independent tradition of preaching and self-help. Many social institutions – youth clubs, credit schemes, educational facilities – are intimately linked to the churches.

But Caribbean people have also given Christianity their own emphases and influences; in some cases religious practices from Africa were mixed in with the teachings of the testaments to produce local faiths. Trinidad's Shango, for instance, is a cult made up of African traditions blended with elements of Roman Catholic and Baptist Christianity.

In other cases, African belief systems have remained more or less unadulterated. Obeah, a form of sorcery originating in West African folklore, is still widely believed in throughout the islands, although few people will admit to it. Similar to Haitian voodoo practices, it can involve the use of magic spells and exotic potions either to cause harm to others or to seek cures for all sorts of problems. The Obeahman or Obeahwoman is still a figure who merits some considerable respect, not to say fear, in the community.

## The Rastafari movement

Although originating in Jamaica, the Rastafari movement has spread throughout the

*The Rastafari movement has made its mark in all parts of the Lesser Antilles.*

Lesser Antilles, and is typical of the synthetic development of religious ideas. Its adherents, in fact, regard it as a way of life rather than a religion. A mix of literal Old Testament reading and African mysticism, it seeks to right the wrongs suffered by black people across the world by reuniting them in the promised land of Ethiopia.

Ras Tafari was the name of the late Emperor Haile Selassie (1892–1974), who is revered as a god by members of the movement. Not all of its adherents believe in a real return to Africa, but most are attracted by a lifestyle that is both rebellious toward authority and stringently devoted to a cause.

## Diversity and tolerance

The Indo-Caribbeans are also in evidence through their religion. In islands such as Trinidad and Guadeloupe, where indentured immigration was greatest after abolition, the landscape is dotted with Hindu temples, adorned with images of Krishna, Shiva, or Rama. Prayer flags flap outside village houses or amidst clumps of banana or bamboo, and Indian communities celebrate feast days, such as Hosay, Phagwa (celebrating the arrival of spring), and Diwali (the Hindu Festival of Lights), with traditional music and dancing. Mosques add another dimension to the religious landscape, and Eid-ul-Fitr, celebrating the end of Ramadan, is an important occasion in Trinidad.

> *Duppies, or ghosts, are kept out of the house at night by sand left on the doorstep as, before entering, they must count every grain – an impossible task even for a ghost to perform before dawn.*

It is a tribute to local tolerance that such a heady mix of religious faiths has rarely produced friction between differing practitioners. The established churches used to campaign against African religion, denigrating it as "superstition" or "black magic," but that is largely a thing of the past. The US-inspired evangelicals may be inclined to preach against Obeah and its ilk, but their message is not widely followed.

This tolerance extends to many walks of life and may explain why the Eastern Caribbean islands, although poor and deprived by some definitions, have not witnessed the social strife that experts predicted in the transition toward independence (but see page 63 for more on Caribbean attitudes toward, and laws concerning, homosexuality, one area to which very little tolerance is extended).

It is always dangerous to generalize about any society, and stereotypes can be condescending, even when well-intentioned. Yet terms like "laid-back," known as "liming" on the islands, contain a grain of truth about local attitudes to life and personal relations, suggesting with some accuracy a general distaste for unnecessary stress and conflict.

# The darker side of life

**While the Caribbean islands may be blessed with many things, life is not always a bed of roses – especially for those who face discrimination.**

Tolerance does not extend to every sector of society in the Caribbean. Religious groups, and therefore much of the population, are notoriously homophobic, particularly in the British Commonwealth countries, still adhering to Victorian legislation criminalizing homosexual acts; and there is no cohesive system of human rights monitoring. Gay tourists will rarely be discriminated against, as long as they do not display in public acts of affection that might offend local citizens, but a Trini gay man will face "battyman" insults if not outright violence.

There is little political will to reform legislation and in a recent UN resolution to condemn arbitrary killings on the basis of identity features, nearly all Commonwealth Caribbean countries voted to exclude the category of "sexual orientation." The only voice to speak out so far is that of the prime minister of St Kitts and Nevis, Dr Denzil Douglas, who urged fellow political leaders to review discriminatory legislation, but has not so far done so in his own country. The move is linked to securing finance for HIV/AIDS prevention, as funding agencies will not allow access to treatment programs until homosexuality is decriminalized.

## Living with HIV

The Caribbean has the second-highest prevalence of living with HIV in the world after Sub-Saharan Africa. Most of the Lesser Antilles are not as badly infected as, say, the Bahamas (3 percent) or Jamaica (1.7 percent); but high rates are seen in Trinidad and Tobago (1.5 percent) and Barbados (1.4 percent). Contrary to popular belief, the principal route of transmission is heterosexual sex, much of it associated with prostitution. More than half of people living with HIV in the Caribbean are women, vulnerable due to gender inequality, sexual taboos, early initiation to sexual acts, and economic need. Nevertheless, it is likely that the proportion of new infections from sex between men is higher than figures show: men get overlooked because homophobia has led to denial and under-reporting.

## Death in paradise

Crimes against tourists are rare, but receive huge publicity when they occur. The murder of a newlywed couple in their hotel room in Antigua or the shooting of a 14-year-old cruise ship passenger caught in the crossfire of gang warfare in St Thomas are broadcast worldwide. Theft from hotel rooms and rental villas is more common but is under-reported to avoid alarming the tourist industry. Robbery of cruise ship passengers on tours is posted on websites as a warning. So powerful is this media attention that cruise lines do not hesitate to withdraw an island from their itineraries if they think including it will damage business.

*Cocaine seized off the coast of Martinique.*

The high rates of murder in Jamaica and Trinidad are legendary, but drugs-related crime means the rates in the USVI are also high. Over 50 percent of the cocaine shipped from South America to the US and Europe passes through the Caribbean and St Thomas sits on a crossroads, with drugs coming from the south and guns from the north. Gangs, "posses" in the Caribbean, flourish in times of economic recession, especially around the drug trade where there are battles over local distribution networks.

The more prosperous islands are the safest for tourists. Top of the table in the region are Montserrat, St-Barths, the BVI, Bonaire, and Dominica. The majority of visitors, just like the islanders themselves, take reasonable precautions with their property and personal security, and have no problems at all.

# SPECTATOR SPORTS

**The West Indies are rightly known for their prowess in cricket, but soccer engenders equal enthusiasm, and sports of every kind are played and enjoyed at all levels.**

West Indies cricket is the major sport of the region that anyone can watch, from a village team to an international match. First-class teams in the region are the Leeward Islands (including the USVI and Sint Maarten), the Windward Islands, Barbados, and Trinidad and Tobago, and players from these teams (and Jamaica and Guyana) are picked to represent the West Indies in international cricket. The men's West Indies cricket team won the ICC World Twenty20 in 2012 and the women's team won the 2010 ICC Women's Cricket Challenge Twenty20 International Tournament and came second in the Women's Cricket World Cup in 2013.

Soccer is played by every small boy with a ball and many girls now take it up at school too. Soccer pitches in the Caribbean can be a sorry sight with little grass and lopsided goal posts, but they are well used. Every island's national team competes in CONCACAF regional tournaments. Aruba, the USVI, Anguilla, and Montserrat are ranked at the bottom, but the Trinidad and Tobago team, the Soca Warriors, holds the record of being the smallest nation ever to qualify for the World Cup Finals, in 2006, where they scored one point.

*There is nothing like a day out at the cricket in the West Indies – beer, music, and boisterous fun in the sunshine with a crowd of passionate supporters.*

*Tricia Liverpool of Trinidad and Tobago looks to pass in the 2011 World Netball Championships in Singapore, in which they came seventh, Jamaica came fourth and Barbados also competed.*

*Kim Collins, of St Kitts and Nevis, became World Champion in the 100-meter sprint in 2003.*

*Sir Viv Richards, an Antiguan cricket legend.*

## AUDIENCE PARTICIPATION

The people of the Lesser Antilles are sports mad. Athletics, cricket, soccer, netball… they are world-class authorities. The latest results will be mulled over every evening over a game of dominoes and a rum – criticism can get quite animated, with heated exchanges as the finer points of a match are debated. If someone asks you where you are from, don't be surprised if he knows every member of your local soccer team and where they stand in the league. High up in the rainforest canopy of Dominica, you could be discussing the merits of the latest transfer list in English soccer with your guide, who wears the football shirt of his favorite Premier League team.

West Indies cricket crowds are legendary and the supporters have influenced audiences worldwide. The game is greeted with a cacophony of sound, from whistles to drums, which quietens as the bowler runs up, and explodes again as the batsman hits the ball to the boundary. During intervals the audience may be entertained by characters such as the (now retired) cross-dressing cheerleader, Gravy, who still occasionally puts on a cameo performance.

*Rodrigue Beaubois, of Guadeloupe, plays basketball for the French national team as well as for the Dallas Mavericks.*

*Polo is played by the affluent elite in Barbados, where there are several polo fields for matches against visiting teams from abroad. Here, Prince Harry competes in a charity cup match.*

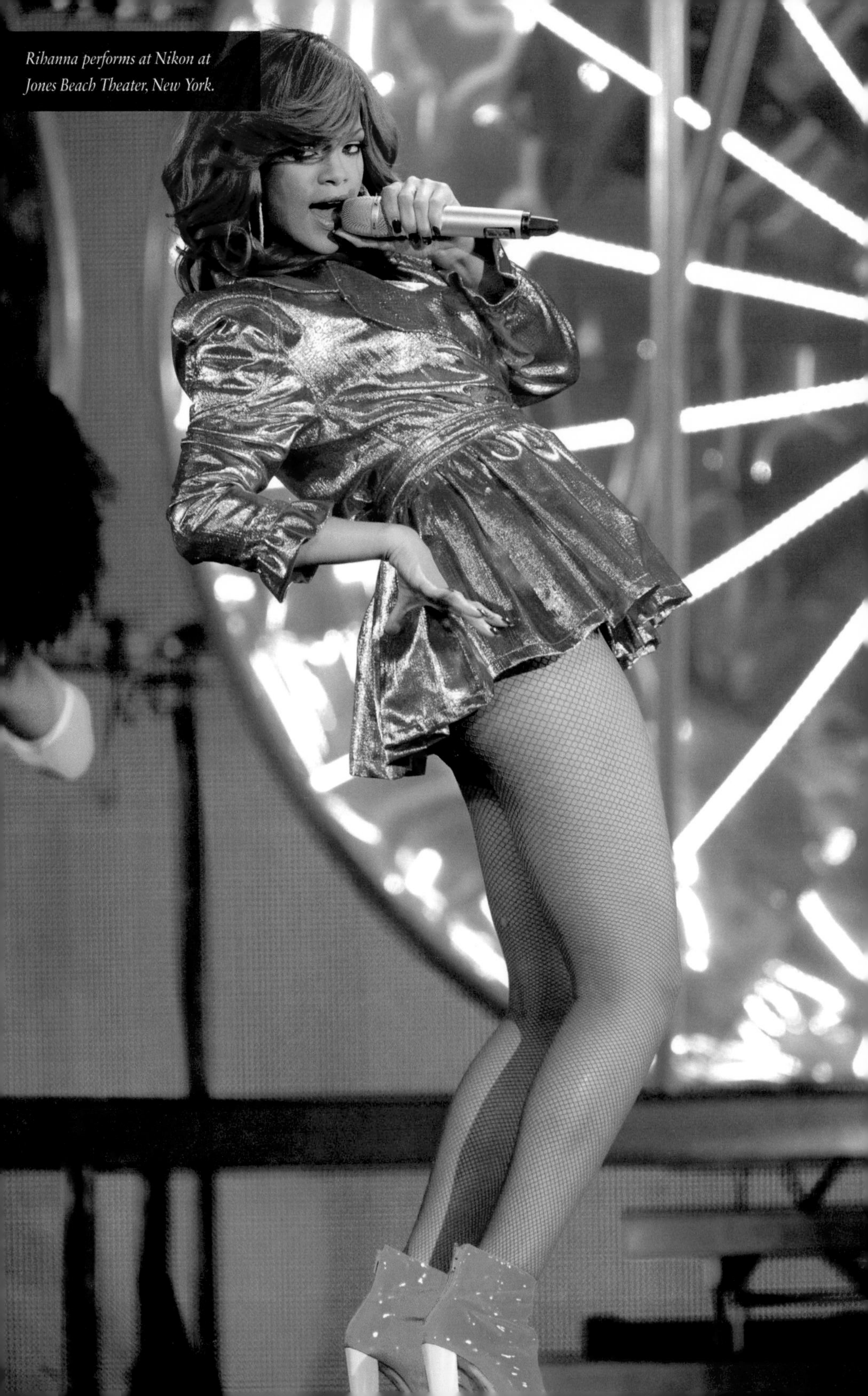
*Rihanna performs at Nikon at Jones Beach Theater, New York.*

# AND THE BEAT GOES ON

Caribbean music never stands still and the eastern islands, where fusion is a way of life, are among the most exciting musical regions in the world.

Think of Caribbean music, and what do you come up with? Reggae would be an obvious first choice. Almost everybody can recognize the sound that took the world by storm in the 1970s with artists like Bob Marley and Peter Tosh and which is still a force to be reckoned with. And then what? Salsa became a phenomenon in the 1980s, with Cubans, Puerto Ricans, and mainland Latin Americans setting the pace. Then there's calypso and steel pan, the infectious good-time music that seems to evoke the region in its every note.

*The award-winning Bajan sensation that is Rihanna exploded on the music scene in 2005, when she was just 17. Now one of the best-selling artists of all time, she tours worldwide with her mix of R&B, pop, reggae, and dance.*

African drumming.

But these four totally different types of music are just the tip of an ever-growing musical iceberg. Leaving aside the bigger islands, such as Jamaica, Cuba, and Puerto Rico, even the smaller territories of the Lesser Antilles reveal an extraordinary diversity of styles and sounds that run from A to Z. In between Trinidad's aguinaldo and Martinique's zouk you will find genres such as bélè (French islands), jing ping (Dominica), raggasoca (Barbados), and tambu (Dutch islands). And that's not to mention bouyon and parang.

## Medley of influences

This baffling array of musical forms is testimony to the creativity and individuality of each Caribbean island. It also reminds us of the many different influences – linguistic as well as musical – that have left their mark on the region. European colonizers from Britain, France, and Spain brought their music and instruments with them, recalled today in dances such as the quadrille of Martinique and Guadeloupe. From Africa came the drum-based rhythms and tradition of collective participation that underlie almost all contemporary styles in the region. Indian migrants contributed distinctive instruments and harmonies, especially in multicultural Trinidad. More recently, American jazz, rock and roll, rap, and hip hop have been incorporated and adapted into local forms, together with everything from Latin brass sections to Country & Western.

Caribbean music never stands still. Constantly borrowing and developing, it keeps pace with technological advances while remaining

> A Calypsonian is… not only an articulator of the population, he is also a fount of public opinion. He expresses the mood of the people, the beliefs of the people. " Mighty Chalkdust, Trinidadian teacher and Calypso Monarch

Predecessors included the tamboo bamboo orchestras, which pounded bamboo tubes on the ground or beat them with sticks (used instead of drums, which were banned by the British colonials as they thought they would encourage rioting) at folk dances, funeral wakes, and, of course, Carnival. Other percussionists resorted to biscuit tins, dustbins, and kitchen pots until the versatility of the imported oil drum, a feature of Trinidad's booming petroleum industry, was discovered.

To begin with, steel pan and its players suffered a serious image problem. Associated with

The steel pan is at the heart of the Caribbean sound and linked to Trinidad especially.

rooted in age-old traditions. In a region where so many cultural influences, good and bad, have been absorbed, fusion is a way of life. No wonder the Caribbean has a reputation for being one of the most exciting musical regions in the world.

## Steel pan – a by-product of oil

You will hear steel pan throughout the region, but Trinidad justifiably claims not just to have invented it, but to be the world leader in playing it. There are still arguments over who it was who first realized the musical potential of a discarded oil drum in the 1930s. But there is no dispute that rhythm and percussion were already well established on the island.

the slum areas of Port-of-Spain and tainted by regular violence, as gangs formed around competing bands to fight turf wars among themselves and against the police. It was only with the advent of corporate sponsorship and the commercialization of Carnival that the violence subsided. With the threat of companies withdrawing band sponsorship, a degree of peace broke out, and the previously violent rivalry subsumed into Panorama, the annual national steel band competition.

## Calypso – voice of the people

The calypsonian was – and still is – the people's orator. In post-Emancipation times, as people flocked to the city in search of jobs and away from the plantation, the calypsonian took on the traditional role of the chantwell, the improvising vocalist who used to sing boastful and comic songs during rural stick-fighting sessions. His function involved the dissemination of gossip, the spreading of news, and the mocking of those in authority. By the early 20th century, his performances were taking place in special tents, in front of discerning audiences who judged the artist's topicality and originality.

Today, little has changed, although there are now female performers, and subjects such

and Lord Kitchener. The Mighty Sparrow is a Grenadian by birth, while Arrow (Alphonsus Cassell, who died in 2010), the singer of the 1980s' worldwide hit Hot *Hot Hot*, came from Montserrat.

That song, in fact, is actually more soca than calypso, a faster-paced, dance-oriented style that has evolved from the fusion of Afro and Indian influences within the Trinidadian music scene (the word "soca" was originally "so-kah" – letters of the Hindi alphabet). Soca turned calypso into a more modern, danceable form, which appealed to younger generations.

*Brass is integral to soca, traditional carnival party music.*

as feminism and domestic abuse provide up-to-date inspiration. The calypsonian's armory contains spontaneous improvisation, wit, and picong (biting, literally piquant, observations). His (or her) songs may be narrative, oratorical, or extemporaneous, but it's likely that they will focus on sex, scandal, and what is known as "bacchanal."

Calypso is part of Trinidad's cultural lifeblood, which permeates through the whole of the Caribbean, and the climax comes each year at Carnival – or Crop Over in Barbados – which provides the background for fierce competition, lucrative prizes, and front-page headlines. Trinidad's hall of fame includes legends such as Roaring Lion, Attila the Hun,

## A CHRISTMAS TRADITION

The build-up to Christmas in Trinidad wouldn't be the same without the Afro-Spanish tradition known as parang (from the Spanish *parar*, meaning "to stop at" or "put up at somebody's house"). The music is named after the roving performers who would move from house to house at the festive season with violins, cuatros, mandolins, guitars, and maracas, along with the African-descended box drum and box bass. Deeply traditional in form, the styles include Spanish names such as *aguinaldo*, *galerón*, or *paseo* and are largely descended from the carol singing of 18th- and 19th-century Spanish settlers.

And the musical evolution continues to gain momentum with the creation of raggasoca, the fusion of Jamaican dancehall and local soca.

## Ceremonial tuk

One thriving aspect of Barbados's annual Crop Over festival (historically held to mark the end of the cane-cutting season) is the tuk band. These percussive outfits are believed to date from as far back as the 17th century and later accompanied the island's local friendly societies, known as "landships," in ceremonies and outings. They are also thought to have modeled themselves on the marching bands of 18th-century British regiments.

Today's tuk band is made up of bass, snare and kettle drums, a penny whistle or flute, and usually a triangle. Despite what might seem at first to be a limited musical range, the bands' versatility is amazing and is often shown off in a wide repertoire of songs, covering the spectrum from European classical pieces to negro spirituals and current *Billboard* (Top Ten) hits. But it is the original, Caribbean-flavored material that brings out the best in the musicians, and thanks to the efforts of calypsonian Wayne

*Kassav band-member Jacob Desvarieux performs at the Pan-African Cultural Festival in Algeria, 2009.*

## ROUND-UP OF MUSIC FESTIVALS

Many islands stage music festivals in addition to annual Carnival celebrations:
**January** St-Barths Music Festival (classic, folk, jazz)
**February** Mustique Blues Festival
**March** St John Blues Festival
**April** Holders Season, Barbados (opera); Carriacou Maroon & String Band Music Festival; Tobago Jazz Experience
**May** St Lucia Jazz and Arts Festival; Union Island Maroon Festival; Gospelfest, Barbados; Rapso Month, Trinidad; Grenada Drum Festival; Aruba Soul Beach Music Festival; BVI Music Festival; Terre-de-Blues Festival, Marie Galante

**June** St Kitts Music Festival; Antilles Music Festival, Martinique and Guadeloupe
**July** Gwo Ka Drum Festival, Guadeloupe
**August** Curaçao Salsa Tour Festival; Pic-o-De-Crop Calypso Finals, Barbados
**September** Curaçao North Sea Jazz Festival
**October** World Creole Music Festival, Dominica; Festival de las Américas, Aruba; Jazz Festival, Antigua and Barbuda; St Croix Music and Arts Festival, USVI
**November** Gwadloup' Festival, Guadeloupe; Martinique Jazz Festival
**December** Carriacou Parang Festival; International Ilojazz Festival, Guadeloupe

"Poonka" Willcock and his group Ruk-a-Tuk International, tuk music has been staging something of a comeback in local festivals.

## Begin the beguine...

The earliest authentic style to have come from Martinique and Guadeloupe is generally agreed to be the beguine, its bolero rhythm a firm favorite among dance orchestras from the 1930s to the 1950s. Over the following two decades, the French Antillean soundscape underwent significant changes due to migration and freshly imported influences. An important new ingredient was brought by Haitian immigrants in the form of kadans or "cadence," a subtle blend of musical accents, syncopation, and instrumental color derived from the fast-paced merengue, the national dance music of the neighboring Dominican Republic.

From kadans evolved zouk in the 1980s, a genre which was less a fad than a true phenomenon, reaching beyond the confines of the Caribbean to touch the continents of Africa, America, and Europe. Zouk trailblazers were the Guadeloupean band Kassav, whose founders, Pierre-Edouard Décimus and Jacob Devarieux, captured the festive mood and euphoria that marked the local *vidé* (spontaneous street carnival parade), and integrated old-style rhythmic dance elements into a modern good-time sound.

The success of Kassav and others marked the entry of French Caribbean music into the international marketplace. It also offered an original, rather than borrowed, model, including a long overdue emphasis on women's voices, that appeals not only to the Caribbean as a whole, but to aficionados of dance music from all over the world.

Sandwiched between French/creole-speaking Martinique and Guadeloupe, the island of Dominica has long been influenced culturally and musically by the two French *départements*. But even if its rhythms are similar to those of its Gallic neighbors, there has still been room for innovation. Dominican cadence-lypso, commonly referred to as kadans, fuses Haitian konpa dance music with calypso, and the island's long-serving popular Windward Caribbean Kulture (WCK) is a band specializing in bouyon, an eclectic mix of cadence-lypso and traditional jing ping, resulting in a compelling cocktail of pulsating drums *à la digital* and keyboards.

## Jazz fusions

The Afro-American art form of jazz has also found a home in the Caribbean, and has been mixed smoothly into the melting-pot of influences. Some 30 jazz festivals are held in the region

> The late Trinidadian composer, Andre Tanker, was considered to be one of the great unsung musicians of the 20th century. His style influenced the island's modern rock groups, such as Orange Sky and Jointpop.

*A steel drummer and his gleaming pans.*

each year. Meanwhile, musicians from the local region have tirelessly experimented with a variety of fusions which embrace New Orleans rhythms and their own distinctively Caribbean flavors.

Notable jazz exponents from the Lesser Antilles who can be seen at many of the festivals (see panel for a music festival round-up) include St Lucia's Luther François, a gifted saxophonist and one of the region's leading jazz composers; Barbadian saxophonist Arturo Tappin, who merges jazz with reggae; Ken "Professor" Philmore (Trinidad), who plays steel pan jazz; Nicholas Brancker (Barbados), who plays funk/jazz bass and keyboard; and Trinidadian Clive Zanda, who performs jazz inspired by calypso and folk music.

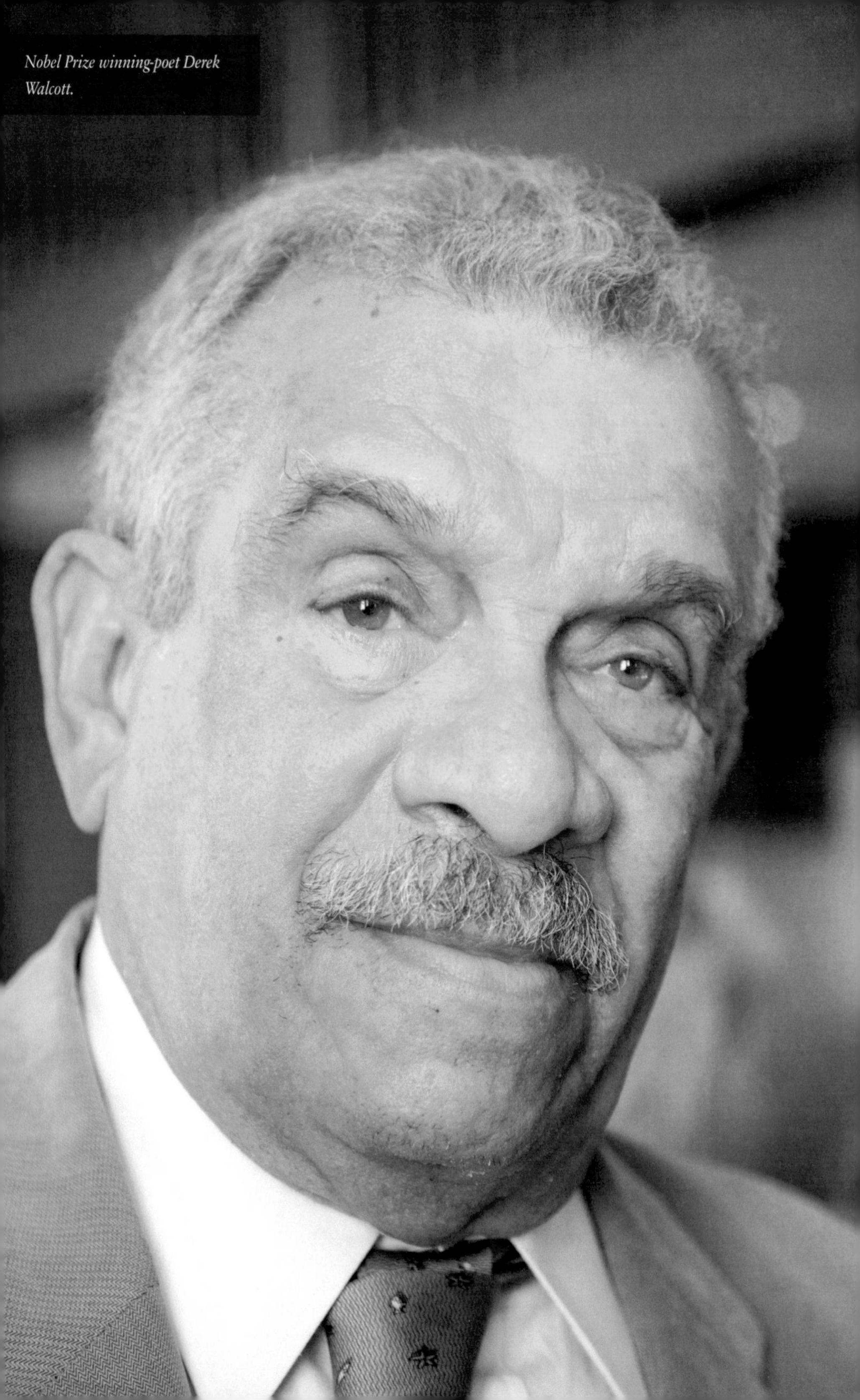

*Nobel Prize winning-poet Derek Walcott.*

# PASSION AND POETRY

The Lesser Antilles has a rich literary tradition – albeit a relatively young one, because for centuries stories and poems were passed down by word of mouth.

The islands of the Eastern Caribbean inspire passion and poetry in equal measure. And in impressive quantity. Few parts of the world can have produced so many top-class writers from so small a population. Although many of them today live abroad, the landscapes, language, and people of the islands fill their work with the unmistakable flavor of home.

Yet literature is a relatively late arrival in the Caribbean. The great Barbadian novelist George Lamming was guilty of only slight exaggeration when he said in the 1960s that Caribbean writing was just 20 years old. However, there has, of course, always been plenty written about the region – from the 17th century, priests, merchants, and other itinerant observers sent back their impressions of island life, to be replaced in the 19th century by travel writers who invariably made their trip "down the islands" with a book in mind.

> Love for an island is the sternest passion: pulsing beyond the blood through roots and loam. Phyllis Allfrey, Dominica

George Lamming explored his Barbadian childhood in his novel: "In the Castle of my Skin."

## Early storytellers

But literature by local people was for a long time in short supply. Slavery, illiteracy, and constant inter-colonial warfare were not ideal conditions for a thriving literary culture, while most slave owners or landlords tended not to be bookish by inclination. Significantly, one of the earliest examples of Caribbean poetry is *Barbados* (1754) in which Nathaniel Weekes offers useful, if unromantic, advice to the island's planters:

*"To urge the Glory of your Cane's success, Rich be your Soil, and well manur'd with Dung, Or, Planters! what will your Labours yield?"*

The culture of the slaves was oral rather than written, and their tales, riddles, and proverbs were handed down by storytellers in spoken form. Since slave-owning societies actively discouraged the formal education of the black majority, it was hardly surprising that few books were read, let alone written.

Even some time after Emancipation, the Lesser Antilles lagged behind larger territories like Cuba and Haiti in literary output. The small islands lacked publishers, bookstores, libraries, and, above all, a reading public. Amid widespread poverty and lack of education, only occasional clerics or dilettantes put pen to paper, but their poetry tended to be little more than tropical adaptations of well-worn European conventions.

One remarkable exception to the rule was John Jacob Thomas, a self-educated black Trinidadian. In 1888, Thomas read *The English in the West Indies*, which was a study of British coloni-

> And yet it was a land of verdant hills and clear waters, beneath a sun every day more radiant. Simone Schwarz-Bart (Between Two Worlds)

*Nobel Prize winner V.S. Naipaul at the 2011 Venice Literary Festival.*

alism in the Caribbean by the eminent Oxford professor, James Anthony Froude. Incensed by Froude's patronizing and prejudiced view of black society, Thomas wrote a devastating riposte, *Froudacity: West Indian Fables Explained* (1889), in which he accused the pompous professor of "fatuity" and "skinpride."

## On the literary map

Several factors coalesced in the 1940s and 1950s to put the region on the literary map. World War II and the immediate post-war years witnessed a massive increase in migration and mobility as islanders seized work opportunities in Europe and the US. Young men like

Lamming, and Trinidadians V.S. Naipaul (knighted in 1990 and Nobel Literature Laureate in 2001) and Samuel Selvon found themselves in London, exposed to a range of new influences. It may have been cold and hostile (as comically described in Selvon's masterpiece, *The Lonely Londoners*, 1956), but it had publishers and literary reviews eager for fresh material.

Other would-be writers from the English-speaking islands went to New York or Canada, while those from Martinique and Guadeloupe reveled in the cultural ferment of post-war Paris. From these experiences of self-imposed exile emerged some of the enduring themes of Caribbean literature: identity, rootlessness, nostalgia, the bitter-sweet reality of returning home.

This period was also one of political and cultural re-evaluation as the islands moved toward independence or greater autonomy, creating a sense of nationalism, of regional identity, long suppressed by colonialism. Fast disappearing were the days when schoolchildren would have to write essays entitled *A Winter's Day*, and writers began to find a distinctive, Caribbean voice. Often this voice was satirical, mocking the colonial system and values that had dominated for centuries. The title of Barbadian Austin Clarke's memoir, *Growing Up Stupid Under the Union Jack* (1980) is typical of the anti-colonial genre.

## Home-grown talent

As writers and intellectuals reassessed their mixed cultural heritage, the beginnings of a local literary establishment emerged. Most early authors were published in London or New York, but a handful of literary journals such as *Bim*, founded in Barbados in 1942, began to publish the work of home-grown talent. The 1950s was the decade in which Caribbean literature finally established itself overseas. Three novels created international reputations for their authors and set out some of the principal themes and attitudes which were to follow in much more fiction.

Lamming's *In the Castle of My Skin* (1953) explored the decline of British colonialism in Barbados and the awakening of new aspirations within a small rural community. Selvon's *The Lonely Londoners* (1956) followed a group of Trinidadian emigrants to Britain and the ensuing culture shock they endured. Naipaul's *The Mystic Masseur* (1957) painted a bitter-sweet picture of incompetence and pretentiousness in colonial Trinidad. Each novel, in its own way, dissected the legacy of British rule and the question of contemporary Caribbean identity.

The smaller English-speaking territories started producing top-rank literature in the 1970s and 1980s with work by Derek Walcott (St Lucia), Edward "Kamau" Brathwaite (Barbados), Jamaica Kincaid (Antigua), Earl Lovelace (Trinidad), and Caryl Phillips (St Kitts). Phillips, now based in England, continues to produce both fiction and non-fiction exploring the timeless themes of belonging, identity, and race.

Official recognition came in the 1990s for two authors whose work is rooted in the region. In 1992, Derek Walcott received the Nobel Prize for Literature, in tribute to his long and productive career as a poet and playwright. In 1990, his magnificent *Omeros*, a reworking of the Homeric legend amid a fishing community in St Lucia, had confirmed his status as one of the world's leading poets. The previous year, the Martinican novelist Patrick Chamoiseau had won the Prix Goncourt for his complex novel *Texaco*, a sought-after sign of approval from the Parisian intellectual establishment.

While not specifically from the Lesser Antilles, Marlon James's 2015 Man Booker Prize win for his third novel, *A Brief History of Seven Killings* shone a highbrow spotlight on Caribbean literature. James became the first ever Jamaican writer to receive this distinction. His novel tells the story of an 1976 attempt to take Bob Marley's life and explores several decades of Jamaican turbulent history, from the 1970s to the 1990s.

### Vibrant French literary scene

The literary productivity of two of the French overseas regions – Martinique and Guadeloupe – is as impressive as that of their Anglophone neighbors. The white Guadeloupean poet St-John Perse won the Nobel Prize for Literature in 1960 (although it is generally known he disliked his island of birth), while Martinique's Aimé Césaire wrote the trail-blazing surrealist epic, *Return to My Native Land*, in 1939.

Nowadays, thanks to first-world levels of education and opportunity, the two islands enjoy a vibrant literary scene, which is taken more and more seriously by big Parisian publishers. Interestingly, many of the most prominent novelists from Martinique and Guadeloupe are women, who mix specifically female themes into the wider theme of French/Caribbean identity – Maryse Condé, Simone Schwarz-Bart, and Gisèle Pineau are three of the better known.

### Influences from abroad

There are some common themes. Many authors continue to examine the relationship between the islands and the European powers. Michael Anthony's *Butler, till the Final Bell* (2003) has as its setting the fight by oil workers in Trinidad for better wages and living conditions under the British. The reclamation of African identity has also been a pervasive theme, as shown in Earl Lovelace's novel, *Salt*, which won the Commonwealth Writers' Prize in 1997.

The influence of the US, from tourists to CNN, is another widespread motif as writers

*The work of Gisèle Pineau explores French/Caribbean identity.*

### TWO OF A KIND

The small, mountainous island of Dominica is the birthplace of two celebrated novelists, both women from white families. After a Bohemian career in 1930s Europe, Jean Rhys disappeared until her book *Wide Sargasso Sea* (1966) became a cult classic. Its atmosphere of tropical menace and madness (the book is a prequel to Charlotte Brontë's *Jane Eyre*, with the protagonist a re-imagining of the "madwoman in the attic") bears some resemblance to the decadent island world described in *The Orchid House* (1953) by Phyllis Allfrey. The two women never met, but they corresponded extensively.

struggle to define what is culturally distinctive about their homelands. US TV soaps feature prominently in *Tide Running* (2001), an unsettling study of sexploitation in Tobago, written by Grenadian Oonya Kempadoo.

In this context, language itself is an important issue, and many authors highlight the richness of local creole or patois. Trinidadian Joanne Haynes, in her coming-of-age novel, *Walking* (2007), even includes a glossary of terms for other English speakers. In the French islands, in particular, writers such as Chamoiseau and Raphaël Confiant have championed their expressive creole against the dominance of "official" French. Dialogue has become very colorful.

Writers are beginning to explore more recent periods of history. Monique Roffey's novel *The White Woman on the Green Bicycle* (shortlisted for the Orange Prize in 2010) is set at the time of Eric Williams and the political upheavals of the 1960s in post-colonial Trinidad, as seen through the eyes of an outsider, a white woman. Earl Lovelace's most recent novel *Is Just a Movie* (2011), winner of the 2012 OCM Bocas Prize for Caribbean Literature, is set in 1970 just after the failure of the Black Power rebellion and

*Raphaël Confiant.*

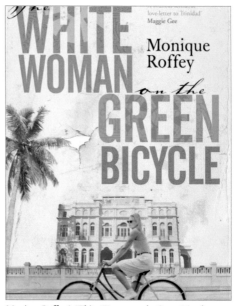

*Monique Roffey's White Woman on the Green Bicycle was shortlisted for the Orange Prize 2010.*

## CARIBBEAN TRAVEL WRITING

Many travelers through the islands in the 20th century felt moved to put pen to paper to describe their experiences and their findings. These were often idiosyncratic. Colonial government of all nationalities came under critical scrutiny for allowing the people to live in unrelenting poverty, but sometimes it was just the weather that wore down early seafaring travelers. Unremitting rain while stuck in port or in a run-down, leaking hotel leaves lasting memories. The classics include: Patrick Leigh Fermor, *The Traveller's Tree*; Alec Waugh, *The Sugar Islands*; Martha Gellhorn, *Travels with Myself and Another*; James Pope-Hennessy, *West Indian Summer*.

follows the daily lives of villagers re-examining their community.

The modern Caribbean writer is above all aware of the fragility of his or her island home in an age of mass tourism and rampant development. In accepting his Nobel Prize, Walcott spoke of a way of life threatened by such progress: "How quickly it could all disappear! And how it is beginning to drive us further into where we hope are impenetrable places, green secrets at the end of bad roads, headlands where the next view is not of a hotel but of some long beach without a figure and the hanging question of some fisherman's smoke at its far end."

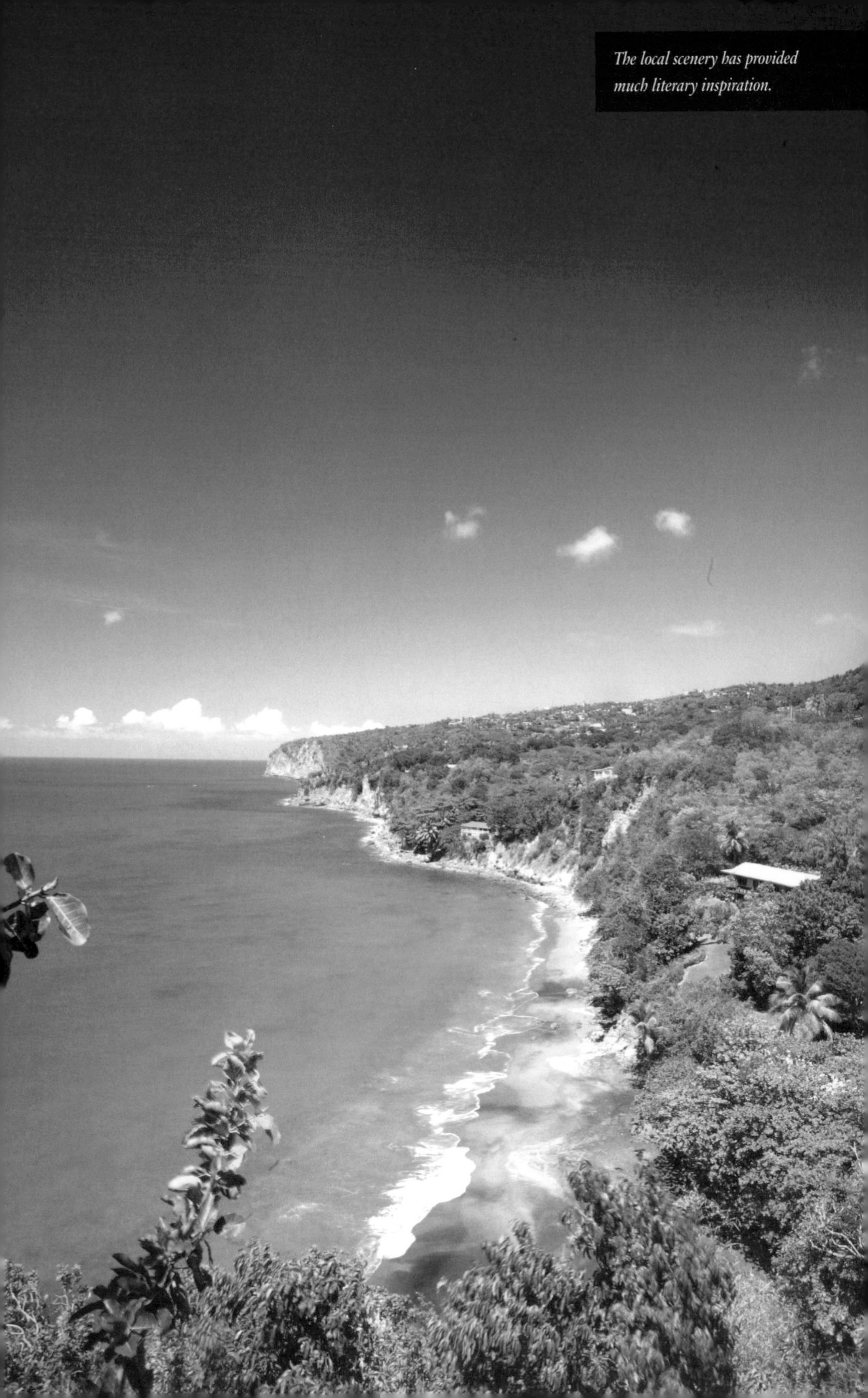

*The local scenery has provided much literary inspiration.*

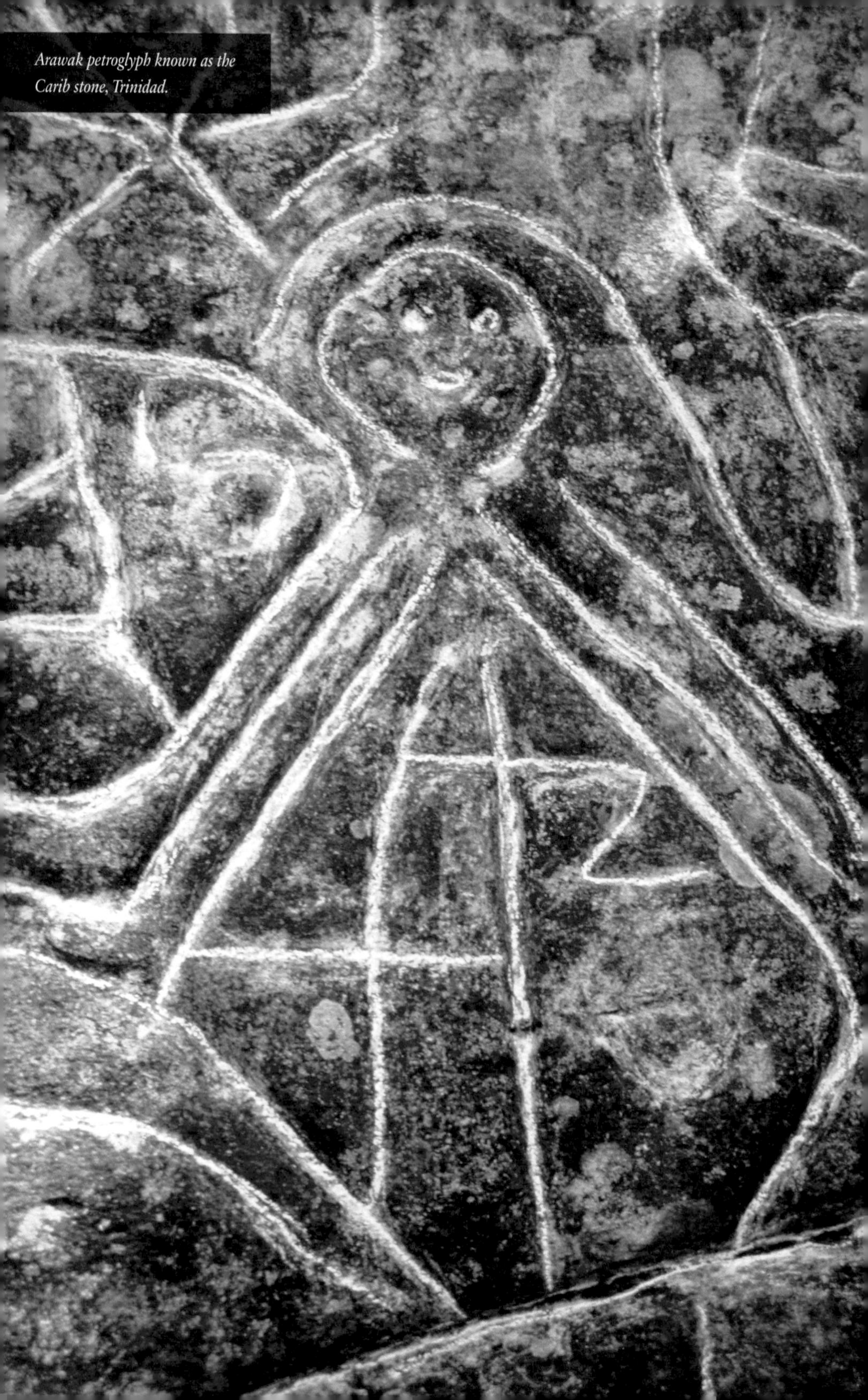

*Arawak petroglyph known as the Carib stone, Trinidad.*

# ART – PALETTE OF ISLANDS

From petroglyphs to performance art, ancient Amerindian ceramics to a modern creole Carnival, the Lesser Antilles motivate a wide range of artistic endeavors.

People have been inspired by the beauty of the islands and their natural surroundings for thousands of years. The greens of the forests, the blues of the sea, the reds and yellows of the flowers conspire to create a palette of color that assaults and pleases the senses in equal measure. The first artists in the islands were the Amerindians, who scratched their drawings on rocks by rivers or on the walls of caves thousands of years ago. Many are clearly representative of their gods and religious symbols, but the meaning of others is less clear.

Later arrivals brought the technology for making ceramics, which allowed greater possibilities for artistic expression. The earliest pottery found has a red background with white paint picking out a simple design. Some 1,400 years ago, however, the style changed with a new influx of migrants. The Ostionoid culture incised their pottery and used less painted decoration. By the time Columbus arrived, they were creating religious artifacts such as *zemi*, or spirit stones, as well as distinctive polychrome and incised pottery styles. Vessels were made with lugs shaped like human or animal heads molded onto the rim of vessels and they developed fine ground stone and shell work. Their legacy continues today principally in Dominica, where the Kalinago still make traditional, intricately woven baskets and mats and carved calabash bowls.

Handmade baskets, Dominica.

## Colonial art

As with literature, art during the colonial days of slavery was a European activity, out of reach of the majority who toiled the soil with little time for creative expression. Colonial visitors replicated what they saw, a utopian vision of well-tended plantations with masters and slaves living contentedly off the fat of the land. The illiterate slaves, however, could not wield a pen to describe their lives, let alone afford a paintbrush and paints to depict the harsh reality of their existence.

## Early 20th-century art

It was only in the 1920s that notable artists started to emerge from the Caribbean and these often catered to the taste in Europe for "primitive" cultures, following in the steps of Paul Gauguin's artistic paradise. The political awakening of the population with the rise of the trade-union movement, the birth of political parties, the growth of a culturally nationalist middle class, and eventual independence had a huge impact on intellectual and artistic life in the islands. These trends took place at the same time as the "new negro" philosophies of the Harlem Renaissance took the US by storm in the 1930s.

For the first time, art was taught in schools, talented students went on to art college and some managed to follow their dream of devoting their lives to art, either at home or abroad, or both. The blockade during World War II had an impact on the French islands, in particular, with several French artists and writers stranded

*Aimé Césaire, French poet and former mayor of Fort-de-France, Martinique.*

there for the duration and nothing better to do than set up painting and sculpture workshops open to all. This was the time when Aimé Césaire and others were developing their literary ideas on "négritude," challenging the status quo, denouncing European colonial racism and defending Afro-Caribbean identity. The cultural complexity of the region, the emergence from slavery and dependency, the Amerindian and African heritage, and the presence of European and North American itinerant artists have all influenced the islands' diversity.

The combination of pressures and influences meant that early Caribbean art was a hodgepodge of styles, although local themes were increasingly explored as part of the creole communities' desire for autonomy. Some artists stuck with the rigorous discipline of traditional figure and landscape painting, putting down on canvas the world around them. Some experimented with Impressionist and Post-Impressionist painting styles while others delved into the spiritual matters of African art and sculptors attempted Art Deco forms.

## Arts and crafts

Running in parallel with these artistic developments, there was a growth in creativity by artisans and craftsmen, self-taught artists whose work is more directly related to traditional and spiritual African art, as seen in their use of patterning and color. Techniques were also similar, particularly in the case of carvings and the methods of selecting, honing, drying, and polishing woods, and these sculptures often had medicinal and spiritual meanings bound up in Afro-Christian religions such as Obeah, Santería, the Rastafari movement, and Vodou.

## Late 20th century art

The 1960s and 1970s were a time of political turbulence in the islands, with the rise of Black Power, the Cuban Revolution, and US-backed dictatorships a backdrop for the increasing clamor for independence. Some Caribbean artists who had been trained abroad became disillusioned with small-island art movements, abandoning the local vernacular in favor of a more international modern style, while others concentrated even more on their African roots and African imagery. Identity became a key issue as artists explored their links with the African diaspora and their feelings of alienation. Racial and class awareness under the guise of political allegory challenged Western styles and values to become a platform for contemporary Afro-Caribbean art.

Tumelo Mosaka, curator at the Brooklyn Museum (NY) writes: *"Today, consistent throughout most islands is the division between mainstream artist movements more closely related to European stylistic trends and often rooted in national development, and self-taught artists whose art works reflect ritual preoccupations related to spiritual movements such as Revivalism, Santería and Vodou and less exposure to art movements abroad. More recently, contemporary artists influenced by post-modernism's concerns with identity have found ways to fuse both forms, resulting in art that appear peculiarly unique to their Caribbean experience".*

## Contemporary art scene

Today, the Lesser Antilles are home to a wide range of artists, whose studios are often open to the public and whose work is widely exhibited. Some artists were born in the islands, some are foreigners attracted to the lifestyle and the inspiration. Some are self-taught, others are graduates of art schools at home or abroad. All forms of art can be found, from figurative

social allegory, and his work is exhibited at the National Museum and Art Gallery, Trinidad; The Studio Museum of Harlem, New York; the Royal Victoria Institute of Trinidad; and the National Collection of Jamaica, as well as in many private collections. One of his recent exhibitions, presenting his 110 acrylic drawings, "Eye Hayti... Cries... Everywhere," was held in 2015 at the National Museum and Art Gallery of Trinidad and Tobago in Port of Spain (www.leroyclarke.com).

Llewellyn Xavier OBE (b. 1945, St Lucia) is known for his collages, his most important

*St Lucia's Llewellyn Xavier is known for his collages.*

to Naïve or symbolic, together with graphic design, installation art, and performance art. Carnival is the prime example of popular artistic expression, bringing together all strands of the arts with colonial and African heritage.

LeRoy Clarke (b. 1938, in Trinidad) is that island's "Master Artist" and figurehead of Afro-Caribbean art. A prolific, self-taught artist and poet, his first major body of work, called "Fragments of a Spiritual," was an epic personal, ethnic, and cultural narrative, reconstructing the spiritual dimension in the aftermath of slavery and colonialism, through post-colonial turbulence and political disillusionment. He is known for his huge, complex and layered paintings, full of symbolism and

work being a collection of recycled materials called "Global Council for the Restoration of the Earth's Environment," 1993, which included signatures from leading environmentalists and conservationists.

More recently, a conceptual work of art entitled "Environment Fragile," calls attention to the destruction of the environment. The works in the series are made from recycled cardboard, representing the destruction of the forests; industrial paint, representing the end of the world's resources; and gold, symbolizing the preciousness of the environment. Xavier was awarded an OBE in 2004 for his contribution to art in the British Commonwealth (www.llewellynxavier.com).

A man cutting into fresh lobster.

# CREOLE CUISINE

**Between American fast-food joints and the international haute cuisine of the big hotels there is the delicious food of the Caribbean to be enjoyed.**

As the word "creole" generally means "born in the islands but originating from the outside world," it seems an appropriate collective name for the region's home cooking, given its history. However, despite the common thread uniting the creole cuisine of the islands, the miles of water that separate them, along with their diverse historic influences from the outside world, ensure that the food of each one is usually quite distinct.

The common thread is provided by the region's rich Amerindian and African heritage; the readily available fresh produce of the fertile land, with its year-round growing season; and the abundance of superb seafood from the surrounding Caribbean Sea and Atlantic Ocean. Meanwhile, the wonderful variation within the styles of cuisine has been created by the diversity of the European countries that colonized the islands, the introduction of indentured labor from the east, and the wide range of differing topography throughout the region.

*Fruit vendor in Ste-Anne, Martinique.*

## Fresh from land and sea

When the European settlers started arriving, there was already some wild game on the islands, such as agouti, iguana, deer, hogs, land tortoises, and guinea pigs, and they added chickens, cattle, sheep, goats, and pigs. Today, people in the country are still happy to run a small farm or raise their "stocks" on whatever pasture is available. On land the swamps and rivers can supply crabs and crayfish, but the best and most plentiful source of protein is the fish and other seafood which abounds in the ocean.

Caribbean seafood can be rated as some of the best in the world. As a result of the generally short distance from the sea to the table, it is served particularly fresh, which contributes to its intense flavor. Grouper, barracuda, kingfish, swordfish, sea bream, jacks, parrotfish, snapper, tuna, albacor, bonito, and dolphin are the names of fish most heard in these islands. Dolphin (also called dorado and mahi mahi) is an ugly, scaly fish not to be confused with the friendly mammal, which is known as a porpoise, often referred to as a dolphin. Flying fish are widely served in Barbados, where the intricate skill of deboning them has been perfected and passed on down the generations.

The Caribbean waters also contain plenty of sea crab, spiny lobster, conch (sometimes called lambis) with their large beautiful shells, sea egg (sea urchin), octopus, and, in the south, very large shrimps, also referred to as "giant prawns." The result of this exciting array of fresh ingredients, prepared in a variety of tantalizing ways, is an exotic culinary extravaganza.

## A culinary legacy

Foods that can be traced back to the Amerindians are still found throughout the islands. Pepperpot stew, a mixture of meats, vegetables, and hot peppers, cooked in black cassava juice

*The barbecue is intrinsic to Caribbean culinary culture.*

### A FAIR EXCHANGE

In the early days of colonization and exploration, there was a tremendous exchange of horticulture and agriculture around the world. While the Caribbean gave the world the pineapple, pepper, cashew, cocoa, avocado, runner bean, potato, sweet potato, and tomato, to name some of the more famous produce indigenous to the region, the outside world returned the favor with many of the fruits, vegetables, and herbs that are now frequently associated with this area – such as mango, lime, orange, banana, coffee, sugar cane, pigeon pea, yam, okra, nutmeg, cinnamon, clove, ginger, shallots, thyme, parsley, breadfruit, and coconuts.

(casareep), a natural preservative, was originally a means of preserving the hunter's bounty. Once brought to the boil daily, it will not go off. Even in this day and age, some establishments and households keep a pepperpot on the stove for months, in a traditional pottery *coneree*, adding fresh ingredients as required. Pepperpot soup, freshly made with vegetables such as okra, pumpkin, and yam, has been only slightly modified since the Amerindian days, with the introduction of imported salt meat.

Another Amerindian favorite, and still a popular snack, was roasted corn. The husk is removed and the corn cooked over an open fire until completely black. It was these highly self-sufficient people who gave the world the barbecue, derived from their word *barbacoa* meaning cooking over a fire. Street food today is usually based on the barbecue, using an oil drum full of charcoal to cook on. Several islands have a fish-fry one day a week in one fishing village or another, where you can find delicious lobster in season or the catch of the day, fresh from the sea, basted in seasoned oil and put straight on the griddle, accompanied by roasted corn, bread, and various vegetables and sauces.

The Amerindians also made delicious bread from cassava (*casabe*) and corn (*fungi* or *funchi*). Fresh bread made with bran and wheat flour is the most common staple and can be smelled baking in the early morning in virtually every village and town.

## An African inheritance

The African slaves were given rations of rice, imported salt cod, salt meat, and dried peas and beans. They were also given small plots of land to grow produce to supplement this meager fare. From this paltry larder came the basis of the delicious food served today. Every island has its own recipe for rice and peas, usually made with salt beef or pork and fresh herbs such as shallots and thyme. Fish cakes, made of salt fish, flour, a variety of pepper and herbs, dipped in batter and deep fried, have an irresistible aroma. Salt fish is still commonly eaten for breakfast.

To season their food, slaves grew thyme, marjoram, mint, sage, rosemary, shallots, and peppers. Today, every island has its own "seasoning" made from finely chopped herbs, onions, garlic, and pepper; and each one offers its own version of a fiercely hot pepper sauce, which should be sampled with caution.

Chicken, roasted, fried, or stewed; roast pork, garlic pork, pickled pig's head, tail, and trotters, pork stew, whole suckling pig roasted on a spit, and ham have always been weekend and cel-

*Most citrus comes from the Pacific region but the grapefruit originated in Barbados in the 18th century. It is a cross between a sweet orange and a bitter citrus fruit called a shaddock, brought from Polynesia by a Captain Shaddock.*

such as rice or yam, to which is added any vegetables, seasonings, fish, meat, or chicken the cook can find to make a tasty and nutritious meal. Because of the ingenious use of herbs and spices, stews in the Caribbean are full of flavor.

An interesting observation about Caribbean cuisine is that the Amerindians, when first encountered by Europeans, were preparing many foods in exactly the same way as some West Africans thousands of miles across the Atlantic Ocean. For example, *cou-cou* or *fungi* – ground corn, boiled up with okra and mashed into a thick paste – is an indigenous dish of

*Harvesting the sugar crops, Barbados.*

ebration fare – not a piece of the pig is spared. All the islands prepare variations of black pudding, made from pigs intestine stuffed with the blood mixed with sweet potato and seasoning.

## One-pot cook-ups

With most of the cooking being done over an open fire, usually with only one pot, many recipes developed for "one pot meals" which included a large variety of tasty soups such as split pea soup, *callaloo*, made from eddoe leaves and crab, pumpkin soup, fish soup, peanut soup, and a "big soup" that you can stand the spoon up in, made with an assortment of root crops and fresh vegetables. Other one-pot meals known as cook-ups are based on a starch

both the Caribbean and Africa. Still enjoyed today, it's usually served with a pungent salt fish, fresh fish, or beef stew.

## Caribbean sweet tooth

With the introduction of sugar cane in the 17th century, Caribbean people developed a very "sweet tooth," blending sugar with island fruits to create such delicacies as tamarind balls, guava cheese, coconut sugar cakes, toolum, comforts, and shaddock rind – candies that have been prepared for generations of children. Preserves of lime and orange marmalade, guava jelly, nutmeg jelly, chutney, and fruit jams are of a very high quality because the golden crystals of Caribbean sugar are bursting with tangy flavors.

Traditional desserts are a combination of British heritage and Caribbean style: bread 'n' butter pudding, rich fruit cake laced with rum, banana and coconut bread, jam puffs, chocolate pudding, and coconut turnovers. Restaurants everywhere include their own versions of the delicious coconut pie on their dessert menu.

## European flavors

The islands generally have a very separate and distinct cuisine from each other, depending on who they were colonized by. The French brought their *pâtisserie* (pastries), stuffed crab back, tomato and herb fish stews reminiscent of Provence, escargots in garlic, and frogs' legs (coyly called mountain chicken in Dominica).

Jug Jug, a Christmas dish of pigeon peas, guinea corn flour, salt meat, and herbs, a corruption of the Scots haggis, was introduced to Barbados by the Scots when they were exiled there after the Monmouth Rebellion of 1685.

The Spanish left Trinidad a delicious legacy: *pastelles* (meat and grated corn steamed in a banana leaf), *escoviche* (pickled fish), *buljol* (salt fish, tomato, lime, pepper, garlic, and avocado),

*The strawberry guava, one variety of this immensely versatile fruit.*

### REFRESHING DRINKS

The abundance of fruit on the islands means that fresh fruit juices are served everywhere: guava, mango, and soursop are some of the most exotic. Mauby is a bitter-sweet drink made from tree bark, and sorrel is a traditional Christmas drink created from the dried bright red blossom of a type of hibiscus. Sea-moss is a mixture of algae, milk, and vanilla, not to everyone's taste. Herbal teas are usually freshly picked and blended for medicinal purposes. Cocoa tea is served at breakfast. Recipes vary, but generally a length of cocoa stick is melted in hot water with the addition of cinnamon and sugar.

to name just a few. Later, Indian and Chinese food was introduced to Trinidad by immigrants from Asia, and the roti – a thick curry wrapped in a chapati – is sold throughout the region, keeping the American burger joints on their toes. Trinidadian Chinese cooking has also evolved into a new and delicious style, modified by the use of different ingredients.

The Dutch islands enjoy an Indonesian flavor to their dishes, due to the Netherlands' connections with the Far East. So the food of the Caribbean is as diverse as the origins of its people – a multitude of exotic flavors, all drawn from the sun-blessed, fertile land, the bountiful seas, and the creative genius of generations of multiethnic cooks and chefs.

# Rum

**It didn't take long to discover that sugar was not just a sweetener but could constitute the basis of a highly alcoholic drink – rum.**

Rum has long been associated with pirates, smugglers, and sailors and featured in many a classic "Boys' Own" adventure story as barrels of the liquid gold were rolled on to British shores by the light of the full moon – duty free.

It didn't take long to discover that a forceful fiery liquor could be produced from sugar cane, and in Barbados in the 1640s the first batches of locally distilled spirits were introduced, or, rather, experienced! Referred to as "kill-devil" by the English Royalist refugee Richard Ligon in *A True and Exact History of the Island of Barbados* in 1657, the drink was strong and barely fit to drink; those who imbibed it quickly felt its effects. As Ligon wrote, "It lays them to sleep on the ground."

Or else, too much of it ended in a "rumbullion," an old English word for a noisy brawl – hence the name rum. Another early visitor to Barbados wrote that "the chiefe fudling they make on the Island is Rumbullion, alias Kill Divill, and this is made of sugarcanes distilled, a hot, hellish and terrible liquor."

Rum is usually made from molasses, the thick, black treacle left after the juice from the sugar cane has crystallized, although the French islands make theirs from sugar-cane juice. Spring water – in Barbados it is filtered through coral rock – is then added and it is left to ferment. After distilling, more fresh water is added to what is now a colorless liquid of almost 95 percent alcohol, and it is poured into oak barrels to slowly mature; the best rum is stored for at least 7 years. The golden color develops from the secret ingredients added by the master blender, which may include vanilla, almond extract, caramel, or older types of rum, combined with the smoked interior of the barrel, which are often recycled Bourbon whiskey barrels. It remains colorless when kept for a short time in stainless steel barrels.

Many of the islands have their own rum factories with their own brand that they are fiercely proud of. For example, Barbados, where it all began, has Mount Gay and Cockspur; Trinidad has Angostura; and Martinique produces several kinds, including Trois Rivières and St Clément.

## Keeping up naval morale

For sailors in the British Royal Navy, rum was an important ingredient in their daily rations – it helped keep them upright in stormy seas and raised morale. But they were extremely upset in 1731 when Admiral Vernon ordered that the spirit should be diluted with water. This concoction was disparagingly called a "grog" after the admiral, whose nickname had been Old Grog because he always wore a cloak of a coarse material called grogram.

Since then rum has been diluted with a wide variety of juices and mixers, creating some wonder-

*An old advert for Clement Rum Distillery, which still operates on Martinique today.*

ful cocktails and punches. However in the rum shops on islands such as Trinidad and Barbados (where you will find one in most villages) rum is drunk neat or "on the rocks." A rum shop is not merely a bar; it is a village store, a community center, an arena for fiercely competitive domino-playing, a place where tongues are loosened, politics discussed, and rumors spread. "Man, leh we fire one on that!" is the exhortation prompted by a happy event.

It is still largely the province of men: "Men in de rum shop; women in de church," so the saying goes. And Lord Byron may have been thinking along the same lines when he wrote, "There's nought no doubt so much the spirit calms/as rum and true religion."

# GINGERBREAD AND BALLAST BRICK

**Caribbean architecture reveals influences from Amerindians, Africa, and the European colonizers, from simple Kunuku cottages to opulent Great Houses.**

When Columbus hit upon the West Indies at the end of the 15th century, the dwellings he found there were nothing compared to what he was used to in Europe, and he wrote to a friend that the "[Indians] live in rocks and mountains, without fixed settlements, and not like ourselves." In fact Amerindians slept in round or oval-shaped huts built of timber and covered with a conical roof made of palms or grass from swamps.

The first Europeans left on islands to set up trading posts, and then the settlers, copied these Indian shelters, but soon introduced wall construction with wooden beams and shingles for the roofs. However, even after Emancipation the slaves rarely built with stone, and single-roomed thatched houses with walls of clay and straw were still in use in the 20th century.

## A medley of styles

When the sugar trade to Europe started, many ships brought huge amounts of red brick and stone in their hulls as ballast. Wealthy planters and merchants on islands like Barbados and Antigua built their Great Houses with it. In Statia's heyday ballast was used for the warehouses on the waterfront. Several styles developed, the Spanish adopting Moorish traditions while the French introduced cast iron. Later, the American invention of mechanical saws gave rise to the intricate wooden lacework – gingerbread – on many facades.

*Shady verandahs and shutters help keep rooms cool, even when there is no air conditioning. They also encourage outdoor gatherings.*

*Dutch colonial architecture in Willemstad, Curaçao, is replicated by new hotels and other buildings with fanciful gables and colorful walls.*

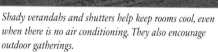

*Cathédrale St-Louis, Martinique, known as the "iron cathedral," was built in 1895 to withstand hurricanes.*

*Chattel house, Barbados.*

## CHATTEL HOUSES: MOBILE HOMES

For the black population of Barbados, mobility was once essential to survival. After Emancipation the planters had to employ labor and, still wanting to control the freed slaves, allowed them to establish small settlements on their land. This made the workers dependent on their employer's goodwill, and they were rapidly chased off the land if there were any problems. So the chattel house was developed: a small wooden "sleeping box" easy to dismantle and take along on a cart to another plantation.

Supported by big rocks or concrete blocks so that rainwater can pass underneath, the one-room house with an optional partition inside is made up of wooden planks fixed to a framework. Makeshift steps lead up to the only door, opening on to the family's living space. Here parents and children, and often grandparents as well, used to sleep in one room. The cooking was done outside, as was any entertaining of neighbors and friends.

This nucleus of a family home – with one or two extensions – is still a common sight in Barbados, especially in the more remote country districts, and only a few years ago a whole village moved from a hilltop to a valley, where running water was available.

*Stollmeyer's Castle was inspired by Scottish and German castles and is one of the Magnificent Seven colonial mansions built between 1904 and 1910.*

*Planters modeled their homes on European styles, adapting them to suit the climate with thick walls. The elegant Rose Hall in Jamaica is a calendar house – with 365 windows, 52 doors and 12 bedrooms.*

*Vermont Nature Trail, St Vincent.*

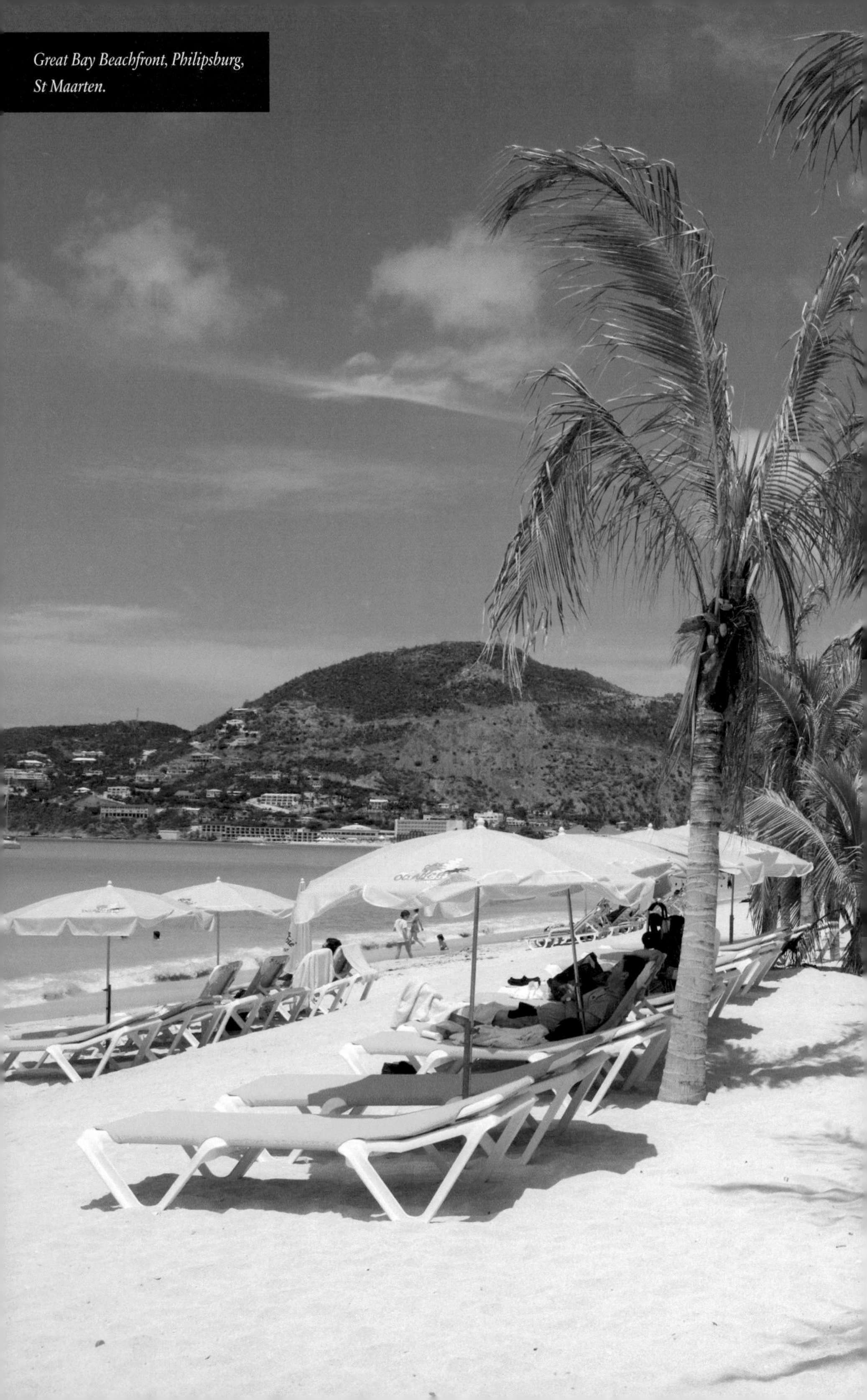

*Great Bay Beachfront, Philipsburg, St Maarten.*

*Granite boulders at The Baths, Virgin Gorda, British Virgin Islands.*

# INTRODUCTION

A detailed guide to the entire Lesser Antilles, with principal
sites clearly cross-referenced by number to the maps.

*The dive sites off the Cayman Islands are some of the best in the world.*

The Lesser Antilles are made up of hundreds of islands forming a broad, sweeping arc around the eastern side of the Caribbean Sea, effectively a barrier between this sea and the Atlantic Ocean. Almost universally, the islands have calm, pretty beaches on their western shores, lapped by the Caribbean, while the eastern seaboards are buffeted by the Atlantic winds and waves, making them dangerous for swimming but a great adventure for windsurfers and kitesurfers.

While most of the islands are volcanic – green peaks of ranges peeping above the water lapping their shores – some of the northern, Leeward Islands and the southern, Dutch islands off the coast of Venezuela are principally coral atolls. So, if your priority is finding a white-sand beach, stretching as far as the eye can see, head for Anguilla or Barbuda in the north or Aruba in the south. More adventurous activities such as canyoning or hiking can be enjoyed in the mountains of Dominica, Martinique, or St Lucia.

*Guana Island, British Virgin Islands.*

Each island has a character of its own and conveys a different mood. In the US Virgin Islands, St John is peaceful and dedicated to nature, whereas St Thomas, only a few miles away, is consumer-driven and go-getting. Tiny St-Barthélemy is as chic as the French Riviera, while miniscule Saba next door is modest and sensible. The colonial history, immigration, topography, and environment of each island have led to startling differences. Each island is individual – unique.

The surrounding waters conceal dramatic underwater scenery with coral reefs, walls, drop-offs, pillars, and wrecks. Divers and snorkelers are spoilt for choice with numerous marine parks preserving natural treasures and sea life. Conditions are perfect for sailing and, whether you are cruising "down the islands" on an ocean liner, a yacht, a ferry or taking a sunset catamaran trip, you should spend a few hours on the water. You may want to base yourself on one island, but the Lesser Antilles are perfect for island-hopping and exploring the pleasures on offer.

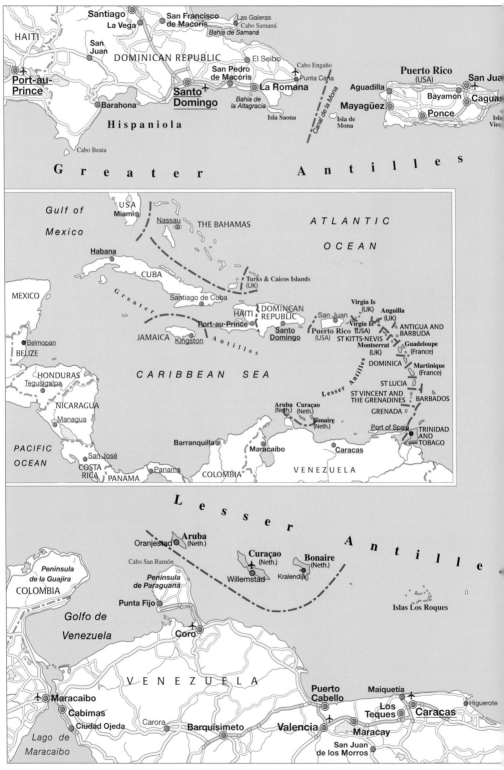

**Greater Antilles (top section)**

Santiago
La Vega
San Francisco de Macoris
Las Galeras
Cabo Samaná
Bahía de Samaná
HAITI
San Juan
DOMINICAN REPUBLIC
El Seibo
Cabo Engaño
Punta Cana
Puerto Rico (USA)
San Jua
Port-au-Prince
San Pedro de Macoris
Aguadilla
San Ju
Santo Domingo
La Romana
Bayamon
Cagua
Barahona
Bahía de la Altagracia
Mayagüez
Ponce
Isla
Vie
Hispaniola
Isla Saona
Canal de la Mona
Isla de Mona
Cabo Beata

G r e a t e r    A n t i l l e s

**Middle section**

Gulf of Mexico
USA
Miami
Nassau
THE BAHAMAS
A T L A N T I C    O C E A N
Habana
CUBA
Turks & Caicos Islands (UK)
MEXICO
Santiago de Cuba
DOMINICAN REPUBLIC
Virgin Is (UK)
Anguilla (UK)
San Juan
Virgin Is (USA)
ANTIGUA AND BARBUDA
HAITI
Port-au-Prince
Puerto Rico (USA)
ST KITTS-NEVIS
Guadeloupe (France)
Belmopan
BELIZE
JAMAICA
Kingston
Santo Domingo
Montserrat (UK)
DOMINICA
Martinique (France)
CARIBBEAN    SEA
ST LUCIA
HONDURAS
Tegucigalpa
ST VINCENT AND THE GRENADINES
BARBADOS
NICARAGUA
Managua
GRENADA
PACIFIC OCEAN
Aruba (Neth.)
Curaçao (Neth.)
Bonaire (Neth.)
Port of Spain
TRINIDAD AND TOBAGO
San José
Barranquilla
Maracaibo
Caracas
COSTA RICA
PANAMA
Panama
COLOMBIA
VENEZUELA

**Bottom section**

L e s s e r    A n t i l l e
Peninsula de la Guajira
COLOMBIA
Aruba (Neth.)
Oranjestad
Curaçao (Neth.)
Bonaire (Neth.)
Cabo San Ramón
Peninsula de Paraguana
Willemstad
Kralendijk
Punta Fijo
Islas Los Roques
Golfo de Venezuela
Coro
V E N E Z U E L A
Maracaibo
Puerto Cabello
Maiquetía
Higuerote
Cabimas
Los Teques
Caracas
Ciudad Ojeda
Carora
Barquisimeto
Valencia
Maracay
Lago de Maracaibo
San Juan de los Morros

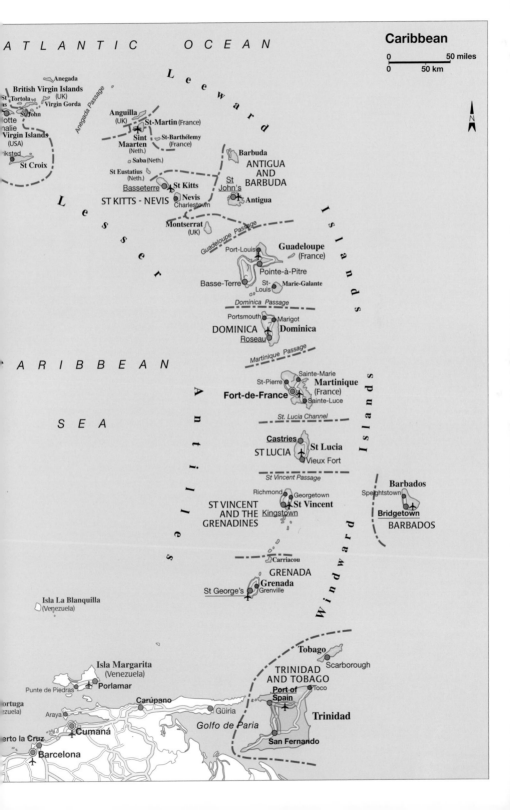

Caribbean

*Jabberwock Beach, Antigua.*

*A diver looks through a crevasse in the waters off the Virgin Islands.*

# THE US VIRGIN ISLANDS

Cruising, sailing, diving, beautiful beaches, and a national park teeming with wildlife – the US Virgin Islands, or USVI, have them all, shared between St Thomas, St John, and St Croix.

**G**reen volcanic islands peer from the never-ending blues of the Caribbean for as far as the eye can see, their submerged feet a vast underwater landscape. No one knows for certain how many islands there are but Columbus, on his second voyage of discovery in 1493, felt there were too many to count and named them after the 11,000 martyred virgins in the legend of St Ursula. However many there are, the USA has 68 of them, amounting to 136 sq miles (352 sq km), and Britain has around 50 (see page 115).

Situated at the top of the Lesser Antilles chain, only four of the USVI are inhabited: St Thomas (pop. 51,600) is the most developed and can have up to eight cruise ships visiting on some days; neighboring St John (pop. 4,100) is mainly taken up by a national park; St Croix (pop. 50,600), 40 miles (64km) to the southwest, is the largest but poorer and more tranquil than St Thomas. Water Island, off St Thomas, has a few residents and is known as the fourth Virgin Island. When sugarcane production bowed out of the economy in the 1960s, the US started developing the islands' potential as a "holiday paradise" for Americans, and today more than two million visitors descend on them every year, the majority arriving by cruise ship or under sail – only about a third fly in.

St Thomas, with USVI capital Charlotte Amalie, is the recipient of the largest proportion of vacationers, and there is very little of the island that hasn't been built on, which gives it rather a crowded feel: the airport runway, a paved stretch of landfill, juts out into the sea – there is no other place for it.

## A thriving Danish colony

Columbus met with a hail of arrows on his visit to the Virgin Islands and as a result of such Carib ferocity, no European settlement was established

**Main Attractions**

Charlotte Amalie
St Thomas Skyride to
  Paradise Point
Coral World Ocean Park
Tillett Gardens
Virgin Islands National Park
Trunk Bay Beach
Christiansted
Estate Whim Plantation
  Museum
Buck Island National
  Monument

*View of the busy town of Charlotte Amalie, St Thomas.*

until the 17th century when the Danes took St Thomas and St John.

St Croix, on the other hand, was settled first by the Dutch and English in around 1625, then by the Spanish in 1650, followed briefly by the Knights Templar of Malta under the sovereignty of France. Finally in 1733, St Croix was sold to Denmark, and the Danish West Indies officially became a colony in 1754.

The colony thrived with sugar growing on St Croix and a roaring slave trade in St Thomas, also an important stopping-off port for ships after crossing the Atlantic. However, by the beginning of the 20th century, as a result of the abolition of slavery, the drop in the price of sugar, and the technological advances in shipping, it was no longer necessary for ships to stop at St Thomas and the economy went into decline.

Meanwhile, the USA had been eyeing up the colony, anxious to protect the Caribbean and the Panama Canal (opened in 1914) from the Germans, and bought the islands from Denmark for US$25 million in 1917. They were then ruled by the US Navy until 1931, when a civil government was established. The inhabitants were given

US citizenship a year later but even now they don't have the right to vote in presidential elections: the status of the USVI is as an unincorporated territory with a non-voting delegate in the House of Representatives.

After World War II, the islands were neglected until American conflict with Cuba sent tourists looking for new white beaches, coral reefs, and azure waters. The construction industry boomed, labor had to be imported from other Caribbean islands, and at the same time new industrial centers and an oil refinery opened up on St Croix.

## St Thomas – a popular island

The main island of St Thomas is often called "Rock City" because it is essentially one big mountain – its highest point being 1,550ft (470 meters) – with one main town, Charlotte Amalie, the capital of the USVI, on its central south shore. The remainder of the 32 sq mile (83 sq km) island's coastline is a garland of beach resorts around a wooded interior of private homes – bright red, corrugated tin-roofed eyries set into the steep hillsides.

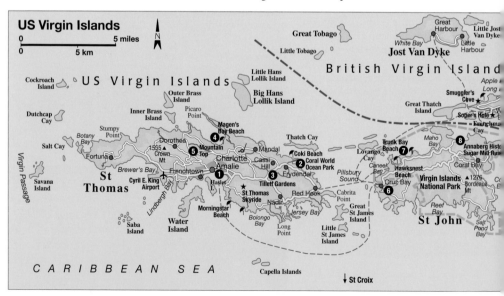

## Charlotte Amalie – a shopper's paradise

Built by the Danes on the south coast of St Thomas and named after the Queen of Denmark in 1692, **Charlotte Amalie ❶** (pronounced "Ah-mahl-ya"), the capital of all the USVI, is a congested town set round an equally congested harbor. Tax-free shopping is the name of the game here, and you can wander along the narrow streets lined with old Danish shipping warehouses, all converted into shops and restaurants. All the streets retain their Danish names, displayed on corner buildings – Kongens Gade (King's Street), Dronningens Gade (Queen's Street), which is also called Main Street, and so on.

Two blocks north of Main Street along Raadets Gade, you come to **Crystal Gade** and **St Thomas' Synagogue.** Constructed in the 18th century, but rebuilt three times since, it remains the second-oldest synagogue in the Caribbean (the oldest is in Curaçao). The present hurricane-proof building with an original sand floor dates from 1833, although its congregation was formed by Sephardic Jews from Amsterdam and London in 1796. The adjacent **Weibel Museum** (tel: 340-774 4312; www.onepaper.com/synagogue; Mon–Fri 9am–4pm; donations welcome) charts the history of St Thomas' Jewish community.

Wandering eastwards along the waterfront you can see the lines of docked boats, sleek yachts, and sailboats in the harbor. St Thomas hosts the St Thomas International Regatta (formerly the Rolex Regatta; www.stthomasinternationalregatta.com) at the end of March, a major yachting event attracting many competitors. The USVI competed in the Americas Cup for the first time in 2000. Sailing gets into your blood on these islands. The ferry that runs every 2 hours to St John waits here alongside the inter-island cargo ships: round-bellied boats with smoke stacks and circular windows; rusted hulls and lamp-lit, lived-in cabins furnished with little cooking stoves, clothes-strewn bunk beds, and radios. Each has a backboard hanging off the side rail, listing their destinations: "Accepting cargo for St Martin, Dominica, St Lucia, and St Kitts."

Behind the wharf is the red-painted **Fort Christian.** Built by the Danes in 1680, it is the oldest building in continuous use on the island and is a National Historic Landmark. Among

*An American paradise and a high crime rate often go hand in hand. It is unsafe to walk around Charlotte Amalie at night or go to remote beaches alone.*

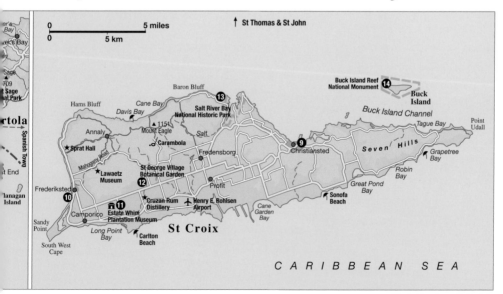

*Feel the power of the wind in the sails of a catamaran or trimaran on a one-day, half-day, or sunset cruise.*

*Yachts are synonymous with the USVI.*

many uses, it served as a prison, with the last prisoner leaving in 1982. The dungeon had housed the **Virgin Islands Museum** (tel: 340-776 4566) displaying valuable Amerindian artifacts, local history, and colonial furniture but since 2007 the fort has been closed for renovation. On Government Hill above the fort is the **Seven Arches Museum** (tel: 340-774 9295; www.sevenarchesmuseum.com; call to make an appointment; donations welcome), a striking example of Danish West Indian 19th-century domestic architecture, now a private museum and art gallery housing artifacts from that era.

## To the yachting havens of the east

Traffic jams are a constant factor in Charlotte Amalie. They are peculiarly "island" traffic jams – not so much the result of too many cars as they are of the relaxed attitude of local people who come upon a friend and stop for a chat through the car window.

Leaving the town along the Waterfront you soon come to **Havensight Mall**, a major shopping center where the cruise ships dock; Denmark owned all this until 1993. Nearby is the **St Thomas Skyride to Paradise Point** (tel: 340-774 9809; www.ridetheview.com; every ship day 9am–10pm), a cable car that will take you up to a beautiful view point. From **Yacht Haven Marina** you can charter a yacht for the day, go light-tackle fishing, or deep-sea fishing for blue marlin – St Thomas is often referred to as the blue marlin capital of the world. Past the turn-offs to the dazzling **Morningstar Beach** (where the people dazzle as well) and the idyllic **Secret Harbour**, after half an hour you come to **Red Hook**, at East End, and the **American Yacht Harbor** offering more sailing of all sorts and a choice of ferries running regularly to neighboring islands. Don't forget, the British Virgin Islands are another country and so passports need to be shown. There is a plethora of beautiful islands out there and you can explore them at speed but not in peace by renting a power boat from the marina.

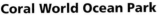
## Coral World Ocean Park

A fascinating underwater observatory in which you, the visitor, become the contained curiosity, and the fish the passing curious, **Coral World Ocean Park ❷** (tel: 340-775 1555; www.coral worldvi.com; Nov–Apr Sun–Thur 9am– 4pm, May–Oct times vary) is 15–20 minutes northeast from Charlotte Amalie at Coki Point. The centerpiece is a three-level underwater observatory from which to view an enormous range of marine life, but the highlight is watching divers from the observatory when they come to feed the sharks, moray eels, and stingrays in the predator tank. There is also a Nautilus semi-submersible – an enhanced glass-bottomed boat tour, or Sea Trek, where you don a specially designed helmet to follow a trail along the sea floor.

If that inspires you to swim down there among the exotic fish, the Orange Cup corals, and the colorful sponges in the underwater gardens off **Coki Beach**, Coki Beach Dive Club offers beginners' courses close by, with practice dives on the shallow reefs between St Thomas and St John.

Many of the 15 dive companies on the island also give lessons in underwater photography.

On the road back to the capital (a 20-minute drive away) lies **Tillett Gardens ❸** (tel: 340-775 1405; www. tillettgardens.com) an old Danish farm that was converted into an arts and crafts center in 1959. Outbuildings in the grounds hold an art gallery, with local artists' work for sale, and screen-printing and crafts studios, and you can combine a visit with lunch in the pretty garden restaurant. During the winter season, there is a series of chamber music concerts, and twice a year the Arts Alive Arts and Crafts Festival, a fusion of art and music, is held here.

Back on the coast road, continue west for another 3 miles (5km) or so, past the spectacular cliffside 18-hole **Mahogany Run Golf Course**, and you reach **Magen's Bay Beach ❹**, a sheltered horseshoe bay once voted "one of the 10 most beautiful beaches in the world" by *National Geographic*. All the fun of the beach can be had here on this mile-long stretch of sand that is perfect for children but does

*St Thomas is a popular port for cruise ships.*

*Tying the knot in the US Virgin Islands, a prime spot for weddings.*

get very crowded. Follow the marked trail to **Little Magen's Bay** for legal sunbathing in the nude – but don't get burned. The picturesque Route 35 back to Charlotte Amalie passes **Drake's Seat**, just a concrete bench in a layby but believed to be the spot used by Sir Francis Drake as his lookout.

For more views and the "world's best banana daiquiris" there is **Mountain Top ❺** (daily), the highest viewpoint on the island, nearly 2 miles (3km) from the capital, which offers more duty-free shopping. Once called Signal Hill, at 1,500ft (457 meters), it was of strategic importance to the US in the 1940s. Now it is commercialized, and best visited when there are few or no cruise ships in port. But it is still worth the trek for photos of the beauty of Magen's Bay – a bright green tear drop of calm, protected waters in a shell of white sand – toward St John and the British Virgin Islands.

Winding your way back down to Charlotte Amalie as evening falls, the boat lights in St Thomas Harbor look like felled constellations bobbing on the water. Island nightlife then kicks

*Cruz Bay, St John.*

into gear as revelers gather to dance in the bayside bars around **Frenchtown** and the former World War II submarine base to the west of the harbor – away from downtown, which is not a desirable place at night. Frenchtown was first settled by immigrants, mostly fishermen, from St-Barthélemy in the late 19th century and many of the older people here still speak creole. Here you find the Quetel Fish Market, where the catch from little fishing boats is sold, the small **French Heritage Museum** next to the ballpark, and waterfront restaurants, which are great attractions.

Offshore is **Water Island**, the fourth inhabited Virgin Island, reached by ferry from Crown Bay Marina. The US bought the island from Denmark in 1944 to use as a military base and for weapons testing, but it has been in private hands since the 1950s. The freshwater ponds that gave the island its name are now salt ponds. **Hassel Island**, also in the bay, is part of US National Parks and uninhabited, although you can get a water taxi to take you there for hiking and a picnic to enjoy the views.

## St John – a nature island

Lying 5 miles (8km) east of St Thomas, **St John** is a small, green atoll, worlds apart from its overcrowded neighbor. The roads are steep, twisty, and rocky but the deeply indented bays afford spectacular views of forested hills, sandy bays, and turquoise sea at every turn. Essentially, St John's fate was sealed when Laurence Rockefeller bought about half the island in the 1950s. He then deeded his portion of the 28 sq mile (70 sq km) mountainous island to the National Park Service. The **Virgin Islands National Park** (www.nps.gov/viis) was opened in 1956 and now covers about two-thirds of the island, although some land in the park is still privately owned and not open to visitors.

The ferry from Red Hook on St Thomas to St John takes just 20 minutes. There are no high-rise hotels here and a four-wheel-drive is the best mode of transport. If you are over just for the day, taxis offer a 2-hour trip around the island.

The main town, **Cruz Bay ⑥**, is the sort of place where people come to meet a friend at the ferry, pick up their mail, get some groceries, and then retreat back into the woods. Taxi drivers mill about and there are T-shirt shops, moped rental shops, open food stands, bars, and restaurants. **Wharfside Village** is a beachfront shopping mall with a working spice factory. The road to the left goes to **Mongoose Junction**, another mall a few minutes' walk away, and the **National Park Visitors' Center** (tel: 340-776-6201, ext. 238; daily 8am–4.30pm), where there are informative displays and you can pick up maps and books and sign up for tours and activities.

*Clocktower on St Croix.*

## Beautiful Northshore Road

The **Northshore Road** from Cruz Bay to Coral Bay follows the lush green coastline through the park to beach after beach of soft, white sand. At **Caneel Bay**, a few minutes' drive outside town, the rich and famous enjoy going without their digital distractions in the genteel, luxury hotel on the beach, created by Rockefeller in 1956.

**Hawksnest Beach** (with changing rooms and picnic tables) in

*Wharfside Village, Cruz Bay, St John.*

### WEDDINGS IN PARADISE

The USVI has become a prime spot in which to get married. After all, what could be more romantic than a wedding ceremony on a white sandy beach or in an exotic tropical garden? What could be more original than tying the knot under the sea in a coral garden or on top of a mountain with a spectacular panorama as a backdrop? Of course you can get married the traditional way in a church, or at any time of day from sunrise to sunset. And how about chartering a luxurious yacht for you and your guests? The choice of settings in the USVI is endless.

As the islands are an American Territory, US marriage laws still apply, so there is just an 8-day waiting period after the Territorial Court of your chosen island has received your application. Then, with the help of the tourist office, which has long lists of addresses and telephone numbers, you can contact the army of wedding consultants, planners, florists, and photographers necessary to achieve the "wedding of your dreams."

Weddings are big business here and yacht charterers are used to working with wedding planners to enable a trouble-free ceremony and reception on the sea, even providing diving gear if desired. And you won't have to go far for your honeymoon – that can be laid on, too.

*Hiking along one of the National Park's many trails.*

the next bay is a dream of a beach, popular with local people and film-makers alike. The cream of the crop, so it does get crowded, is **Trunk Bay Beach ❼** (with bathhouse, snack bar, snorkel-gear rental, shop, and life-guards), where snorkelers can follow the well-marked, 675ft (210-meter) long National Park Underwater Trail. Around the corner are two camp-grounds: Cinnamon Bay offers basic cottages, large tents, or bare sites on the beach backed by tropical vegeta-tion; and a little further on, Maho Bay concentrates on deluxe camping with tent cottages.

## Park trails and mill ruins

There are 20 hiking trails in the National Park, ranging from 15 min-utes to 2 hours, and many of them start from the Northshore Road. From Leinster Bay, just past Maho Bay, you can take a 30-minute walking tour of the **Annaberg Historic Sugar Mill Ruins ❽**, where there are the remains of the mills (wind- and horse-pow-ered), the sugar factory, and the rum still. The mortar between the stones of

the buildings is made of flour, molas-ses, and sea shells, so you've essentially got very old, hard cakes in front of you. Cultural demonstrations of tradi-tional skills take place Tuesday to Fri-day from 10am to 2pm. The trail back to the parking lot is lined with small, low-growing, fern-like plants known locally as *greeche greeche*. The plant's tiny leaves fold up when touched.

The walking tours with rangers through the park are an eye-opener, especially if you're curious about the indigenous flora (there are 800 species of plants and 50 species of birds breed-ing here, while many more migrants visit in the winter) and their various medicinal uses. On the 3-mile (5km) **Reef Bay Trail** (reservations at the Visitors' Center), you see the Reef Bay sugar mill ruins and petroglyphs (Amerindian stone pictures) and have a boat ride back to Cruz Bay.

## St Croix – an island with a difference

A seaplane – "It's fun to land on water" says the sign at the St Thomas termi-nal – takes you to the waterfront of

Christiansted on **St Croix** (pronounced "Croy" as in toy), 40 miles (65km) to the south of St Thomas. Very different from St Thomas, it takes longer to get around, and from east to west there is a dramatic change in the landscape – from low, grassy seaside hills that are reminiscent of Cornwall in England, to lush rainforests. Nearly 20 miles (33km) long and at 84 sq miles (210 sq km), St Croix has room for changing climates; it's drier in the east and prone to drifting mists over the west end.

In the bars you'll hear many conversations comparing one island to another, declaring what one has over the other. You hear a lot of that from the resident aliens who make up one-third of the population here – those from other Caribbean islands who've migrated to the USVI to find work and who are known as *garotes*, after a local bird that flies from island to island; North Americans, called Continentals, who have made their home here. They all say they want to keep St Croix quiet and modest, not like St Thomas.

## Christiansted – a Danish preserve

You feel the Danish influence everywhere, especially in the main town of **Christiansted 9**, in the northeast, where the cream-colored buildings are made of bricks that the Danish ships brought over as ballast. Christiansted is a town built for the tropics, with overhanging balconies and cool arcades. Many of the red-roofed buildings constructed in the prosperous years of the 18th century by rich merchants have been restored and the whole of the historic area, including the harbor area, is maintained by the US National Park Service. Christiansted National Historic Site, established in 1952, consists of 7 acres (3 hectares) and six historic buildings: Government House (1747), Steeple Building (1753), Danish West India & Genia Company Warehouse (1749), Custom House, Scale House (1856), and Fort Christiansvaern (1738).

The majestic, colonial **Government House** on King Street is used for many government and social functions. You can visit the ballroom, gardens, and the Court of Justice (tel: 340-773 1404; daily 8am–7pm; free). In the square on the waterfront, the **Old Danish Scale House** was where sugar and molasses were weighed before being shipped out. Close by, **Fort Christiansvaern** (visitor center tel: 340-773 1460; www.nps.gov/chri; daily 8am–5) has been well preserved and you can see the dungeons and punishment cells plus an exhibit on how to fire a cannon. Across Hospital Street, the **Steeple Building** (Mon–Sat 10am–5pm, Sun noon–5pm, in winter until 4pm), originally built as a Lutheran church, is now a museum of the island's early history. Since its deconsecration in 1831, the building has also been a bakery, school, and hospital. Behind the Boardwalk where the seaplane checks in, **King's Alley Walk**, developed after the 1995 hurricanes, penetrates a fascinating maze of arcades and alleys lined with shops, restaurants, and bars. Several times a year, whether the area needs it

*The Annaberg Historic Sugar Mill Ruins.*

**TIP**

Guided horseback nature rides are arranged from Paul and Jill's Equestrian Stables alongside Sprat Hall Plantation just north of Frederiksted (tel: 340-772 2880; www.paulandjills.com). For the more hale, mountain bike tours of 2–6 hours take you up through lush rainforest (Freedom City Cycles, 2 Strand Street, Frederiksted, tel: 340-772 2433; www.freedomcitycycles.com).

or not, shopping is actively encouraged with "Jump Up," when bands play in the streets, Mokojumbie dancers (stilt walkers) chase away evil spirits and a party atmosphere prevails.

## Frederiksted

The only other town on the island is tiny **Frederiksted** ❿, 17 miles (27km) away on the west coast. A small network of shops greets the cruise ships as they dock at the modern 1,500ft (450-meter) pier. Sights include the renovated 18th-century, red and white **Fort Frederik**, with a museum and art gallery (Mon–Fri 8.30am–4pm, Sat if a cruise ship is in) and the **Caribbean Museum Center for the Arts** (tel: 340-772 2622; www.cmcarts.org; Thur–Sat 10am–5pm), promoting regional art. The town has seen its fair share of natural disasters, from hurricanes to fires, but still retains its narrow streets and alleys lined with colonial buildings.

## Every plantation tells a story

*History is preserved at the Estate Whim.*

Between the two towns is the rural heartland of St Croix, where cattle and sugar have been the traditional farming activities. The **St Croix Heritage Trail** runs the length of the island following the routes of 18th-century roads (now upgraded to modern standards). A self-guided experience, it offers a cross-section of the island's history and culture. Guided walks and tours round plantation houses and ruins are offered on a regular basis by **St Croix Landmarks Society** (52 Estate Whim, Frederiksted; tel: 340-772 0598; www.stcroixlandmarks.com). One of these is the **Estate Whim Plantation Museum** ⓫ (Wed–Sat 10am–3pm). Whim is the oldest sugar plantation museum in the Virgin Islands and is a fascinating window on to the lives of the people who lived and worked there, as well as the economics and technology of sugar making. The estate is typical of plantations laid out by the Danish West Indian Company in the early 18th century, with first cotton, then sugar being grown, and finally cattle being reared here.

Another visit is to the **Lawaetz Museum** (Tue–Sat 10am–4pm) 3 miles (5km) away at Little La Grange, the

beautifully preserved family home of Danish farming immigrants, several generations of whom lived and farmed here.

Putting the sugar plantations into context in the modern age, it is worth visiting the **Cruzan Rum Distillery** (3 and 3A Estate Diamond, Frederiksted; tel: 340-692 2280; www.cruzanrum.com; tours Mon–Fri 9am–4pm, Sat–Sun10am–2pm), for a view of the production process. The Nelthropp family have been on St Croix for many generations and were among the first distillers to experiment with flavored rums, still popular with visitors today.

## Exotic flora

Also in this area, on Route 70, a collection of more than 1,000 species of tropical and exotic flowering trees, vines, and shrubs can be seen among the ruins of an 18th- and 19th-century plantation village in 16 acres (6.5 hectares) at **St George Village Botanical Garden** ⑫ (tel: 340-692 2874; www.sgvbg.org; gardens daily 9am–5pm, museum Tue–Fri 9am–5pm and weekend cruise ship days; charge to enter gardens). A small museum in a former slave house details the history of the area from the first Amerindian settlers to the Danish planters. An archeological site has dated Amerindian habitation of the area to AD 100.

## The north coast

On the north coast, just 4 miles (6km) from Christiansted, is **Salt River Bay** ⑬, where Columbus landed looking for fresh water (he found hostile Carib Amerindians instead) and which is now a National Historic Park. It has a large mangrove forest and an underwater canyon, which is ideal for scuba diving. **Northshore Road** runs along many of the island's beautiful beaches. Unprotected by reefs, the surfing is good off these shores and divers love the drop-off wall at Cane Bay. Heading south on Route 69 past the **Carambola Golf Course**, Robert Trent Jones's pride and joy, you reach **Mahogany Road**, which leads west

through the heart of the rainforest – a rich, bowered darkness with vines hanging from giant mahogany trees, kapoks, and the tidbit, also called the mother-in-law tongue, for the way its long seed castings rattle in the wind.

## An underwater park

**Buck Island Reef National Monument** ⑭ covers around 850 acres (340 hectares) of dry land, crystal-clear water, and barrier reef just off St Croix's northeast shore. Dive shops on the waterfront at Christiansted organize scuba diving and snorkeling trips to the island. There's a stretch of beach to the west that boaters like to sail up to, where there are changing facilities and picnic tables and two underwater trails (charter a boat; there are plenty on offer, and it will come ready equipped with lunch, and snorkeling and diving gear). The sea's most exotic and psychedelic renderings pass you by like a pre-arranged fashion show: the dusky damselfish, the redbanded parrotfish, the yellowhead wrasses, and the lookdown moonfish – you can just check them off in your program.

*Snorkeling in the USVI.*

# THE BRITISH VIRGIN ISLANDS

Once a pirates' refuge, today this peaceful archipelago with white powdery beaches washed by crystal-clear waters is a mecca for sailors and divers.

British Virgin Islands

Caribbean Sea

Only a few miles away from the glitz of the US Virgin Islands, the BVI, as the British Virgin Islands are affectionately referred to, do not cater for mass tourism. On the main islands of Tortola, Virgin Gorda, Jost Van Dyke, and Anegada, out on a limb to the north, there are no high-rise developments, flashy hotels, or casinos and most of the other 50-plus islands are uninhabited or have only one exclusive hotel or villa. For a long time, they managed to evade the whirlwind of change that enveloped most of the Lesser Antilles and are now capitalizing on their simple treasures: a pleasant, gentle citizenry and long, unspoiled beaches of powdery white sand bordering clear seas that give new meaning to the word "blue".

Here, all the action takes place above and beneath the surface of the water: sailors love the warm breezes that blow them from island to island where they can sample the secret coves only accessible by sea, and divers have a rich underworld of reefs to explore. This natural wealth forms the basis of the islands' economy and up-market resorts have developed around marinas offering yacht and hotel accommodations combined – it's the yachties the government wants to attract, along with those seeking somewhere quiet and beautiful to escape to. Up on the

mountain slopes, hairy lianas (vines) hang from ancient mahogany trees in snatches of remaining forest.

All the islands are of volcanic origin apart from Anegada, a flat coral and limestone atoll 30 miles (48km) north-east of the largest island, Tortola (21 sq miles/55 sq km). Both Tortola and Virgin Gorda, 14 miles (20km) away, rise steeply from the sea, each with a volcanic peak – Tortola's Mount Sage is 1,709ft (540 meters) and Gorda Peak is 1,369ft (415 meters). Getting anywhere in a hurry on Tortola

**Main Attractions**

Soper's Hole
Smugglers Cove
Mount Sage National Park
Cane Garden Bay
The Baths
Gorda Peak
Bitter End Yacht Club
Prickly Pear Island

*Little Dix Bay, Virgin Gorda, British Virgin Islands.*

*The Crafts Market in Road Town.*

is impossible. Some of the roads are easily on a par with alpine passes in Europe, with altitude differences of nearly 1,000ft (300 meters) within a couple of miles. The asphalt road encompassing most of Tortola was only completed towards the end of the 1980s; before then, anyone from Sea Cow Bay in the south who wanted to go to Cane Garden Bay in the north went either by donkey or by boat.

## Pirate haunts

Christopher Columbus may not have been all that impressed by these seemingly haphazardly located volcanic rocks when he discovered them in November 1493. But who was looking for good beaches at that time? Gold was what he was after, and there wasn't any. The predominantly steep terrain of Tortola provided the English with a handful of plantations later on, and there were enough fish in the sea to keep the slaves well fed. To protect the plantations and settlements from the incursions of pirates, forts were built along Tortola's south coast. One famous pirate dropped

anchor here on numerous occasions: Sir Francis Drake, for whom the strait between Tortola and the southern islands is named. His fleet was often in the area from 1568 to 1595 to keep the Spanish and Dutch in check, which also entitled the English to plunder their gold. Sometimes the forces of nature helped by dashing the ships on to the reefs north of Anegada – more than 300 vessels lie on the seabed here. Other pirates roamed the southern islands, feeding the imagination of story-tellers for years to come. The BVI have been in British hands since 1666 and today are mainly self-governing as a British Overseas Territory.

## Road Town –Tortola's capital

The yachting harbor, built around the artificial moles of Wickhams Cay 1 and 2, and the attractive marina beneath the renovated walls of the Fort Burt Hotel to the southwest, have given **Road Town ❶** a bustling maritime character – "road" is the nautical name for a protected and safe place to

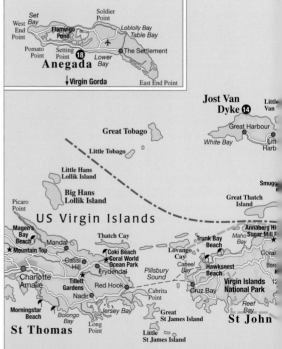

drop anchor. Waterfront Drive on the landfill area is a wide road sweeping around the harbor linking the marinas, the government buildings on **Wickhams Cay**, and the cruise ship landing area.

Palm trees and shrubs are taking root on this once barren area of reclaimed land, and modern structures such as the Government Building came in for quite a bit of stick when first constructed. Caribbean T-shirts emblazoned with tropical patterns dangle from stalls in the **Crafts Market** close by, alongside colorful fish mobiles, napkin rings, and other delightfully impractical items.

On picturesque **Main Street**, once the waterfront road, the typical West Indian-style wooden buildings now house banks, insurance companies, boutiques, and souvenir shops. The **Virgin Islands Folk Museum** (tel: 284-494 3701 ext. 5005; Main Street; Mon–Fri 8.30am–4.30pm; free) documents the colonial era, alongside marine exhibits and Amerindian artifacts in a typical old West Indian wooden building. Near the **ferry**

**docks** a few minutes' walk southwards – where boats leave regularly for other islands including St Thomas and St John – **Pusser's Co. Store & Pub**, an attractive gingerbread-style house that's hard to miss, has all the atmosphere of a British harbor pub. This is the place to try the Admiralty Rum, or Pusser's Painkiller, a notorious rum cocktail, and listen to maritime yarns. Through a door, Pusser's Store (branches in Soper's Hole, Marina Cay, and Leverick Bay) provides items with a nautical flavor.

At the bottom of Main Street, fronted by some spectacular flamboyant trees, the smart new government offices overlook the harbor. The **Old Government House** (tel: 284-494 4091; Mon–Fri 9am–3pm, weekends by appointment) on Waterfront Drive, a national landmark, has been converted from the official governor's residence into a museum of local history.

The first government house was destroyed by a hurricane in 1924. When government outgrew its replacement (now the museum), a new governor's office building

*Decanters emblazoned with a yachting theme at Pusser's Store.*

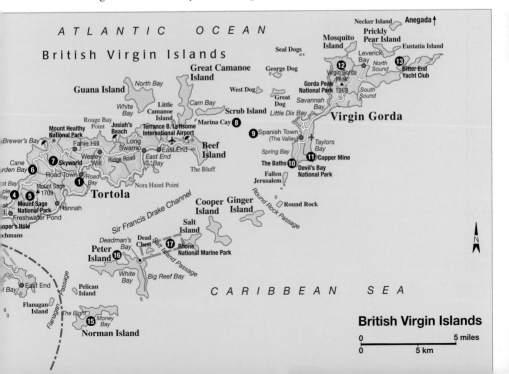

**British Virgin Islands**

0 — 5 miles

0 — 5 km

was constructed on the eastern side of the garden in the 1980s. A new government house was built in the western part of the garden and completed in 2003, with public areas downstairs, and living quarters for the governor and his family upstairs.

To the north of the town, next to the police station, the **J.R. O'Neal Botanic Gardens** (daily; donations welcome), with an avenue of palm trees, beautifully portrays the various vegetation zones of the islands and includes an orchid house, fern house, and medicinal herb garden.

## Tortola's west end

Winter in the BVI means only a few hours of rain every now and then. It never gets cold or unpleasant; big warm raindrops fall onto the hot ground, and the sun's rays appear from time to time through dramatic cloud formations. Then in summer the islands look exotic and green. Bougainvillea covers the houses with its magnificent blossoms, and the gardens are full of bright red hibiscus. The marina at **Soper's Hole** ❷ on

Frenchman's Cay, 8 miles (13km) west of Road Town, Pusser's Landing, the yacht charter buildings, the galleries, and the shops all combine with the surrounding countryside to create a magnificently colorful scene, especially just before sunset. Ferries to the US Virgin Islands and Jost Van Dyke (see page 122), 5 miles (8km) away, leave from Soper's Hole.

All the beaches in the BVI are public, but you're certain to find a quiet spot near the elegant hotels in **Long Bay** at the end of the steep road over Zion Hill. The bumpy track westwards past Belmont leads to **Smugglers Cove** ❸, a delightful sandy inlet with sunshine practically guaranteed until evening, and wonderful snorkeling. Around to the west, dramatic rocks rise from the sea at **Steele Point** and smart villas decorate the steep slope behind.

## Trophies and shells

When Hurricane Luis passed this way in 1995, it seems to have had something of an effect on **Bomba's Surfside Shack**, in **Apple Bay** ❹. In

*Tortola, as seen from the sea.*

a venue popular with locals, yachties, and surfers jumping the waves in the bay, a few more oddities were added to the collection of trophies plastered over the ramshackle walls: an ancient bra, a pennant from New Zealand, T-shirts and other flotsam, many bearing personal dedications to the shack's owner. This place has become a real institution and one of the best-known nightspots in the BVI – the "full moon parties" and weekly reggae nights are quite an experience: hips sway amidst the barbecue smoke, and the fun spills out on to the road.

At the other end, in **Carrot Bay**, a more traditional collection can be seen at the North Shore Shell Museum Bar & Restaurant where, after a drink or a meal of cracked conch, grilled lobster, and good Caribbean cooking, you can see exhibits of local crafts alongside the countless shells.

## Panoramic hairpins around Mount Sage

The coast road winds up from Carrot Bay along spectacular Windy Ridge toward Cane Garden Bay and branches off into **Mount Sage National Park** ❺, a protected area of tropical forest spared from clearance in the plantation era. Giant mahogany trees with complex roots cling on to the rock face of the 1,709ft (543-meter) **Mount Sage**, and lianas, moss, and numerous orchids leech moisture from tree trunks and hollows; tree frogs start their chorus just before sunset. As water takes longer to seep through volcanic rock than through limestone, the vegetation grows profusely here on an annual rainfall of less than 12ins (30cm).

Rum plays a major role in the BVI, but much of it actually comes from other islands. There were once seven family-run firms producing the "liquid gold" in **Cane Garden Bay** ❻ but now only the fine Arundel Cane

Rum is produced at the 200-year-old tumbledown **Callwood Distillery** (tel: 284-495 93 83; Mon–Sat 7.30am–5pm; free). The secret of the rum's high quality, according to owner Michael Callwood, is that it is made from the sugar-cane juice rather than the molasses left behind in the sugar refining process.

The gently curving bay in front is one of the Virgin Islands' top beaches: deckchairs and sunshades are for rent, yachts move slowly past buoys on the turquoise sea, all types of watersports are on offer, and calypso bands strike up outside the bars just before sunset. **Brewer's Bay** farther north is far more provincial: the sand is much darker, and don't be surprised to see the odd cow walking across it. The roads around here are very steep and signposts point to the ultimate viewing spot at **Skyworld** ❼ on Ridge Road where there is a 360-degree panoramic view of Road Town, surrounding islands, and the rolling hills to the east: a perfect place for a picnic before hitting the challenging mountain

**TIP**

The best surfing can be experienced from November along Tortola's north coast at Apple Bay, the eastern end of Cane Garden Bay, and Josiah's Bay.

*Blooms of the heliconia genus.*

**FACT**

Every March the BVI Spring Regatta & Sailing Festival (www.bvispring regatta.org) attracts around 100 yachts and sailors from all around the world. Participants enter in 18 classes and race in three race areas, and the weeklong event, starting at Nanny Cay, is accompanied by fantastic Caribbean parties. In 2016 the regatta celebrated its 45th anniversary.

road once more to Long Swamp and East End, 7 miles (11km) away. From there turn steeply northward and over the summit to the Lambert Beach Resort where, with a drink on the terrace, you can gaze in wonder at the creamy white beach edged by palms and ancient seagrapes around **Elizabeth Bay**.

**Beef Island**, where the Terrance B. Lettsome International Airport is sited, is connected to East End by the Queen Elizabeth Bridge. Off the coast, the tiny 6-acre (2-hectare) island of **Marina Cay** ❽, only slightly higher than the surrounding coral, looks as if it could easily disappear under a large wave. Free ferries ply to and from the island, 5 minutes away, around 10 times a day from **Trellis Bay**, just east of the airport and a popular windsurfing spot. Once owned by the author Robb White, who used it as the setting for his book *Our Virgin Isle* and the film version *Two On The Isle* with Sidney Poitier in the 1950s, Marina Cay is now a private resort belonging to Pusser's and offers a wide variety of water sports such as snorkeling, underwater safaris, kayaking, and deep-sea fishing.

## The fat Virgin and her giant "marbles"

If Columbus had been thinking of St Ursula and her 11,000 virgins when he named this archipelago, why should a granite island have been named Virgin Gorda (Fat Virgin)? Speculation abounds, one notion being that, from afar, the 10-mile (16km) long island looks like a reclining woman with a protruding stomach. **Spanish Town** ❾, also known as The Valley, is the main town on Virgin Gorda and until 1741 was the capital of the entire group of islands. The houses are dotted across various parks and gardens, and souvenir hunters will find a handful of colorful boutiques near the modern and well-equipped **Yacht Harbour**, south of the ferry dock.

From here taxis can take you across the southern part of the island past huge rounded granite blocks looking like giant marbles scattered all over the place, to **The Baths** ❿, where the house-high boulders have formed natural grottoes and pools perfect for swimming and snorkeling. There's an easy trail between them, with ladders and bridges over the tricky parts. Geologists refer to this phenomenon, which is part of the **Devil's Bay National Park**, as "woolsack weathering" – long ago, a thick layer of soil covered the stone, and acids from the humus gradually worked their way into hairline fissures in the rock, wearing it away. As the topsoil gradually disappeared, wind, heat, and salt particles continued to erode the rough granite so that some look as if their shells are about to break.

Noticing that the granite southeastern coast of Virgin Gorda was similar to that of Cornwall, where copper mining was a lucrative industry in the early 19th century, the British

*Aerial view of Devil's Bay, Virgin Gorda, British Virgin Islands.*

speculated that there must be some copper here too. They were right, and Cornish miners worked the **Copper Mine ⓫**, not far out of Spanish Town, for around 30 years. The chimney of the old mine, ruins of old stone buildings, a copper-ore pit, and remains of a smelting furnace can all still be seen.

## Yachting in the north

Just 5 minutes north of Spanish Town lies **Little Dix Bay**, where in 1964, after his success with Caneel Bay Resort in St John (see page 109), Laurance Rockefeller opened the BVI's first hotel, geared expressly toward family vacations, and put Virgin Gorda on the map.

At the narrowest point of the island, less than 980ft (300 meters) of land separate the spray-covered coast to the east from gorgeous **Savannah Bay**. On weekdays this coastline is like one long private beach – all yours. The road continues north, branching off to **Gorda Peak ⓬** (1,369 ft/417 meters), a National Park where the views from

the observation point, reached after a short walk through some protected mahogany forest, are quite dizzying. Then it's downhill all the way to the happy and colorful Pusser's hotel at **Leverick Bay.**

The North Sound Express launch stops off at the hotel on its 45-minute journey from Tortola across the deep water of the North Sound to the **Bitter End Yacht Club ⓭** at John O'Point. Here the yachties rule and the beach and water sports facilities are awe-inspiring. Instead of staying in any of the discreet-looking villas dotting the hillside or next to the beach, you can spend your holiday on one of their 30ft (9-meter) yachts.

On the northeastern edge of North Sound lies **Prickly Pear Island**, which has a beautiful long white beach at **Vixen Point**, with the Sand Box beach bar. The island is a National Park, home to resident and migratory birds, and there is a trail from the beach bar to North Beach. No ferries stop here, so you must have your own boat.

**TIP**

Sailing, kiteboarding, and windsurfing courses for all ages are available from the Bitter End Sailing School at Bitter End Yacht Club (tel: 284-494 2746) and you can also learn about live-aboard cruising (www.beyc.com).

*The Baths, Virgin Gorda.*

*The beach at Prickly Pear Island.*

*The world-famous Soggy Dollar Bar on Jost Van Dyke, British Virgin Islands.*

## Jost Van Dyke – a tranquil retreat

The moment the speedboat to **Jost Van Dyke** ⑭ from Soper's Hole has docked, all the passengers disappear into Great Harbour except for the tourists, who stand gazing around them in astonishment. Time seems to stand still here: a handful of houses in a bay, and green hills under a scorching sun – indeed, electricity was only brought to the island in 1991. A few people stand in front of the Customs House, and goats graze peacefully in the cemetery. A pink sign bears the words "water-taxi" together with a phone number. What on earth do people spend their time doing here? Some, such as Foxy in his beach bar, have become accomplished storytellers.

The water-taxi quickly takes you westward round to White Bay where you have to paddle barefoot through the waves to the beach. Pant and dress hems get wet, but dry out again almost as quickly while you're lying in the hammocks among the palm trees at the aptly named Soggy Dollar Bar. Every day feels like Sunday here. The atmosphere is perfect, and so romantic that it is almost a cliché: palm and seagrape trees, ultra-fine sand, gentle hills on the southern horizon, and all of it at the place where a painkiller cocktail (Pusser's Painkiller) was supposed to have been invented. What ailments needed to be cured in this paradise? Surely it can only have been the pain of having to leave.

## Treasure islands

Forming the southern edge of the Sir Francis Drake Channel, south of Tortola, is a collection of tiny islands that provided perfect hiding places for pirates and inspired romantically inclined 19th-century authors such as Robert Louis Stevenson (1850–94). This Scottish novelist and poet is supposed to have chosen the uninhabited **Norman Island** ⑮ as the location for his *Treasure Island* (1883), and treasure hunters have done a great deal of digging ever since, to no avail. The real treasures, however, are under the water around the reefs of the

### THE DOG ISLANDS

The Dog Islands are a collection of tiny islets 2.5 miles (4km) northwest of Virgin Gorda. They got their name because sailors who anchored there heard barking and thought there were dogs on land. They soon discovered, however, that the noise came from barking Caribbean Monk seals, which they promptly caught and ate. Now, the islands are a stopping place while sailing from North Sound to Jost Van Dyke, and are popular with divers for the canyons and bridges underwater, as well as other interesting rock formations. Great Dog is the largest island, followed by West Dog Island and George Dog Island. There is a sub-grouping of Seal Dog Islands, off Great Dog Island, the smallest of which delights in the name of Cockroach Island.

protected bay known as **The Bight** which are bountiful in colorful fish; the caves along the rocky west coast, reached by boat, offer snorkelers a magnificent show.

When it's time to come up for air, cold drinks and Caribbean food are served up by the galley team on the *William Thornton II* (tel: 284-496 8603; VHF channels 16 or 74; www.williamthornton. com), a replica of an old Baltic trading vessel, in The Bight. More underwater caves and reefs give divers and photographers a fascinating few hours around **Pelican Island** and the pinnacles of rock called **The Indians**.

Despite the name, **Deadman's Bay** on the north coast of **Peter Island** ⑯ is often ranked as one of the top romantic beaches in the world – a white-sand beach fringed with palm trees and lapped by a gentle turquoise sea has to be irresistible. Cacti and enormous agaves cover the island, owned by the environmentally conscious Peter Island Resort. Gold-medal-winning chef Alson Pont's Caribbean specialties can be sampled at the beach restaurant.

With a view of **Dead Chest**, where the pirate Blackbeard is said to have left 15 sailors to die – "Fifteen men on a dead man's chest/ Yo ho ho and a bottle of rum" – the diving boats set off toward the buoys surrounding the *RMS Rhone* in the **Rhone National Marine Park** ⑰. In 1867, this 320ft (100-meter) long Royal Mail vessel sank just to the west of **Salt Island** during a hurricane. One passenger and 20 crew members were rescued and to thank the Salt Island rescuers, Queen Victoria gave them ownership rights to it in return for one English pound of salt a year.

Several of the boats that take divers out to explore the colonies of coral and sponge fore and aft of this ship – which lies 70ft (20 meters) below the surface and has an enormous propeller – dock at Salt Island. The last resident and salt-gatherer died in 2004 and is buried on the island.

## Anegada – an island of beaches and wrecks

The flat island of **Anegada** ⑱ is easy to overlook, at 11 by 3 miles (17 by 5km), its highest point being a mere 28ft (9 meters). But, with a continuous white beach from the Anegada Reef Hotel in the south, round West End along the north shore, where turtles nest, to East End, it would be a mistake if you did. For snorkelers, the reef offshore contains caves, drops, and tunnels awash with colorful fish and turtles. Farther out, beyond the reef, scuba divers can explore several wrecks, home to angelfish, stingrays, and grouper. Fishermen still provide the hotel with the best lobster in the BVI – it's also a top spot for bone fishing.

Two short strips of tarmac meet up in **The Settlement**, where most of the 300-strong population live. The controversial decision to introduce flamingos to the lagoon in 1992 proved a success when wild ones joined them and they reared some young. Anyone just here for a day would do well to hire a jeep to visit **Loblolly Bay**, on the north coast, which is flanked by two bars.

**FACT**

British entrepreneur and head of the Virgin empire Sir Richard Branson couldn't resist the idea of owning a Virgin Island and he famously owns Necker Island and Moskito Island, north of Virgin Gorda. Luxury houses have been built on both islands which are available to rent at luxury prices (www.virgin limitededition.com).

*A wooden dock at Anegada.*

# LIFE ON THE OCEAN WAVE

**The steady northeasterly trade winds that carried Columbus into the New World have made the Caribbean one of the top sailing destinations.**

The image of sailboats cruising in the gentle waters around the Grenadines seems like a dream – quiet sand-fringed bays below rolling hills, rustic harbor towns, and lively beach bars. Visitors from all over the world flock to the Caribbean harbors during winter months, either with their own boats, on bareboat charters, or renting large yachts with a skipper and a crew. The season kicks off with the arrival of yachts from Europe taking part in the Atlantic Rally for Cruisers just before Christmas in Rodney Bay, St Lucia. The old English seafaring tradition has influenced international regatta competitions in the British Virgin Islands and in Antigua, but you can find yacht clubs on most of the bigger islands organizing inter-island races at different times of the year. For local color, look out for races between traditional wooden fishing boats, such as at Anguilla's Carnival in August, or beautiful schooners, ketches, and sloops built as early as 1909 racing off English Harbour during Antigua's Sailing Week (April).

*Sailboats at the Antigua Classic Yacht Regatta, Antigua and Barbuda.*

*The south coast of Barbados is one of the best places for kite surfing in the Caribbean, its winds attracting keen surfers from around the world.*

## Island hopping

Sailing during the night and fun-filled days spent on different islands: cruises on the luxurious all-inclusive waterhotels are big business. Cruise ships mainly begin their routes in Florida, San Juan, or Barbados and offer guests 24-hour entertainment with a break during the day to explore an island or shop in tax-free malls. Some cruise lines offer themed holidays such as those for gay travelers or even romantic novelists.

*Day sails along the west coast of Barbados or the leeward side of any of the Lesser Antilles are a popular excursion.*

*A Carib man building a boat near Castle Bruce, Dominica.*

## IT'S ALL IN THE GAME

When visiting the Carib Territory in Dominica you will see large wooden canoes carved out of a single tree trunk. These are identical to the canoes used by the tribes on their migrations from the Guianas and the Orinoco basin northward up the island chain centuries ago. They also used them when they went to war and for fishing. They were skillful at killing fish by using spears or by throwing branches of *matapisca* – the local name for the **Jacquinia** tree – into the sea, which would slightly paralyze even large fish, but didn't harm humans. They also caught fish using baskets, nets, or lines; fish and shellfish were their main source of protein and most of their settlements were close to the sea.

Today, big-game fishing enthusiasts fight tuna, marlins, and wahoo while strapped to comfortable seats on motor boats. Equipped with special rods, private charter boats offer day-trips on many of the islands, or you can book a whole week's adventure on the waves. Smaller companies also provide angling gear, but the tale of the blue marlin or grouper that got away is up to you.

*While small or mid-sized cruise ships may lack the facilities of the larger ships, they have the advantage of being able to visit small harbors off the beaten track.*

*Kayaking is a popular activity around the coasts of most islands, exploring the mangroves or rocky coves and marine parks, as here at Anse Chastanet Resort, St Lucia.*

*Deep sea fishing in the Caribbean, whether on a day trip or competing in a tournament, is a thrill for any fisherman.*

A father and daughter play tag on one of Anguilla's empty beaches.

# ANGUILLA

Romantic, long white sandy beaches, exclusive hotels, and a feeling of seclusion make this small British outpost, where the strong-minded people are welcoming and courteous, a paradise.

Caribbean Sea — Anguilla

The low coral island of Anguilla sits at the top of the Leeward Islands chain, a serene, remote place of empty beaches with powdery white sand and untouched cays and reefs, adrift in the wide blue sea. Nothing much happens on this tiny British territory, far from the mainstream of a busy world. And this tranquility is the island's main asset. Since it stood up and flexed its muscles against its governing partners St Kitts and Nevis in the late 1960s, Anguilla seems content to retain its sleepy character, proud and protective of its 12 miles (19km) of well-kept beaches, crystalline waters, and exquisite coral reefs teeming with a wide variety of marine life, a magnet for sun worshippers, water sports enthusiasts (but no jet-skis), and divers alike.

At 16 miles (26km) long and 3 miles (5km) wide, Anguilla (Spanish for "eel") is one of the drier islands, covered in tangled vegetation and low, tough scrub, foraged by hundreds of goats. Trees have never really been a feature here, especially after the ones they had were uprooted by Hurricane Luis in 1995 (a disaster the islanders have put well behind them), but now, thanks to a concerted effort by a band of Anguillians to beautify the island, they are shooting up all over the place. Topsoil is scarce and

only a few acres are fertile enough to support some hardy crops: pigeon peas, cassava, yams, corn, and tropical fruits. However, modern technology, in the form of hydroponic agriculture, has permitted a small industry, growing vegetables for the local market as well as for the restaurants of St-Martin (see page 133), 5 miles (8km) to the south.

## A quirky history

This impoverished land endowed Anguillians with a social history

**Main Attractions**
Wallblake House
Sandy Ground
Sandy Island
Shoal Bay
Island Harbour
Heritage Collection

*Dive right in.*

*Goats roam everywhere.*

that, like its political history, is quirky. Archeological excavations have unearthed evidence of Amerindian presence on the island dating from 1300 BC, centuries before the Arawak-speaking tribes are believed to have settled the Caribbean chain (at around the time of Christ). Remains from Amerindian villages have also been discovered at Rendezvous Bay, Sandy Ground, and Island Harbour, making Anguilla one of the most archeologically interesting places in the region. By the time the first British settlers arrived in 1650, the island was uninhabited.

The colonizers tried to plant tobacco and, later, sugar. Because of the dry climate and poor soil, these cash crops never took root and, to a large extent, neither did slavery. Still, slaves were duly imported, although they were freed long before Emancipation in 1834, as beleaguered planters could barely feed themselves.

Thus, Anguilla's flat, barren land left its people almost free of the scars of slavery, evolving into an extraordinarily egalitarian and color-blind society, where everybody owned their land and helped each other through frequent droughts and hurricanes, and to overcome the lack of fresh water and arable soil. Nevertheless, one resource, besides their character, was left to the Anguillians – the sea. Unlike other West Indians, landlocked by the success of plantations, Anguillians became expert boat builders, sailors, and fishermen.

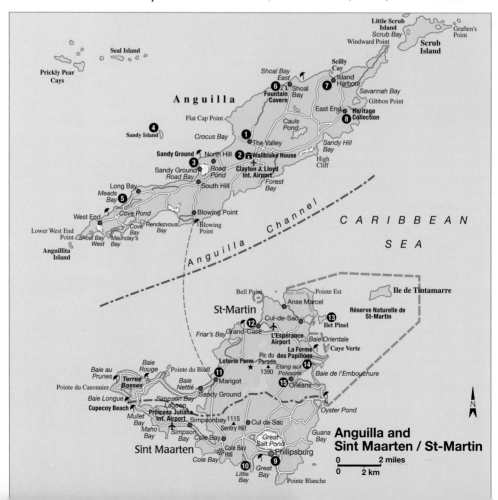

Anguilla and Sint Maarten / St-Martin

## Up in arms

Such strength of character, sense of community, and loyalty, however, were severely tried when, in 1967, against the Anguillians' wishes, Britain, in an attempt to divest itself of its dependencies, made Anguilla and the much-resented St Kitts and Nevis, 70 miles (110km) away, an Associated State. More autonomy was directed from St Kitts, sparking the Anguilla Revolution (see page 133).

Today, Anguilla is content to be one of Britain's few remaining Overseas Territories. Local government handles most domestic affairs, while a British governor takes care of the civil service, police, judiciary, and foreign affairs.

## Tasteful tourism

Much of Anguilla's charm lies in what it lacks. There is no mass tourism, although the extension of the runway at Clayton J. Lloyd International Airport in 2004 now allows medium-sized jets to land, as well as the small island-hopping planes. Most visitors arrive by sea at **Blowing Point**, on the south coast, on ferries from Marigot in St-Martin, just 20 minutes away. With only around 13,000 full-time residents, everybody knows everybody else and cars don't pass without a nod, a wave, or a honk. There are no casinos, scarcely any crime, and the church – Methodist, Anglican, Baptist, and Seventh Day Adventist – is still the center of Anguillian life.

The islanders have adopted a tasteful approach to tourism, restricting development to small, expensive resort-hotels, such as the exclusive Cap Juluca at Maunday's Bay and Malliouhana (the Arawak name for the island) in Meads Bay. Moreover, they seem deeply committed to protecting their natural assets, introducing measures to assure the conservation of the fragile ecology, and enforcing strict regulations to protect the marine environment.

## The Valley

Since the island has been reaping the financial rewards of tourism and a thriving offshore finance sector, **The Valley** ❶ has grown from a few houses on a country crossroads to a small commercial center with banks, business places, and a shopping mall. In the renovated old Customs Building across from Ronald Webster Park is the **Anguilla National Trust** (tel: 264-497 5297). The National Trust plays a leading role in island conservation, creating wildlife protection schemes and youth programs and running heritage tours, highlighting the flora, fauna, and history of the island.

Heading south out of The Valley toward Sandy Ground, you come to **Wallblake House** ❷ (tel: 264-497 6613; http://wallblake.ai/history.html; Mon, Wed and Fri 10am–2pm; tours by appointment). Built in 1787 by Will Blake, and recently restored, it is the oldest plantation house on the island and all its buildings are intact, including the kitchen, slave quarters, and stables. Cut stone had to

**FACT**

When a major cruise line proposed to develop a cay as an island getaway for its passengers, the Anguillian owners of the land turned down the deal, worth millions of dollars, preferring to preserve the unspoiled islet for their children.

*Wallblake House after 7 years of dedicated restoration.*

be hauled across the island from the East End or Scrub Island and burned coral, shells, and molasses were mixed into the mortar. The restored house is home to the Roman Catholic priest of **St Gerard's**, the tiny modern chapel next door with walls of open stonework.

Farther along the road is the **Old House** (tel: 264-497 2228). Built around 1800, it was home to a succession of Magistrate-Doctors, representing the British Crown. The two-story wooden structure has been restored and is now a restaurant.

## A salty heritage

Anguilla was famous for its salt, mined from saline ponds dotted around the island. They are home to a wide variety of birdlife, visiting and resident, such as the great blue heron and white-cheeked pintail. The last bag of salt was processed at Road Pond in **Sandy Ground ❸** in 1985, and at the northern end of the bay, which sweeps round in a horseshoe of white sand, the mini-museum in **The Pumphouse Bar** (www.pumphouse-anguilla.com), once the old salt factory, documents the story of salt "picking." A few doors away, **Johnno's** is said to be one of the best beach bars in the Caribbean, and jumps to live music on the weekends.

## Beautiful beaches

Many people come to Anguilla just for the beaches, and the west coast has an uncrowded long stretch of perfect, white sand. From Sandy Ground it's a 5-minute boat ride (from the pier; on the hour 10am–3pm) to **Sandy Island ❹**, a desert island of sand, with a beach bar and restaurant. The surrounding coral reef offers fascinating snorkeling, and farther out to sea, divers can explore the spectacular underwater canyon by **Prickly Pear Cays**, another short boat ride away.

**Meads Bay ❺**, 3 miles (5km) along from Sandy Ground, is one of the trendiest, attracting film stars and the super-rich, while **Shoal Bay West** on the other side of West End Point is more remote. Sheltered **Rendezvous Bay** on the south coast looks over to St-Martin and offers good windsurfing. Reputedly one of the best beaches of the Caribbean, **Shoal Bay East, ❻** miles (5km) north of The Valley, is perfect for swimming, snorkeling, and relaxing.

## Archeological treasure

**Fountain Cavern**, just inland of Shoal Bay, is a Unesco World Heritage Site, but not yet open to the public. The cavern and the area around it are to be developed by a subsidiary of the Anguilla National Trust into the island's first National Park, with plans for an interpretive center, museum, and easy access to the cave (preparatory work was commenced in May 2015). A natural spring in a large underground cavern, this is an important archeological site where magnificently preserved petroglyphs have been found alongside a 16ft (5-meter) stalagmite carved

*A hotel at Meads Bay, Anguilla.*

into a head, believed to be that of Yucahú (giver of cassava/yuca), the most important Amerindian deity. Archeological excavations indicate that Amerindians used the site for ritual purposes around AD 400–1200, making it the oldest known and the longest used ceremonial cave site in the entire Caribbean, representing an extraordinary example of Amerindian cultural heritage.

## The national passion

Island Harbour ❼, 3 miles (5km) to the north, is a pretty working fishing village where brightly painted, prosperous-looking boats line the beach. Nearby, **Big Spring** (tel: 264-497 5297), which served as the village's water source, is in a partially collapsed cave with Amerindian petroglyphs. Fishing has always been a booming business here, where sweet and luscious spiny lobsters are so plentiful; they are exported to St-Martin, Puerto Rico, and St Thomas. After the day's catch, sacks of them are spilled onto the sand for prospective buyers.

Now powered by outboard motor, the fishing fleet once flourished under sail and fishermen would race home from their grounds 30 miles (50km) out to sea. Racing became a passion and today the traditional boats are built solely for that purpose; sailing is on a par with cricket in popularity. On holidays and in Carnival Week in August, the whole island comes to watch and place bets on boats that race from Sandy Ground, Meads Bay, Blowing Point, and Rendezvous Bay to a marker out at sea.

## Island museum

Two miles (3.2km) south of Island Harbour, in the small locality of **East End**, you will find the only museum on Anguilla, **The Heritage Collection** ❽ (tel: 264-235 7440; www.offshore.com.ai/heritage; Mon–Sat 10am–5pm). It is owned and curated by local historian and writer Colville Petty, with historical artifacts, including those from the ancient settlements of Arawak Indians and from the period of the Anguilla's Revolution.

*Anguilla's beaches are reason enough to visit.*

### "WE WANT ENGLAND!"

Animosity began between St Kitts and Anguilla after 1825 when Britain incorporated the two islands with Nevis into one colony. The Anguillians resented the St Kitts government, which treated them as country bumpkins and did little to help them through some lengthy droughts.

Several pleas to London for direct British rule were ignored and the situation finally came to a head in 1967 when Britain tried to join the three islands together permanently as an Associated State of St Kitts-Nevis-Anguilla. Anguillians rebelled saying, "We don't want statehood, we want England," set the 13-strong St Kittitian police force adrift in a boat, and mounted an 18-man attack on St Kitts, which then fizzled out.

Until then, Anguilla had been poor and undeveloped with inadequate public and health facilities, including no electricity or piped water, and high unemployment.

The St Kitts administration still didn't help and Britain remained blind to their plight, so the Anguillians took over their own management. Finally, in March 1969, 400 British paratroopers, marines, and policemen invaded Anguilla to a great welcome, returning it to Britain. Today, the Revolution remains a crucial part of the islanders' psyche and they celebrate the anniversary every year.

# SINT MAARTEN/ST-MARTIN

A busy island shared between the Netherlands and France, it is a haven for shoppers and sunseekers. While the French side excels in gourmet restaurants, the Dutch part is a gambler's delight.

**Main Attractions**
Philipsburg
Baie Longue
Marigot
On the Trail of the Arawaks museum
Loterie Farm
Butterfly Farm

According to legend, the border of Sint Maarten/St-Martin was defined when a Dutchman and a Frenchman stood back to back, then walked around the island until they met face to face. The Dutch side is smaller, supposedly because the Dutchman was fat, or slow, or drinking gin as he walked, or all three. Crossing the border today is an affair of total informality, quite in keeping with the character of this tiny "freeport" island, with nothing but a monument erected in 1948 to commemorate the 1648 Treaty of Concordia which divided the island between the two nations. Despite such informality, the border holds great symbolic value to the islanders, marking peaceful co-existence and distinguishing two communities which are the same and yet different.

Sint Maarten/St-Martin's border bisects the smallest landmass – 37 sq miles (96 sq km) – in the world shared by two countries. The smaller southern half – Sint Maarten – has been one of the four constituent countries of the Kingdom of the Netherlands since "independence" in 2010. Sint Maarten had long resented being governed from Curaçao when it was part of the Netherlands Antilles, and now benefits from greater self-government while still under the protection of the mother country. The northern side of the island constitutes the French overseas collectivity of St-Martin. As of 1946, French St-Martin was technically an *arondissement* of Guadeloupe, which is a *département* of France (in the same way that Hawaii is a state of the US), but in 2007 (after a referendum in favor of secession in 2003), St-Martin gained COM status and a local assembly was elected. The difference between the two nations is immense: St-Martin is quintessentially French in style, developed on a small scale but including Parisian shopping and gourmet food, whereas

*A dish of snails – St-Martin's cuisine is typically French.*

*White and tawny rums made by Rhum Clément, the island's leading producer of Rhum Agricole (made from fresh sugar cane rather than molasses.)*

*The Courthouse in Philipsburg.*

Sint Maarten has large resorts, casinos, and fast-food chains.

## Contrasting landscapes

The west end of the island is an atoll of low land surrounding a lagoon, while the east end consists of a range of conical hills, the highest being Pic du Paradis (1,390ft/420 meters). Dotted around are a number of salt ponds. There is no drama here. The hills are low and easy to climb, the beautiful white beaches are sheltered. It's a fertile landscape of soft hills and pasture, cattle and horses. Green and hawksbill turtles nest on the shores and the fishing is good.

## A sharing mentality

French colonists arrived in the north of the island in 1629 and in 1631 the salt ponds in the south attracted Dutch settlers. The two groups lived amicably apart. Holland was at war with Spain, and Spain had a monopoly on European salt, an essential commodity for the preservation of food in the days before refrigeration. Spain reconsidered its earlier decision not to colonize

the island and occupied it from 1633 to 1648. It was while the Dutch were trying to recapture the island in 1644 that the young Peter Stuyvesant, then governor of Curaçao, lost his leg to a Spanish cannonball at Cay Bay (3 years later he became governor of the Dutch colony on present-day Manhattan). The Spanish abandoned the island 4 years later, and the Dutch moved back with the French, dividing the territory between them. The border has survived unchanged to this day, despite several armed incursions in both directions and persistent attempts by the Dutch in the 18th century to buy the French side outright. The island has changed hands 16 times, including brief occupations by the British, and the last Dutch–French accord was in 1839, since when peace has reigned.

At the height of colonialism, sugar and salt became the island's most important exports, until slavery was abolished and the plantations went into decline. Salt was shipped to the US and to Holland where it was used in the herring industry until that too ground to a halt in 1949.

### A COSMOPOLITAN STEW

The relative prosperity of the island over the last few decades has attracted thousands of immigrants to work in construction and the hotel industry, mostly on Sint Maarten. While the French side is decidedly French, the Dutch side is a more cosmopolitan mix in which Dutch, American, Caribbean, and Asian segments play equally important roles.

In St-Martin, everyone speaks French, creole, and often English, whereas in Sint Maarten, although Dutch is the official language and taught in schools, everyone speaks English and signposts and notices are all in English too. Papiamentu has been spoken on the island since 1960 when it arrived as the language of an imported labor force from other Dutch islands, and Spanish is often heard, too.

## Philipsburg – the Dutch capital

In 1733, a town was founded on the sandbar that separates the Great Salt Pond from Great Bay. It was named **Philipsburg** ❾, in honor of John Philips, the Scotsman who did so much for the early development of Sint Maarten. The sand is still very much in evidence; all over town there are unobtrusive welcome mats to keep as much of it outdoors as possible. But what's left of the pond is easy to ignore – a stretch of stagnant water with some long-term plans to clean it up and make it a bird sanctuary – so who would realize that when Back Street takes a strange course, it's avoiding the ghost of a huge storage pile of salt?

By day, Philipsburg is a lively, crowded, commercial town, usually packed with cruise ship visitors. Its two main roads, the parallel Front Street (Voorstraat) and Back Street (Achterstraat), are linked by a series of narrow alleys (steegjes) running down to the beach, crammed with duty-free shops: "the shopping center of the Leewards." In the middle of everything

is the **Courthouse**, built on **Wathey Square** in 1793, and still in use. This was the venue for Sint Maarten's independence celebrations on 10.10.10, when the Netherlands Antilles were disbanded and Sint Maarten became an independent country within the Kingdom of the Netherlands. A whole book has been written about its history, but now this is the place to pose for photos and pay parking tickets. The square is lined with former merchant residences that became shops as the population moved out of the developing town. Directly in front of the square, the town's characteristic excitement begins as cruise ships' tenders, sometimes four at a time, unload crowds of passengers onto the pier, all bent on the task of spending money for pleasure.

The main shopping area, **Front Street**, has undergone a beautification program including tree-planting and benches for weary shoppers. The duty-free shops are stocked with designer goods such as Gucci, Kohinoor, and Little Switzerland, but soon buildings with ornamental fretwork known as

**FACT**

Tourism in Sint Maarten/ St-Martin took off after World War II as the island had been left with a ready-made airport. Juliana airport was built as a military airfield by the US in 1943 while the island was occupied by the Allies, during the Occupation by Germany of France and the Netherlands.

*The promenade at Philipsburg.*

**FACT**

Seashells found only in the deepest waters were discovered on beaches after Hurricane Luis struck the island in 1995. The storm closed the island to tourists for 3 months and wrecked many livelihoods.

West Indian "gingerbread" (see page 88) come into view. The characteristic architecture that developed in the 18th and 19th centuries is still evident in a few two-story structures around Wathey Square, with a warehouse or shop below, living quarters above, and steps from the street up to a front gallery or verandah. But since Hurricane Luis swept through in 1995 there are not many left.

A fascinating video showing the devastating effects of the hurricane can be seen at the small **Sint Maarten Museum** (Museum Arcade, 7 Front Street; tel: 590-599-542 4917; www.museumsintmaarten.org; Mon–Fri 10am–4pm; donations welcome), upstairs at the eastern end of Front Street, and you can stop off for a drink at the **Pasanggrahan**, originally a government guesthouse, and now the oldest inn on the island, which has an atmosphere of disheveled charm (www.pasan-hotel.net). The name comes from the Indonesian word for "guesthouse".

Queen Wilhelmina and her daughter, the future Queen Juliana, stayed here during World War II and their bedroom is now the Sydney Greenstreet Bar. While relaxing with a drink, perhaps the island's famous Guavaberry liqueur – a rum-based cocktail mixed with the wild red berries that grow wild on the hills – you can watch the boats going in and out of the marinas on trips around the island and to St-Barths, St Eustatius, and Saba.

**Great Bay Beach** is a wonderful place with an attractive boardwalk that stretches along the entire length of the sand. Restaurants, bars, and stalls entice promenaders to pause and take in the view. While the tiny Wathey Square cannot match Marigot's wideopen waterfront, efforts to make it more "people-friendly" have been successful and have given Philipsburg a much-needed focal point.

## Fortress viewpoints

The historical sites around Philipsburg are only worth visiting for their views: from Fort Hill, the site of **Fort Willem** to the west, you can look over the capital below; **Fort Amsterdam** commands Great Bay from the west, looking across to the **Old Spanish Fort** on Pointe Blanche, and over Little Bay on the other side.

The forts guarded the earliest Dutch settlements, which were located on the sand bar and around **Little Bay** ❿. Now sprawling along the peninsula in direct contrast to the historic ruins of Fort Amsterdam is the modern 220-room Divi Little Bay Resort (www.diviresorts.com).

## Around the popular west coast

Getting in and out of Philipsburg and Marigot, the capital of the French side, at rush hour, or traveling the main routes between Philipsburg, Simpson Bay, and Marigot can be nothing short of a bother. The road from Philipsburg climbs to the brow of Cole Bay Hill from where there is a justly famous vista of **Simpson Bay Lagoon** and neighboring islands. Beyond, the road drops to **Simpson Bay** and to the

*A man playing his steel drum, Philipsburg.*

hotels and white beaches that circle the west end. Alternatively, another road heads up the east side of Simpson Bay Lagoon direct to Marigot, passing the international border monument.

Simpson Bay Lagoon is bisected by the international boundary and has an outlet to the sea on either side. The road from Philipsburg to the airport crosses the bridge over the southern outlet, and this can become a bottleneck for traffic. The bridge opens three times a day to allow large boats into the lagoon, where there is a harbor for mega-yachts.

Past Juliana airport the road reaches the built-up resorts of **Maho** – famous not only for its casinos and Sunday beach parties but also for the location of the beach at the end of the runway, tempting sunbathers to duck as the planes swoop down to land. Hang on to your towel or it will be blown into the sea. **Mullet** is the most popular beach, although it can get very crowded at weekends. Surfing is good here if the swell comes from the north, and you can rent beach chairs, sunshades, etc. Limestone and marl sediment laid in nearly horizontal beds has created low, richly colored cliffs along the shore of the quieter **Cupecoy Beach**, the most westerly beach on the Dutch side, where clothes are optional.

Across the border, beaches are unspoiled and secluded with sandy **Baie Longue** stretching for 1 mile (1.5km) along the south coast, graced by just one small, up-market hotel, **La Samanna**. Round Pointe du Canonnier, the western tip of the island, is **Baie aux Prunes** (Plum Beach), which is good for snorkeling at the points at each end and for surfing in the center. **Baie Rouge** is a long sweep of sand with cliffs at the eastern end. **Baie Nettlé** is another good beach but access to it is difficult because of the hotels built along it. At its eastern end, at **Sandy Ground**, as you approach Marigot, there is a bridge over the second outlet from Simpson Bay Lagoon to the sea, but this is only used by fishing boats and other small craft.

## Marigot – a touch of southern France

After the sometimes crass commercialism of Philipsburg, **Marigot** ⑪

*Marigot, with its southern French overtones.*

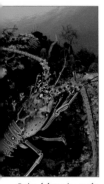

*Spiny lobster is caught on the Saba Bank, a shallow part of the sea between Saba, about 25 miles (40km) south of Sint Maarten.*

*Tourists at the Les Mardis du Grand Case Festival, Saint Martin.*

seems both more European and more Caribbean at the same time; more appealing, more colorful, and equally lively. There is more than a touch of southern France here, especially in the morning **fruit and vegetable market** (best on Wednesday and especially Saturday) on the quay. Wide open to the sea, the quay is a welcoming recess where, unlike its Dutch counterpart, it invites you to stop and sit in the cafés, bars, and excellent restaurants that spill out onto the streets. It seems entirely right to sit and watch the ferries loading for Anguilla while eating chicken barbecued over a halved oil drum, salt cod (once the food of slaves) served with rice and peas, or fresh fish with lime and garlic and spices – delicious Caribbean fare.

Or, if you prefer, you can survey the market square over an espresso and *pâtisserie* in a café like **La Vie en Rose**, opposite the harbor. It is then a 15-minute walk (or a short car journey) up to the ruins of **Fort St-Louis** for some magnificent views of the town and Anguilla, 5 miles (8km) away.

There is fine shopping to be done along **rue de la République** and in the chic boutiques around the **Marina Port La Royale**, which embraces the boat-filled northernmost finger of Simpson Bay Lagoon with elegant shops and cafés. On Thursday nights a carnival atmosphere pervades as shops stay open late, bands play, and the restaurants fill up with onlookers and satisfied shoppers. Those too busy to sit down and eat can grab a barbecued snack at one of the many *lolos* (food stalls) scattered around the town. Significantly, much of the town still takes a siesta from noon until 2 or 3pm, unthinkable among the driven merchants of Philipsburg, where midday belongs to the cruise ships.

On the way up to Fort St-Louis, St-Martin's museum, **On the Trail of the Arawaks** (7 rue Fichot, Place de l'Eglise Catholique; tel: 590-690-871 499; www.stmartinisland.org; Mon–Fri 9am–1pm, 3–5pm), includes exhibits from pre-Columbian times up to the 20th century and provides excellent information about the island. Ceramics and figurines in the museum have

been dated as far back as 550 BC, the oldest so far discovered in the Caribbean. Remains of a half dozen or so Amerindian camps have been unearthed to date, especially around the beaches of Terres Basses, on the southwestern shore of Simpson Bay Lagoon, revealing that the island was used as a resort or hunting ground. They referred to the island as Sualiga, "a place to get salt" and Oualichi, "a place to get women." The arrival of Amerindians on the island is believed to date back to 3350 BC, but the island was uninhabited when the French and Dutch arrived. The museum's curator, Christophe Henocq, leads tours to the archeological dig at Hope Estate, where many of the relics were found.

## Into the hills

Leaving Marigot to the north, the road skirts past the central hills where there is a network of hiking trails punctuated by viewing points. Several lead to the **Pic du Paradis**, which is densely wooded and alive with colorful forest birds. The country to the north, around Grand Case, supported many of the sugar plantations in the 18th century and it is apparent that cane was planted virtually on the hilltops. It ushered in a long period of prosperity, which lasted until slavery was abolished in 1848 on the French side, and 15 years later in the south, causing a lot of grief, especially where several plantations straddled the border.

**Loterie Farm** (tel: 590-590 878 616; www.loteriefarm.net; daily sunrise–sunset) is a former sugar plantation on the slopes of Pic du Paradis. Now a tourist attraction with a nature reserve, it offers activities for all the family: hiking trails through the forest, zip-lining for children or adults, a restaurant using home-grown fruits and vegetables, a tapas bar, and a huge, free-form swimming pool with cascades.

## Grand Case – the gastronomic capital

It has been said of the little town of **Grand Case** ⑫ that its only industry is eating, but there are also art galleries here and, of course, a beach. The most touted creole creativity in St-Martin is culinary, and this village alone offers

*Scuba diver exploring a wreck off St Maarten.*

*Looking out over Marigot from Fort St-Louis.*

dozens of choices, lined up along the beachfront road.

The sand at Grand Case and **Friar's Bay**, just to the south, is golden, not white, and the light seems different in this part of the island, with tones of ochre and gold. The road leads round to the east, south of the salt pond, which attracts an abundance of bird life, through the rolling countryside and mangrove swamps of **Cul-de-Sac**, where there are boats that go over to **Ilet Pinel** ⓭, an offshore island that offers excellent snorkeling and a choice of places for lunch. Sheltered **Anse Marcel** to the northwest is a favorite spot with yachties who take advantage of the large Radisson resort there, the shopping mall, and the marina.

### St-Martin Nature Reserve

Much of the north of the island is a protected nature reserve where fishing and hunting are forbidden. The **Réserve Naturelle de St-Martin** (St-Martin Nature Reserve; Anse Marcel; tel: 590-590 290 972) covers more than 7,400 acres (3,000 hectares) of sea and 370 acres (150 hectares) of land, including the islands off the east coast: Pinel, Petite Clef, Caye Verte, Tintamarre, the small islets off the Baie de l'Embouchure, and Créole Rock overlooking Baie de Grand Case, as well as reefs lying within 200yds/meters of shore. The marshlands and mangroves on the east coast at Etang aux Poissons and the Salines d'Orient at Baie Orientale are also protected.

### Quiet beaches

Along the rough Atlantic shores of the east coast, there are several isolated beaches off the road to Orléans, and windsurfing and kitesurfing are popular here. At **Baie Orientale**, a lively place with bars, restaurants, and small hotels, you should take care when swimming as there is a powerful undertow. The Club Orient is a naturist resort at the east end of the beach for those who wish to acquire an all-over tan. On the bandstand next to the club, calypso and reggae bands play in the afternoon, creating a party mood.

On the western bank of the Etang aux Poissons is **La Ferme des Papillons** ⓮ (Butterfly Farm; tel: 590-590 873 121; www.thebutterflyfarm.com; daily 9am–3.30pm), which has a fascinating collection of butterflies and caterpillars. The best time to visit is in the morning when they are most active. **Orléans** ⓯, farther south, was the capital of French St-Martin until 1768, but only graves and a dueling ground recall those days. Local artist Roland Richardson lives here. He has a gallery in the former *mairie* (town hall), a restored West Indian building on the rue de la République in Marigot.

Beyond are the beaches of **Oyster Pond**, and reefs that lure scuba divers to their caves and cliffs. Oyster Pond is also home to a yacht club and the bay is busy with boats. The coast itself is wild, with windswept scrub and cacti, including the striking Pope's Head, growing around **Guana Bay** (named for the iguanas once found here); the beach here is where body-surfers come for the best rides.

*A reveler at St Maarten Carnival.*

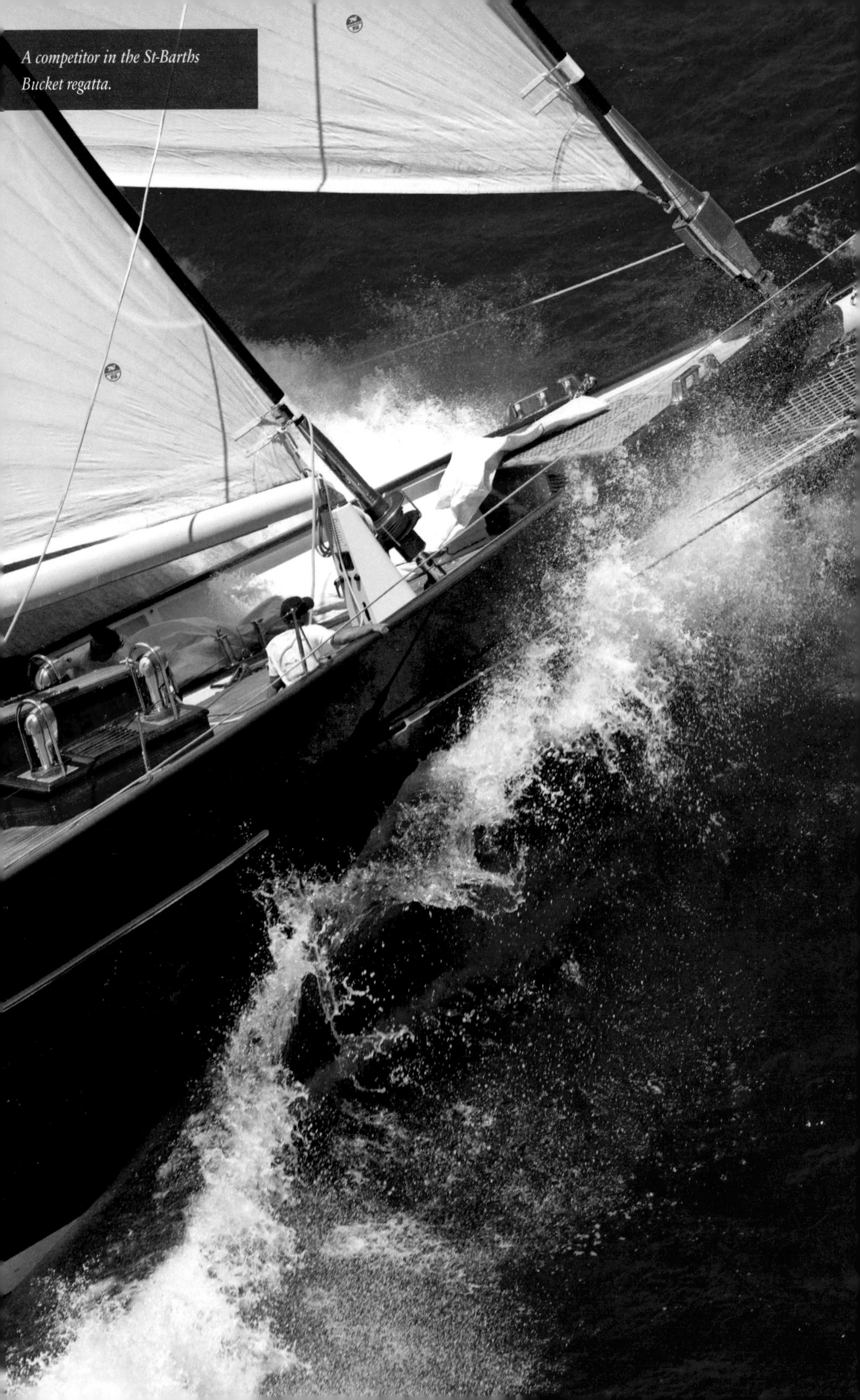

*A competitor in the St-Barths Bucket regatta.*

# ST-BARTHÉLEMY

Known affectionately as St-Barths, this ultra chic
French haunt of the rich and famous is a Caribbean
St-Tropez with magnificent yachts in the harbor
and Parisian chefs in the restaurants.

**W**ith an international renown that far outstrips its 10 sq miles (25 sq km) of white beaches and craggy hills, this tiny French island at the top of the Leeward Islands is a magnet for the rich and famous. As a result St-Barthélemy harbors some of the world's most sought-after real estate. Like St-Tropez in southern France, sky-high prices only serve to enhance the allure of St-Barths, as it is popularly known.

This is the very essence of France in a tropical haven, and it smells of France, too – *baguettes* baking in the *boulangeries* and coffee wafting from the street cafés. The island's network of narrow roads has given rise to the sensible use of the now ubiquitous compact Smart car. It is perfect for the terrain of St-Barths, particularly in the high season when the place is crowded and parking spaces are at a premium.

## French settlers and pirates

Columbus sighted the island in 1496, naming it for his younger brother, Bartholomew, and it first appeared as a mere fly-speck on a Spanish map in 1523, identified as San Bartolemé.

French settlers from St Kitts set up home here in 1648, only to be massacred by a passing band of Carib warriors several years later. Undeterred, a group of Huguenots from Brittany and Normandy arrived, establishing

the first permanent settlement, which thrived, not on farming and fishing, but on piracy. St-Barths became a clandestine rendezvous for pirates, plundering the passing Spanish galleons laden with treasure. The island's rocky, arid hills, with no fresh water supply and lack of savannah, made a sugar industry unthinkable, although some cotton and tobacco were cultivated. Few slaves were imported and the people continued to live the peasant life they had in France. The French government reported them to be

| Main Attractions |
| --- |
| Gustavia |
| Corossol |
| St-Jean |
| Anse de Colombier |
| Anse de la Grande Saline |

*The harbor at Gustavia.*

"good people, very poor, honest, rather ignorant, and quite quarrelsome."

## Sold out to the Swedes

Nevertheless, in a most unexpected and bizarre trade, in 1784 the neglectful government of Louis XVI gave St-Barths to King Gustaf III of Sweden in exchange for trading rights in the port of Göteborg (Gothenburg). The Swedes immediately got down to turning the island into a model possession. The capital was given its decidedly non-Gallic name of Gustavia while the port was declared duty-free.

Spared the terror and dissolution that were about to overtake her French sister islands during the French Revolution (1789–95), the island flourished. The local administration worked to organize the population, not as Swedes, but as people of St-Barths, with their own traditions and heritage. A rational pattern of streets was laid out around the harbor, warehouses were built, the roadways cobbled. By 1806 the island wallowed in relative prosperity, with a population bloated

to about 6,000. However, during the following decades St-Barthélemy experienced a series of devastating disasters – natural and economic – and in 1878 Sweden sold the island, with the 1,000 remaining French descendants, back to France.

St-Barths, together with St-Martin 15 miles (24km) away, came under the administrative umbrella of Guadeloupe, an overseas department of France (see page 133), but pressure grew for more autonomy. A referendum was held in 2003 on separation from the administrative jurisdiction of Guadeloupe, and in 2007 St-Barths finally became an Overseas Collectivity (COM). It has a governing territorial council, the Hôtel de Ville (Town Hall) is now the Hôtel de la Collectivité, and a senator represents the island in Paris.

## Gustavia – a Gallic town with a Swedish heritage

Set around a yacht-filled harbor and careenage too small for cruise ships (small ships can anchor in the outer harbor), the picturesque buildings of

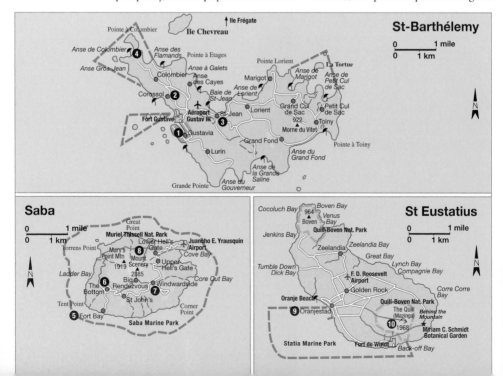

the capital climb up the steep hillside behind. **Gustavia ❶** is still a free port, and the latest haute fashions from Versace to Saint Laurent and Prada to Valentino are all available right here in the exclusive boutiques, along with Gucci leathers and Louis Vuitton suitcases. Boat-loads of shoppers arrive from Sint Maarten, and cafés spill out onto the streets Parisian style, buzzing with a young, chic French crowd. There are no beggars or hucksters here, no ramshackle shops or rums, and no colorful, aromatic market clogs the waterfront – only four makeshift vegetable stalls on a side street, operated by a half dozen women who sail the 125 miles (200km) from Guadeloupe weekly.

The feel, sound, and smell of the capital is French, but the Swedish influence can still be seen in the architecture and the names. The harbor is attractive and well cared for, with plenty of interest for a brief walking tour. In the southeast corner by the promenade there is a huge anchor on the waterfront. Weighing 10 tons and dating from the late 18th century, it is marked "Liverpool…Wood…London" and probably came from a British frigate.

Opposite the anchor stands **St Bartholomew's Anglican Church**, built in 1855 from local stone, with bricks for the steps brought from France and dark lava cornerstones from St Eustatius. Go round the corner and up rue Gambetta and you come to a stone **bell tower**, all that is left of an old Lutheran church destroyed by a hurricane. The bell, cast in Sweden in 1799, was used until the 1920s for celebrations and to ring the curfew at 8pm. In 1930 a clock took over this role, but until then children used to toll the bell at sunrise and sunset. Further up the hill, so its sound would carry further, is the bell tower of the Roman Catholic Church, **Notre-Dame de l'Assomption**,

The Swedes bequeathed three forts – Oscar, Karl, and Gustav – at strategic points around the town, and beneath Fort Oscar is the **Musée Municipal de Saint-Barthélemy** (tel: 590-590 297 155; www.saintbarth-tourisme.com; Mon, Fri 8.30am–1pm, 2.30–5pm,

FACT

During the Christmas period, the likes of Leonardo DiCaprio, Paul McCartney, Beyoncé, and Kate Moss can be found hiding out here, along with assorted billionaires, supermodels, minor royalty, and the scores of day-trippers who come over from St-Martin every day to try to spot them.

*The sophisticated waterfront.*

*Rudolf Nureyev built a house on the Pointe à Toiny on the rocks where the waves often sprayed him on his sundeck. The house is available to rent as a holiday villa.*

*A secluded coastline on St-Barths.*

Wed, Sat 9–1pm). On rue Avater in the **Wall House** building, the museum has exhibitions of local history, and costumes and island crafts. Another local private museum containing St-Barth curios, le P'Tit Collectionneur, has been opened on rue des Marins (www.saintbarth-tourisme.com; Mon–Sat 10am–1pm, 4–6pm), and the owner, André Berry, gives an interesting tour of his collection.

A 5-minute walk past the ruins of Fort Karl brings you to **Anse de Grand Galets**, also called **Shell Beach**, which, as the name suggests, is covered with shells. There is a pleasant beach bar for drinks or a meal.

## Around the island

Going west out of Gustavia, you soon reach the tradition-bound fishing village of **Corossol ❷**, on a brown-sand beach lined with colorful fishing boats and lobster traps. The women sit outside their houses weaving latania palms into hats, mats, and baskets, which are for sale in the village.

**St-Jean ❸**, on the northern shore, has the most popular beach, divided in two by a spit of rock on which stands the rebuilt **Eden Rock** hotel, where Greta Garbo once stayed. You can lunch on freshly caught lobster, surrounded on three sides by a turquoise sea. On the west side of Eden Rock is the airport runway, which ends in the sand. If you are on the beach there you'll be able to see the whites of the pilots' eyes as they negotiate landing and take-off. St-Jean is a lively place and a focal point on the north coast. It is not a particularly large village, but there is a lot going on here. Behind the beach are shopping plazas, lots of small and medium-sized hotels, gourmet restaurants, bars, snack bars, and other entertainment, giving an atmosphere of the French Riviera.

Farther east, **Lorient**, where the first French settlers lived, offers good surfing or snorkeling depending on the mood of the sea. Paths lead down to the beach between rental villas. The village is quieter than St-Jean and traffic is lighter, but it has a couple of good supermarkets if you want to stock up with French food and wine.

## Plentiful beaches

St-Barths has at least 14 beautiful white sand beaches, and one of the best of the secluded ones is **Colombier** ❹ at the tip of the northwest peninsula, where sea turtles come back year after year to lay their eggs. The beach cannot be reached by car, but the 30-minute walk from the village is well worth it for the magnificent island views en route. Another way in is by boat from Gustavia. Around the point to the east, the wide stretch of sand edged with latania palms and seagrapes at **Flamands** is rarely crowded despite a few small hotels with lots of facilities for water sports, a variety of which are available here as it is not in the marine reserve, although it is another turtle nesting site from April to August.

Much of the coastline and offshore waters in the northeast are protected within the **Réserve Naturelle**, where there are three horseshoe-shaped bays sheltered by a reef: Anse de Marigot, Anse de Grand Cul de Sac, and Anse de Petit Cul de Sac. **Marigot** is very quiet, with crystal-clear water, rocky outcrops, and good snorkeling. Windsurfers and kitesurfers head for **Grand Cul de Sac**, which has a sandy bay backed by a large salt pond. It is so well protected by the reef and peninsula that it has the appearance of a lagoon, with shallow water of all shades of blue and green. Sand fleas can be a problem here, as they sometimes are on **Anse de la Grande Saline**, in the south, a long white beach also next to a salt pond. Surfers gather here for the waves while waterfowl enjoy the pond. They know a good place to stay when they see it. This is one of the loveliest beaches in the Caribbean, backed by sand dunes and protected by cliffs at either end. There are no facilities on the beach but there are several restaurants by the salt pond for a good lunch.

**Anse du Gouverneur** can be reached from Gustavia via Lurin, where there is a satellite mast on the hilltop. A very steep road leads down to the beach, where parking is available. The pretty bay is delightfully quiet and unspoiled. Pirate treasure is rumored to be buried here, but the booty of 17th-century Montbars the Exterminator has never been found.

*It's all part of the St-Barths allure.*

## EXTREME AIRPORT

Only tiny commuter planes carrying fewer than 20 passengers can land at St-Barths' Gustav III airport. They have to surmount Mt Tourmente on the approach, where there is busy traffic and a roundabout, then suddenly the plane dives steeply and lands, with brakes squealing, stopping just short of the sea and the beach of St-Jean.

The History Channel program, *Most Extreme Airports*, ranked it as the third most dangerous airport in the world. Pilots are required to have special training to land here, and for passengers, especially on a windy day, the landing is quite an adventure. It's a tourist attraction in itself, and people park their cars on the hilltop to watch the action while sunbathers on the beach keep an eye on the other end of the runway.

# SABA

Saba
Caribbean
Sea

**A tiny volcanic peak jutting out of the crystal clear waters of the Caribbean and Atlantic, Saba's dramatic mountain scenery matches the magnificent underwater world around it.**

**Main Attractions**
The Bottom
Windwardside
Mount Scenery
Saba Marine Park

*Saba's craggy coastline with the nail-biting airport runway just visible.*

There are no white sandy beaches on the Dutch island of Saba (pronounced "Say-bah"). This miniature volcanic island's rocky slopes climb steeply out of the tropical sea, rising to 2,885ft (870 meters) at the top of cloud-covered Mount Scenery. Rugged cliffs, the refuge for a variety of seabirds, support 5 sq miles (13 sq km) of green, mountainous terrain dotted with small villages of pretty, pristinely kept, white houses with red roofs, which were once linked only by hundreds of steps.

Fewer than 2,000 people live here, half of them light-skinned and the other half dark-skinned, and they all speak English, although Dutch is the official language. As no plantation economy ever existed, slaves were only brought over to help on the small farms and carry goods up and down its paths.

As on St-Barths, 30 miles (50km) to the northeast, landing on Saba is a nerve-wracking experience. The pilot heads straight for a vertical rock face, only to fly a sharp, cool curve to the left just as you feel that your time has come, and then lands seconds later on a runway the length of an aircraft carrier – 1,300ft (398 meters) to be precise – so that his 10 or so passengers can disembark safely. Saba's airport, completed in 1963, is only open when the trade winds are gentle enough. Getting here has never been easy: in earlier days, arriving by sea was not much better as there were no natural harbors for protection against the strong currents and fierce gusts of wind.

## Shipwrecked

Christopher Columbus "discovered" Saba in 1493, but it was only in 1632 that the first Europeans – a couple of shipwrecked Englishmen – first set foot on the island. Later, eager Dutch settlers from St Eustatius, 17 miles (27km) to the southeast, managed to brave the waves that crash regularly against the steep coastline. Ruled a dozen different times by the Spanish, French, and English, Saba was finally taken over for good by the Dutch in 1812. In 2010, on the dissolution of the Netherlands Antilles, its status became that of a public body (often referred to as a "special municipality") of the Kingdom of the Netherlands.

## Fort Bay

The only inlet in the towering cliffs where boats are able to dock is at **Fort Bay** ❺, which is a relatively flat bay by Saban standards but with none of the luxuries of a proper harbor. Before 1972, when the pier was built, anyone who disembarked here – or at Ladder Bay on the west coast – always got their feet wet after being rowed ashore in wooden jolly-boats. The first vehicle on the island, a jeep, was landed in 1947 on two sloops lashed together to form a makeshift raft. These days, day-trippers from Sint Maarten, 28 miles (45km) to the north, arrive on high-speed ferries almost daily and the dive shop in Fort Bay gets very busy.

The first part of the road that staggers across the craggy terrain to the airport was built in 1943, under the auspices of Josephus Lambert Hassell. After Dutch engineers had declared any road construction to be impossible, Hassell took a correspondence course in civil engineering and proved them wrong. Before that, on landing at Fort Bay, people had to walk up hundreds of stone steps to the main village of The Bottom, and cargo had to be carried, including once a piano that took 12 men to get it to its destination.

## From The Bottom to the top

At 820ft (250 meters) above the sea, **The Bottom** ❻ does not live up to its name. In fact it is derived from *de botte*, the Dutch word for a bowl, as it stands on a small piece of flat land surrounded by mountains. With around 500 inhabitants, the village functions as the island's capital, and the government building is surrounded by the hospital, school, **Cranston's Antique Inn** – the first guest house, established in the 1830s – and a few bars. American students from the small medical school there give it a youthful ambience.

*A tide pool at Saba.*

*The idyllic setting of Windwardsid.*

*The Saban anole – from the African name meaning "little devil" – is a lizard endemic to this island.*

*A church on the island.*

The road only reached the picturesque village of **Windwardside** ❼, 900 steps farther up, in 1951 and, despite the souvenir shops selling Saba lace, a bank, some dive shops, and a few small hotels and restaurants, it still remains very much a Dutch Caribbean idyll in its peaceful setting against a green mountain ridge between the haze-covered Mount Scenery and Booby Hill. Pretty white wooden houses on granite foundations, and gardens full of flowers in vivid bloom, decorate the village.

The red roofs are all very clean – they have to be as they are used for collecting rainwater, for there are no rivers on the island. What at first appears to be a family crypt in the vegetable gardens or orchards turns out to be the property's own cistern, which is crucial to survival, and you may see a grave beside it – there is little room for cemeteries here.

The **Harry L. Johnson Museum** (www.museum-saba.com/HLJohnson; Wed, Fri 11am–2pm, Sun 1.30–3pm), set in a flower-filled meadow, was once a sea captain's house, built in 1840, and it still has the original kitchen. A wall covered with ships' masters' certificates shows how closely the men of Saba are associated with the sea. For centuries, they earned a living as fishermen and mariners, plying the Caribbean trading routes. One Saban sailor is reputed to have been paid in gold for smuggling escaped French prisoners from Guyana to Trinidad.

Nearby, the home of road builder and engineer Josephus Lambert Hassell has been converted into a little shopping mall with an art gallery and a restaurant. Farther up the village are the tourist office with helpful staff, a bank, a shop, and a post office.

## Climbing Mount Scenery

It is not a good idea to wait for a completely clear day before climbing **Mount Scenery** ❽, as you might have to wait a very long time – the summit rarely peeks out of its thick cloud veil. The ascent begins on the outskirts of Windwardside (on the road to The Bottom) and you don't need to be an expert climber, although good shoes will make the 3-hour tour easier because the 1,064 steps along the way are steep and often wet.

Lizards scurry across the path at the start of the trail and the bright red and yellow artificial-looking heliconia that grace the lobbies of smart hotels all over the world grow wild among the trees. The higher you climb, the more luxuriant the vegetation becomes: the trees are covered in lianas (tropical vines), massive leaves darken the path, and the fog closes in. Then, just beneath the summit, a 210ft (64-meter)-high radio tower (brought up in just one day by a helicopter) comes into view. The stormy wind whips through the trees and whistles through the steel structure, and behind it Mount Scenery drops away.

### Muriel Thissell National Park

Other hiking trails around Saba may not be so dramatic but are just as satisfying. On land that used to be

owned by the Sulfur Mining Company, the **Muriel Thissell National Park** extends from Mount Scenery to the north coast and the sulfur mine, and has a choice of trails in forest and scrubland. Before you set off, you should register at the **Saba Trail Shop** (Windwardside, tel: 599-416 2630; www.sabapark.org; Mon 1–4.30pm, Tue–Fri 9am–4.30pm, Sat–Sun 10.30am–2.30pm) where you must pay a maintenance fee.

## Volcanic underwater landscapes

Do you get cold hands after a 50ft (15-meter) dive? That will be no problem at the **Hot Springs** site, where divers can plunge their hands into the warm sand. From 1987, the waters around Saba have been protected as part of the **Saba Marine Park**, concealing a vast, spectacular volcanic landscape rich in sea life and accessible to divers.

A small entrance charge to this colorful experience is charged by the diving schools, or by the organizers of boat excursions from Sint Maarten. The 26 diving grounds – only accessible by boat – provide divers at all levels with unbelievably beautiful spots, such as **Tent Reef Wall**, encrusted with corals and sponges, or the gently sloping reefs where elegant stingrays cruise and nurse sharks sleep in the sand.

At **Third Encounter**, what must once have been an underwater volcano rears up to just 100ft (30 meters) below the surface. A pillar of coral, called Needle's Eye, has grown up on its western flank over the millennia – a unique collection of tube and barrel sponges, star coral, elephant ears, and brain coral.

The **Saba Bank**, 2.7 miles (4.3km) southwest of Saba, is the largest submarine atoll in the Atlantic Ocean and has some of the richest diversity of marine life in the Caribbean Sea, providing a nursery for fish, lobster, and other marine life. It is the world's fourth-largest submerged coral island, rising 0.6 miles (1,000 meters) from the sea floor, and it is still growing. It is enclosed by an Exclusive Economic Zone of the Netherlands and it is forbidden for tankers, cruise ships, or other large vessels to anchor on the bank.

### DRINK

Everyone has a secret recipe for the aromatic dessert drink, Saba Spice. The main ingredient is always rum, while the mix of brown sugar, cloves, fennel, and other flavorings tends to vary. Try it and see.

*French angelfish off the coast of Saba.*

# THE SPLENDORS OF THE DEEP

**The dramatic seascape of the Caribbean is still a largely unexplored realm of beauty, even though generations of settlers have changed the landscape.**

Tourism has set off the spirits of invention: more and more tiny submarines seating about 20 or so passengers are being launched throughout the region to give the ordinary visitor a chance of sharing the kind of underwater experience previously only available to the rapidly growing crowd of scuba divers.

## The pool is open

With its warm and shallow waters, 75°F (24°C) being the average temperature, the Caribbean Sea is an ideal spot to learn to scuba dive. Hundreds of dive shops certify beginners after four or five days of theory and practice in shallow waters (PADI, NAUI courses). More advanced divers and budding marine biologists will also meet instructors to help them find the best sites and produce exquisite underwater photography.

Some of the most beautiful dive sites are located in protected marine areas. The boom in tourism – more fish to be caught, more sewage water to be disposed of, more beach pollution and reef damage from ships' anchors – has severely endangered the fragile and highly complex reef ecosystem. The tiny island of Bonaire was the first to protect the coastal waters around the island as a marine park; others such as Saba and the British Virgin Islands followed suit. Jacques Yves Cousteau initiated a marine park on the western shore of Guadeloupe; St Eustatius protects its historic treasures below the water line, and most islands now have protected marine areas.

*It is essential to carry out the routine safety checks with one's diving buddy before taking to the water.*

*The rainforest of the sea – diverse and abundant multi-colored coral reef sponges filter huge quantities of sea water and are more numerous in the Caribbean than reef-building corals.*

*Gorgonians, known as sea fans, move with the current as though blown by a breeze. These soft corals come in many colors, and are often home to seahorses and flamingo tongue snails.*

*A wreck off Curacao.*

## RECAPTURED BY THE SEA

Off the western shores of Aruba, around 33ft (10 meters) below land, are the remnants of a tanker, the *Pedernales*, torpedoed during World War II. It is only one of a growing number of wrecks attracting divers close to the island. Aruba is the westernmost island of the Netherlands Antilles, offering an assortment of underwater wrecks, including planes. At 460ft (140 meters) long the *Antilla*, off the coast of Aruba, is the biggest wreck in the Caribbean and living proof of nature's rapid move to integrate: corals, sponges, anemones, and other invertebrates have attached themselves to the huge hull and transformed it into a multicolored patchwork, where Spotlight parrotfish and Queen angelfish enhance the dazzling scene. Its storage room in the bow is as big as a church. There are plenty of books on each island documenting their shipwrecks and other man-made sites. Old anchors can be found around St Eustatius, and you can explore the shipwreck *Proselyte* in Great Bay (St Maarten) or the RMS *Rhone* in the Rhone Marine Park, off Tortola, or investigate a load of old cars, which tumbled from a barge off Vaersenbaai, Curaçao.

*Bonaire has a pristine underwater world and is known for its superb snorkeling, as well as being a prime scuba diving destination.*

*Wrecks soon become encrusted with coral, offering shelter to fish, eels and other sea creatures. They are easily spotted by scuba divers.*

*Spotted eagle rays can reach up to 30ft (9 meters) in length.*

*Silhouetted palm trees at dusk.*

# ST EUSTATIUS

Peace and quiet is what you will find on this small Caribbean hideaway, along with a network of hiking trails and a vast underwater landscape just waiting to be explored.

St Eustatius
Caribbean Sea

D ominated by the dormant volcano called The Quill (1,968 ft/600 meters) with a lush rainforest center, this tiny Dutch island has so far avoided appearing on the beaten tourist track, making it a peaceful place to escape to. Colloquially called Statia, this 11 sq mile (28 sq km) haven, with Oranjestad its only town, has a fount of fascinating tales to tell about a more prosperous era.

In 1775, minuscule Statia was a thriving trading center, known as the Golden Rock, and had as many as 10 ships a day calling at Oranjestad, then a busy town. Janet Schaw, a touring Scottish gentlewoman, strolled along the seafront and recorded her impressions in her *Journal of a Lady of Quality:* "From one end of the town of Eustatia to the other is a continued mart, where goods of the most different uses and qualities are displayed before the shop doors. Here hang rich embroideries, painted silks, flowered Muslins, with all the Manufactures of the Indies. Next stall contains most exquisite silver plate, the most beautiful indeed I ever saw, and close by these iron-pots, kettles, and shovels. Perhaps the next presents you with French and English Millinary-wares. But it were endless to enumerate the variety of merchandize in such a place, for in every store you find everything…"

*Ocean view.*

This "lady of quality" would have difficulty recognizing Statia today. A few crumbling ruins, some under water, are all that is left of the warehouses and merchants' offices along the seafront. Things are a lot quieter now.

## Ill-gotten gains

St Eustatius was "discovered" by Columbus in 1493 and taken by the Dutch for the West India Company during the 1630s. Twenty-two changes of flag later, the island finally succumbed to the Dutch.

**Main Attractions**

Oranjestad
St Eustatius Historical
    Foundation Museum
The Quill
Diving the Marine Park

**EAT**

In 1781, after invading St Eustatius, Admiral Rodney is supposed to have found most of his booty buried in the graveyard of the Dutch Reformed Church. He ordered the coffins to be opened after an abnormal spate of funerals had taken place.

Plantations on the central plain – where the airport now lies – gave the islanders a good living, but their jewel was the safe harbor. Well positioned on major trade routes, in the 18th century Statia was made a duty-free port and reaped the rewards. Valuable goods filled the coffers at the numerous local trading offices and the island became a center for the slave trade, too. During the American Revolution (1775–83) arms and gunpowder were smuggled through the island in barrels of rum and molasses via the merchant ships bound for New England – and the population is reported to have swelled to 20,000.

Such was the island's support for the rebellious British colonies in North America that in 1776 soldiers fired a salute when they sighted one of their warships, the *Andrea Dorea*. This was the first salute ever fired by another land in honor of the recently formed United States of America and moved Statia to the front of the world stage. The Americans were delighted, but, needless to say, the British were absolutely furious.

However, signals of that kind were normally only employed to greet trading vessels, and the Dutch government assured the seething British that they had no intention of recognizing the sovereignty of the USA, so it is not clear whether the guards up in Fort Oranje recognized the importance of the American flag.

## Rodney's revenge

Britain finally settled the score when Admiral George Rodney attacked St Eustatius in 1781 and ransacked the warehouses, banishing the merchants and capturing their ships. He sent back to England £5 million worth of booty. This started a steady decline in the fortunes of the island, and the end of slavery in 1863 finished off the small plantation economy. The population dwindled to less than the 3,000 it is today, and the island's main source of income is now an oil depot on the northwest coast where supertankers load and unload. Otherwise, the Statians live by subsistence farming, money sent home from relations abroad, and Dutch support.

*Print of the British naval assault on St Eustatius.*

However, poverty has not prevented the Statians, who mostly speak English, from showing their warmth and friendliness to visitors, and there is very little crime to speak of. They are still proud of their historical gesture and on November 16 each year, they celebrate Statia-America Day, when cannons are fired from Fort Oranje and the islanders get together and sing a hymn that includes the lines: "Statia's past you are admired/Though Rodney filled his bag/The first salute fired/To the American flag." The flags of the 13 American colonies are then hoisted above the fort to mark the occasion.

## Oranjestad – a fallen town

Not long after Admiral Rodney's sojourn in **Oranjestad** ⑨ a mighty undersea earthquake caused much of the lower part of the town, where all the warehouses were, to crumble into the sea. Now some of the submerged ruins and sunken ships provide great snorkeling and there are plans to restore the parts of the Lower Town left on dry land. The Old Gin House, built with the bricks of an 18th-century cotton gin,

is now an attractive hotel and restaurant on the waterfront. The Old Slave Road winds up to the top of the 130ft (40-meter)-high cliff where **Fort Oranje** (daily), dating from 1636 and restored in 1976 for the US bicentennial celebrations, guards the bay, the cannons pointing at imaginary enemies. There's a fine view down to the mile-long dark sand of **Oranje Beach,** Statia's best swimming spot. Memorial plaques on the fort from Franklin D. Roosevelt and the "St Eustatius Commission of the American Revolution" commemorate the island's fateful salute.

Close by, in Doncker-De Graff House, an 18th-century building once inhabited by an extremely wealthy Dutch merchant during Statia's heyday, is **St Eustatius Historical Foundation Museum** (also known as Simon Doncker House; tel: 599-318 2288; www. steustatiushistory.org; Mon–Thur 9am–5pm, Fri until 3pm, Sun until noon). This is where Admiral Rodney made his headquarters for 10 months in 1781 before the French pushed him out. One of the best historical museums in the region, the house gives a genuine feel

*Creatures of the deep – a green turtle and a French angelfish.*

*Face painting goes down well with kids.*

of what prosperous colonial life must have been like and has some excellent collections of Amerindian pottery, a skeleton, tools used by the early settlers, and detailed documentation of the ignoble slave trade. Excavations at Golden Rock near the airport uncovered a large Amerindian village, with round houses of different sizes, some capable of accommodating up to 30 people, and supported by timbers up to 25ft (8 meters) high set in deep holes. A complete floor plan is shown in the museum. People from the Orinoco region arrived in Statia about 1000 BC, but left in AD 700–1000.

The center of town around Fort Oranje is preserved as part of the Historic Core Renovation Project. Many small, wooden houses, typical of Dutch colonial architecture, with arcaded porches and balconies with gingerbread trim, have been restored and preserved.

**Honen Dalim Synagogue** was burned by Admiral Rodney and the large Jewish population was expelled. Built in 1739, its walls of yellow brick, brought over as ships' ballast and

*St Eustatius Reformed Church.*

unusual at that time, enclose a broad, two-story room, but the outside steps lead to nowhere. The walls were restored in 2001 as part of the renovation project, but funds have not as yet been secured for a new roof.

The congregation of the **Dutch Reformed Church**, the island's largest church, a few minutes' walk farther on, also departed with the drop in prosperity. The massive tower made of dark volcanic stone in 1775 is still standing after renovation in 1981, but the broad nave is roofless.

## Green giants in the crater

The Statians shot several worried glances at **The Quill** ⑩ when Montserrat (see page 180) started erupting in 1995. Old paintings of the island show massive plumes of smoke above Mazinga, the old Amerindian name for the volcano. Nothing happened, however, and both the slopes and the crater are accessible to hikers. A sometimes steep but largely pleasant path starts in the outskirts of Oranjestad on the road leading west out of town, and continues up to the rim of the crater. When you reach the edge, you can actually descend into it and explore the primary rainforest growing there. Small geckos race across the ground, and tiny hummingbirds dip into the orchids growing wild on the trees. Most startling are the hermit crabs that tumble to the sea inside their shells to reproduce, before making the arduous return journey back up to the crater.

In the early morning, swathes of fog hang above the gigantic trees inside the crater. This is the best time for the 3–5-hour tour with guides provided by the St Eustatius National Parks Foundation (STENAPA, Gallows Bay; tel: 599-318 2884; www.statiapark.org). Some of the ancient trees along the route have been given biblical names by local people. Moses, for instance, is a mighty old tree covered with aerial roots.

Other hikes, all marked on the STENAPA map, are found in the area called **Behind the Mountain** on

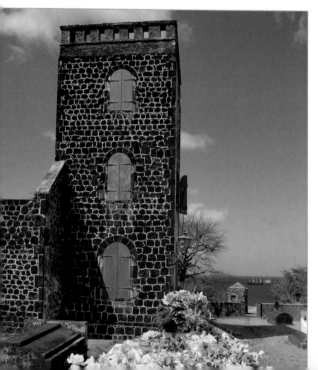

the southeastern slope of The Quill, where STENAPA has the **Miriam C. Schmidt Botanical Garden** (sunrise–sunset, suggested donation), complete with a visitor center, protecting the secret habitat of the rare, endemic, pink-flowered morning glory. In the lonely bush and meadow landscape in the north more trails extend as far as the **Boven** (964ft/294 meters).

While walking around the island you may come across archeological digs. Statia's wealth of history is constantly being uncovered, from pre-Columbian times as well as the days of plantations and slavery. The St Eustatius Center for Archeological Research (SECAR, tel: 599-318 0066; www.secar.org) welcomes volunteers to help protect and develop the island's resources and educate local people and visitors alike.

## Treasures in the deep

Statia has at least a dozen interesting dive sites with a historical slant, and is a very rewarding destination for under-water fans, however experienced or inexperienced they may be. Sometimes an ancient clay pipe may be seen on the ocean bed, but leave it there; it's against the law to remove historical artifacts. STENAPA has established a Marine Park on the leeward side of the island on the same scale as Saba's (see page 148). Three dive centers in Lower Town offer, among other things, beginners' courses and snorkeling around the **Old City Wall** in the bay. Between the ruined walls of Lower Town's submerged buildings swim brightly colored parrotfish and angelfish.

The boat trip out to the other diving grounds only takes a few minutes. The finest ones are illuminated by the morning sun, such as **Barracuda City**, where dozens of these silvery glinting fish glide around 65–80ft (20–25 meters) down, beside a miniature precipice. An anchor has been lying here since the 18th century, and there are more at **Anchor Point and Lost Anchor**. Two wrecked ships at **Double Wreck** have undergone a sea change over the past 200 years and now stingrays, flying gurnards, and spotted morays live inside their hulls and cabins alongside vast communities of sponges and sea anemones.

*The swimming position of the seahorse is more or less vertical, in the direction of travel.*

*The rainforest in the crater of The Quill.*

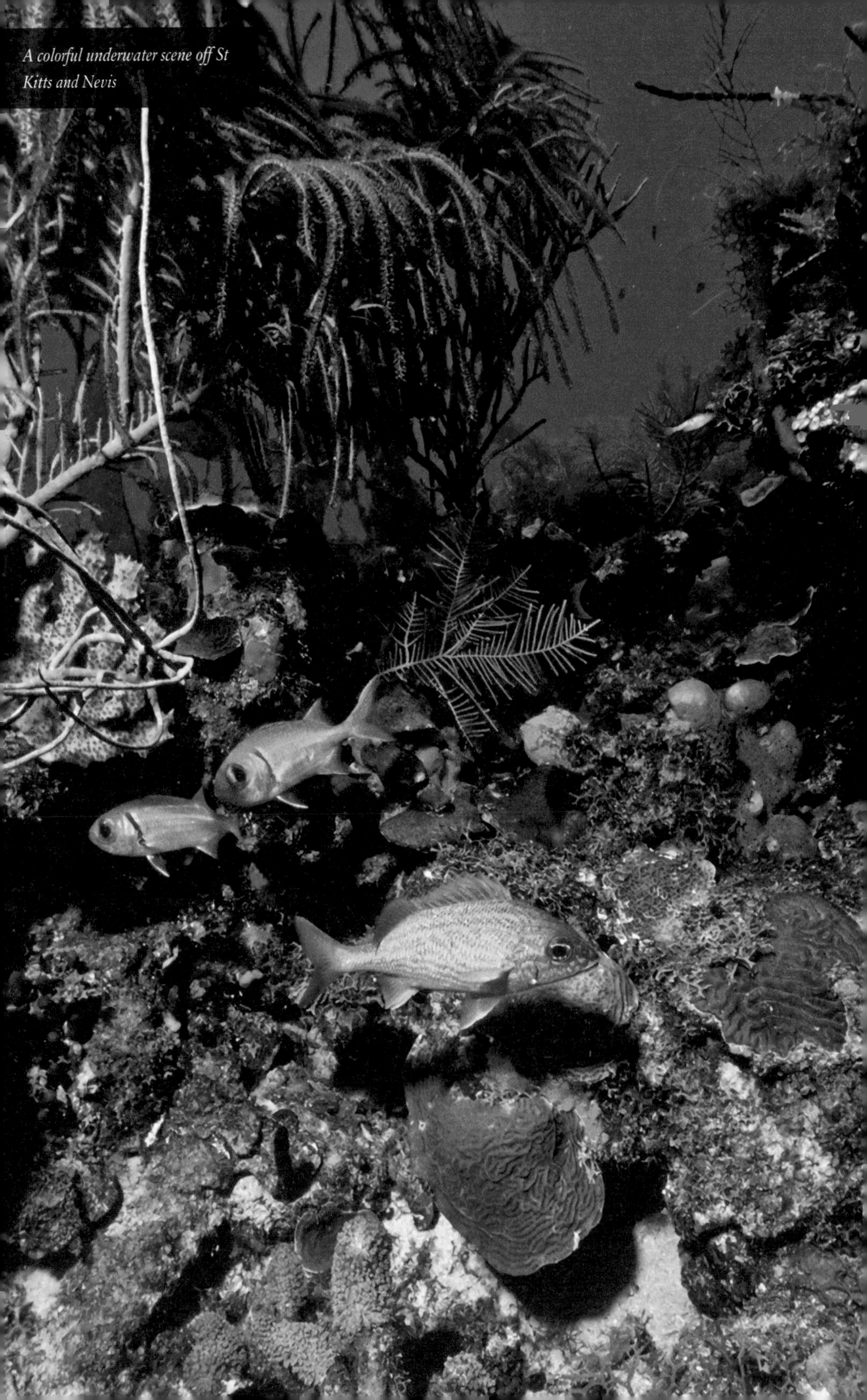

*A colorful underwater scene off St Kitts and Nevis*

# ST KITTS AND NEVIS

**St Kitts and Nevis have left behind their plantation economy and woken up to what they have to offer the discerning visitor – a relaxed way of life and luxury hotels in elegant Great Houses or on the beach.**

W hen the last Sugar Train too-
ted at the sugar factory at
Needsmust on St Kitts on
July 30, 2005, it signaled the end of a
chapter in the Federation of St Kitts
and Nevis. Certainly, it was the end
of many years of toiling in the fields
for the last 1,500 islanders employed
in the industry. However, cane still
grows around the island, since the
crop protects the land from erosion,
at least until another use is found for
it. As Kittitians waved goodbye to the
sugar industry, tourism was becoming
a profitable prospect. But even with a
growing number of visitors this still
remains a place to relax and enjoy the
tranquility of an unrushed society.

The Amerindians called St Kitts
Liamuiga (The Fertile Isle) and Nevis
Oualie (Land of Beautiful Water).
Columbus named the former St
Christopher, still its formal title, and
the latter Nuestra Señora de las Nieves
(Our Lady of the Snows – in reality,
clouds). St Kitts sits on a land area of
65 sq miles (168 sq km), while Nevis,
separated by a 2-mile (3km) stretch of
choppy sea, is smaller at 36 sq miles
(93 sq km).

## First British settlement

The arrival on St Kitts in 1623 of British
settlers was followed closely by a group
of French colonists and for many years
the island was shared between them,

with Britain occupying the northwest
and France the southeast. Partition
was ended with the Peace of Utrecht
in 1713 and St Kitts was finally recognized as a British colony in 1783 under
the Treaty of Versailles.

By that time the islands were thriving sugar and cotton producers supported by a vast army of African slaves,
a situation that continued way beyond
Emancipation in 1834. In the 1780s,
tiny Nevis had become a more significant commercial center than New York,
a veritable Caribbean social nexus ("The

| Main Attractions |
| --- |
| Basseterre |
| Romney Manor and |
| Wingfield Estate |
| Brimstone Hill National park |
| Fortress |
| Mount Liamuiga |
| Turtle Beach |
| Charlestown |
| Nevis Peak |
| Botanical Gardens |
| Montpelier Great House |
| Nisbet Beach |

*Schoolchildren at Basseterre, St Kitts.*

Queen of the Caribbees"), complete with palatial planters' mansions and a fashionable hotel-spa. Horatio Nelson, sent to enforce the Treaty of Versailles, was an attractive and eligible addition to the social whirl, despite annoying the planters by chasing away the "foreign" American traders vital to their economy.

Never big enough to warrant individual attention, from 1816 St Christopher, Nevis, Anguilla, and the British Virgin Islands were administered as a single colony. In 1871 this was replaced by the Leeward Islands Federation. In 1958–62, St Kitts and Nevis belonged to the West Indies Federation. The road to independence was a rather messy process. In 1967, the three islands of St Kitts, Nevis, and Anguilla, long jointly administered, became an Associated State of the United Kingdom. Almost immediately Anguilla ceded, eventually regaining its Crown Colony status, and the islands of St Kitts and Nevis – never very compatible bedfellows – were left to sort out a joint constitution prior to their formal independence on September 19, 1983. The secession of Nevis, long a burning issue, has now taken a back seat after a referendum in 1998 failed to gain the approval of two-thirds of the electorate.

## The pulse of development

With the demise of the sugar industry, the government put great emphasis on investment in tourism to generate employment and wealth distribution. Spending on infrastructure has made St Kitts unrecognizable from only 20 years ago. There is a thriving cruise ship port complex and new roads have been built to take pressure off traffic in Basseterre. Among major developments are the Warner Park Sporting Complex, with a cricket stadium used in the 2007 ICC Cricket World Cup, and the Silver Jubilee Athletic Stadium, used for the carifta Games, both of which are valuable magnets for sports tourism. Not to be left out, Nevis is constructing a geothermal power plant, and new villas, spas, and other tourist projects have also been built.

The government also initiated a fast-paced public-housing program so that today tiny, mostly well-kept dwellings speckle the landscape. Cable TV and

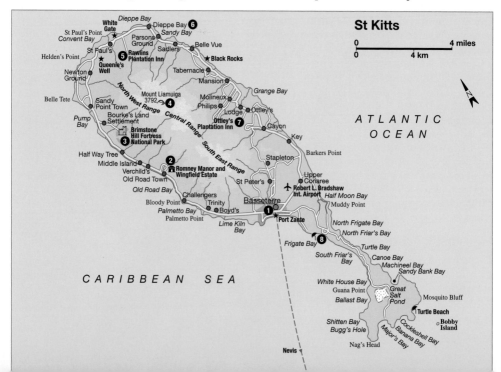

the internet are no longer a luxury and almost everyone has a cellphone or two. The flimsy wooden cottages of the past are being replaced by "wall" (concrete) homes and SUVs are increasingly seen on the roads.

## Basseterre's revival

This knack for patiently waiting to pick only the choicest fruits of progress, while preserving the best of the old ways, is nowhere more evident than in **Basseterre ❶**. After a long descent into shabbiness, this elegant old West Indian town, which became the official British capital in 1727, is enjoying a second debut.

A campaign to restore the town's graceful but dilapidated commercial buildings and dwellings has resulted in one of the greatest success stories in Caribbean architectural preservation. Careful and sensitive restorations have revealed the buildings' original charm, with their lower floors of rough-cut volcanic stone and upper stories of fanciful wooden gingerbread. What began as an exercise in civic pride has become an economic success story as well. More

and more cruise ship passengers enjoy the town's beauty, and business is growing, with attractive shops offering duty-free products opening up everywhere.

Yet Basseterre still booms with an irrepressible Caribbean vigor. Crisply dressed traffic police sort out the snarls at the intersections around the **Circus** where an ornate cast-iron clock tower, the **Berkeley Memorial**, regards the swirling scene; visitors and locals peer down from the balcony of the **Ballahoo**, a meeting place and restaurant, at the frenetic salesmanship of the cab drivers ("Man, you gotta want a taxi – s'way too hot to walk, man").

**Independence Square** nearby is a pretty park, overlooked by 18th-century houses. Where once there was a slave market is now a network of paths in a Union Jack design with a fountain in the middle.

## The bayfront

Just off the bayfront, **Port Zante** has emerged on 30 acres (12 hectares) of reclaimed land, now almost completely covered with stores and restaurants catering mostly for cruise ship visitors.

**TIP**

The St Kitts Music Festival features well-known artists from the Caribbean and all over the music world. This spectacular 4-night event in June is held in the grounds of the Warner Park Stadium, which was refurbished for the Cricket World Cup in 2007.

*Scenic railway journey, St Kitts.*

*Green vervet monkeys on Nevis.*

**Bay Road** runs the full length of the ocean front in Basseterre, linking Port Zante to the downtown area where locals live and work. On Bay Road is the bus terminal and in the same complex is the ferry terminal, where ferries go back and forth between St Kitts and Nevis. In true Caribbean style, mangoes, soursop, pears, herbs, and every type of tropical fruit and vegetable line the sidewalks just next to the terminal, wooing the discerning shopper towards the local market just steps away on the other side of the road.

## The St Kitts circular

If Basseterre is basking in a vibrant new life, then the rest of St Kitts, as enjoyed on the 32-mile (51km) loop drive, remains mostly in a sleepy haze, although there is evidence of an island in transition. The island's main road wriggles through villages of pastel-shaded wood and breeze-block cottages with tin roofs, overlooking black-sand beaches and backed by fields of sugar cane climbing up to the fringes of the rainforest around Mount Liamuiga (once Mount Misery).

Remnants of old sugar mills abound and the round stone towers, now bereft of their sails, dot the landscape. A handful of the plantation houses have found a more productive use as elite inns and private homes. The little railroad has been renovated and is still busy, carrying tourists (principally cruise ship visitors) on a 3-hour circular tour of the island. The **St Kitts Scenic Railway** (tel: 869-465 7263; www.stkittsscenicrailway.com) passes ruined sugar estate buildings and offers a better view of the countryside than you get from a car. The narrow-gauge railway was built in 1912–26 to take the cane from the fields to the sugar mill in Basseterre, and it was this innovation that caused the closure of the small sugar windmills on the estates.

By car, head west out of Basseterre on the coast road through fishing villages to **Old Road Town**, where the first British settlers landed. Above the village are the ruins of Wingfield Sugar Estate and the lush rainforest gardens of **Romney Manor ❷**; the old estate house was destroyed by fire in 1995. Here are the workshops of **Caribelle Batik** (tel: 869-465 6253; www.caribellebatikstkitts.com;

Mon–Fri), where you can buy batik clothes and material and watch their creation. There are 6 acres (2.4 hectares) of glorious gardens containing a saman tree believed to be more than 350 years old. At 24ft (7 meters) in diameter, it covers half an acre.

A three-minute walk from Romney Manor is **Wingfield Estate**, with the ruins of a mighty sugar mill and rum distillery. Knowledgeable guides will explain the processes to you, and there is a café. Wingfield is also the place to come for the **Sky Rides** zip line tour (tel: 869-466 4259; www.skysafaristkitts.com), where cablevs allow you to fly through the rainforest over Wingfield River.

Farther northwest, **Brimstone Hill Fortress National Park** ❸ (www.brimstonehillfortress.org; daily 9.30am–5.30pm), a Unesco World Heritage Site, is history preserved atop an 800ft (245-meter) volcanic plug of andesite edged by limestone protrusions. A great graystone fortress peers out over a panorama of ocean. Begun in 1690, the fortress was confidently known as Britain's "Gibraltar of the West Indies," until its humiliating capture by the French in 1782, just prior to their final ejection a year later. Today a series of small museum rooms gives a useful overview of island culture and history, and a café provides a welcome rest. It is one of the best-preserved historical fortifications in the Americas: don't miss it. After touring the fortress you can follow nature trails and spot green vervet monkeys larking about. The views are tremendous and you should be able to see several neighboring islands from the top.

## Mount Liamuiga

High above the fort, the rainforest begins abruptly. Guided walking tours to the 3,792ft (1,156-meter) picture-postcard volcanic crater of **Mount Liamuiga** ❹ are available from tour operators in Basseterre, although it is possible to do most of it independently from the village of St Paul's. Follow sinuous paths up through the cane and enter the gloom where the trade wind breezes suddenly cease. Buzzings and rustlings in the undergrowth and tree tops suggest a lively retinue of residents and possible sightings of

*Jason Holder of Barbados Tridents in action during the 2014 Limacol Caribbean Premier League Final, 2014.*

### GENOCIDE AT BLOODY POINT

Both St Kitts and Nevis were inhabited by Amerindians when Columbus passed by in 1493. They were named Caribs by the subsequent colonizers, and the Kalinago chief, Ouboutou Tegremante, initially welcomed Sir Thomas Warner and his family when they arrived at Old Road Bay from the Guianas in 1623. Leaving his family behind, Warner then sailed to Britain to bring more settlers to the island in 1624. When they were joined the following year by the crew of a French ship that had been attacked by the Spanish, the Amerindians began to be worried about the pace of colonization.

Kalinago chiefs from St Kitts, Nevis, and Dominica planned to attack the settlers in 1626, but they were betrayed and the local Amerindians were killed in their beds. Warner and his men prepared themselves for the expected retaliation and faced an invasion force of some 3,000–4,000 warriors. Two thousand of them were massacred in a deep ravine and bodies were piled high on the beach – called Bloody Point – by the combined British and French forces, whose casualties numbered about 100. Subsequently, African slaves were imported to work on the sugar plantations and Sir Thomas Warner died a very wealthy man in 1649. He is buried in an ornate tomb in St Thomas' churchyard at Middle Island.

*Picture-perfect views from the terrace of Rawlins Plantation Inn.*

*Spice Mill's inviting daybeds on Cockleshell Beach.*

green vervet monkeys. There are beautiful wild orchids and other flowering plants in the forest. You can climb into the crater, holding on to vines and roots, and from here to the summit a guide is essential. The hike will take all day and is only for experienced hikers.

## Plantation Inns

On the northern slope of the volcano, off the circular road, **is Rawlins Plantation Inn ❺**, a 17th-century plantation house and ruined mill transformed into a lovely British colonial-style hotel surrounded by beautiful gardens. It is a pleasant place to stop for lunch or afternoon tea on the terrace while touring the island, or you can go a bit farther round the northern tip to the **Golden Lemon Inn**, at **Dieppe Bay ❻**. The main building was once a warehouse and shop, with the family living quarters above. The beach, looking across to Statia, is black sand, and it is a good spot for birdwatching, with lots of water birds paddling and fishing.

Continuing along the north coast road, you come to **Black Rocks**, an interesting rock formation where lava flowed into the sea and solidified. Farther along this Atlantic side of the island, **Ottley's Plantation Inn ❼**, another converted sugar estate, offers a spring-fed pool and short and easy rainforest walks. The Ottley family came from Yorkshire in the 18th century, but the Great House has been much altered and expanded since then. The present building is gracious and elegant, on a hillside overlooking the ocean.

## The southeast peninsula

At the entrance to the 14-mile (22km) southeast peninsula, **Frigate Bay ❽** embraces both the Atlantic and the Caribbean with pale sandy beaches offering water sports. This is the main island resort area so far, with a large Marriott hotel and golf course as well as other, more intimate places to stay. From Frigate Bay a 6-mile (4km) road runs down the narrow, hilly peninsula to Major's Bay. From the top you can see **Friar's Bay**, with a wild beach on the Atlantic Ocean on one side and a calm beach on the Caribbean Sea on the other and Nevis in the distance.

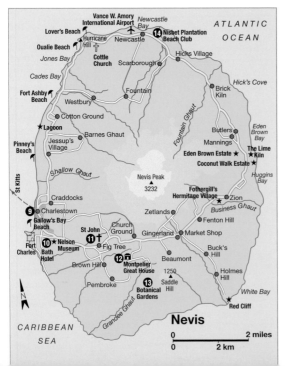

Construction has begun on the huge **Christophe Harbour** project covering 2,500 acres (1,012 hectares), which includes a five-star luxury hotel (to open in 2016), a 300-acre (120-hectare) marina village capable of accommodating mega-yachts and Customs and Immigration facilities, villas, spas, beach clubs, and a Tom Fazio golf course. One of the agreements between the developers and local government was that they maintain the environmental integrity of the island, including sensitivity to the salt ponds, lagoons, coral reefs, monkeys, tropical birds, and vibrant sea life.

**Great Salt Pond** is being developed for the marina, with a channel giving an outlet to **Ballast Bay on** the Caribbean. Excavated sand is to be used to replenish the beaches at Ballast Bay and **White House Bay**. The latter has long been popular as a yacht anchorage and there is good diving on old wrecks there. **Sandy Bank Bay,** on the Atlantic, is a sheltered, curved bay with plenty of sand, as its name suggests, but while you can splash around in the shallow water, swimming is dangerous because of the undertow. It is a marine sanctuary and no boat moorings are permitted. Christophe Harbour Beach Club is here, and a large residential development is planned.

**Turtle Beach** is heaven for birdwatchers and nature lovers, or visitors can just lunch in the Beach House restaurant, take a swim, and admire the view of Nevis. It is very romantic in the evening as the moon rises and the lights come on over the water on Nevis. Luxury bungalows have been built here for a select few guests so far.

There are other luxury resorts under development: Silver Reef Resort and Ocean's Edge Resort in Frigate Bay, and Cockleshell Bay Resort, to be the Caribbean's first Park Hyatt Hotel. Spice Mill is a lovely beach bar and restaurant on **Cockleshell Beach,** with four-poster daybeds and sun loungers on the sand, often with live music to complete the process of relaxation.

## The slow boat to Nevis

While regular short-hop flights are available between St Kitts and Nevis every day, ferries linking Basseterre to Charlestown provide an unforgettable 30- or 45-minute, 12-mile (19km) nautical experience – a slice of island life in its most chaotic and charismatic form. Whether you want to reach Nevis quickly and in style or on the slow cargo boat MV *Sea Hustler* is up to you; there is no difference in the price. An alternative in transport to Nevis from St Kitts is the sea bridge: owners drive their vehicles onto the barge and take an interesting journey to Nevis, where they simply drive off when they arrive.

The ride is choppy as the ferry rolls past the velvety hills of the southeast peninsula, catching the bigger waves in The Narrows between the islands. Outside the spray-splattered windows, the classic volcanic profile of Nevis Peak rises 3,232ft (985 meters) into perpetual cloud cap. Dense rainforest shrouds the higher slopes; lower down are fields and the remnants of old sugar mills, and below that the line of **Pinney's Beach** – 4 miles (6km) of golden

*The ferry linking St Kitts to Nevis.*

*Downtown Charleston, Nevis.*

sand shaded by palms, backed by the luxury Four Seasons Resort. With bars and restaurants, this is the island's busiest beach and it still looks deserted.

## A gingerbread capital

Emerging from its palmy setting, **Charlestown** 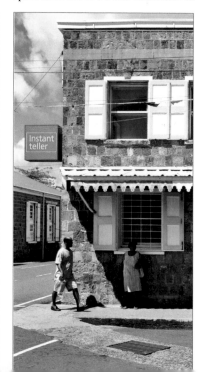 (pop. 1,800) is a colorful sprawl of pastel walls, tin roofs, and shady gardens. At the pier a hand-painted sign reads "Welcome to Nevis. Birthplace of Alexander Hamilton."

After Nevis' heyday in the 18th century, the town's fortunes fluctuated, hit by hurricanes and other disasters and the slackening demand for its Sea Island cotton and sugar cane. However, Charlestown has retained a quaint dignity and architectural unity in its high-roofed, verandah-shaded, gingerbread-trimmed buildings on Main Street and around **D.R. Walwyn's Plaza**.

At the top end of Main Street is the **Alexander Hamilton Museum** (www. nevis-nhcs.org; Mon–Fri 9am–4pm, Sat 9am–noon) in a Caribbean Georgian house on the site where the 18th-century American statesman Alexander Hamilton was born in 1755 or 1757. Set in a

beautiful garden by the sea, growing typical Nevisian plants and trees, the museum charts the life of Hamilton and the island's history. The museum is on the first floor; upstairs is the island's House of Assembly.

Back at the Plaza, huckster ladies sell vegetables and trinkets near the **Nevis Handicraft Co-op,** where home-made fruit wines – pawpaw, sorrel, genip, and gooseberry – are for sale in old soda bottles, along with some fiery pepper sauce. Around the corner at the **Nevis Philatelic Bureau**, visitors can buy first-day editions of colorful Nevis stamps. On Saturday, by 7.30am the town is bursting with life as Nevisians crowd into the fish, meat, and vegetable market down by the docks.

## The Nelson era

The 18-mile (30km) road around Nevis meanders southward out of Charlestown to the shell of the once-fashionable **Bath Hotel** ⑩ (Mon–Fri; charge). Built in 1778 to accommodate the cream of colonial society visiting the natural sulfur spring nearby, the hotel spa is believed to be one of the first in

### HORATIO AND FANNY

Horatio Nelson came to the Caribbean as Captain of the *Boreas* in 1784, to keep an eye out for any illegal trading. After American independence, the new nation's ships were no longer allowed to trade with British colonies, but when Nelson impounded the goods of four disguised American merchant ships lying off Nevis, the island's merchants, who were going to do business with them and whose livelihood depended on them, sued him for £40,000. Their anger was such that Nelson had to hide on his ship for 8 weeks until John Herbert, the president of Nevis and Fanny Nisbet's uncle, bailed him out.

Based in Antigua in English Harbour, Nelson hated the "infernal heat" of the West Indies and sought diversion on Nevis, which represented the height of fashion at the time. His charm and his friendship with the future William IV, who was also based in Antigua for a time, made him a welcome guest in Nevis's Great Houses, and he was soon seen with the attractive young widow, Fanny Nisbet, on his arm.

He married Fanny in March 1787, and Prince William wrote: "Poor Nelson is head over ears in love. I frequently laugh at him about it… he married Mrs Nisbet on the twelfth of March [it was the 11th] and I had, my Lord, the honour of giving her away…."

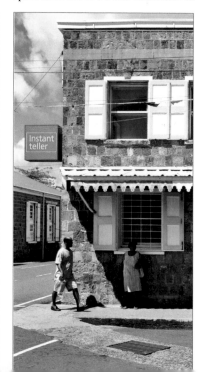

the Caribbean. The Spring House, built over a fault that supplies hot water at a constant 102°–108°F, is closed because of hurricane damage, but an outdoor pool has been constructed for anyone wanting to sample the healing powers of the mineral waters.

The British sea captain Horatio Nelson was stationed here in the mid-1780s when he married Fanny Nisbet, a Nevisian society widow (see box), and the **Nelson Museum** (www.nevis-nhcs.org; Mon–Fri 9am–4pm, Sat 9am–noon) has a marvellous collection of memorabilia of his time in the West Indies. Their marriage certificate is on display in the 300-year-old **St John's Fig Tree Church** ⓫, 2 miles (3km) away, which also has a fascinating array of tombstones.

The road continues eastward, circling **Nevis Peak** whose forested slopes hide a web of hiking trails, and wriggles past bursting bushes of bauhinias and untidy bark-dripping gum trees. The spine-laden trunk of a sandbox rises out of a tangle of Mexican creepers and lantana. A turning to the right leads to **Montpelier Great House** ⓬, the sugar estate where

Horatio and Fanny tied the knot. In the 1960s, a plantation house-style hotel was built on the site, which is now surrounded by lovely gardens, and past guests have included British royalty. It is one of several tastefully converted estates on the island, where you can recapture the atmosphere of the old plantation days.

Close by, the **Botanical Gardens** ⓭ (tel: 869-469 3509; www.botanicalgarden nevis.com) are well worth visiting for their spectacular collection of plants from around the world, highlighted by statuary and fountains. There is a conservatory designed as a mini Kew Gardens, a good copy of the one in England, a replica Great House, a shop, and café.

On the north coast, popular opinion has it that the **Nisbet Plantation Beach Club** ⓮, near Newcastle, has the best beach in Nevis, although **Oualie Beach** gives it a good run for its money, with water sports, snorkelling, scuba diving, and even cycling. Beaches on the Atlantic side of the island, such as **White Bay,** have good views of Montserrat, but the sea is rough and dangerous.

**FACT**

Eden Brown Estate on the east coast is supposed to be haunted by a bereft bride, Julia Huggins. Her husband-to-be and his best man, her brother, held a duel on the eve of their wedding in 1822. The fiancé killed the brother, and the bride's father would not let her marry a murderer. She remained a recluse in the house and islanders say that she has often been heard crying there.

*Manicured lawns at the Botanical Gardens, Nevis.*

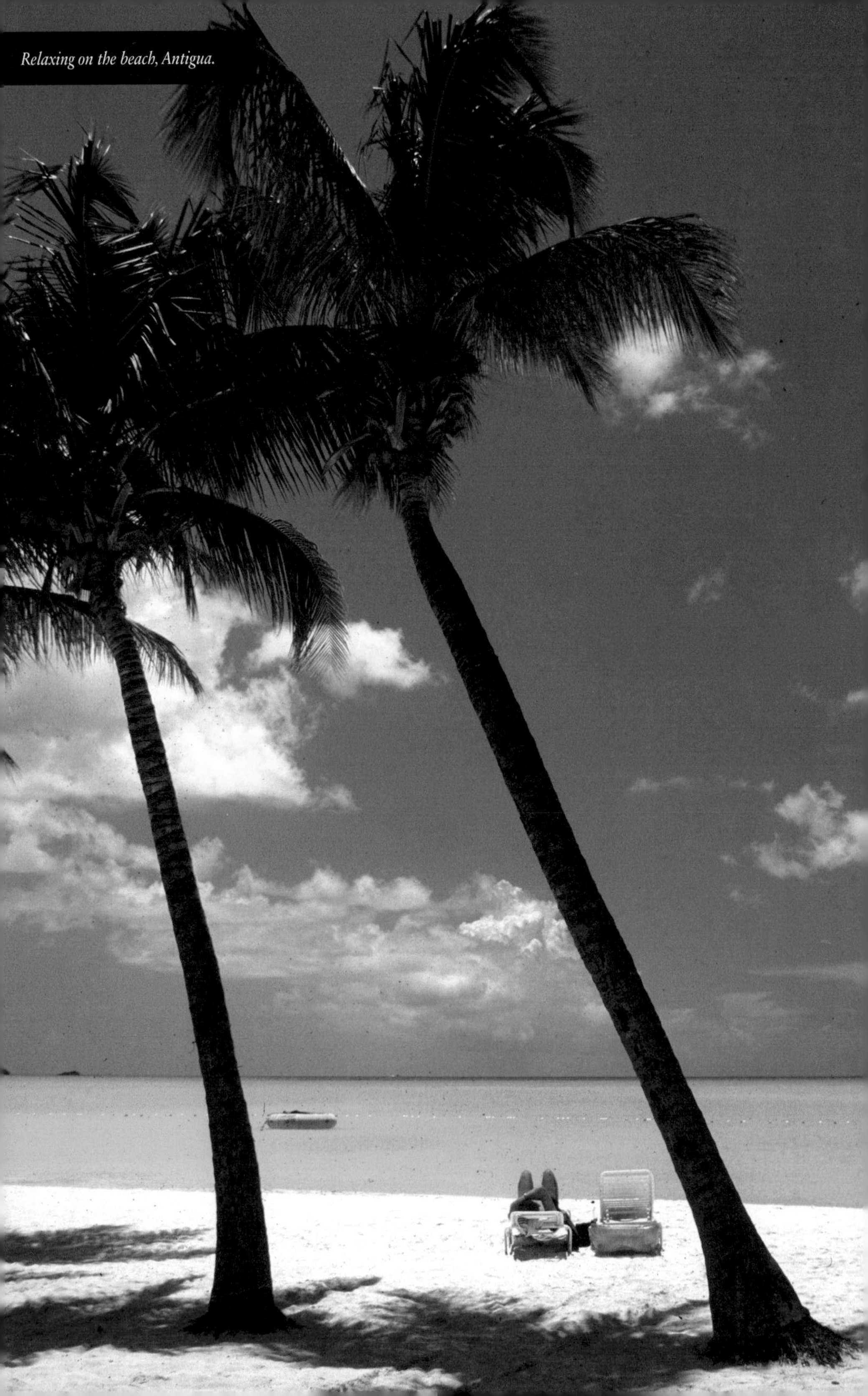

*Relaxing on the beach, Antigua.*

# ANTIGUA AND BARBUDA

With a white sandy beach for every day of the year
and waters licked by the steady northeasterlies,
these islands, set in the heart of the Caribbean, are
a haven for beach lovers and sailors.

**S**haped like a heart, the Leeward island of Antigua (pronounced An-tee-ga) shimmers in the heat of the Caribbean sun as the airplane comes in to land. For many, landing on this 108 sq mile (270 sq km) flat island of volcanic rock, coral, and limestone is their first taste of the Antilles as they wend their way to other islands. At the heart of the Caribbean archipelago, Antigua, with islands Barbuda and the uninhabited Redonda, is edged by a beautiful coastline abundant with bays, coves, and natural harbors. There are 365 white sandy beaches in all, so the tourist brochures say, and water sparkling in every shade of blue and turquoise between the Caribbean and the open Atlantic.

The vegetation on Antigua is limited to low scrub and dry grassland, and the only real scenic variety is provided by a few green hills and scraps of forest in the southwest. But water sports enthusiasts love Antigua. Divers explore the barrier reefs surrounding the island, while windsurfers and sailors enjoy the steady trade winds. Every April, the international yachting set breeze in for Antigua Sailing Week, when partying vies with sailing. The gentle Caribbean Sea on the leeward side is perfect for swimming and once, during a state visit, even enticed the queen of England into its warm, soothing waters.

*Hobie Cats, Jolly Beach Resort.*

## An experienced nation

Antiguans can look back on a lot more experience than most of their neighbors where tourism is concerned. During World War II, the USA used Antigua as a base for reinforcements and air power, building a modern airport that created a suitable infrastructure for tourism after the war. By 1965, there were more than 50,000 visitors to the island, and, today, around 250,000 people arrive by air and some 540,000 come on cruise ships each year, contributing about two-thirds

**Main Attractions**
St John's
Dickenson Bay
English Harbour and
    Nelson's Dockyard
Shirley Heights
Half Moon Bay
Barbuda's palm beach
Barbuda's Frigate Bird
    Sanctuary

of the country's revenue. Most of the population of 90,000 today make their living from tourism.

## Wadadli and its "rulers"

In 1493, on his second journey to the New World, Christopher Columbus sighted the island and named it after a church in his home town of Seville in Spain: Santa Maria de la Antigua. It was first named Yarumaqui, meaning the island of canoe-making, by the Tainos, and then the Caribs called it Wadadli, meaning eucalyptus oil, after the trees which the British cut down so that they could plant sugar cane. The name can still be seen today on the bottle caps of a local beer.

The British established a settlement on Antigua in 1632. During the Anglo-French colonial wars in the 17th and 18th centuries, Antigua served as the Caribbean base for the British fleet. In 1666 the French briefly captured the island, after which it became a British sugar colony. The first sugar plantation was cleared by Sir Christopher Codrington, who leased Barbuda to grow provisions for his slaves.

Barbuda's settlement is named after him. When sugar prices dropped in the late 1800s, and then dramatically collapsed in the late 1960s, the plantation owners' houses fell into disrepair; now, only the ruined windmills are left.

## The big Birds

Part of the crown colony of the Leeward Islands until 1956, Antigua was given associated status with full internal self-government within the British Commonwealth in 1967, and in 1981 it finally became independent with Vere Cornwall "Papa" Bird as prime minister. From 1946, Bird and his Antigua Labour Party (ALP) had steered the fortunes of the island, and in 1994, he was "succeeded" by his son, Lester.

The Bird clan has a huge private fortune, and critics have accused the "family business" of a level of corruption that is unique even by Caribbean standards, involving fraud, arms smuggling, drug running, money laundering, and so on, interlaced with the fierce rivalry between two of Papa Bird's sons, Vere Jr and Lester. In her story *A Small Place* (1988) the Antiguan writer Jamaica

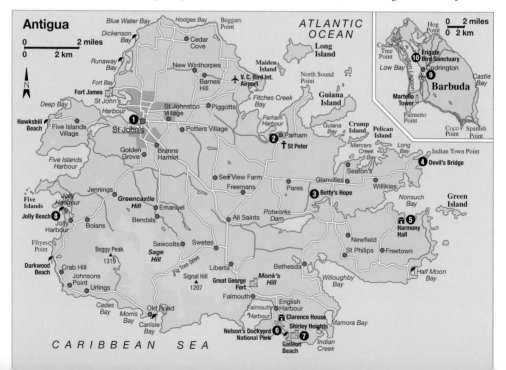

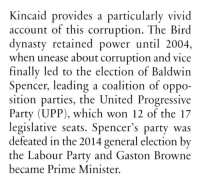

Kincaid provides a particularly vivid account of this corruption. The Bird dynasty retained power until 2004, when unease about corruption and vice finally led to the election of Baldwin Spencer, leading a coalition of opposition parties, the United Progressive Party (UPP), which won 12 of the 17 legislative seats. Spencer's party was defeated in the 2014 general election by the Labour Party and Gaston Browne became Prime Minister.

## St John's – a thriving town and harbor

St John's ❶ (pop. 81,000) in the northwest is Antigua's capital and is set around its largest and most important natural harbor. The streets in the center are lined with typically Caribbean wooden houses; most of the historic buildings date from the late 19th and early 20th centuries, because a large part of the town was destroyed by a seaquake in 1843.

Old warehouses by the Deep Water Harbour have been converted into shopping centers within reach of the cruise ships: **Heritage Quay** offers a Las Vegas-style casino and duty-free shopping, and **Redcliffe Quay**, which used to accommodate enslaved Africans before they were auctioned off at the market, has been restored, retaining many of its historical features, and now has restaurants and souvenir shops. Both are pleasant places in which to relax in air-conditioned surroundings. A third quay, **Nevis Street Pier**, can accept the latest mega-ships.

At the southern end of Market Street a block or two up the hill, is the colorful **Public Market** where produce from the island is sold right on the street. The busiest days are Friday and Saturdays. There is also a covered market here. No stroll through St John's would be complete without a visit to the **Museum of Antigua and Barbuda** (tel: 268-462 4930; www.antiguamuseums.net; Mon–Fri, 8.30am–4.30pm, Sat 10am–2pm; donation) on Long Street, at the other end of Market Street. Located in the Old Court House (1844), this collection of oddities provides an insight into local cultural history. It ranges from Siboney and Taino excavation finds to steel drums that you can try out for yourself.

*Stocking up on beachwear in St John's.*

The most attractive items are in the geological section and include large coral skeletons.

The finest view of the busy capital is from the Anglican **Cathedral of St John the Divine**, two blocks eastward on Church Street. Its distinctive twin towers can be clearly seen from all over the old town. This Anglican episcopal church is actually the third structure to be built on the site. The first church, built in 1682, was made completely of wood, while the second (built in 1789) fell victim to the quake of 1843. The present structure dates from 1845–8 and, despite its exposed location, it turned out to be sturdy enough to withstand hurricanes that devastated the rest of the island. The two statues of St John on the south gate were actually planned for a church in Guadeloupe, but an English warship stole them during shipment.

Across the road, the **Antigua Recreation Ground** is the hallowed home of Antiguan cricket, and the spot where local hero Sir Vivian Richards, the "Master Blaster," knocked off the fastest century in cricket. The new ground built for the 2007 ICC World Cup and subsequent Test matches is named after him.

The harbor entrance is protected by two 18th-century bastions: **Fort Barrington** to the south, and on the northern promontory **Fort James**, which still has cannon dating from the colonial era and has wonderful views. The beach in the bay below is St John's local beach and popular for parties at weekends. Otherwise, the impoverished-looking huts along the northern suburbs make it clear that not everyone on Antigua has profited from tourism; and, ironically, the luxury cruise liners are within full view, creating two worlds that could scarcely be more different from one another.

## The white beaches of the north

When driving in Antigua you need to get used to amazingly fast minibuses, whose drivers prefer to hoot rather than brake. There are no buses in the north, however, nor to the airport. Bumpy tracks included, Antigua has no more than 60 miles (100km) of road altogether.

*The waterfront at St John's.*

The stretch of coast to the northwest of St John's provides perfect conditions for Antigua's premier industry, tourism. **Runaway Bay** and **Dickenson Bay** both have good, sandy beaches with a clutch of hotels, restaurants, and beach bars. Dickenson Bay is well equipped for water-based activities, with glass-bottomed boats, various diving schools, jet-ski rental, and other water toys. The farther north you go, the quieter beach life becomes.

On the north and northeast coasts there are long stretches of sand, but this is the Atlantic coast and it is windy – great for kitesurfers and windsurfers – and there are a couple of schools for beginners and advanced surfers.

## Quiet coasts and Betty's Hope

Broad, sandy bays nestle between weathered limestone crags along Antigua's eastern coastline, which is pounded by the Atlantic. **Parham** ❷, tucked away in a sheltered harbor, is where, in 1632, the first British colonists from St Kitts arrived. The village church of **St Peter's**, built in 1840, is an unusual octagonal shape. Nearby, the shoreline is bordered by several mangrove swamps which are now, owing to development, a rarity on Antigua. From Crabs Peninsula to the east, you can look over to Guiana Island, 100yds/meters offshore.

About 4 miles (6km) away to the south and east, in the middle of dry bushland, on the other side of the small village of Pares, stands the remains of **Betty's Hope** ❸ (tel: 269-462 1469; Mon–Sat 9am–4pm), the first sugar plantation to be established on a grand scale in Antigua, in 1674, and now an open-air museum. In the midst of such a barren landscape, and plains dotted with husks of sugar mills, it is not that hard to imagine vast fields of sugar cane here. The plantation was developed by the British officer Christopher Codrington, who came to Antigua as governor of the Leeward Islands. His family lived in the Great House, named for his daughter, for many generations until 1921 when they abandoned sugar and moved to the US. The mill has been restored and occasionally grinds in full sail. Other plantation buildings

*St Peter's church.*

Cricket on the beach.

Nelson's Dockyard, one of the Caribbean's iconic sights.

remain in ruins for lack of finance, but there is a small visitors' center.

**Devil's Bridge** ❹, nearly 5 miles (8km) away at the most eastern tip of the island near Long Bay, is a natural rock bridge with several blowholes formed by the incessant pounding of the Atlantic surf.

A good beach is **Half Moon Bay** in the southeast; because of its perfect, almost circular shape, many consider it to be the finest on the island. Just before you get there, take a left turn to **Nonsuch Bay** 2 miles (3km) away, to **Harmony Hall** ❺ (tel: 268-460 4120; www.harmonyhallantigua.com; daily). A former plantation house, it is now known for its art and crafts gallery and boutique (10am–6pm), a small hotel, and an excellent Italian restaurant. The bar is tucked away in the old stone mill tower and moorings are available in the bay. A ferry will take you to the beaches on Green Island, just offshore.

## Nelson's Dockyard and English Harbour

The quickest way to reach the southwest coast from St John's is to take the much-used All Saints Road. The first small town you pass is **Liberta**, which commemorates the first slaves who settled here after they were freed by the British in 1834.

A 30-minute walk takes you up Monk's Hill to the ruins of **Great George Fort** and panoramic views across **Falmouth Harbour**, splattered with white sails. **English Harbour** is tucked away inside the bay, and was made a National Park in 1985. The potential of this magnificent, protected, natural harbor was realized as early as 1671, and while tropical storms damaged numerous Royal Navy vessels in most other parts of the West Indies, here in English Harbour and Falmouth Bay they were protected from the worst. Completely hidden from the enemy out at sea, the dockyard was a safe place in which to repair the ships. Admirals Hood and Rodney stayed at **Admiral's House** on several occasions during their battles against France toward the end of the 18th century, and from 1784 to 1787 the young Horatio Nelson, commander of HMS *Boreas*, was based here.

Today, the former naval base, **Nelson's Dockyard** ❻ (www.nationalparks antigua.com/visiting/nelsons-dockyard; daily 8am–6pm) is a picturesque yachting harbor. Warehouses and powder magazines have been restored with an affectionate eye for detail and transformed into a museum, romantic restaurants, and nostalgic hotels. The **Admiral's Inn** and the **Copper and Lumber Store** are two sensitively restored and atmospheric hostelries, with walls of brick brought over from England as ships' ballast. A lively place at the best of times, Nelson's Dockyard really comes into its own during the big regattas, such as **Antigua Sailing Week**, when the bars and restaurants stay open all night and there's dancing till dawn.

## Shirley Heights

Across the harbor, high up on the hilltop, stand the ruins of the once protective fortress of Shirley Heights. At the foot of the hill is **Clarence House**, built especially for Prince William, the duke of Clarence, when he was transferred to Antigua in 1787 as commander of HMS *Pegasus*. This typically Georgian colonial building, with a pretty verandah and shuttered windows, now serves as the British governor's guesthouse and country residence. But official visitors don't get exclusive access, as the rooms full of period antiques are open to the public when the governor is away (tours are free, but a tip is appreciated).

There's a perfect, 360-degree panoramic view from **Shirley Heights** ❼. In 1781 Governor Thomas Shirley instigated the construction of the fortifications to protect the harbor, and on clear days the excellent view extends as far as Montserrat, 28 miles (45km) southwest, and Guadeloupe, 40 miles (64km) to the south. The observation point and restaurant at the top are both called **The Lookout** and every Thursday and Sunday there is a barbecue and live music here – steel bands from 4pm followed by reggae on Sunday after 7pm.

The feared attack by the French, which the bastion was supposed to prevent, never actually materialized. Most of the soldiers who died at English Harbour did so from tropical diseases rather than in battle. A marked path leads from The Lookout to the cemetery in which they

**TIP**

Learn more about English Harbour on an historical boat trip (departs noon, daily from outside the Copper and Lumber Store), or during the multimedia show at the Dow Hill Interpretation Centre (daily; charge) on the way to Shirley Heights.

*Sailboat racing.*

## ANTIGUA SAILING WEEK

Arriving in Antigua at the end of April you won't see many suitcases on the luggage bands, just bulky sailors' bags by the hundred. Antigua Sailing Week (www.sailingweek.com), more than four decades on, is one of the top five yachting events in the world, attracting more than 200 yachts, 1,500 participants, and 5,000 spectators – from the world-class cup-winners to the amateur sailing enthusiast. Alongside the 5 days of racing off the shores of Antigua are 7 days and nights of intensive partying.

Two days are wholly set aside for organized fun and frolics in Falmouth's shallow harbor waters: Lay Day falls after 3 days of racing, when climbing a greasy pole, tug-of-war, and a wet T-shirt competition judged by a "bishop" and other honorary majesties are all part of the festivities; Dockyard Day celebrates the finish in an even more raucous fashion.

Although to some sailing is just a sideline of the week, there is serious racing all around the island for a range of classes. All sorts of boats join in from the small (with a handicap) to the high-tech 58-footer (18-meter) with fiberglass sails and a crew of 20-plus. And at lookout points, it's a wonderful sight to see the boats turn into a westerly course and release their colorful spinnakers.

lie buried; the ruins of several barracks, stables, and cisterns can also be seen, giving some idea of the harshness of garrison life. **Galleon Beach**, right beneath Shirley Heights, is an ideal place for a subsequent swim, accessible by car or water-taxi from English Harbour.

## Green hills and soft sand

Just north of Liberta, **Fig Tree Drive**, the most scenic road on Antigua, winds down toward the southwest coast. The figs are not figs at all but wild banana plants which, together with a few giant trees and lianas, provide a vague idea of what the rainforest here was once like. At Old Road, the trip continues north, hugging the coast all the way, and soon **Boggy Peak** (1,319ft/402 meters), the island's highest point, comes into view.

Two of Antigua's finest beaches, **Cades Bay** and **Darkwood Beach**, which each have a bar and restaurant, have astonishingly few visitors. In contrast, just around the next point, **Jolly Beach** ❽ (plus the yacht-filled Jolly Harbour) is lively and busy, with hotels, villas, restaurants, a supermarket, a golf course, and lots of entertainment.

## Beautiful Barbuda beaches

**Barbuda**, 25 miles (40km) to the northeast, offers a desert island remoteness for those who want to get away from it all. The population is only 1,300 and its attraction is **Palm Beach**, the seemingly endless, shimmering, slightly pinkish coral beach on the Caribbean side. The landscape on this 68 sq mile (170 sq km) island is flat as a pancake and scrubby apart from the eastern "Highlands," which rise to a maximum height of just 128ft (40 meters).

There are at least two daily 10-minute flights from Antigua to Barbuda and you can arrange an all-in day trip with a visit to the frigate bird sanctuary, and to caves containing Amerindian drawings, plus lunch and some time on the beach included. Alternatively, take the catamaran, *Barbuda Express* (90 minutes from St John's; www.antiguaferries.com), which also offers tours of the island.

Situated on the eastern edge of the 8-mile (13km)-long lagoon, **Codrington** ❾, the main town (or village really), where most of Barbuda's inhabitants live, is named for Sir Christopher. The sugar baron was leased Barbuda by

*Down at the pier, Codrington.*

Charles II in 1685 and the family kept it as a source of provisions and labor for their sugar estates on Antigua. The village is mostly made up of single-story houses on the edge of the lagoon. There is very little of note except the well, where people used to draw water until the 1980s, and the remains of parts of the stone walls used to demarcate the boundary of the settlement within which everyone had to live until 1976. After emancipation in 1834, the ex-slaves were left with no jobs, no land, and no laws, as everything belonged to the Codringtons. After many years and many disputes, Antiguan law was applied, but although Barbudans may own their houses, all land now belongs to the government.

The **Frigate Bird Sanctuary** ⑩ to the north of Codrington Lagoon is truly impressive and the largest outside the Galápagos. Nesting sites of the unusually tame frigate birds are mainly located in the mangrove swamps, and can be reached by boat. It is a breathtaking sight to see some 10,000 frigates in courtship displays and raising their young on the tops of the mangroves.

## Redonda – a fantasy monarchy

The third island in this small nation, **Redonda**, 24 miles (38km) southwest of Antigua, is uninhabited – except for birds. This half square mile (1 sq km) rocky island, where guano was collected until the middle of the 20th century, has a history of its own. In 1865 an eccentric Irishman named Matthew Shiell celebrated the birth of his son by landing on Redonda and claiming it as his kingdom. Although Britain annexed the rock in 1872, the title was not disputed and Shiell abdicated in favor of his son, a novelist, who took the title of King Felipe in 1888. On his death in 1947, the title was passed on to the poet John Gawsworth, who "reigned" as King Juan I from 1947 to 1967 and liberally appointed new members of the Redondan aristocracy, such as Dylan Thomas, both Lawrence and Gerald Durrell, Diana Dors, and Dirk Bogarde. Nowadays, the monarchy is hotly disputed, with at least one king living in England and another in Spain. To discover more about this fantasy monarchy, check www.redonda.org.

*Redonda, an island home to birds.*

*A frigate bird nesting site.*

# MONTSERRAT

Montserrat
Caribbean
Sea

**Where once Montserrat was a sleepy backwater, the still-active volcano has put the island on the map, making it a tourist attraction like no other.**

*Dramatic view from the Volcano Observatory.*

The people of Montserrat are still rebuilding following the volcanic eruptions in the Soufrière Hills that started in July 1995 and which destroyed much of the infrastructure in the southern part of the island. The mountain above Long Ground, which spewed pyroclastic flows of rocks, ash, and gases over the crater rim at 80mph (130kmph), destroying many homes and livelihoods, continues to be active. After the initial explosion, subsequent flows devastated villages and towns, including the capital Plymouth, and in

June 1997, 19 people died. Then, following a relatively quiet period, its dome collapsed again in May 2006, removing about 100 million cubic meters of lava and making it the second largest collapse of the eruption. The explosions sent ash nearly 12 miles (20km) up into the air, the highest recorded so far. The island is still on the alert.

Before the eruption 11,000 people called the island home; now fewer than half remain. There is a resilience and determination in those who wouldn't, or couldn't, leave, and those who returned to rebuild the island.

## How Montserrat used to be

Life "before the volcano" had been normal. This tiny, pear-shaped island of 11 by 7 miles (18 by 11km) – a British Overseas Territory – formed a gentle society. Its people were mainly farmers cultivating the rich volcanic soil, civil servants, construction workers, or in the tourist industry. Visitors loved "old-fashioned" Montserrat ("How the Caribbean used to be" was the marketing phrase) and, at one time, rock stars such as Paul McCartney and the late David Bowie came to record at Sir George Martin's Air Studios, which was a victim of Hurricane Hugo in 1989 and ceased operations.

Plymouth had once been pastel pretty, with gingerbread houses in the Caribbean vernacular style. Everywhere had been green, except for the beaches, which were volcanic black.

## An Irish-Catholic sanctuary

By the time Columbus saw the island during his second voyage to the New World – and named it Montserrat (Serrated Mountain) after the mountainous ridges near the abbey of the same name outside Barcelona – the original Amerindian inhabitants were no more. The first recorded settlers in post-Columbian times were Irish and English Catholics seeking sanctuary from Protestant persecution on St Kitts.

By the middle of the 17th century, a typical Caribbean colonial structure, with an economy based on sugar, had been established: a small Anglo-Irish planter class developing a social, economic, and political power base over a growing number of African slaves. When the sugar industry collapsed, and a post-Emancipation society developed, limes and cotton were introduced, soon becoming the backbone of the economy. Gradually, a greater degree of autonomy was won from the British. Today, there is a locally elected government with a British governor responsible for security and external relations.

## Life in the "safe zone"

The island is now divided into the northern "safe" zone and the southern "exclusion" zone. Everyone lives in the northern areas untouched by the volcano. Its wilder landscape ends in steep cliffs, and beyond the dark sea are the purple outlines of St Kitts and Nevis on one side and Antigua, on the other. The infrastructure has been rebuilt in this safe part of the island – protected from the volcano by the **Centre Hills** running from east to west through the middle of the country. Access to all areas south of Foxes Bay and Jack Boy Hill to Bramble airport and beyond is prohibited. There is also a maritime exclusion zone around the south coast, which has inadvertently benefited the local marine life. The dive sites off the north coast are also doing well, with healthy coral teeming with fish and a variety of sponges.

A new airport, now called John A. Osborne airport, was built near the village of **Gerald's**. Funded by the British government, it opened in 2005 and is the main link to other islands; there

*A green turtle at close quarters.*

*A fisherman casts his nets.*

**TIP**

The *Guide to Centre Hills*, on sale at the Montserrat Tourist Board (www.visit montserrat.com) and the Montserrat National Trust, contains descriptive and detailed information about the species, hiking trails, and plants found in the forest on Centre Hills.

is also a ferry service between Little Bay and St John's, Antigua.

## An island tour

Signposting on the island isn't always as good as it should be, so if you rent a car don't be afraid to ask directions. The roads in Montserrat wiggle, climb, and plunge, so proceed with caution. Alternatively hire a taxi for a day.

The **Montserrat Volcano Observatory ❶** (visitors' center tel: 664-491 5647; www.mvo.ms; Mon–Thur 8.30am–4.30pm) is located in a purpose-built complex uphill from Salem in Flemings. Staff at the observatory issue weekly updates on volcanic activity, which is monitored constantly. You can get a spectacular view of the volcano, Belham Valley, and ash-covered Plymouth from the viewing deck. Visits are self-guided and there is an interesting documentary describing the history and impact of the eruption (hourly 10.15am–3.15pm).

Downhill and north of Salem, the **Montserrat National Trust ❷** (tel: 664-491 3086; www.montserratnational trust.ms; Mon–Fri 9am–4pm) in the

Oriole complex, Olveston, stages several exhibitions each year and has a botanical garden, a research library, and a gift shop. They can also provide information on a series of nature trails in the hills. Hiking and birdwatching are increasingly popular on Montserrat and forest rangers are on hand to guide visitors. The Centre Hills Project is helping to protect species such as the Montserrat oriole, the mountain chicken (actually a frog), and the galliwasp lizard, as well as many endangered plants.

The **Runaway Ghaut** is half a mile (800 meters) from the National Trust, on the main road. A ghaut is a ravine or channel taking rainwater from the mountains out to the sea. Visitors can walk the mile-long scenic track to the west coast, following the line of the last retreat of the French who constantly fought the British for control of the island. Two black-sand beaches on this part of the coast are **Woodlands Beach**, which has a covered picnic area on the cliff above the beach, and **Bunkum Bay**, which has a beach bar. The sea at Woodlands is for strong

*This bar in Cudjoe Head has a volcanic backdrop.*

swimmers only, because the beach shelves very quickly and the waves can be quite strong.

Most of the island's shops, banks, the tourist office, and government buildings can be found in **Cudjoe Head** or in **Brades**, or on the road between the two. Just north of Brades is **Carr's Bay**, where there are the remnants of an old fort, with cannon pointing out to sea.

## A new capital

**Little Bay ❸** port and town are being developed as the new capital for the island. Already there are several bars, restaurants, a nightclub, and dive center. A cultural center (tel: 664-491 4242; www.themontserratculturalcentre. ms), built by former record producer Sir George Martin as a gift to the people of Montserrat, opened in 2007. Built into the hillside, it is the largest building on the island and has an auditorium seating 500 and an amphitheatre with capacity for 2,500. Little Bay is also the location of **Festival Village**, an entertainment venue by the sea, and a new cricket ground.

Just round the bluff to the north of Little Bay is the island's only pale-sand beach, at **Rendezvous Bay ❹**. You can either hike from Little Bay or take a short boat ride, or kayak. There is good snorkeling on the reef offshore. The 1-hour trail starts behind the concrete-block company in Little Bay, climbs over the hill and steeply down the other side to the beach.

North and beyond the airport is the village of **Drummonds**, a good place to begin a walk to **Silver Hills ❺** (1,322ft/403 meters). There is a communications tower at the top of the hill, and from here, on a clear day, you can see over Montserrat's northern coastline to Antigua, 27 miles (44km) away. There is a second trail to Rendezvous Beach from here, but it is a long, hot hike of 3.5 hours with no shade, so take a hat, sunscreen, and plenty of water. There is a picnic spot and another excellent viewpoint at **Jack Boy Hill ❻**, on the east coast, where you can see the old airport in the valley below, and look south to where the pyroclastic flow wiped out the villages in its path.

*In 1907 Mrs Goodwin won a competition with this design for Montserrat's emblem. It portrays Ireland, as Erin, embracing Christianity with the Irish harp and reflects the island's early Irish connections.*

*A little confusingly, the giant ditch frog is known locally as the mountain chicken.*

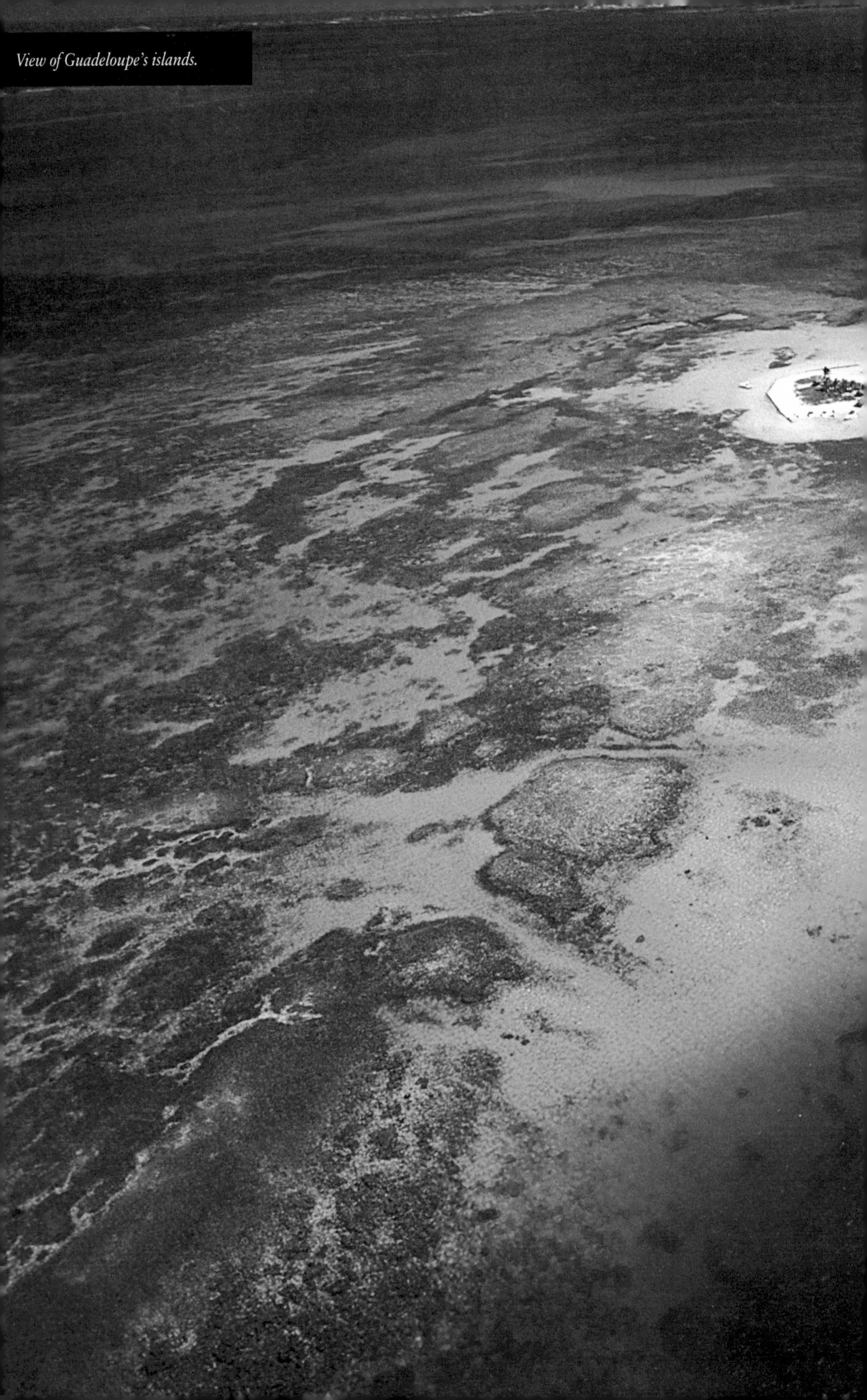

*View of Guadeloupe's islands.*

SAFRAN
€UROS
FRANCS
ROUCOU
€
F
€UROS
FRANCS
*Spices on sale at St- Antoine Market, Guadeloupe.*

# GUADELOUPE

French, but proudly Guadeloupean, this is an island of contrasts, from the arid lowlands and white beaches of Grande-Terre to the volcanic mountain forests and diving grounds of Basse-Terre.

B utterflies have a short lifespan, but the two unequal wings of Guadeloupe – one dry and rocky, edged with a white ring of beaches, the other mountainous, verdant, and crisscrossed with hot and cold rivers – have been spread for centuries. It is said that when Columbus first set eyes on Guadeloupe in 1493, he immediately encased it in a casket and presented the jewel to the Catholic king of Spain.

At 555 sq miles (1,438 sq km) Guadeloupe is one of the larger islands of the Lesser Antilles and is not only diverse, but also complex. Banana plantations crawl up the sides of volcanoes, flat expanses of sugar cane grow alongside winding mangrove swamps, international hotels contrast with wooden huts perched on four stones, and major highways cross paths leading over the mountains through giant ferns and dense forests.

## A piece of France

Guadeloupe, along with surrounding islands – Marie-Galante, Les Saintes, and La Désirade – is a *département* of France and therefore part of the EU. These islanders, like Martinicans, have French citizenship and French passports and have the same rights as those living in France, around 4,500 miles (7,000km) away. Arriving in Guadeloupe from another Caribbean island may make you wonder if you have taken a wrong turning somewhere: the four-lane highway from the airport is jammed with French cars, the large supermarkets and furniture stores are the same as those in France.

Guadeloupe's main export is bananas – most of which are eaten in France – and sugar cane, mainly used for making rum, still accounts for 40 percent of agricultural land. However, tourism is rapidly taking over as the country's biggest earner.

**Main Attractions**

Le Gosier
Musée Archéologique Edgar Clerc
Morne-à-l'Eau cemetery
Chutes du Carbet
Réserve Cousteau
La Soufrière
Terre-de-Haut

*Antillean creole dress.*

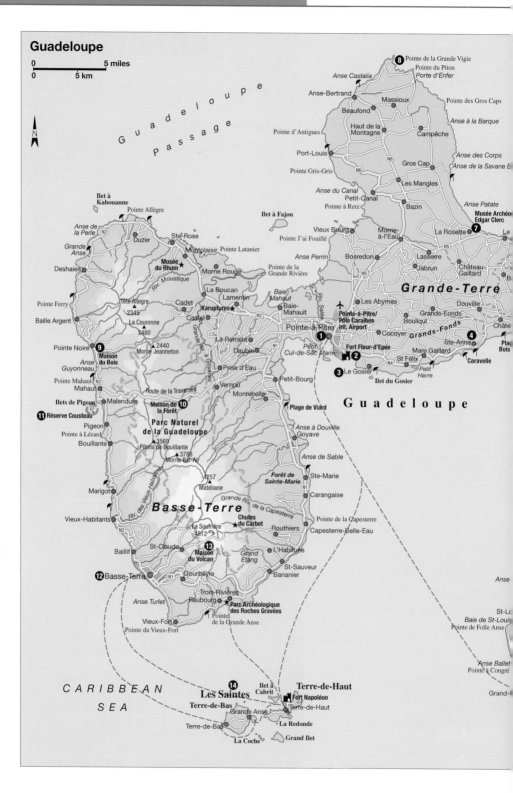

# Guadeloupe

0 ___ 5 miles
0 ___ 5 km

N

Guadeloupe Passage

Pointe de la Grande Vigie ⑧
Pointe du Piton
Porte d'Enfer
Anse Castalia
Anse-Bertrand
Pointe des Gros Caps
Massioux
Beaufond
Anse à la Barque
Haut de la Montagne
Pointe d'Antigues
Campêche
Port-Louis
Anse des Corps
N8
Anse de la Savane B
Gros Cap
Pointe Gris-Gris
N6
Les Mangles
Anse du Canal
Petit-Canal
Anse Patate
Pointe à Retz
Bazin
Musée Archéo
Edgar Clerc
Vieux Bourg
Morne-à-l'Eau
La Rosette ⑦
Le
Pointe J'ai Fouillé
Anse Perrin
Bosredon
N5
Lasserre
Château-Gaillard
Jabrun
B

Ilet à Fajou
Pointe de la Grande Rivière

Ilet à Kahouanne
Pointe Allègre
Anse de la Perle N2
Duzer
Ste-Rose
Montplaisir Pointe Latanier
Grande Anse
Musée du Rhum
Morne Rouge
Deshaies
Riv. Moustique
La Boucan
Lamentin
Baie Mahaut
Pointe Ferry
Tête Allègre
2345
Cadet
Karuptures
Baie-Mahault
Grande-Terre
Les Abymes
Douville
Baille Argent
La Couronne
2480
Castel
Grande Riv.
Grands-Fonds
La Retraite
N2
Pointe-à-Pitre/Pôle Caraïbes Int. Airport
Grands-Fonds
Pointe Noire ⑨
2440
Morne Jeanneton
Daubin
N1
Pointe-à-Pitre ①
Bouliqui
Cocoyer
Châte
Maison du Bois
Prise d'Eau
Petit Cul-de-Sac Marin
Fort Fleur-d'Epee
Ste-Anne ④
Plac Bois
Anse Guyonneau
Route de la Traversée
Vernou
②
St Félix
Mare Gaillard
Pointe Mahaut N2
Montébello
Le Gosier ③
N4
Petit
Havre
Caravelle
Mahaut
Ilet du Gosier
Ilets de Pigeon
Malendure
Maison de la Forêt ⑩
Plage de Viard
Guadeloupe
⑪ Réserve Cousteau
Pigeon
Parc Naturel de la Guadeloupe
Anse à Douville
Goyave
Pointe à Lézard
3569
Bouillante
Pitons de Bouillante
Anse de Sable
3788
Morne-Bel-Air
4257
Matéliane
Forêt de Sainte-Marie
Ste-Marie
N1
Marigot
Carangaise
Basse-Terre
Grande Riv. de la Capesterre
Vieux-Habitants
N2
Pointe de la Capesterre
Chutes du Carbet
Routhiers
Capesterre-Belle-Eau
La Soufrière
4812
L'Habituée
Baillif
St-Claude
Maison du Volcan ⑬
Grand Etang
Gourbeyre
St-Sauveur
Bananier
⑫ Basse-Terre
N1
Anse
Trois-Rivières
Faubourg
Anse Turlet
Parc Archéologique des Roches Gravées
St-Lo
Pointel de la Grande Anse
Baie de St-Louis
Pointe de Folle Anse
Vieux-Fort
Pointe du Vieux-Fort
Anse Ballet
Pointe à Congré

CARIBBEAN SEA

⑭
Ilet à Cabrit
Terre-de-Haut
Les Saintes
Fort Napoléon
Terre-de-Bas
Terre-de-Haut
Grand-I
Grande Anse
La Redonde
Terre-de-Bas
Grand Ilet
La Coche

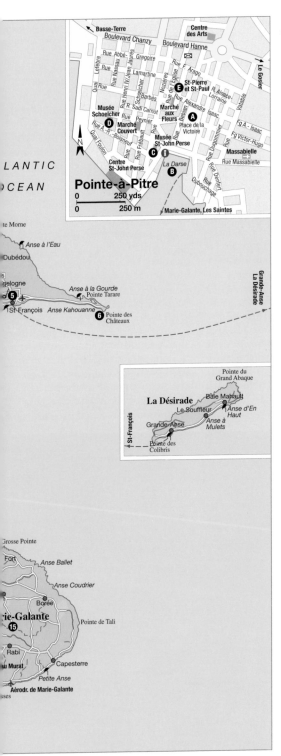

Basse-Terre
Boulevard Chanzy
Rue Abbé Grégoire
Rue Nassau
Rue Lefèbre
Rue Henri IV
Rue Jean Jaurès
Lamartine
Quai Rue
Rue Schoelcher
R. Sadi Carnot
Rue Barbès
Musée Schoelcher
Rue Peynier
Marché Couvert
Rue A.-R.-Boisneuf
Rue Frébault
Quai Foulon
Musée St-John Perse
Centre St-John Perse
Rue Mozières
Boulevard Hanne
Centre des Arts
Rue de l'Église
Rue F. Arago
St-Pierre et St-Paul
Rue Alsace Lorraine
Rue Alexandre Isaac
Place de la Victoire
Marché aux Fleurs
Fg A.-Isaac
Fg Victor-Hugo
Rue Duplessis
Massabielle
Rue Massabielle
La Darse
Rue Oubouchage
Rue Vatable
Rue Bébian
Rue Peynier
Le Gosier
Valable
Rue Denfert

**Pointe-à-Pitre**
0    250 yds
0    250 m
Marie-Galante, Les Saintes

L ANTIC
OCEAN

te Morne
Anse à l'Eau
Dubédou
gelogne
St-François   Anse Kahouanne
Anse à la Gourde
Pointe Tarare
Pointe des Châteaux
Grande-Anse
La Désirade

Pointe du Grand Abaque
**La Désirade**
Baie Mahault
Le Souffleur
Anse d'En Haut
Grande-Anse
Anse à Mulets
St-François
Pointe des Colibris

Grosse Pointe
Fort
Anse Ballet
Anse Coudrier
Borée
ie-Galante
Pointe de Tali
Rabi
u Murat
Capesterre
Petite Anse
Aèrodr. de Marie-Galante
sses

# Land of beautiful waters

The Spanish made several attempts to settle the island after Columbus had dropped by long enough to name it for the Virgin of Guadelupe in Spain. However, they were foiled by the resident Caribs who tenaciously guarded their Land of Beautiful Waters (Karukera) until the arrival of the French in 1635. Within 5 years, the Amerindians had been suppressed, and soon a thriving sugar economy was in operation, underpinned by the labor of African slaves.

The British cast a greedy eye on the island, invading twice and taking control in 1759. They agreed in the 1763 Treaty of Paris to return the island to Louis XV – in exchange for keeping Canada.

Life took a downward turn for the *békés* (rich white planters) when during the French Revolution slavery was abolished in the French colonies and a revolutionary commissioner, Victor Hugues, was sent to Guadeloupe in 1794 to enforce it. This he did with gusto, defeating the British, who had been invited in by the *békés* to maintain the status quo, and then guillotining 850 royalist planters.

When Napoléon came to power, Hugues was replaced and slavery reinstated until abolition was decreed in the 1848 Revolution that established the Second Republic in France. After that, 40,000 East Indians came to work on the sugar plantations.

Guadeloupe and Martinique went into decline during the two world wars; thousands of islanders went to fight for France, and in World War II they suffered an Allied blockade during the German occupation of France, cutting off the import of basic essentials. Afterward, in 1946, integration into the Third Republic as *départements d'outremer* (overseas departments) of France seemed the only way toward economic recovery for the French islands.

There have been several groups advocating independence and many Guadeloupeans who, although not wanting to break away, resent France because of the way top jobs are given to incoming French when unemployment is high (3–4 percent of the population leave each year to work in metropolitan France); they also feel that their créole culture – a mix of African, East

*St-Antoine market, in the capital.*

*The streets of Pointe-à-Pitre.*

Indian, and West Indian – is being swamped by all things French.

## Pointe-à-Pitre – the unofficial capital

Pointe-à-Pitre ❶, the economic capital of Guadeloupe, has little architectural beauty. But if you close your eyes to the low-cost housing developments and delve into the old town, you discover its appeal. In some places its balconied wooden houses rival those of the French Quarter in New Orleans.

**Place de la Victoire** Ⓐ is bordered by sidewalk cafés and old colonial buildings. This is the historical heart of Pointe-à-Pitre, and several monuments in honor of local personalities and events are exhibited here. The square opens out onto **La Darse** Ⓑ (the harbor) with boats that go to the islands of Marie-Galante and Les Saintes. La Darse continues along the wharf where for three centuries the import-export houses traded their goods, but the buildings have now been transformed into the modern US$20-million **Centre St-John Perse**, housing 80 shops, restaurants,

and a hotel. Cruise ships drop anchor at the cruise terminal several times a week.

Behind, the small **Musée St-John Perse** Ⓒ (9 rue Nozières and rue A R Boisneuf; tel: 590-590-900 192; Mon–Fri 9am–5pm, Sat 8.30am–12.30pm) celebrates the life and work of the Guadeloupean poet who was born into a *béké* family as Alexis Saint-Léger in 1887. Although he left the island when he was 12, never to return again, he idealized the Caribbean in his poetry and was awarded the Nobel Prize for Literature in 1960.

Mingle with the crowd thronging the **rue Frébault**, Pointe-à-Pitre's busiest street, another block away from the harbor. Stop at the **Marché Couvert** (Covered Market) close by, bordered by rues St-John Perse, Schoelcher, Frébault, and Peynier. It is at its bustling, colorful best in the morning. Here you can pick up stylish cotton clothing, straw bags, and local crafts, and feast your senses at stalls piled high with fragrant spices and exotic fruits such as sugar apples, sweetsops, soursops, mangoes, and passion fruit,

or tubers such as yams, sweet potatoes, cassava, and madera, as well as home-grown vegetables.

A few minutes to the west on rue Peynier is the **Musée Schoelcher ⓓ** (24 rue Peynier; tel: 590-590-820 804; Mon–Fri 9am–5pm), dedicated to the French politician Victor Schoelcher, who persistently campaigned for the abolition of slavery in the French colonies and signed the decree in 1848.

On the way back to place de la Victoire turn left up rue Nozières and, nearby, tucked away to the right, is the **Marché aux Fleurs** (Flower Market) in front of the sand-colored facade of the basilica of **St-Pierre et St-Paul ⓔ**. Built in the 1830s with metal supports and exquisite stained-glass windows, it successfully withstood the huge earthquake in 1845.

## Exploring Grande-Terre

On Grande-Terre the flat landscape of sugar-cane fields is dotted here and there with the massive stone silhouette of a sugar mill, the dark green foliage of a mango tree, or the scarlet splash of a flame tree. On leaving Pointe-à-Pitre on the N4, the south coast road, you come to Guadeloupe's main resort area, starting with one of the biggest marinas in the Caribbean at **Bas du Fort**, about 2 miles (3km) from the center. On the hilltop above, looking across to Marie-Galante and the mountains of Basse-Terre, is the coral-built, 18th-century **Fort Fleur-d'Epée ❷** (daily; free) which holds art exhibitions and has lovely gardens.

**Le Gosier ❸**, 2 miles (3km) farther on, is the hub of the holiday scene, where there are countless little restaurants. The service is slow, but a Ti-punch (rum with sugar-cane syrup) helps to pass the time. Try the humbler dishes not to be found on every menu, such as breadfruit *migan* (breadfruit slices cooked slowly with lemon juice and salt pork) and *bébélé* (plantains, green bananas, congo peas, tripe with salt pork) from Marie-Galante, or maybe a *bokit*, a large round fried sandwich, the local answer to fast food. This is the real Guadeloupe. The town comes alive at night to the sound of zouk emanating from the nightclubs.

**FACT**

The two "wings" of mainland Guadeloupe are divided by the Rivière Salée. Paradoxically, the smaller, flatter eastern "wing" is called Grande-Terre, which means large or high land, and the large, mountainous western "wing" is Basse-Terre, meaning low land. It is believed they were named by sailors for the winds that blow greater in the east and lower in the west.

*Traditional Caribbean Creole houses in Grand Terre, Guadeloupe.*

There are several sandy beaches along the south Atlantic coast but the typical French West Indian village of **Ste-Anne 4**, 9 miles (14km) away, sits on one of the best, while the Club Med resort enjoys another fine beach at Caravelle. The road slopes down a farther 9 miles (14km) to **St-François 5**, once a quiet little fishing village and now an upmarket resort with its own airport for light aircraft and private jets, and a golf course. Ferries depart regularly from the opulent marina for the island of La Désirade, 6 miles (10km) away. The road out of the town ends 7 miles (11km) on at the craggy **Pointe des Châteaux 6** where, as a final gesture, the rocks have been lashed by the Atlantic at its juncture with the Caribbean into spectacular castle-like formations. You can walk up to the cross planted at the Pointe des Colibris in 1951 for some fine views.

## Pre-Columbian treasures

Back on the N5 heading north, after about 8 miles (13km) you reach **Le Moule**, once the capital and now the surfing capital of the island. The beach restaurants are perfect for lingering over a plate of seafood. Just outside at La Rosette is the **Musée Archéologique Edgar Clerc 7** (Mon–Tue, Thur, 9am–5pm, Wed, Fri 9am–1pm; free), which houses one of the Caribbean's largest collections of pre-Columbian items, and other treasures.

Follow the coast road and take a swim in one of the many sheltered, hidden coves, or push on farther north, on the N8, which cuts across country of thornbushes and acacias for about 15 miles (24km) to the **Pointe de la Grande Vigie 8**. Here the land ends. Only a few years back this area was a wild and desolate place, but is now the haunt of scuba divers and strong swimmers who are not duped by the apparent calm of the blue, blue water.

On your way back to Pointe-à-Pitre, stop off at **Morne-à-l'Eau**, home of the island's most magnificent cemetery, which is a true city of the dead, with funeral palaces of black and white checkered tiles. On All Saints' Day in November the cemetery at night is aglow with the flickering of tiny candles.

*The dense forest around Capesterre-Bell-Eau.*

## The Basse-Terre mountains

Now for the western wing, the mountainous **Basse-Terre**. From Pointe-à-Pitre, the N1 heads down the eastern coast. You can stop at places such as **Les Jardins de Valombreuse** (www.valombreuse.com; daily 8am–6pm), lovely gardens in a rainforest setting, where you can buy flowers, have them packed for export, and collect them at the airport. **Capesterre-Belle-Eau** is the third-largest town, notable for its seafront avenues of flamboyant trees and royal palms. South of the town at St-Sauveur, turn inland on the D4 (Route de l'Habituée) to reach the **Chutes du Carbet**, three spectacular waterfalls with pools of warm, sulfuric water you can swim in.

Back on the N1, head towards the **Parc Archéologique des Roches Gravées** – ancient rocks etched with images of men and animals, which were carved by the Amerindians who originally inhabited Guadeloupe – at Trois Rivières on the southeast coast.

Alternatively, the N2 heads west round the north coast of Basse-Terre. Modern art lovers should stop in the town of **Lamentin**, a 15-minute drive west of Pointe-à-Pitre. Massive modern-art sculptures, called Karuptures, pop up at intersections, in school yards, in the countryside, and at the fishing port. For rum *aficionados*, there is the **Domaine de Séverin** distillery at La Boucan, where they still use a paddle wheel; and the **Musée du Rhum** at the Distillerie Reimonenq, Ste-Rose. Heading down the west coast you get to **Pointe Noire**, where you can visit the **Maison du Bois** ❾ (tel: 590-590 981 690; under renovation), a woodworking center which has an exhibition of wooden household implements.

The N1 and the N2 are linked by a dramatic road bisecting Basse-Terre. The **Route de la Traversée** cuts across the 60,000 acres (24,000 hectares) of the **Parc Naturel de la Guadeloupe** (www.guadeloupe-parcnational.com). About halfway along the 15-mile (24km) route, edged with giant ferns, bright red flamboyants, and rainforest, is the **Maison de la Forêt** ❿ (Nov–Apr and July–Aug Mon–Sat 8.30am–1pm, 1.45–4.30pm, Sun 9am–1.15pm, May–June and Sept–Oct Mon–Fri 9am–1pm, 1.45–4.30pm; free), a good information center that provides maps for well-signposted walks, some lasting only 20 minutes – such as the one to the beautiful **Cascade de l'Ecrevisse** – others, like the Pigeon Trail, taking 3 hours. South of the junction with the N2 you quickly come to the dark sands of **Malendure**, the launching pad for the **Réserve Cousteau** ⓫, a marine park around the Ilets de Pigeon.

The N2 twists and turns along the coast for about 16 miles (26km) to **Basse-Terre** ⓬, the administrative capital of the *département* of Guadeloupe. Under the shadow of the smoking **La Soufrière**, which last yawned and fell back to sleep in 1976, the old, colonial port, founded in 1634, has neatly planned squares, narrow streets, a 17th-century cathedral, and the well-preserved ruins of **Fort Louis Delgrès**, named after the black

*The raccoon is a rare sight in Guadeloupe and is the emblem of Basse-Terre's massive Parc Naturel.*

*Bois bandé (the local Viagra), for sale in the market.*

**FACT**

The popular British-French TV comedy-drama series *Death in Paradise*, starring Kris Marshall and Joséphine Jobert (following the departure of original leads Ben Miller and Sara Martins), has been filmed on Guadeloupe since 2011. In 2015, the show's creator Robert Thorogood published a novel, *A Meditation on Murder (A Death in Paradise novel)*, featuring characters from the series.

*Les Saintes, Guadaloupe.*

commander who died resisting the re-imposition of slavery.

Several roads lead up through lush countryside to the smart resort of **St-Claude**, 4 miles (6km) into the foothills of La Soufrière, where there is an informative **Maison du Volcan**  ⓭ (Bains-Jaune, Route de la Soufrière; daily 9am–1pm, 2–4pm) and the start of some scenic trails. You can drive farther up the mountain to a parking area at Savane à Mulets by steaming fumaroles, and those fit enough can tackle the arduous 90-minute climb to the often cloud-covered crater.

## Trips to the islands

At **Trois Rivières** on the coast south of the volcano, ferries make the 25-minute trip to **Les Saintes** ⓮ where, in 1782, Britain's Admiral Rodney foiled the French fleet's planned attack on Jamaica in the Battle of the Saintes. Of this huddle of eight islands, only two – **Terre-de-Haut** and **Terre-de-Bas** – are inhabited. Their tiny population is of Breton origin, descended from the pirates who used to stake out the seas. Today, they are skilled sailors or fishermen, identifiable by their wide hats, called *salakos*. It is worth staying the night in one of the several small hotels and inns on Terre-de-Haut to experience the tranquility of a beautiful island with white-sand beaches after the day-trippers have left. While you are here, try the delicious seafood, or buy *torment d'amour* (torment of love) cakes at the ferry port.

From Pointe-à-Pitre boats go daily to Les Saintes and to the circular 60 sq mile (155 sq km) island of **Marie-Galante** ⓯, which Columbus named for his own ship. Bordered by white sandy beaches, one of the most secluded being the hidden coves of **Anse Canot** on the northwest coast, the island still grows sugar to make rum. Tour one of the rum distilleries and visit the atelier of local sculptor Armand Baptiste.

**La Désirade**, a melancholy place not typical of Guadeloupe, is reached by ferry from St-François, on the southern coast of Grande-Terre (an hour's drive from Pointe-à-Pitre along the N4); the island once served as a leper colony and was often a final destination for its inhabitants.

## COUSTEAU'S SILENT WORLD

When Jacques-Yves Cousteau (1910–97) was filming his award-winning film *Le Monde du Silence* (1955) at Ilets de Pigeon, he discovered what he considered to be one of the best dive sites in the world. As a result of the enthusiasm of this French underwater explorer and cameraman *extraordinaire*, the Réserve Cousteau, a large 2,471-acre (1,000-hectare) submarine park was set up around the tiny islands off Malendure on the western coast of Basse-Terre. The reason this site is so much more beautiful than most others is because the hot volcanic springs around the islands have created a wonderful warm environment for a much wider variety of sea life than other Caribbean coasts. Forests of hard and soft corals and large communities of magnificent tube and barrel sea sponges in violets, yellows, flaming red, and greens give shelter to a universe of fish in all shapes, sizes, and color schemes. Gorgonias gently sway in the silvery gentle sea in temperatures of around 82°F (28°C), and the visibility is still perfect at depths of 65–130ft (20–40 meters).

To experience such a spectacular site, well-equipped dive shops with licensed instructors at Malendure organize individual dives or courses. You can also rent tanks for beach dives, as the underwater scenery starts close by.

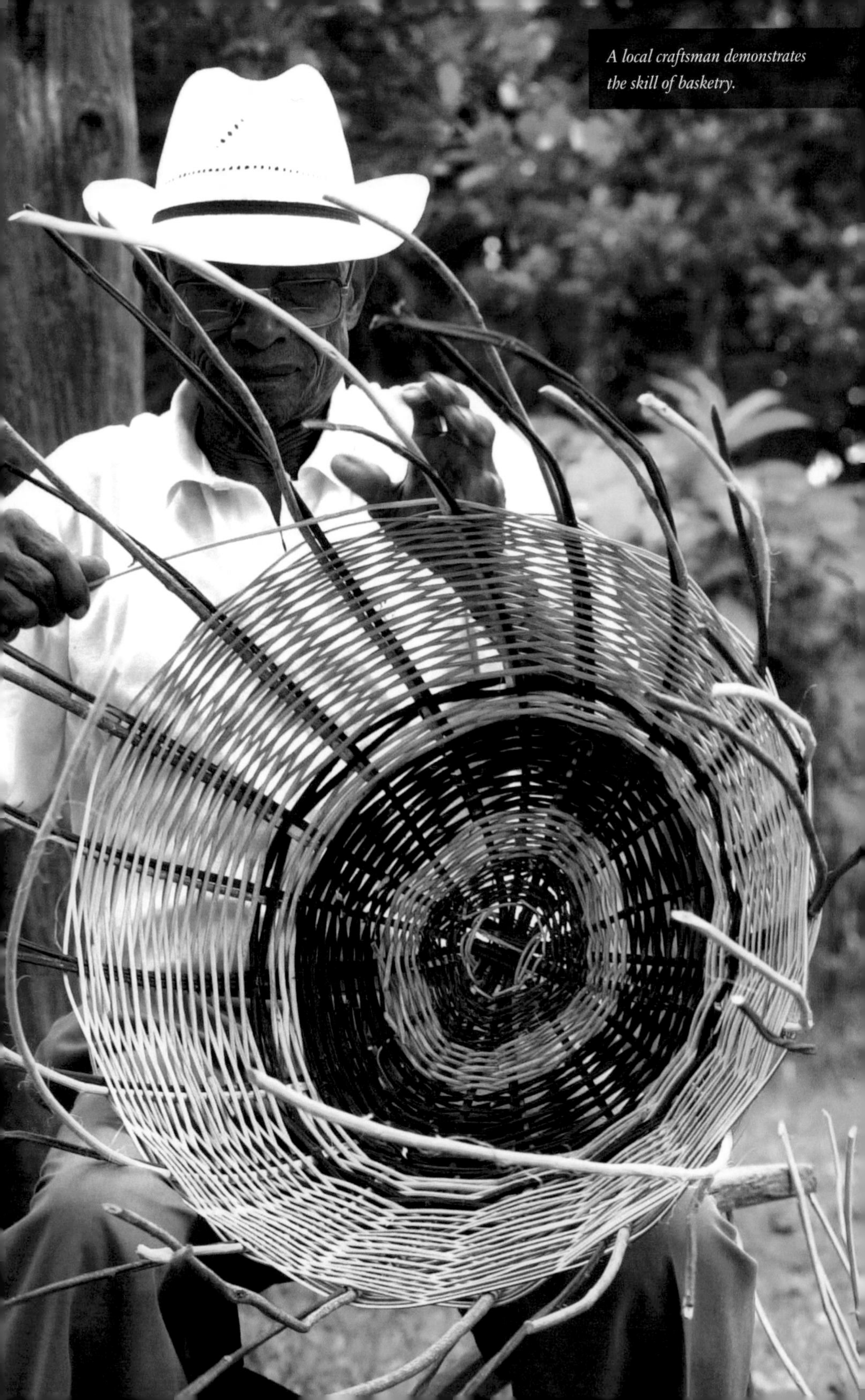

*A local craftsman demonstrates the skill of basketry.*

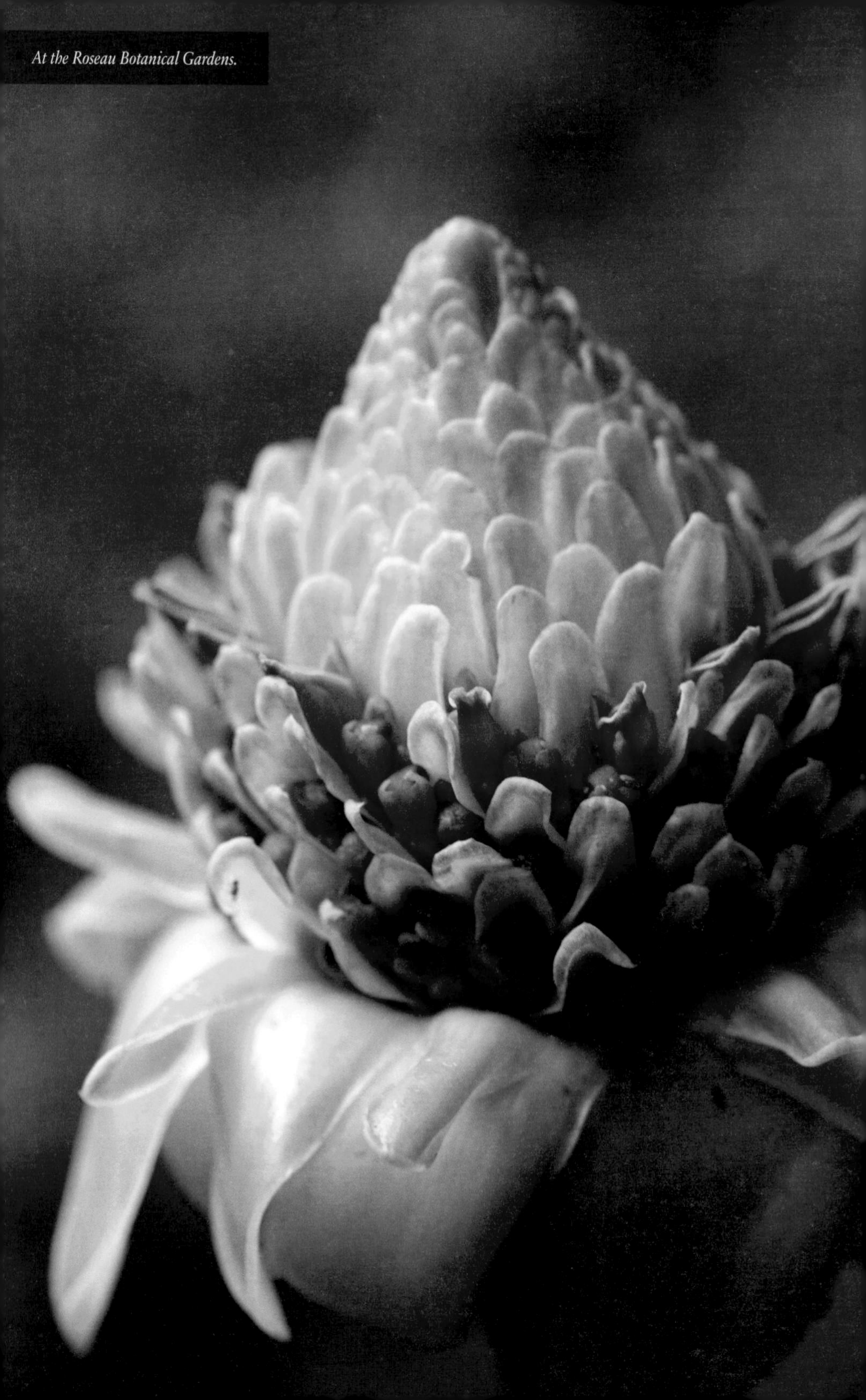

*At the Roseau Botanical Gardens.*

# DOMINICA

**Untamed and beautiful, this lush volcanic island has jungle trails, sulfurous pools, and coral reefs. Above and below sea level it is a magnet for nature lovers, from birdwatchers to whale spotters.**

As Mr Rochester, the hero of Jean Rhys's novel, *Wide Sargasso Sea*, toiled up the path toward his honeymoon home halfway up a Dominican mountainside, he lamented: "Too much blue, too much purple, too much green. The flowers too red, the mountains too high, the hills too near." It is not only fictional characters who have been overwhelmed by the physical presence of Dominica (pronounced Dom-in-*ee*ka). From Columbus, who sailed into Prince Rupert Bay in 1493, to the 19th-century British imperialist J.A. Froude and the 20th-century travel writer Patrick Leigh Fermor, all have been somewhat in awe of the rugged island of Dominica.

The largest of the Windward Islands (15 by 29 miles/25 by 46km), Dominica lies between Guadeloupe and Martinique. From the air, it has a dark presence: volcanic mountains disappearing into its dense, cloud-covered spine, forested ribs of ridge and valley, carved out by the numerous rivers rushing down to the sea, while a road hugs the coastline. With much of its surface still covered in some of the finest rainforest and cloudforest in the region, its 72,000 people live in scattered communities beside the sea, mainly on the sheltered leeward side, or along the ridges.

*Dominican sugarcane is a popular delicacy.*

## A protecting environment

The magnificent environment of this "Nature Island" has been both a protection and a constraint. In the past, it protected the island from total exploitation by even the most grasping of European adventurers and settlers as, with only small patches of flat land, there were no great riches to be made.

Although the colonizers managed to drive the resident Caribs – or Kalinago, as they called themselves – from the leeward coast into the mountain fastnesses and to the remote northeast,

**Main Attractions**
Roseau
Trafalgar Falls
Papillote Wilderness
   Retreat
Morne Trois Pitons National
   Park
Waitukubuli National Trail
Kalinago Barana Auté
Cabrits National Park
Fort Shirley
Whale watching

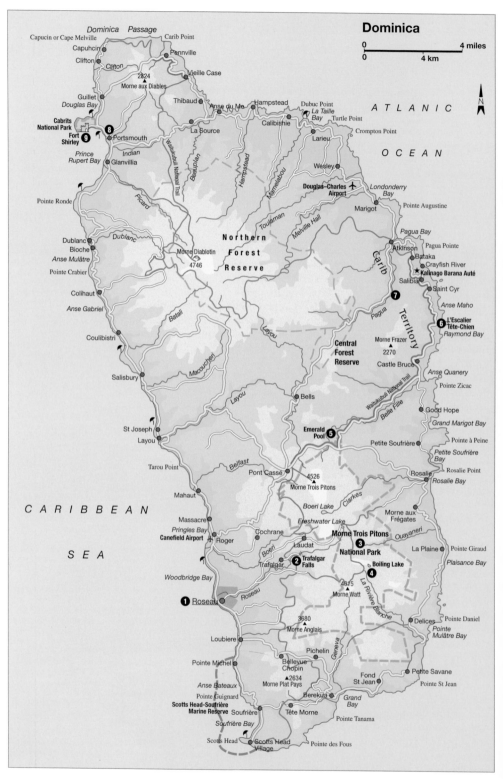

Dominica

they were not entirely wiped out. The environment protected them. Again in the 18th century, the forests provided a sanctuary for the maroons (escaped slaves), and it also enabled a strong-minded independent peasantry to develop, cultivating "gardens," as they still do, in forest clearings.

The early settlers, at the end of the 17th century, were small-timers, Frenchmen from Martinique, who traded with the Kalinago, cultivated tobacco, and later coffee and cocoa, on estates whose names alone – *Temps Perdu* or *Malgré Tout* – evoke a sense of loss and resignation.

When the British finally took control in 1783, wresting the island from the French (who continued to skirmish with the British through the Napoleonic Wars), sugar, then limes, and eventually, in the 1930s, bananas became the main crops. The banana industry grew spectacularly in the 1960s, becoming known as "green gold" (see box). Now challenged by the large Latin American competitors, modern Dominica, independent from Britain since 1978, is looking to tourism as a main provider of income and source of employment.

## Island pursuits

There is no mass tourism in Dominica, partly because of the small airport, and no long-distance direct flights. Visitors who make the effort to get here are active, inquisitive, and hardy. They bathe in rivers whose cliffs are smothered in vines, giant ferns, and the yellow-red claws of the dramatic heliconia plant. They hike into the forests, up trails that are still used by Dominicans to reach their forest "gardens," past the buttressed trunks of great trees, such as the chatanier, or the giant of the forest, the gommier, from which the Kalinago still make their canoes.

They explore the seabed, where there are majestic underwater seascapes, from submerged pinnacles to corals and sponges populated by reef fish. Despite run-off from the 365 rivers on the island, due to steep drop-offs the sediment falls away and visibility is excellent in the unpolluted water. Whale and dolphin watching are other popular activities, and boats

**TIP**

For a scuba site with a difference, head for Champagne by Scotts Head in the southeast, where you can swim through underwater hot-spring bubbles and watch myriad sea life – it's even better at night.

*A tree house at Rosalie Forest, part of the Three Rivers Eco-Lodge accommodations.*

*Coffee, a stalwart in Dominica's agricultural identity.*

with sonar equipment have a remarkable success rate in locating a number of species living in or migrating through Dominica's waters. As well as all these activities, there is kayaking, canyoning, canopy tours, birdwatching, or even relaxing on a beach.

## Tropical storm Erika

In August 2015, Dominica was badly hit by tropical storm Erika which caused massive landslides and rock falls, burying villages and blocking roads; many bridges were taken out and services (telecommunications, electricity etc) cut off. At least 31 people were killed; around 900 homes were destroyed; 14,000 people were temporarily left homeless; and the total damage amounted to CA$482 million. The village of Petite Savane suffered the most severe devastation in the country. Fortunately, the top Dominican sites were unaffected by Erika. Following the storm, Dominica has been rapidly recovering, in part due to considerable international assistance; as of December 2015, most accommodations are operational and all major roads passable. The

*Roseau, capital of Dominica.*

restoration of access to some segments of the Waitukubuli Trail was still under way at the end of 2015.

## On the banks of the Roseau River

Not even **Roseau** ❶ (pronounced Ro-zo) – with its department stores and supermarkets – can escape the impact of the island's hinterland, the essentially agricultural base of Dominican society. For every Saturday – from before first light until mid-morning – the capital (pop. 16,000) hosts market day. There, beside the mouth of the Roseau River with its backdrop of mountain and forest, is laid out the bounty of the land. From armfuls of ginger lilies to sacks of yams, from coffee beans to avocados, watercress to coconuts, all are gathered into this place of plenty, an endlessly festive endorsement of Dominica's national motto: *Apres Bondie Cest La Ter* (After God it is the land).

The capital is squeezed between the sea and the mountains, with outlying villages running up the valleys and along the coastal road. Slightly ramshackle, with narrow streets, it has

a small, 18th-century French quarter, with additional 19th-century buildings, their wood and stone houses with tin roofs supporting overhanging verandahs and gingerbread fretwork. Now that middle-class Dominicans (known in the old days as the *gros bourg*) prefer to live in the cooler suburbs up in the hills, many of the old town houses have been replaced by somewhat charmless concrete buildings. The once narrow waterfront has been extended to create the Bay Front, which includes the cruise ship pier.

The small **Dominica Museum** (Bayfront; closed until further notice) is housed in the old post office, and covers everything from island geology and economy to the history of the slave trade. Behind it is the Old Market Plaza, still used by vendors of crafts and souvenirs, containing the old, red market cross. A walk up King George V Street will lead you to the **Botanical Gardens**, the main recreational park, used for cultural events. In 1979, Hurricane David devastated the vegetation, leaving uprooted trees that are still visible, including an African baobab tree. There is still a varied collection of tropical trees, however, proof that everything in Dominica grows at a rapid rate and there is an aviary for Dominica's endangered sisserou and jacquot parrots.

## Volcanic wonders

Heading inland up the Roseau Valley for 5 miles (8km) past the Botanical Gardens, you will reach **Trafalgar Falls** ❷ (daily), two spectacular waterfalls. They are a 10-minute walk from the tropical gardens and inn at **Papillote Wilderness Retreat** (see box). You may be besieged by guides here but you will only need to engage one if you want to go farther than the viewing platform.

More active and intrepid visitors may prefer to try **canyoning** (also called rappeling or abseiling) in the river gorges, or wading, swimming, jumping over cascades, climbing or rappeling through waterfalls. The island is beginning to receive international attention – in 2015, Dominica was rated third in a ranking of islands for Best Caribbean Destination for Adventure in USA Today's 10 Best Reader's Choice Awards.

*Tour the rainforest canopy by aerial tram.*

## ISLAND GARDENS

All Dominicans are wedded to the land, from the first Amerindians, who brought with them many of the fruits and vegetables now native to the island; the maroons, who survived in the forests; and the slaves, with their provision grounds; to the colonizers, who saw that plants from other parts of the world could flourish in the Caribbean.

Dominicans welcome visitors to their lovingly tended patches, whether they be the market gardens of **Giraudel** or the botanic gardens of **Papillote Wilderness Retreat**, near Trafalgar Falls (tel: 767-448 2287; www.papillote. dm; daily; garden tour charge), where an array of tropical flowers complements the natural contours and vegetation of the rainforest. "They blend from nurtured collections into wilderness," says creator Anne Jno Baptiste.

The experienced and caring staff at Extreme Dominica (tel: 767-295 7272; www.extremedominica.com) will make sure everyone achieves their goal. Dominica's volcanic origins and numerous rivers make this one of the best canyoning destinations in the Caribbean for both beginners and experienced abseilers – you can even rappel down waterfalls onto beaches.

The magnificent **Morne Trois Pitons National Park** ❸, a Unesco World Heritage Site, covers 17,000 acres (6,800 hectares) of the southern central part of the island. Those with more than an average dose of energy can hike to the **Boiling Lake** ❹, the second-largest cauldron of bubbling hot water (220ft/66 meters wide) in the world, which lies in the heart of the park. This geological phenomenon is, in fact, a flooded fumarole, from where hot gases escape through vents in the earth's molten crust. It's a tough but extraordinary journey (an 8-hour round trip), which starts at **Titou Gorge**, close to the village of **Laudat**, 6 miles (10km) northeast of Roseau. The track plunges and rises,

*On the Waitukubuli Trail.*

crosses streams and climbs up to narrow ridges opening up into a lunar landscape of steaming vents and geysers, hot pools of boiling mud, and mineral streams streaked with blue, orange, black, and yellow. This is the **Valley of Desolation** – and beyond that the Boiling Lake itself.

## Waitukubuli National Trail

The Kalinago called the island Waitukubuli, meaning "how tall is her body," and this name has been adopted for the new **Waitukubuli National Trail** (www.dominica.dm/index.php/waitukubuli-national-trail), opened in 2011, which runs 115 miles (184km) from the far south at Scotts Head to the far north at Capucin, touching both east and west coasts, going up and down mountains, across rivers, and through forest reserves. The trail is divided into 14 segments, and local communities have been involved in clearing their own sections, renovating old slave roads, smugglers' trails, Kalinago paths, and donkey tracks, installing steps, bridges, and handrails. You can walk just one segment or the whole lot, and accommodation can be arranged in small village bed-and-breakfast places, in homestays, or on campsites.

## From west to east

The road north out of Roseau goes past Woodbridge Bay and the deep-water harbour to Canefield, where there is a small airport for local flights. You can either keep on the Leeward Coast road up to Portsmouth, or turn inland. This road, known as the Transinsular Road, is the main route to the international Douglas-Charles airport. At the Pont Cassé roundabout, take the second exit to continue on the Transinsular Road, or the third exit to skirt the northern edge of the Morne Trois Pitons National Park.

At the next junction you can turn right for **Rosalie Bay**, where there is a turtle-watch program. Green, hawksbill, and leatherback turtles all nest on the black-sand beach here, right in front of a luxury hotel.

If you turn left instead, heading for Castle Bruce, you will come to the pretty **Emerald Pool** ❺, in the heart of lush green rainforest, where you can have a picnic, then stand behind the 40ft (12-meter) waterfall, and cool off with a dip.

**Castle Bruce**, on the Atlantic coast, on a lovely bay with good views from the hills around, marks the start of Carib Territory. **L'Escalier Tête-Chien** ❻ (The Snake's Staircase), farther north along this dramatic coastline, a rock formation that looks like a stone serpent slithering up out of the ocean, features extensively in Kalinago folklore.

## A Carib settlement

Today, the surviving 2,200 Caribs/Kalinago live along the northeastern seaboard in the **Carib Territory** ❼ between Castle Bruce and Atkinson, on land set aside for them in 1903 by a well-meaning British administrator called Hesketh Bell, who thought they would die out unless they were

guaranteed a "reservation" of their own. Today, the area is not in itself distinctive but you will see houses built on stilts, and roadside stalls display the unique basketwork of the Kalinago (finely woven in three colors from a forest reed) and other handicrafts, the lingering legacy of an ancient culture. As well as growing coconuts and bananas, and making these lovely baskets, the Kalinago survive on fishing and carving.

In the Carib Territory is a model village, **Kalinago Barana Auté** (Crayfish River; tel: 767-445 7979; www.kalinago baranaaute.com; charge), where guides explain the culture and history of the people, and you can watch women weaving baskets, before a singing and dancing folklore troupe bids visitors a traditional farewell.

## The north coast

The Transinsular Road joins the coast road at Atkinson, on Pagua Bay, the northern boundary of the Carib Territory. Continue to head north, past Douglas–Charles airport, to the lovely beaches in the Calibishie area, with

*A boat trip up the Indian River.*

*Village hut in Carib territory.*

*Dominican fishermen.*

a view of Marie-Galante. Sandstone cliffs and pale sand characterize this north-facing coast. It is not so battered by the Atlantic as the eastern seaboard because of protective reefs and islands, but you still need to take care on rough days. There are several small and pleasant places to stay around here.

## Cabrits National Park

The spectacular headland of the **Cabrits National Park**, 25 miles (40km) north of Roseau and close to the second town of **Portsmouth** ❽, is covered with dry tropical forest that is typical of the Caribbean coast: bay, mahogany, sandbox, white cedar, and logwood. And there in the heat among the silent trees are the lovingly restored buildings of the 18th-century British fortifications, **Fort Shirley** ❾ (daily), one of the most important military sites in the West Indies, complete with gun batteries, storehouses, and officers' quarters. During the colonial wars, it housed up to 600 men, protecting both the north of the island and Prince Rupert Bay to the south. The Cabrits peninsula has the added attraction of

*Boiling Lake, Morne Trois Pitons National Park, Dominica.*

being surrounded by a **marine park**, rich in underwater life and excellent for snorkeling and diving.

The town of Portsmouth is of little tourist interest, but is busy with hundreds of students from the Ross University Medical School campus. South of town are the wetlands around the **Indian River**. It was into this bay that Columbus sailed on November 3, 1493, the day he first sighted Dominica, and it was the Kalinago of the Indian River area who provided subsequent European sailors with water and shelter, pineapples and cassava. The boat trip from the coastal road at the river mouth up this haunting gray-green waterway follows the route European sea captains took to greet the Carib chief. More recently the swamps and forests were used as film locations for the movie *Pirates of the Caribbean*.

## South to Soufrière

The road south out of Roseau hugs the coastline, past the dive lodges of Castle Comfort to the villages of Soufrière and Scotts Head at the tip of the island. The area from Anse Bateaux to Scotts Head peninsula encompasses the Scotts Head-Soufrière Marine Reserve. Brightly painted fishing boats are hauled up on shore and the scene, with its mountain backdrop and Martinique in the distance, is picturesque. There are plenty of buses from the capital to this area and several informal places to eat fresh fish; just ask around and you'll be directed to an unmarked hut where you can get a cheap meal.

**Soufrière Bay** is an extinct volcano and the lava chute plummets down, providing scuba divers with fascinating sites such as Crater's Edge, Scotts Head Pinnacles, and the amazing sulfur springs where the rising bubbles have been named Champagne. On Scotts Head point is an old gun emplacement where a battalion of Scots Guards used to fire warning cannon when French ships approached. This is the starting point for the Waitukubuli Trail.

# Whale-watching trips

**Dominica is known as the whale watching capital of the Caribbean: 22 species have been spotted and some of them are residents.**

One of the features of Dominica's underwater landscape is the steep drop-off very close to the shore, which provides deep water and feeding grounds for whales. Dominica is the ideal place to spot pilot whales, pygmy whales, melon-headed whales, false-killer whales, mixed pods of sperm whales and spotted whales, as well as Atlantic spinner, spotted, Rissoís, Fraser, and bottle-nosed dolphins. Between November and March, a classic whale and dolphin safari offers a 90 percent success rate in spotting whales and dolphins, and the island has become known as the whale-watching capital of the Caribbean. While six species are seen on a regular basis, 22 of the 33 species known to frequent Caribbean waters have been spotted off Dominica. Sperm whales are resident in Dominican waters and can be seen at any time of year, although November to March is best, when there are more adult males present. Scotts Head, at the southern tip of the island, is a good place to spot them from land. A bull sperm whale can grow to 67ft (20 meters); it is the largest toothed animal in the world and has the largest brain of any animal. Researchers have monitored the females and young males and have built up a picture of their family life and social interaction. They can recognize individual family members and know how they relate to each other.

The skippers have boats equipped with sonar, backed up by a lookout scanning the surface for telltale signs, including the distinctive musky, oily scent of a sperm whale. The boats head along the west coast, stopping regularly to take soundings and listen for each creature's signature tune, from the singing of humpbacks and the clicking of sperm whales to the pinging of pilot whales and the whistling of dolphins. The humpback whale is more often heard than seen, but the flipping of any great black fin tail creates a frisson of excitement, particularly as a whale can dive as deep as 6,000ft (2,000 meters). The pilot whale prefers to travel in pods of 60 while the sperm whale might be accompanied by 20ft (6-meter) calves. As for dolphins, acrobatic spotted and spinner dolphins love to surf the wake of the boat and provide ample consolation for any missed whale sightings. You may also see turtles, fish, and lots of seabirds and you get a wonderful view of the rugged beauty of the island, making the boat trip rewarding on many levels.

## Choosing a trip

Whale-watching trips of 3–4 hours are offered by several of the dive operators, including Dive Dominica (Castle Comfort Lodge; tel: 767-448 2188; www.divedominica.com; trips Sun 2pm; US$50 per person), Anchorage Dive Center (Anchorage Hotel, Castle Comfort; tel: 767-448 2638; www.anchoragehotel.dm; trips Wed, Sat 2pm, and Sun by reservation; US$50 per person), and JC Ocean Adventures (Mero Beach; tel: 767-449 6957; www.jcoceanadventures.com; trips on demand, US$50 per person for four to six people, US$100 per person for two to three people on the boat). There is also a fishing charter boat offering whale watching for small groups. Contact Captain Jerry of Island Style Fishing (tel: 767-265 0518; www.islandstylefishing.com; US$65 per person, minimum four people) for a personal and informative tour. Customized tours can be arranged, but if you want to get in the water with the whales you will have to obtain a permit from the Dominica Fisheries Division first.

*Sperm whales (Physeter catodon).*

# TROPICAL BOUNTY OF THE ISLANDS

**Flowers of the forest, fruit of the trees, vegetables from the ground – under the blazing sun there's a treasure trove of color, dazzling greenery, and food.**

Like the people of the Eastern Caribbean, the flora of the region is a great melting pot. There were plants that were here before man, plants brought by the Caribs in their canoes when they paddled from South America, those which came from Africa during slavery, and those brought from all over the world by the adventuresome Europeans.

For visitors to the region from North America or northern Europe, familiar only with expensive house-plants nurtured in a centrally heated room or the exotic fruit and vegetable section in the supermarket, the sudden sight of these magnificent plants growing naturally in a tropical landscape is intoxicating.

## Market day

Venture into a local market in the rainier, more mountainous islands and explore the unfamiliar: the knobbly soursop (it makes an excellent juice); the pale green christophene or cho-cho of the squash family; tiny green and red peppers, some fiendishly hot. Drier islands will not have such a range, but there will be "ground provisions" – the root vegetables, such as yams, which are part of the staple diet. And there are the cut flowers: the amazing red or pink gingers, artificial-looking anthurium, and dramatic torch gingers. Everyone grows something somewhere.

And while there are the formal botanical gardens, and gardens of former estate houses to visit, don't forget to admire the ordinary backyard garden growing an amazing range of vegetables, fruit, and exotic flowers, often in just a tiny space.

*The startling flower of the shaving bush tree, or Bombax ellipticum, native to Mexico but grown in Florida and the Caribbean.*

*The coconut tree is one of many useful varieties of palm that grow throughout the Caribbean.*

*The exquisite torch lilly, also called the wax rose, torch ginger, or ginger lily, can be found from Costa Rica to Barbados.*

*Vanilla stems climb a coconut tree near the water.*

## SPICE AND ALL THINGS NICE

There is a sweetness in the Caribbean air which romantics might attribute to spice, and in particular to the vanilla plant, a straggly plant from the orchid family with an exquisite-smelling flower that opens only for a few hours in the morning. Pollinating is done by hand and the resulting pods give the much sought-after vanilla flavor.

Although spices such as vanilla and nutmeg were once an important export crop, most arrived in the Caribbean in the 18th century from the Far East "spice islands". Once, Grenada grew some 25 percent of the world's nutmeg. You can still see the warehouses at Gouyave on the west coast where the spice is sorted. The outer lacy red covering is ground down into a powder and becomes mace. Visit local markets throughout the region for supplies of nutmeg and cinnamon (dried strips of bark), pale gold rhizomes of ginger, black pepper (grown on a vine), and cloves (dried flower buds).

*Coffee is grown throughout Central America and the mountainous islands of the Caribbean.*

*The tropical fruits of the Caribbean have been delighting visitors for centuries.*

*Nutmeg, once stripped of its red lace covering of mace and the outer shell, can be ground for use in cooking or as an essential oil in perfumes and pharmaceuticals.*

Les Anses d'Arlet.

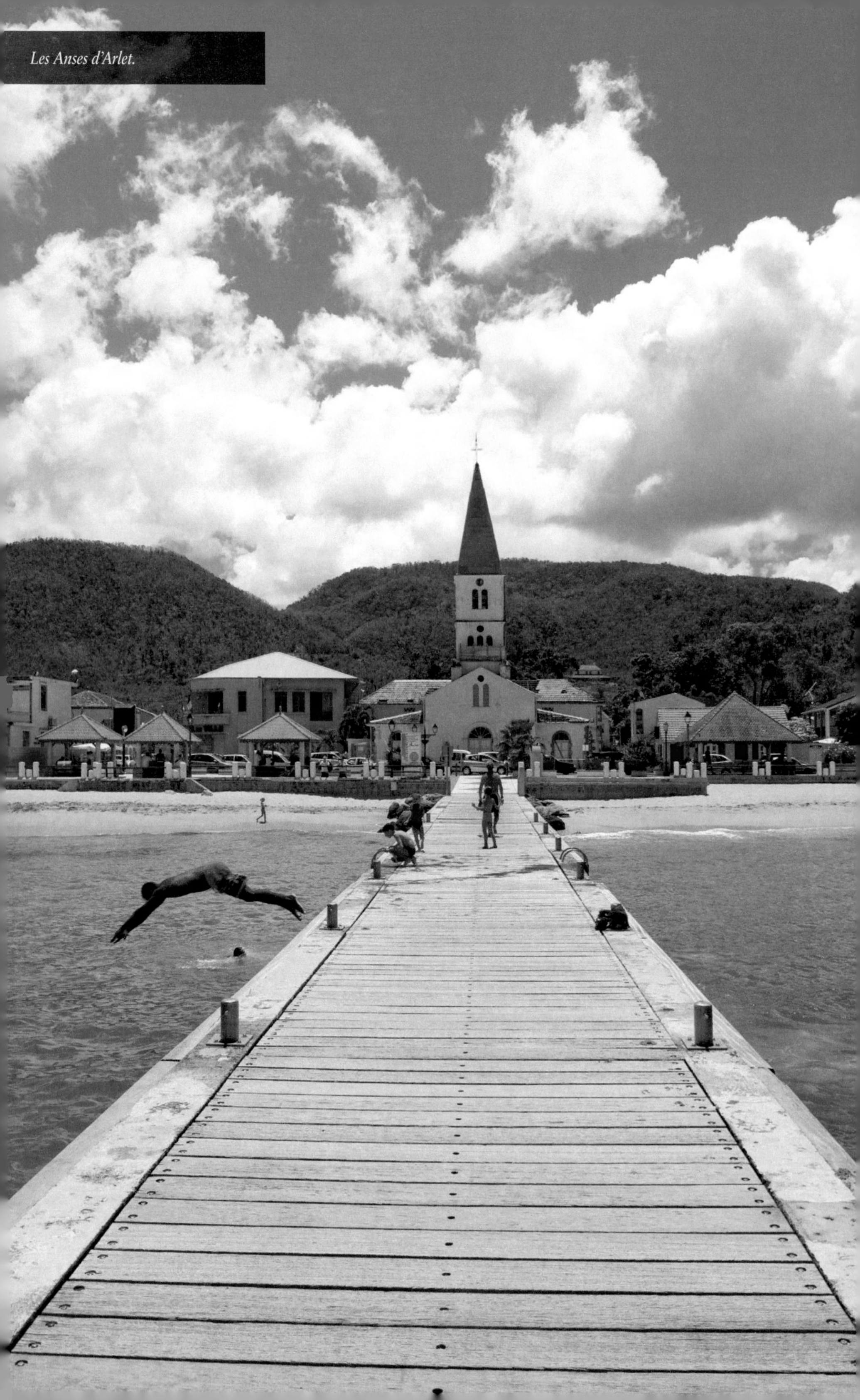

# MARTINIQUE

A piece of France transported to the tropics, this beautiful, mountainous island, famous for its exotic flowers, exudes a sense of sophistication from the black and white beaches to the rainforest.

Martinique
Caribbean
Sea

**W**hen Christopher Columbus landed on Martinique in 1502, he commented, "It is the best, the most fertile, the softest, the most even, the most charming spot in the world. It is the most beautiful thing I have ever seen. My eyes never tire of contemplating such greenery." But he continued on his travels and another century went by before the first French settlers arrived in 1635, led by the corsair Pierre Belain d'Esnambuc, to found St-Pierre and begin the colonization of the island.

## Tropical France

Apart from a few short-lived occupations by the British, Martinique has remained steadfastly French. The first impression visitors have of the island is of a tropical France: amid the palm-fringed beaches, hillside banana plantations, valleys of pineapples, and volcanic mountains, the essence of the motherland can be found in the *boulangeries*, the pavement cafés, the noisy mopeds, the hypermarkets, and Parisian shops in the capital, Fort-de-France. Trinidadian writer V.S. Naipaul wrote in *The Middle Passage* (1962): "Unlike the other islands, which have one main town to which everything gravitates, Martinique is full of little French villages each with its church, *mairie* and war memorial…"

A mountainous island of 417 sq miles (1,085 sq km) – 40 miles (65km)

at its longest, 19 miles (31km) at its widest – its contours ascend gradually from an irregular coastline and culminate dramatically, in the north in Montagne Pelée (4,583ft/1,397 meters), the now-dormant volcano that erupted with a shattering violence in 1902. Pelée is linked to other mountains – Les Pitons du Carbet (3,923ft/1,205 meters) in the center, and La Montagne du Vauclin (1,653ft/504 meters) in the south – by a series of gentler hills, or *mornes*.

Martinique is a largely agricultural island with a racially mixed population

**Main Attractions**

Jardins de Balata
St-Pierre
Gorges de la Falaise
Musée du Rhum St-James
Musée de la Pagerie
Marin
La Plage des Salines

*The coastline at Le Diamant.*

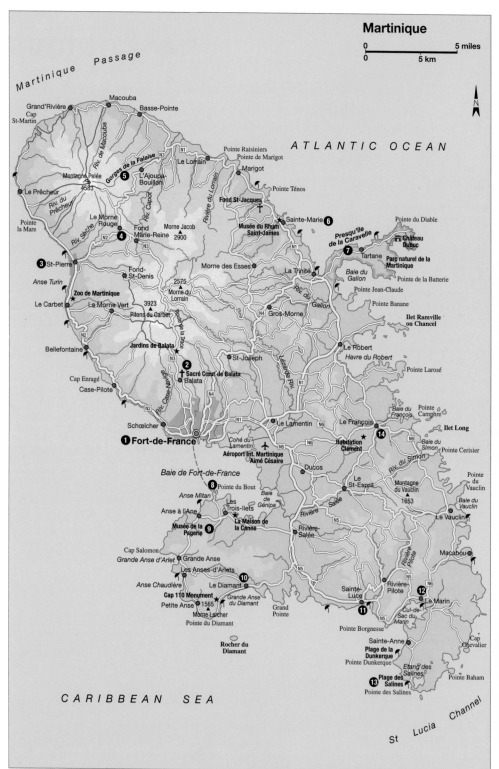

# Martinique

Martinique Passage

ATLANTIC OCEAN

CARIBBEAN SEA

St Lucia Channel

Grand'Rivière
Cap St-Martin
Macouba
Basse-Pointe
Pointe Raisiniers
Pointe de Marigot
Le Lorrain
Marigot
Pointe Ténos
Montagne Pelée
4583
**5** L'Ajoupa-Bouillon
Le Prêcheur
Pointe la Mare
Riv. du Prêcheur
Riv. Sèche
Le Morne Rouge
**4** Fond Marie-Reine
Morne Jacob
2900
Fond St-Jacques
Musée du Rhum Saint-James
Sainte-Marie **6**
Pointe du Diable
Presqu'île de la Caravelle
Château Dubuc
Tartane **7**
Parc naturel de la Martinique
**3** St-Pierre
Anse Turin
Morne des Esses
La Trinité
Baie du Galion
Pointe de la Batterie
Fond-St-Denis
2575
Morne du Lorrain
Pointe Jean-Claude
Le Carbet
Zoo de Martinique
Le Morne Vert
3923
Pitons du Carbet
Pointe Banane
N4 Gros-Morne
Ilet Ramville ou Chancel
Jardins de Balata
St-Joseph
Le Robert
Havre du Robert
Cap Enragé
Case-Pilote
**2** Sacré Cœur de Balata
Balata
Pointe Larosé
Bellefontaine
Schœlcher
**1** Fort-de-France
Cohé du Lamentin
Le Lamentin
Le François **14**
Baie du François
Pointe Camphre
Ilet Long
Aéroport Int. Martinique Aimé Césaire
Habitation Clément
Baie du Simon
Pointe Cerisier
Ducos
Baie de Fort-de-France
**8** Pointe du Bout
Anse Mitan
Anse à l'Ane
Les Trois-Ilets
Baie de Génipa
Le St-Esprit
Montagne du Vauclin
1653
Pointe du Vauclin
Baie du Vauclin
Le Vauclin
**9** Musée de la Pagerie
La Maison de la Canne
Rivière-Salée
Cap Salomon
Grande Anse d'Arlet
Grande Anse
Les Anses-d'Arlets
Macabou
Anse Chaudière
Cap 110 Monument
Petite Anse
1565
Le Diamant **10**
Grande Anse du Diamant
Morne Larcher
Pointe du Diamant
Grand Pointe
Rivière-Pilote
**12** Le Marin
Sainte-Luce
**11**
Cul-de-Sac du Marin
Pointe Borgnesse
Rocher du Diamant
Sainte-Anne
Plage de la Dunkerque
Pointe Dunkerque
Etang des Salines
Cap Chevalier
Pointe Baham
**13** Plage des Salines
Pointe des Salines

0 — 5 miles
0 — 5 km

N

of 386,000. Like the other Caribbean islands, it has been through the horrors of colonialism and slavery; but while most of the British West Indies have sought their own paths in independence, Martinique, with its sister island of Guadeloupe (see page 187), has been absorbed politically and economically into France as a full *département d'outremer* (overseas department) and *région* of the republic.

## Escape from the Revolution

The first French settlers wasted no time in establishing sugar plantations, despite resistance from the Carib population, who moved to the Atlantic coast until they were eventually wiped out by more sophisticated French weaponry and unfamiliar diseases. Slaves were imported and the economy thrived, driven by the *békés*, the traditional white elite. In 1789, at the onset of the French Revolution, their security was threatened by slave unrest and they invited the British to occupy the island to preserve the status quo. As a result, between 1794 and 1802,

unlike Guadeloupe, Martinique's *békés* avoided the guillotine.

After Emancipation in 1848, fought for by French abolitionist Victor Schoelcher, the sugar industry went into decline, although remaining the island's main export with its liquid-gold by-product, rum. Nevertheless, St-Pierre, the capital, grew into a cultural center with a "saucy" reputation, until it was obliterated on May 8, 1902, when a volcanic eruption killed the entire population of 30,000.

Supporters of the Vichy government in World War II, the Martinicans were deprived of their essential imports by the Allied naval blockade and learned to live off their natural resources. Afterward, the black radical Martinican poet Aimé Césaire, who had been educated in Paris and was a member of the French Communist Party, was elected both mayor of the new capital, Fort-de-France, and *député* to the French Assembly on a tide of anti-*béké* feeling. He and many others (not all Communists) were keen to divert power from the local aristocracy to the republic.

*Horseback-riding at Anse Grosse Roche.*

## Fort-de-France

Martinique's capital, **Fort-de-France** ❶, is large by island standards and, with a population of more than 85,000, it is thronged with people, traffic, and noise. If there are cruise ships in port, it can be positively heaving in the old quarter by the waterfront. Like most Caribbean ports, Fort-de-France has had its fair share of fires, earthquakes, and other natural disasters, so there are many modern structures among the more interesting 19th-century (and earlier) buildings. What hasn't changed, however, is the grid of narrow streets, which makes driving a nightmare and walking a pleasure. While the center has a Caribbean atmosphere, highways, office blocks, industrial centers, shopping malls, and concrete apartment blocks spread all the way out to the airport and beyond, emphasizing that this is France, in all but name and climate.

The centerpiece of the town is **La Savane**, a 12-acre (5-hectare) park of lawn, shady palms, footpaths and benches. At the northern end of La Savane stands the headless statue of Napoléon's Joséphine, who was born at Les Trois-Ilets across the Baie de Fort-de-France. Her pedestal shows a relief of Napoléon about to crown her, plus her date of birth (June 23, 1763) and the date of her marriage (May 9, 1796). Many believe that she was behind her husband's decision to reintroduce slavery in 1802 after the Revolutionary Convention banned it in 1794, hence the monument's decapitation. And it remains defaced, a potent symbol of Martinique's tortured past. A second statue is of Pierre Belain d'Esnambuc, the Norman nobleman who led the first French settlers in 1635.

## Constructions of metal

On the northwest corner of La Savane is the magnificent **Bibliothèque Schoelcher** (rue de la Liberté; Mon 1–5.30pm, Tue–Thur 8.30am–5.30pm, Fri 8.30am–5pm, Sat 8.30am–noon; free), a colorful Baroque building crazy with Roman, Egyptian, and majolican tiles, and named for the man most responsible for the final abolition of slavery in the French West Indies. The library contains the abolitionist Schoelcher's private collection

*Schoelcher Library, Martinque.*

*Proud to parade at the Carnaval de la Martinique.*

of books, and often stages exhibitions. Designed by Henri Picq, a contemporary of Gustav Eiffel, it was built of metal in Paris in 1887, then shipped out to Martinique piece by piece.

**Cathédrale St-Louis**, on rue Schoelcher a few minutes away, is another of his metal constructions, built in 1895 to withstand the fiercest hurricanes and earthquakes. Known as the "iron cathedral," its steel-reinforced spire rises 200ft (60 meters) into the sky and it has some fine stained-glass windows.

On the west side of La Savane is the **Musée d'Archéologie et de Préhistoire** (Mon 1–5pm, Tue–Fri 8am–5pm, Sat 9am–5pm; free on the last Sat of each month) with three floors of remnants from Taino and Carib Amerindian tribes. It has the finest collection of pre-Columbian artifacts in the Caribbean: stone, shell, and ceramic.

Southeast of La Savane, **Fort St-Louis**, over the bay, was originally built in 1640 and added to over the years. The fort is still used as a military base and is closed to visitors, except on special occasions such as the annual Journées du Patrimoine, when all the island's historical monuments are open to the public free of charge. These Heritage Days are held over the third weekend in September.

Downtown can be a hot, humid, traffic-dominated place, but it is dotted with colorful street markets. The **Marché aux Poissons** (Fish Market), by Place Clemenceau and next to the river, is the scene of constant activity, as fishermen unload their catch from small boats. In surrounding streets there are several other less pungent markets specializing in flowers, fruit, and vegetables. The **Grand Marché** on rue Blénac is the most tourist-oriented and is full of attractively packaged spices and sauces; it is open every day, all day, but busiest on Friday afternoon and Saturday.

## North to higher ground

Heading for the hills, north out of town, you pass through the prosperous suburb of Didier and, 1 mile (1.5km) or so farther on, join the spectacular **Route de la Trace**, or N3, which zigzags across the mountainous spine of the island to Morne Rouge. Originally carved out by Jesuits, it runs through thick and varied

*The market in Fort-de-France.*

---

**RACIAL HOT POT**

Although the majority of Martinicans can trace their ancestry back to African slaves, a large proportion are descended from East Indian laborers who arrived after the abolition of slavery. Of Tamil origin, they now make up some 5–10 percent of the population. There are also small communities of Syrians, Lebanese and Chinese, in addition to the *békés*, descended from the first French and British settlers and often still the landowning class.

Creole cuisine reflects this mix of cultures, with many dishes containing elements from all of them. One dish that appears to take ingredients from everywhere is the Colombo, a curry of chicken, meat or fish with vegetables, spiced with a masala of Tamil origin, enlivened by tamarind, wine and/or rum, coconut milk, lime juice and cassava.

vegetation with explosions of color from flowering plants. You may do a double-take at the sight of **Sacré Coeur de Balata** ❷ peering out of the hillside, as the church is a copy in miniature of the Sacré Coeur in Paris, but less white, because of the greater humidity of the tropical rainforest.

Nearby, the **Jardins de Balata** (Balata Botanical Garden; tel: 596-596-644 873; www.jardindebalata.fr; daily 9am–6pm, last entry 4.30pm) are tropical gardens with a grand view over Fort-de-France to Trois-Ilets. At their best, after the rainy season at the end of the year, they have a stunning collection of anthuriums, as well as an array of exotic trees and shrubs. Jewel-like hummingbirds flit among the flowers, while lizards scuttle along the paths. Indeed, Martinique has a wealth of parks and gardens to discover – more than 30 dotted around the island.

## A Caribbean Pompeii

*The ruins of Rue Victor Hugo and La Place Du Mouilage, Martinque, 1902.*

At Le Morne Rouge, take the left fork on the N2 for 5 miles (8km) to descend to the Caribbean and the ghost town hugging the coast: **St-Pierre** ❸, the former cultural and economic center of Martinique that was once known as the "little Paris of the West Indies." Behind looms **Montagne Pelée**, the sleeping volcano (now constantly monitored) that, after grumbling for a few days, finally awoke on May 8, 1902, at 7.50am, in a fireball of seething lava and superheated gases. Fires erupted in the town and the sea boiled. Within seconds, 30,000 people were dead. On entering the town, the road passes the cemetery where a large white mausoleum contains the victims' remains.

St-Pierre never recovered. Ruins offer their mute testimony: the burned, broken stone walls of seaside warehouses, the foundations and stairways that lead nowhere, the vanished theater, and on the hill that rises behind it the cell of the sole survivor, Antoine Ciparis, a drunkard locked away the day before and protected by the strength of his dungeon. Ciparis ended up traveling the US in a replica of his cell with the Barnum & Bailey circus.

A new town has grown among the rubble of the old, and there are cafés and restaurants to refresh the curious visitor.

While the memory of the eruption is poignant, St-Pierre is not a gloomy place, and the local tourist office organizes fascinating tours of the ruins. The **Musée Vulcanologique** (tel: 596-596-781 516; daily 9am–5pm), in rue Victor-Hugo, presents evidence of the disaster: large clumps of nails and screws fused by heat, melted bottles, a large church bell deformed by fire, containers of scorched food. In the sunlight outside, knowing that deep down Pelée still seethes, it is a chilling display.

On the coast, south of St-Pierre, is the popular black-sand beach, **Anse Turin**, where the artist Paul Gauguin stayed in 1887 before he went to Tahiti. The **Centre d'Interprétation Paul Gauguin** (former Musée Gauguin; to reopen in 2016) has copies of his letters and works, and also a collection of creole costumes, showing the different dresses and headgear, with an explanation of their significance. **Le Carbet**, the next town south, is where Columbus is thought to have landed. Diving and other water sports are available and there are pleasant restaurants on the beach.

On the outskirts of the town is the **Zoo de Martinique** (www.zoodemartinique.com; daily 9am–6pm, last entry 4.30pm), a beautiful, colorful zoological and botanical garden created on the **Habitation Latouche**. The plantation was established in 1643, making it one of the oldest sugar estates, but destroyed in 1902 by the volcano. Ruins of plantation buildings can be seen, including a viaduct and waterwheel that powered the sugar mill.

## The Gorges de la Falaise

From **Le Morne Rouge** ❹ at the foot of Mont Pelée, the Route de la Trace (N3) heads northeast to the Atlantic coast. After about a mile (1.5km), a rough road leads to within 1,600ft (490 meters) of the volcano summit, where the mountain air is cool. Only experienced climbers with guides should attempt the peak: it rains a lot and is full of hidden dangers. However, there are many trails suitable for different levels of fitness and experience, leading from the village around the mountain. The next town is L'Ajoupa Bouillon on the slopes of Mont Pelée. Look for signs: a hike along the River Falaise leads to the **Gorges de la Falaise** ❺ (daily 8am–5.30pm, closed after heavy rain; charge includes a guide), a series of impressive canyons and dramatic waterfalls in the forest, with trailing lianas and overhanging ferns. Take a swimsuit and shoes with a good grip that can get wet. This is also one of several locations for canyoning along the rivers coming down from Mount Pelée, cutting gorges as they descend to the sea (contact Bureau de la Randonnée et du Canyoning, tel: 596-596 550 479; http://bureau-rando-martinique.com).

## The Rum Museum

Taking the dramatic Atlantic coast road, peppered with beautiful beaches, battered by an angry sea (swimming is dangerous), it is worth stopping off in **Sainte-Marie** ❻ to visit the **Musée du Rhum Saint-James** (www.rhum-saintjames.com; daily 9am–5pm; free) in the St-James rum distillery. Here, exhibits

*Tastings at the Musée du Rhum Saint-James.*

*Islanders are proud of their fine rum.*

*La Maison du Bagnard.*

tell the story of sugar and rum from 1765, and there is plenty to sample and buy. Martinican rum is considered to be among the finest in the world. In 1996 it was awarded the AOC *(Appellation d'Origine Contrôllée)* label, bestowed only on fine French vintages. Rum flavors vary according to climate and soil conditions and all the island's distilleries offer *dégustation*, or rum tasting. There is a little train for visitors, **Le Train des Plantations** (daily; charge) pulled by a tractor, which will take you through the sugar-cane and banana plantations to the **Musée de la Banane** (http://museedelabanane.fr daily 9am–4.30pm) on a working estate, Habitation Limbé. Here you can find out all about the production, packaging, and export of bananas. Former workers' huts are now shops and there are pleasant gardens

The road meanders on down past **La Trinité** to the 8-mile (13km)-long **Presqu'île de la Caravelle** ❼ which, protected by the Parc Naturel de la Martinique, is crisscrossed by nature trails. There are plenty of good beaches offering an assortment of water sports,

particularly surfing. At its tip are the ruins of **Château Dubuc** (daily 9am–4.30pm), a sugar estate rich in legends of smugglers and slavery.

## Joséphine and the south

It takes 15 minutes for the *navettes* or *vadettes* (half-hourly from the quay in front of La Savane) to cross the Baie de Fort-de-France to **Pointe du Bout** ❽, where they tie up in another Martinique. Beaches here are pristine, with smart yachts moored in the marina, restaurants, the Créole Village Shopping Plaza, and a cluster of luxury hotels.

Taxis await to drive you to the **Musée de la Pagerie** ❾ (Tue–Fri 9am–4.30pm, Sat–Sun 9.30am–2pm) just outside Les Trois-Ilets. A rusted metal sign points the way to the birthplace of Empress Joséphine. Marie-Josèphe Rose Tascher de la Pagerie, later rechristened Joséphine by her famous husband, left Martinique for Paris in 1779 to marry the Viscount of Beauharnais. In 1796, two years after the viscount's death by guillotine during the French Revolution, she married Napoléon Bonaparte.

The main village in this area is **Les Trois-Ilets**, where the sidewalks and roofs are made from clay bricks and tiles manufactured at the Village de la Poterie de Trois-Ilets (tel: 596-596-680 344; www.pti-sa.com; Mon–Sat most workshops 9am–6pm). One mile (1.5km) east of Les Trois-Ilets, at Pointe Vatable, is the sugar-cane museum, **La Maison de la Canne** (Tue–Wed 8.30am–5.30pm, Fri–Sat 8.30–5pm, Sun 9am–5pm), within the walls of an old distillery. Machinery and models are used to great effect to show the history of the sugar industry.

Across the southwestern peninsula, on the Caribbean coast, the pretty village of **Les Anses d'Arlets** has a fine sandy beach dotted with restaurants. Next is Petite Anse, and a few miles and many bends later is **Le Diamant** ⑩, a larger village with a good choice of hotels and restaurants and a long beach of soft, white sand. At **Anse Cafard** at the western end of Le Diamant stands the *cap 110* sculpture by local artist Laurent Valère. Overlooking the sea where a slave ship sank in 1830, the 15 large bowed figures are a memorial to the 300 enslaved Africans who perished in the wreck; the sculpture also commemorates the 150th anniversary of the French abolition of slavery.

About a mile out to sea is the unmistakable hump of the **Rocher du Diamant** (Diamond Rock), an outcrop of volcanic stone which, curiously, was once a small part of the British Empire. In 1805, a party of 100 British soldiers, complete with cannons, took possession of the rock to control the channel between Martinique and St Lucia. After 18 months the French ejected them from their uncomfortable position, which they had named HMS *Diamond*.

## Southern splendor

The best beaches in Martinique are on the southern coast. In Diamant, Grand Anse is a lovely stretch of sand but the sea can be treacherous. For calmer waters, head towards **Sainte-Luce** ⑪, the neighboring village, where several beaches are tucked away in calm coves. Further along is **Le Marin** ⑫, a busy seaside town and the center of all yachting activity. Marin has a pleasant, arty feel; on the seafront, restaurants and bars add to the atmosphere with live music and late-night sessions.

**Plage des Salines** ⑬, the finest stretch of white-sand beach and calm turquoise sea on the island, wraps itself for miles around Sainte-Anne and the surrounding littoral forest. Further up the Atlantic coast, **Le François** ⑭ is protected by an immense barrier reef; maritime excursions offer picnics on the islets in the shallow bay. Martinicans say you have not really visited the island until you have drunk a midday Ti-punch in the Baignade de Josephine, a stretch of clear, shallow water between two islands. Le François is also home to **Habitation Clément** (www.rhum-clement.com; daily 9.30am–5pm), a plantation house with a rum distillery and aging facilities producing Rhum Clément; an art gallery; and an arboretum with an important palm tree collection containing specimens from all over the world. If you are going to do a little tasting be aware that traffic police carry out regular patrols.

*Plage des Salines.*

*The magnificent Pitons.*

# ST LUCIA

Plenty of sandy beaches, lush, green, forest-clad mountains, reserves protecting the environment on and offshore, and activities to suit any visitor, beautiful St Lucia has it all.

Caribbean Sea
St Lucia

Fought over for more than 200 years, St Lucia (Loo-sha), lying between Martinique to the north and St Vincent in the south, has earned the grand-sounding title "Helen of the West Indies." A veritable treasure during colonial times for its strategic position, and caught in a power struggle between the British and French, this is an incredibly beautiful and enchanting island, a mixture of luxuriant tropical vegetation on a mountainous landscape, stunning beaches, and typically creole culture.

The most spectacular feature is the Pitons. The two majestic, cone-shaped peaks on the southwest coast, coated with lush forest, appear on the covers of holiday brochures and postcards all over the world. Rising straight out of the Caribbean Sea to a height of 2,600ft (795 meters), these twin peaks are proof of St Lucia's volcanic creation. So is the sand, which shimmers in all kinds of shades: snow-white, cream, anthracite gray, and even black.

But green is the color that predominates as you go inland. At least one-fifth of the 238 sq mile (617 sq km) island is covered by a thick carpet of luxuriant tropical rainforest, home to an assortment of wildlife such as the St Lucia parrot (*Amazona versicolor*) and pygmy gecko, and with orchids, anthurium, and the heavily

scented frangipani just growing wild. The highest peak, Mount Gimie (3,117ft/950 meters), is almost permanently hung with cloud, which provides the fertile interior, the rivers and streams with enough water the whole year round. Banana plantations sweep down to the craggy east coast, dramatically buffeted by the wild Atlantic. Until the 1980s, bananas were export article number one. Since then, tourism has outstripped all other income sources, and now more than 330,000 visitors holiday on St Lucia each year,

**Main Attractions**
Pigeon Island National Landmark
Fond Latislab Creole Park
The Pitons
Anse Chastanet Marine Park
Sulfur Springs
Diamond Botanical Gardens
Edmund Forest Reserve
Maria Islands Nature Reserve

*Biking on St Lucia.*

*Among the meanings embedded in the St Lucian flag, the black and the white stand for the two races, living and working in unity.*

while 650,000 cruise ship passengers also visit.

## Colorful changes of flag

St Lucia's history is typical of the region. Columbus and the Spanish probably noticed the Pitons from a distance, but they were far too busy heading for South America to bother with the island. After that the Caribs used guerrilla warfare to defend their Hewanorra (Land of Iguanas) against half-hearted attempts at invasion by the British and Dutch. It was only in 1650 that some French settlers finally managed to establish a long-term base on the second-largest of the Windward Islands.

In the years that followed, the French flag and the Union Jack alternated with each other 14 times, until the island finally became British for good in 1814. In 1979, the island was granted independence while remaining within the British Commonwealth.

However, French cultural influences have remained a strong factor in St Lucia. English is the official language but the mother tongue is a melodic creole patois – a mixture of West African influences and French – known as kwéyòl, which is spoken in formal and informal arenas. A good 75 percent of inhabitants are Roman Catholic rather than Anglican and, although cricket is played here as elsewhere in the British Caribbean, the people also love dancing the *beguine* from Martinique.

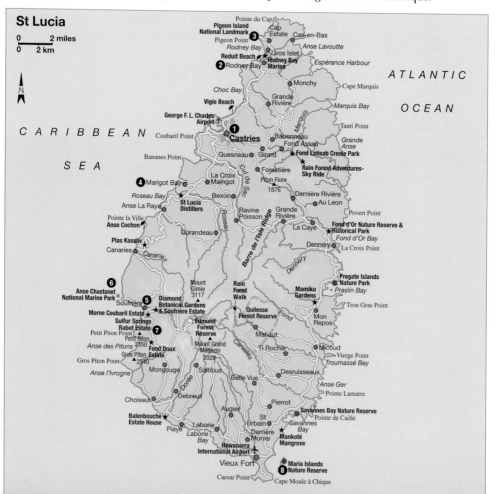

# Castries

Apart from its attractive position in the natural harbor, **Castries ❶** (pop. 70,000), St Lucia's modern capital, has few interesting sights. The town was named after the French naval minister Marechal de Castries, who did a great deal to help the colony's economic development at the end of the 18th century. In 1927 and 1948 two major fires reduced the entire old part of the town to ashes and most of the rebuilding was done in concrete. A stroll through the center, however, provides an exciting glimpse of everyday Caribbean life.

On Friday and Saturday the large **Central Market** heaves with a crowd of country folk, townies, and visitors. Local farmers pile up the fruits of their labors – rose-colored sweet potatoes, papayas, bananas, heavy breadfruit, and all the aromatic spices that flourish in the fertile volcanic soil. Craftsmen lay out their work alongside the fishermen's catch, and men play dominoes as bystanders noisily egg them on.

On the corner of Laborie and Micoud streets is the Roman Catholic cathedral, the **Minor Basilica of the Immaculate Conception** (daily, closed only when Mass is in progress), whose interior walls are lined with colorful murals by the acclaimed St Lucian artist Dunstan St Omer. In 2005, St Omer and his son, Giovanni, created 12 magnificent stained-glass windows for the cathedral, and yellow light floods the building via decorative windows in the ceiling. As you leave the cathedral on Laborie Street, to your left is Brazil Street, which has several wooden buildings with gingerbread fretwork and balconies dating back to the late 19th century, the only ones of their kind to survive Castries' last great fire in 1948.

The main square, bounded by Brazil, Laborie, Micoud, and Bourbon streets, is a well-kept, small green space with a shady, 400-year-old saman tree. Open-air concerts are often held here. Initially called the Place d'Armes in the 18th century, it is now **Derek Walcott Square**, in honor of the St Lucian poet and playwright, who won the Nobel Prize for literature in 1992. Near the bandstand there are busts of Walcott

**FACT**

The St Lucia Jazz Festival (www.stlucia.jazz. org) every May is claimed to be the most successful in the Caribbean, drawing around 18,000 people. Started in 1992 to fill hotel rooms in low season, the event attracts scores of international big names.

*The port of Castries, St Lucia.*

and another eminent St Lucian, Sir Arthur Lewis, who won the Nobel Prize for Economics.

The very best view of the town and island is from Fort Charlotte on **Morne Fortune**, or the "Hill of Luck," 3 miles (5km) south of Castries. Renovated and used as a college, the fort was built by the French and British in the 18th century and has witnessed many a battle between the two colonial powers. Today, you can watch the larger-than-life cruise ships jostle for the prime spot in the port next to **Pointe Seraphine** and **La Place Carenage** duty-free shopping centers.

## Beaches and nightlife in the north

The coastal region to the north of Castries is the island's foremost resort area, with sheltered, white-sand bays, hotels, quaint fishing communities, a marina, shopping malls, and historic landmarks. In the northeast, turtles nest, while rural life inland continues much as it has for generations.

The focus of tourist activity is the growing village of **Rodney Bay** ❷. This former US military base now features a 1,000-berth marina, many hotels, apartments, restaurants, and bars for a vibrant nightlife, as well as a casino and two shopping malls with supermarkets and designer clothes outlets. When the Atlantic Rally for Cruisers (ARC) completes the trans-atlantic crossing just before Christmas, the area heaves with party-goers celebrating the ships' safe arrival. **Reduit Beach**, at the end of the village, is one of the best stretches of sand on the island and you can rent sunloungers, umbrellas, and water sports equipment.

There's a very special kind of party every Friday night from 10pm when the otherwise rather sleepy fishing village of **Gros Islet**, on the north side of the marina, wakes up for a "jump-up" lasting well into the early hours. Anyone can come, and the smell of grilled chicken fills the streets, together with the steady thump from sound systems. Everyone loves a party on St Lucia, so join

*Locals at the market in Castries, St Lucia.*

in and enjoy it, but keep an eye on your possessions.

Connected to the mainland by a causeway near Gros Islet is the **Pigeon Island National Landmark** ❸ (tel: 758-452 5005; www.slunatrust.org; daily 9am–5pm), with inviting beaches and well-tended footpaths. First inhabited by Amerindians, it was later the haunt of French pirates before Admiral George Rodney established his naval outpost here in 1780. The ruins of **Fort Rodney** commemorate the admiral's departure from here in 1782 just before he inflicted his crushing defeat on the French at the Battle of the Saintes, off the coast of Guadeloupe. If you climb up to Signal Peak you will see the strategic advantage of Pigeon Island, with an amazing view all along the west coast of St Lucia and across to Martinique.

Most of the fortress buildings have been left in ruins. The Officers' Mess is the only building to have been renovated, now used as the headquarters of the **St Lucia National Trust**, a small interpretive center, and a pub, which remains open after the park has closed. The park is popular as a wedding venue, and also hosts concerts during the St Lucia Jazz Festival in May.

North of Gros Islet is **Cap Estate**, once heavily forested, then cleared for tobacco and sugar before becoming a desirable residential area around the St Lucia Golf and Country Club (tel: 758-450 8523; www.stluciagolf.com). The far north of St Lucia is the driest part of the island and much of the coast is rocky and rough. The northwest has some pretty beaches in bays where there is usually a single hotel.

On the northeast, Atlantic, side of the island is **Cas-en-Bas**, where there are some rough-and-ready beaches with lots of wind, making the bay popular with windsurfers and kitesurfers. There are coastal paths that offer some nice hiking too.

## Inland attractions

There are lots of activities in the north to tempt you away from the beach to get a feel for the rural interior with its pretty villages dotted between the forested hills. **Fond**

**TIP**

Several boat tours sail down the west coast to Soufrière for lunch and a visit to the volcano, Diamond Falls, and the Botanical Gardens, stopping for a swim and snorkel on the way back.

*Rodney Bay, St Lucia.*

St Lucian bananas are shipped to the UK.

**Latisab Creole Park** (Fond Assau; tel: 758-450 5461; www.fondlatisab creolepark.com; tours by appointment) is a few miles southeast of **Babonneau** via narrow country lanes. The 11-acre (4-hectare) working farm, which cultivates nutmeg, cocoa, and cinnamon and produces its own honey, maintains many aspects of traditional St Lucian culture, some aspects of which are Amerindian, and practices farm techniques that have been passed on from father to son. For example, much communication is done using the ancient art of drumming. Visitors can watch log sawing done to the beating of drums accompanied by a *chak chak* band (named after the sound made by a local instrument). While sawing, the men sing kwéyòl folk songs, accompanied by the band and the drum beats, which help to maintain rhythm and momentum. You can also see local people crayfishing, using traditional bamboo pots, and making cassava bread and *farine* – a fine cassava flour produced from the root vegetable grown on the estate.

*Zip-line through the forest for an adrenaline rush.*

Down the road from Fond Latisab, in Chassin, at the foot of La Sorcière hill, is the popular **Rain Forest Adventures – Sky Rides** (tel: 758-458 5151; www.rainforest adventure.com; Dec–May Tue–Sun). During a 2,5-hour tour, visitors are transported high above the forest in a gondola, offering a bird's-eye view as they glide through the forest canopy. After the ride you can buckle up to zip-line through the forest, an adrenaline rush which is great fun, and only basic levels of fitness and health are required.

## The land of Bounty

Beyond Morne Fortune south of Castries, the road twists and turns and goes up and down through spectacular scenery to **Marigot Bay ❹**, 8 miles (13km) away, up mountains and down past the broad banana plantations of the Roseau Valley, which provide bananas for British supermarkets. Yachties flock to the natural harbor and large marina, where once Admiral Rodney bamboozled the French by disguising his fleet with palm fronds;

and you can enjoy a drink in Doolittle's, which is a boat ride across the bay, and named for the 1966 movie *Dr Doolittle* which was shot here.

The Roseau Valley is now one of the main banana-growing areas on the island, but before bananas were planted the land was given over to sugar cane. Some of that sugar went into producing rum, and although the sugar industry has disappeared, rum is still important. You can visit **St Lucia Distillers** (tel: 758-456 3148; www.stluciarums. com; Mon–Fri 9am–3pm; reservations essential, 24 hours in advance) which produces a wide selection of rums and liqueurs from imported Guyanese molasses. There is an extensive buffet of some 20 rums for tasting after the tour and, of course, there's a shop. Bounty is the dark rum you will most commonly see on the island, while Cristal is the white rum used in cocktails.

## Local treats

The main road now winds its way south across the mountains in a series of hair-raising hairpins; several rivers have formed natural harbor bays along the coast, and the villages of **Anse La Raye** and **Canaries** are filled with colorfully painted fishermen's houses. Every Friday night, Anse La Raye residents put on a "fish fry" accompanied by DJs and loud music in the streets. Stallholders set up coal pots and barbecues in front of the fishermen's huts and lay out tables for people keen to try the catch of the day, and even lobster when in season, washed down with a Piton beer.

Another local culinary treat is on offer just before you reach Canaries. At a curve where the road widens is **Plas Kassav** (tel: 758-459 4050; daily 8.30am–7 or 8pm), where a family bakery uses traditional methods to produce a delicious cassava bread with many different flavors (coconut, peanut butter, cherry and raisin, cinnamon, salt, salt fish, or smoked herring). It is as popular with local people for a snack or lunch as it is with tour parties.

## The scenic route to Soufrière

The road to Soufrière is green and beautiful, with lush vegetation overhanging the road as it twists along the edge of the mountains and cuts through the hills along the coast. To the east is **Mount Gimie** (3,117ft/950 meters), the highest peak on the island, in the midst of forest reserves. As the West Coast Road descends to Soufrière, there are several viewpoints where you can get that picture-postcard photo of the bay and the Pitons, especially pretty if there is a tall ship in the harbor.

At **Soufrière** ❺, the 18th-century French capital of St Lucia, about 5 miles (8km) south of Canaries, old wooden buildings with pretty balconies and gingerbread fretwork line the streets, slender coconut palms border the dark volcanic sand, fishing boats and yachts bob in the emerald-green bay, and the dark-green wooded peaks of **Petit Piton** (2,350ft/743 meters) and **Gros Piton** (2,540ft/798 meters) create a magnificent backdrop. This Caribbean landscape seems too good

### TIP

Experienced climbers can try their hand at scaling Gros Piton, but the difficult ascent may only be made in the company of local guides familiar with the terrain. Call the Tour Guides Association on tel: 758-489 0136.

*The village of Anse La Raye.*

**TIP**

In a mansion house on Cap Estate is **Llewellyn Xavier's Studio** (tel: 758-450 9155; www.llewellynxavier.com), where the work of the St Lucian multimedia artist can be viewed only by appointment. His art is exhibited in the permanent collections of museums and galleries all over the world.

to be true; not even the rain, frequent on the west coast, can spoil the joy of being in a place like this. Louis XIV of France granted around 2,000 acres (809 hectares) of land to the Devaux family, who ran a successful plantation growing sugar, cocoa, tobacco, and cotton. Descendants of the family still own land here and their estates are open to the public.

The dramatic scenery continues underwater at the **Anse Chastanet National Marine Park** , north of Soufrière, where the diving and snorkeling are reputedly the best on the island, with more than 25 different types of coral in the reefs. The dive shop at the resort, Scuba St Lucia, rents snorkeling and diving equipment, runs scuba diving courses, and offers several daily boat and shore dives from its black-sand beach. Just north of Anse Chastanet are two beaches of golden sand, Anse Mamin and Anse Jambon. Anse Mamin is backed by forest and former plantation land from where Bike St Lucia organizes jungle biking trips on trails through the old plantation.

*Snorkelers take in the their surroundings and a large brain coral.*

## Springs and plantations

Not far from the Pitons the pungent odor of hydrogen sulfide in the air heralds the crater region of **Sulfur Springs** (tel: 758-459 7686; daily), called "the only drive-in volcano in the world," because car parking was possible between the bubbling springs of gray-brown mud for quite some time. No longer: now the last few yards have to be covered on foot. The volcano collapsed more than 40,000 years ago and now produces only the foul-smelling gases and hot water that can reach temperatures of 338°F (170°C). In 2004, the Pitons, the marine park, and the Sulfur Springs were designated a Unesco World Heritage Site.

The restorative powers of the steamy springs are harnessed in the water at the historic **Diamond Botanical Gardens Mineral Baths and Waterfall** (tel: 758-459 7155; www.diamondstlucia.com; Mon–Sat 10am–5pm, Sun 10am–3pm). In the middle of a splendid garden, where colorful orchids, flame trees, and hibiscus bushes bloom, the hot water streams out of the ground into tiled basins at a temperature of around 100°C (212°F). A commemorative plaque announces that a creole girl from Martinique named Marie-Josèphe Rose Tascher de la Pagerie (see page 216), Napoléon Bonaparte's wife-to-be, used to spend her holidays here in the 18th century because her father owned a plantation near Soufrière. The estate, still owned by the Devaux family today, also features a restored water mill (1765), which was used to crush sugar cane and to provide Soufrière with electricity.

The region around Soufrière as a whole is just the right place to get a feel for plantation life. A number of the traditional old manors are open to the public. The **Morne Coubaril Estate** (tel: 758-459 7340; www.stlucia ziplining.com; daily; guided tours) is a working plantation with an abundance of fruit trees and bushes such as papaya, coconut, banana, orange, grapefruit, and cocoa; it was owned by the Devaux family until 1960.

The **Fond Doux Estate** (tel: 758-459 7545; www.fonddouxestate.com), between Soufrière and the fishing village of Choiseul, offers tours around its 250-year-old cocoa plantation, serves local cuisine in the restaurant and provides accommodations in the estate cottages.

The **Rabot Estate** (tel: 758-457 1624; www.thehotelchocolat.com), a beautifully rehabilitated 140-acre (56-hectare) cocoa plantation owned by the British *chocolatiers*, Hotel Chocolat, dates back to 1745 and has some very rare old trees of scientific interest – and interest to those who love chocolate. This is a true "bean to bar" experience, as the owners make chocolate from their own cocoa. They have built a boutique hotel Boucan there and there is also a restaurant specializing in chocolate recipes.

Halfway between Choiseul and Laborie, inside an enchanting 70-acre (30-hectare) park, lies **Balenbouche Estate** House (tel: 758-455 1244; www.balenbouche.com; daily; guided tours by appointment). Always atmospheric with the ghostly remains of sugar production permeating throughout, the small family-run hotel is supremely peaceful.

## The green heart of the island

Most of the mountainous heart of St Lucia is forest reserve, partly to protect wildlife and partly to preserve water supply for the island. Trails are maintained by the **Forestry Department** (tel: 758-450 2231, 758-468 5649; tours), and it is possible to hike from one coast to the other.

With advance notice, the rangers will escort you from Fond St Jacques through the **Edmund Forest Reserve** to the **Quilesse Forest Reserve** and down to the rangers' station on the **Des Cartiers Rainforest Trail**, near Mahaut, and to Micoud on the east coast. Alternatively, for a shorter excursion, follow the **Enbas Saut Trail** from the rangers' station above Fond St Jacques. This steep but exhilarating trail winds down 2,112 steps cut in the hillside to a pool and little waterfall on the Troumassée River, providing an opportunity to see elfin woodland,

*The old sugar mill workings at Balenbouche Estate House.*

*Accommodations for rent on the Fond Doux Holiday Plantation.*

*The lighthouse crowning Cap Moule à Chic.*

*Saint Lucia Whiptail (Cnemidophorus vanzoi).*

cloud forest, and rainforest, depending on your altitude. Expect to get wet and muddy, especially after rain, which is frequent. You may be lucky enough to spot a rare St Lucian parrot. They nearly became extinct in the 1970s, but after the introduction of strict protective measures, several hundred of them are thriving on the island again.

## Atlantic coast

The east coast, which has plenty of rainfall, few inhabitants, and a raw Atlantic atmosphere, is rewarding for nature lovers. At the southern tip of the island is **Vieux Fort**, the second-largest town and the location of the international airport. Spectacular views of both sides of the island can be had from the **lighthouse** perched on top of **Cap Moule à Chique**, standing 730ft (223 meters) above sea level. Vieux Fort has a beautiful strip of white-sand beach, **Anse de Sables**, which is popular with windsurfers and kitesurfers for the trade winds blowing onshore. There is a beach bar, a few cabins, and a surf center where boards and equipment can be rented.

Just off the beach is the **Maria Islands Nature Reserve ❽** (restricted access, closed during nesting season; for information contact the National Trust, tel: 758-452 5005). A real birdwatchers' dream, it is home to – among others – the sooty tern, the red-billed tropic bird, and the brown noddy, which tucks its nests under the prickly pear cactus. Also living there are two endemic reptiles: the St Lucia whiptail lizard (*Cnemidophorus vanzoi*) and the non-poisonous kouwess grass snake (*Dromicus ornatus*).

Driving up the east coast you pass a large area of mangrove swamp, **Mankoté Mangrove**, and the **Savannes Bay Nature Reserve**, a protected wetland with good birdlife. About 9 miles (16km) from Vieux Fort is the fishing village of **Micoud**, where the Troumassée River meets the sea. Inland from here is **Mahaut** and there is good walking and parrot-watching in the forest reserves.

## Flora and frigate birds

A good bet for getting to know the island's flora is **Mamiku Gardens** (tel: 758-455 3729; www.mamikugardens.com;

### THE WHIPTAIL LIZARD

The endemic St Lucia whiptail lizard (*Cnemidophorus vanzoi*) is the only whiptail found in the Eastern Caribbean. The males sport the colors of the St Lucian flag: black, white, blue, and yellow. Cats, rats, and mongooses preyed on the population until by the 1960s there remained just a few lizards on the Maria Islands. In the 1990s the Forestry Department and the Durrell Wildlife Conservation Trust started to introduce the whiptail to other predator-free offshore islands in order not to have "all their eggs in one basket." A satellite colony on Praslin Island was hugely successful and in 2008 whiptails from all three islets were moved on to Rat Island, off Castries, in order to widen the gene pool. In 2014, successful breeding was confirmed on Rat Island. A further colony on Dennery Island is planned.

daily 9am–5pm), close to **Mon Repos**. In the 18th century Mamiku Estate was home to a French governor of the island, then became a British military outpost, and is now a banana plantation. With easy walking trails, bright orchids, and a plethora of visiting bird species to spot, Mamiku is a perfect way to spend a relaxed afternoon.

The road continues north to **Praslin Bay**, with the tiny **Praslin Island** lying just offshore. Villagers maintain their old fishing traditions here and you can still see canoes made from gommier trees. In the northern part of the bay a huge resort and golf course have been partially built, but construction has stalled and St Lucia's government is searching for investors who could revive the project. As a result, the **Fregate Islands Nature Reserve** is off limits to visitors. The frigate bird (*Fregata magnificens*) migrates from Cape Verde in Africa to nest here, but their numbers have dropped dramatically.

At **Dennery** the main road turns west into the Mabouya Valley. As the road climbs, the view down to Fond d'Or Bay is spectacular. Nearby, an old fort and plantation ruins have been developed as **Fond d'Or Nature Reserve and Historical Park** (tel: 758-453 3242; daily), with a wooded canopy of coconut palms, an estuarine forest, and mangrove wetlands. Visitors can hike along the forest trails and tour the estate that contains the remnants of the sugar mill, the windmill, and the old planter's house, which is now an interpretive center.

## Transinsular Road

The road now leaves the coast behind and heads inland and uphill into the forest before climbing over the **Barre de l'Isle**, the ridge that divides the island. At the high point there is a stall where Forestry Department guides meet hikers. You can either do the short Barre de l'Isle trail on your own for views of the forest down to Roseau Valley, or hire a guide for the longer **Mount La Combe** hike. As you emerge from the forest the landscape becomes progressively more built-up until the smell from the coffee-roasting factory advises you that you are on the outskirts of Castries again.

*A purple-throated carib hummingbird.*

*A stream running through Mamiku Gardens.*

*Trekking to Soufrière volcano.*

# ST VINCENT AND THE GRENADINES

Volcanic and lush, St Vincent is a nature lover's paradise, while the numerous Grenadine islands have some of the world's finest beaches and a sea of incredible blue for adventurous sailors.

Caribbean Sea

St Vincent and The Grenadines

A savored retreat for West Indians themselves, St Vincent and its 32 sister islands and cays, scattered like shells dropped from a child's overflowing bucket, are still untouched by the overt hand of tourism. There are no neon lights, no high-rise buildings, no traffic jams, no brand-name fast-food joints, no crowds, no noise.

Between St Lucia in the north and Grenada to the south, only eight of the islands are inhabited, accounting for a population of 103,000, most of whom live on St Vincent. The largest, at 18 miles (30km) long and 11 miles (18km) wide, the lush, craggy island of St Vincent is presided over by the somnolent volcano La Soufrière (4,048ft/1,234 meters). The "untouched" islands of the Grenadines, encompassing only 17 sq miles (44 sq km) altogether, are havens of natural beauty whose charms extend across some of the most beautiful beaches in the world into seas of many hues, rich in marine life – perfect for sailors and divers, and for beachcombers in search of privacy.

## The populated islands

Among the populated islands, Mustique and Petit St Vincent are the hideaways of the rich and famous while the coral reefs of Bequia, Canouan, and Mayreau offer spectacular diving and snorkeling. Union Island, the most

southerly, is the sailing gateway to the region. St Vincent and the Grenadines, which receive around 200,000 visitors every year, offer the beauties of nature but with creature comforts such as relatively easy accessibility, comfortable places to sleep, and the pleasure of a good meal in a restaurant. The size of an island's tourist industry is loosely based on the length of the airport runway. The small one at St Vincent's E.T. Joshua Airport allows only small planes to land here, meaning no mass tourism. A new international

**Main Attractions**

St Mary's Roman Catholic Cathedral of the Assumption
Botanic Gardens
Vermont Nature Trail
Falls of Baleine
Black Point Tunnel
Bequia
Tobago Cays

*The jetty at Bequia.*

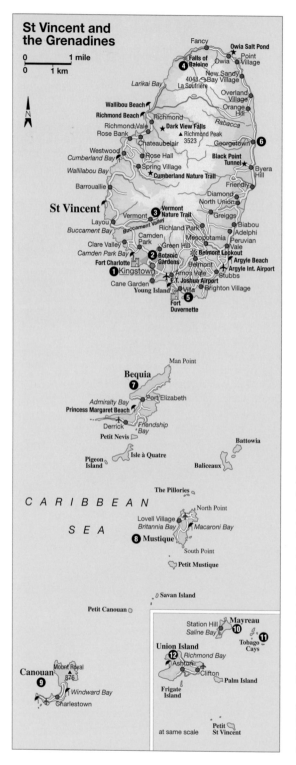

**St Vincent and the Grenadines**

airport, currently under construction at Argyle on the eastern side of St Vincent, is scheduled to open in 2016. It will have four times the capacity of the existing E.T Joshua Airport, so its opening should certainly give a boost to the country's tourism.

## Forceful Caribs

The first settlers on St Vincent in the 17th century were Africans. In 1675, the resident Caribs rescued some shipwrecked slaves, and these were subsequently joined by escaped slaves from St Lucia and Grenada. The mixing of the two produced the "Black Caribs," distinct from the indigenous "Yellow Caribs," and eyewitness reports of the time describe many a battle between them. It was not until the early 18th century that St Vincent was finally settled by the French after many wrangles with the Caribs, who were not going to let go of their domain without a fight. They eventually lived alongside the French in an uneasy truce.

In 1722, the British moved in and until 1783 France and Britain were involved in a tug-of-war over the island, already planted with indigo, cotton, tobacco, and sugar. Alongside this conflict the Black Caribs waged war against the British colonists in what is known as the Carib Wars. These were finally ended in 1797 when 5,000 Caribs were deported to Roatán, an island off Honduras. There is still a small settlement of the Black Carib descendents in the north of St Vincent.

## From prosperity to poverty

By 1829 St Vincent contained 98 sugar estates manned by slaves. After Emancipation, immigrants came from Portugal and India to work the land and the present population is largely a mixture of these three nationalities.

However, natural disasters took their toll in the form of a hurricane in 1898 and an eruption of La Soufrière in 1902 – two days before the catastrophic eruption of Montagne

Pelée on Martinique (see page 214) – which killed around 2,000 people, mostly Caribs, and finished off the plantation economy.

Run-down and poor, St Vincent and the Grenadines was granted independence in 1979, just a few months after another volcanic eruption had wrecked the agriculture of the island, already suffering from a series of hurricanes.

## Kingstown

In the mornings, the cobblestone streets of **Kingstown** ❶ are full of uniformed school children, government workers, cab drivers, people peddling sandals, and old women selling odd collections of goods from upturned cardboard boxes. Hustlers coax tourists on rides to the volcano or to the Falls of Baleine, or try to sell recordings of local calypsonians and bands such as Blaksand and New Direction. As the afternoon heat grips the town, government officers, bankers, and lawyers take their lunch at the **Bounty**, a café on Halifax Street, or the more cosmopolitan rooftop restaurant in the **Cobblestone Inn**, a converted sugar and arrowroot warehouse in Upper Bay Street.

Nonetheless, this town, little more than several dusty blocks carved in a rugged shoreline, is the heart of St Vincent and the Grenadines. There are no buildings of colonial grandeur here, but **St Mary's Roman Catholic Cathedral of the Assumption**, beside Victoria Park to the west, makes up for this by providing a fascinating selection of architectural styles and features in one – Romanesque, Moorish, Byzantine, and Flemish spires, turrets, towers, belfries, crenellations, and castellations are all here – built throughout the 19th century and 1930s. Opposite, the old Anglican **St George's Cathedral** has some wonderful stained-glass windows, which feature red angels.

Kingstown may be the most visible source of activity in this tiny nation, but the real power comes from the rich volcanic soil. This is an island of farmers, a place where almost everyone knows how to furrow a hillside to plant sweet potatoes. On Friday and Saturday you get an idea of just how

*Tropical treats at the beach.*

productive that soil is when farmers ride into town loaded down with their produce: fruit and vegetables like ginger, breadfruit, cashews, dates, and cassava. Trade in the **Central Market** on Upper Bay Street is brisk and colorful.

On the reclaimed land on the harbor in front stands the concrete **Little Tokyo Fish Market**, built with Japanese aid, to nurture support for continued whaling in the region. Minibuses bound for the rest of the island depart from here.

In the port, the dockside hubbub reaches a crescendo once a week when the Geest Industries freighter arrives to ship the week's crop of bananas to the rest of the world. The banana industry suffered when the preferential agreement with the EU ended in 2006, but the crop still accounts for around 35 percent of St Vincent's exports and makes a significant contribution to the island's economy.

## The oldest botanic gardens in the West

*General vista at the Gardens.*

Leaving Kingstown via the Leeward Highway to the west, on the edge of town you come to the **Botanic Gardens ❷** (daily; free), the oldest in the western hemisphere, founded in 1765 to propagate spices and medicinal plants. Chances are young men – unofficial guides – will approach you at the entrance and offer you a tour of the 20-acre (9-hectare) gardens that contain teak and mahogany trees, and nearly every flower and tree that can grow in the Caribbean, including a 50ft (15-meter) breadfruit tree, one of the original seedlings brought to the West Indies in 1793 by Captain Bligh on his famous ship the *Bounty*.

Perched some 600ft (180 meters) on a promontory above the town, 15 minutes' drive to the west, the ruins of **Fort Charlotte**, built in 1806, command spectacular views across the Caribbean to the Grenadines and, on a clear day, as far as Grenada, 60 miles (95km) away. In the barracks a series of paintings (from 1972) portrays the early history of St Vincent.

## Parrots and petroglyphs

The Leeward Highway provides a dramatic 2-hour drive along the west

coast with beaches of gold or black sand. In the **Buccament Valley** about 2 miles (3km) from Kingstown you can wander through rainforest along the 2-mile (3km) **Vermont Nature Trail ❸**. Maps of hikes are provided at the information center and you may see the endangered St Vincent parrot or the whistling warbler, both unique to the island. Fishing villages dot the coastline and in places there are petroglyphs dating back thousands of years. There is one just north of Layou, another in the playground of a school in Barrouallie. **Wallilabou Bay** was a location for the movie *Pirates of the Caribbean*, with copies of 18th-century buildings erected to represent Port Royal in Jamaica. Several of the Grenadines also became movie sets. **Richmond Beach**, under the dark gaze of La Soufrière, marks the end of this beautiful winding road and a boat is necessary to go any farther. Many boat operators offer trips – which can include snorkeling and a lunch stop – to the **Falls of Baleine ❹**, 7 miles (11km) away at the northern tip of the island. There you can swim in the pools filled by these freshwater falls in a river that flows from the volcano.

## Along the Windward coast

The E.T. Joshua airport, east of Kingstown, is about 15 minutes away. Close by is the **Arnos Vale cricket ground**, the home (or shrine) of Vincentian cricket. Vincentians love their cricket and support their team in droves, making a match a festive social occasion with loud music and dancing no matter which team wins.

A little farther east, on the south coast road, **Villa ❺**, colloquially known as "The Strip," is the island's main resort area, with several hotels, guesthouses, restaurants, bars, and water sports facilities. Just 200yds/meters offshore, the tiny, privately owned resort on **Young Island**, linked to the mainland by a small water-taxi, becomes officially child-free between January 15 and March 15. Beside it on a rock is 19th-century **Fort Duvernette**.

The road winds through what the Vincentians call their island's "breadbasket." On the Atlantic side the soil is more fertile and from the

*Breadfruit in the Botanic Gardens.*

*The Grenadines are equally stunning, if not more so, when viewed from above.*

unbarricaded road you have somewhat frightening views of deep valleys dotted with farms and banana plantations. The **Mesopotamia Valley** offers challenging walks through forests and plantations. From the 900ft (275-meter) viewing platform of the **Belmont Lookout** you get a good view over the valley, the remnant of an extinct volcano, and a major agricultural zone, still home to agouti, manicou, and other wildlife.

You may experience the odd traffic jam on the Windward Highway, the narrow coastal road that leads north to Georgetown, but they are usually caused by drivers stopping for a chat, or someone going to inspect fish for sale on the roadside. The island gets drier the further north you go, with yellow sandstone cliffs over black-sand beaches. **Black Point Tunnel** is 350ft (106 meters) long, built in 1815 by Carib and African slaves. After it was blasted through the rock, sugar estates in the north were able to transport their sugar through it to be loaded onto boats at a jetty on Byera Bay for export. This was

*Owia Salt Pond.*

another movie location, for *Pirates of the Caribbean: Curse of the Black Pearl*.

**Georgetown** ❻, the second-largest town on St Vincent, was once the prosperous sugar capital of the island: when the price of sugar fell, the sugar plant that employed most of the laborers in this valley was closed. Now there's a sense of driving through a ghost town, although rum is still produced nearby by **St Vincent Distillers** (tel: 784-458 6221; visits by appointment; free). Formerly the Mount Bentinck refinery, the distillery produces a range of rums using imported molasses, although locally the most popular is the 84.5 percent alcohol Sunset Very Strong Rum.

A little farther on is the **Rabacca Dry River**, once a hot river of lava. You can drive or walk along here to well-marked trails that lead to the crater of La Soufrière. A 6-hour round trip, it is an arduous hike best begun very early in the morning, and only by the fit and healthy, but it is worth the effort when you finally crest the rim and look down into that awesome volcano. It is often cloudy, cold, and wet at the top so come well equipped and take a guide.

At the northern tip of the island is **Owia Salt Pond**, a natural swimming pool protected from the crashing Atlantic surf by volcanic rocks. Facilities have been built here, with parking, a craft center, bar, washrooms, and showers. Owia and the next village, **Fancy**, are where the Black Caribs live and the area is very poor, isolated, and rugged.

## Island-hopping

Most people arriving on an island in the Grenadines do so by sea. Anchorages are provided to protect the coral reefs surrounding the islands. Water-taxis zip around the bays waiting to take yachtsmen on shore, and boys often come out to the boats with goods for sale. Ferries regularly leave Kingstown for the islands, and

Bequia, Mustique, Canouan, and Union Island all have small airports for light aircraft.

The focal point of **Bequia** ❼ (pronounced "*bek-way*"), 9 miles (14km) from St Vincent, is the stunningly beautiful **Admiralty Bay**, an enormous, clear harbor bordered by steep green cliffs, holding several yacht anchorages. Around the island is a Marine Protected Area looking after 30 superb dive sites, many of which are suitable for snorkeling too. **Port Elizabeth** is a thriving little community with guesthouses and a full range of stores including a yacht chandler, bank, and internet café. Along the shore sloops are built by the skillful local boat builders.

During the 19th century, the New Bedford whalers used Bequia as a whaling station. The island's last whale harpoonist, the late Athneal Oliverre, lived in a small house in the south, which he turned into a **whaling museum**. The front door is framed by a whale jawbone and inside is a vertebra of the first one he killed in 1958. When and if a whale is caught (Oliverre caught his last one in 1992 – the International Whaling Foundation permits the islanders to harpoon two a year), the whole island comes to watch.

**Mustique** ❽, 15 miles (24km) south of St Vincent, is a clean and manicured island where privacy and quiet are prized by those who can afford the phenomenally expensive, luxury villas. The whole island, with its beaches and offshore waters, is a conservation area. You can walk around the island, take a picnic to **Macaroni Beach** on the Atlantic side, where there is palm-thatched shade, or snorkel at Britannia Bay or any of the other lovely bays on the Leeward side. Yachties congregate at **Basil's Bar** (www.basilsbar.com), the place to be seen, and there is a path from there to the **Cotton House Hotel**, which is the only other watering hole.

The small, crescent-shaped island of **Canouan** ❾ has some of the Caribbean's best and most private beaches. There is also a luxury resort, complete with the Grenadines' only golf course. Tiny **Mayreau** ❿ is less than 2 sq miles (4.5 sq km) and inhabited by about 250 people. There are no roads, a small salt pond, and one very quiet resort. Nearby a tiny clutch of five uninhabited islands, known as the **Tobago Cays** ⓫, offers spectacular snorkeling and diving, popular with day-trippers. In order to preserve the area a National Marine Park is being developed.

Mountainous **Union Island** ⓬, the most developed of the smaller Grenadines, is the region's sailing center, and an ideal starting point for trips to the surrounding islands. Across the bay is beautiful **Palm Island**, formerly Prune Island and now a popular resort with Caribbean islanders seeking peace.

Farthest south is **Petit St Vincent**, an island resort considered to be one of the best in the region, where exclusive privacy is the order of the day.

*Mustique viewed from Sleeping Dragon.*

*Callaloo Villas, luxury accommodations on Mustique.*

# ENDANGERED BIRDS

**Color and noise characterize the profusion of birds on the islands, providing inspiration for many a Carnival costume, but loss of habitat is endangering many of them.**

Every time a swamp is drained for a beach resort, a mangrove forest cleared for a marina, or a rainforest cut down for growing root crops, the habitat of birds and other wildlife is threatened. They retreat to ever-smaller patches of woodland and their numbers inevitably decline. The variety of birds on the Lesser Antilles is amazing, and is directly linked to the wide range of habitats, from dry, tropical forest to wetlands and rainforest. Migrant seabirds and waterfowl add to the numbers of residents, attracting large flocks of birdwatchers in their wake.

## Forest reserves

On many islands forest reserves protect water supply. Here, parrots flourish in the treetops and doves scuttle about on the forest floor while hummingbirds flit about from flower to flower. The Windward Islands parrots are all of the genus *Amazona*, originally from South America, but most islands have a unique species, such as the versicolor in St Lucia and in Dominica the sisserou *(Amazona imperialis)*, which is critically endangered, and its marginally less threatened relative the red-necked parrot, or Jacquot *(Amazona arausiaca)*. In the 1970s all these flashy green parrots faced extinction, hunted for food and the pet trade while their nesting sites were destroyed by hurricanes or urbanization. Protection, education, and breeding programs have gradually raised numbers but they still remain endangered.

*Barbuda's mangroves are home to over 5,000 nesting frigate birds (Fregata magnificens) nicknamed the Man-o-War bird.*

*The national bird, unique to Montserrat, is the Montserrat oriole, Icterus oberi, a black and gold oriole found along the Centre Hills trail.*

*The endangered St Vincent parrot, Amazona guildingii.*

*Birds in flight.*

## BIRDWATCHING IN TRINIDAD AND TOBAGO

Together, Trinidad and Tobago have more species of birds than any other Caribbean island, as a consequence of their proximity to South America. Estimates put the total at 469, including a staggering 21 species of hummingbirds, 11 of parrots and macaws, and 24 of tanagers. Tobago has half the number of its larger sister, but hosts 12 species of breeding birds not found on Trinidad. Mangrove swamps, marshes, savannah, and rainforest contribute to the islands' biodiversity so attractive to birds, while many of the offshore islets (Saut d'Eau, Konstadt Island, Soldado Rock off Trinidad, Little Tobago, St Giles and Marble Islands off Tobago) are reserves with the largest seabird colonies in the Southern Caribbean, including breeding colonies of red-billed tropic birds and frigate birds.

The most accessible birdwatching sites on Trinidad are the Caroni Bird Sanctuary, the Asa Wright Nature Centre, and the Pointe-à-Pierre Wildfowl Trust. Caroni offers the spectacular sight of hundreds of scarlet ibis coming home to roost at dusk, while a staggering 159 species have been recorded at Asa Wright, including the nocturnal, cave-dwelling oilbirds, a nesting colony of oropendolas, and numerous hummingbirds which come to the verandah to feed.

*Millet Bird Sanctuary Trail is one of the best birdwatching locations on St Lucia with five endemics living in the secondary rainforest around the Roseau Dam.*

*Neither endemic nor endangered but easily seen splashes of color worth identifying are the blue-crowned mot mots (Momotus momota). Watch them being fed at the Old Copra House (Grafton Caledonia Wildlife Sanctuary, Tobago) at 8am and 4pm, a spectacular sight.*

# GRENADA

Known as the Spice Island of the Caribbean, this aromatic island, most famous for nutmeg, and now for cocoa, has mountains, rivers, waterfalls, and white-sand beaches well worth exploring.

Caribbean Sea

Grenada

A colorful gem of an island, Grenada ("gre-*nay*-dah") is, by any definition, small. Only 21 by 12 miles (35 by 20km) in size, it seems bigger than it really is, partly because its mountainous interior looms large and is slow to cross, and partly because its landscape is so varied. Its fertility is largely thanks to the 160ins (406cm) of rain deposited on the island's interior each year by the trade winds. This creates lush and often impenetrable rainforest, streams that cascade down to the sea, and ideal conditions for the generations of small farmers who have worked their smallholdings since the British freed the slaves in 1834.

In 2004, the island was struck directly by Hurricane Ivan, which uprooted trees, caused damage to 90 percent of the buildings, and devastated crops. However, the land is astonishingly fertile; bananas, cocoa, citrus, mangoes, and coconuts grow in dense groves or by the roadside. Farther up in the interior, ferns and mahogany trees drip in the humidity.

Known as the Spice Island of the Caribbean, it is nutmeg that gives Grenada its most delicious and distinctive aroma. Nutmeg has been grown here since the 1780s when the British brought it over from East India and, together with cinnamon,

ginger, and cloves, replaced sugar as the island's main export. Mature nutmeg trees were destroyed by the hurricane and cocoa is now the main crop, but the replanting of nutmeg is ongoing and the crop is still important. Known affectionately as the "retirement tree" as it is thought to guarantee a comfortable old age, the nutmeg tree drops an apricot-like fruit which splits when ripe to reveal its seed and the surrounding red membrane, which makes the separate spice, mace.

**Main Attractions**

St George's
Gouyave Nutmeg
   Processing Station
Levera National Park
Belmont Estate
Grand Etang National Park
Grand Anse
Carriacou

*Grand Anse Beach, Grenada.*

**FACT**

The Queen's Park Stadium, just north of St George's, was refurbished and its seating capacity increased to 20,000 for the ICC Cricket World Cup in 2007. The island is also home to the West Indies' Cricket Academy.

## The prettiest capital

Few would disagree that the capital, **St George's ❶**, is a fine town and has retained its picturesque charm and small-town warmth.

The geography of St George's is unusually attractive, as the town is built around the rim of a volcanic crater, which forms its almost landlocked harbor, and over a promontory, giving a variety of views. There are steep hills, steps, and twisting streets, making driving tricky and even walking challenging. From around the waterfront Carenage, edged with solid stone warehouses, the town rises steeply, houses, churches, and forts ringing the inner horseshoe bay. Over the promontory, where the French-built **Fort George** (www.forts. org; daily) commands panoramic views

of the town and harbor, is another part of town, joined to the Carenage by the 100-year-old Sendall Tunnel. Here, the cruise ship terminal on the Esplanade disgorges thousands of visitors into the town. One of their first stops, **Market Square**, is the scene of hectic and colorful activity on Saturday morning as farmers bring their vanloads of yams, mangoes, and bananas to town. This is also the place to find spices, crafts, nutmeg oil, nutmeg soap, and cocoa balls.

Delicate French provincial architecture rubs shoulders with robust Georgian stonework, a happy consequence of Grenada changing colonial hands several times in the 18th century. Pink fish-scale roof tiles date from the time when they crossed the Atlantic as ballast in French ships. Pastel-colored

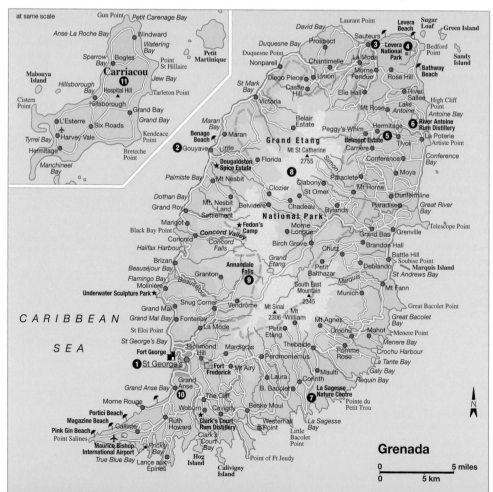

wooden houses clinging to the hill-sides contrast with the dour stone ruins of **St Andrew's Presbyterian Kirk**'s belfry and the imposing walls of Fort George.

The small **Grenada National Museum** (corner Young and Monckton streets; Mon–Fri 9am–5pm, Sat 10am–1pm), near the Sendall Tunnel, is housed in the former French barracks, built in 1704. The British used parts of it as a prison, then later the ground floor was a warehouse and upstairs became the Antilles Hotel. The exhibits are a varied mixture of dusty relics from all stages of Grenada's history, including the "Cuban crisis." One of the best ways to pass the time is simply to sit and admire the view, toward sea or mountains, preferably from the shady terrace of the waterside **Nutmeg**, famous for its rum punches.

## "The intervention"

The town exudes history, but most Grenadians prefer not to discuss the events of October 1983, which brought their island brief notoriety. In 1979, a group of radicals turfed out the eccentric and dictatorial Prime Minister Eric Gairy in a bloodless coup. Four and a half years of People's Revolutionary Government, led by the charismatic Maurice Bishop, ensued and long overdue reforms were introduced. But Grenada's "revo" disintegrated as a hardline faction tried to snatch power. Bishop was arrested, freed by a crowd, and then, in scenes of appalling brutality, was executed with several supporters in the courtyard of Fort George. The US, long suspicious of Grenada's links with Castro's Cuba, seized the opportunity to invade. More than 6,000 US Marines landed in what is euphemistically known as "the intervention."

It seems long ago, but the scars remain. Several of those convicted of the murders have been released, while some remain in jail in **Fort Frederick** on Richmond Hill. Others still mourn their dead.

## Spice of Grenadian life

The center of Grenada's nutmeg industry is **Gouyave** ❷ (pronounced "warve"), on the west coast about 6 miles (10km) north of St George's. A ramshackle one-street fishing community, populated by as many goats as people, it has a pungent **Nutmeg Processing Station** (Mon–Fri), where visitors can see the grading, drying, and packing process. The town is also home to a laid-back weekly evening fish fry, known as Fish Friday, where visitors can enjoy Grenadian fish specialties and local music. Just before Gouyave, down a dirt track, is the crumbling **Dougaldston Spice Estate** (Mon–Fri; free), once a prosperous plantation but now fallen on hard times. Small bags of nutmeg, cinnamon, and cloves are on sale here for a few dollars.

From Gouyave the road follows the coast north, providing spectacular sea views, before turning inland through several poor villages to the small north-coast town of **Sauteurs** ❸. The French name (literally "Leapers") recalls a grisly moment in Grenada's

*The seed of the nutmeg tree.*

**TIP**

Serious hikers can take a 5-hour walk in the Grand Etang National Park to Concord Falls, where it's possible to swim, and on to Fedon's Camp, where a rebel planter held out against the British in 1795. The good news is there is a bus back to St George's from nearby Concord.

colonial past when French forces surrounded the last community of indigenous Caribs in 1651. Rather than surrender, the 40 Caribs jumped from the 100ft (30-meter) cliff into the sea below. On the promontory by **St Patrick's** church there you can peer down onto the rocks and spray.

A rough road leads east out of Sauteurs to the **Levera National Park ④**, a wild and varied area of scrubland, mangrove, and palm-lined beach. From the hilltop there are spectacular views of the offshore and uninhabited **Sugar Loaf**, **Green**, and **Sandy islands**. **Bathway Beach**, looking out to Sandy Island, is a normally deserted expanse of white sand, where seagrapes provide welcome shade. Currents are strong, despite a protective reef, but there is a 33ft (10-meter)-long natural rock pool, perfect for swimming.

## A working plantation

The main road south of Sauteurs takes you to the **Morne Fendue Plantation House**, a gray stone house. Drive south for 15 minutes and between Hermitage and Tivoli there is a turn-off to

*Staff at the Grenada Chocolate Company.*

**Belmont Estate ⑤** (tel: 473-442 9524; www.belmontestate.net; Sun–Fri 8am–4pm), a working plantation offering tours of the organic farm, goat dairy farm, gardens, heritage museum, and cocoa processing facilities, while there is also a restaurant for lunch, using fruit, vegetables, goat's cheese, and chocolate from the property, and also offering specialties such as *callaloo* and pepperpot. Formerly a nutmeg plantation, its trees were severely damaged by Hurricane Ivan and production on Grenada declined by about 75 percent. Cocoa has since replaced it as the island's main crop. The organic cocoa produced here (and by other local organic farmers) is used to make the exquisite, prize-winning chocolate produced by the Grenada Chocolate Factory (www.grenadachocolate.com). If you buy some, don't be worried about it melting in the heat of the tropics. It is so pure that it doesn't melt, but if you are concerned, buy the cocoa powder instead. Just east of here is the **River Antoine Rum Distillery ⑥** (Mon–Fri 9am–5pm), where guided tours demonstrate 18th-century rum

distilling techniques based on a water-powered cane crusher. From here it is a short drive to **Lake Antoine**, a lonely crater lake teeming with birdlife.

## Nature in the raw

At **Grenville**, a sprawling, rather unattractive town with a dirty beach on the east coast, the picturesque coastal road leads to **La Sagesse Nature Centre** ❼, about 10 miles (16km) south. Here, you drive through a banana plantation before arriving at a shaded beach, overlooked by a small guesthouse and restaurant terrace. Within walking distance is a microcosm of Caribbean coastal ecology: a mangrove estuary, salt pond, coral reefs, and cactus woodlands.

But Grenada's natural **tour de force** is the **Grand Etang National Park** ❽, an area that covers the mountainous backbone of the island, from Mount St Catherine (2,755ft/840 meters) to Mount Sinai (2,306ft/703 meters). The Grenville–St George's road winds tortuously up into rainforest and occasional warm mist. About halfway is Grand Etang itself, a water-filled volcanic crater at 1,900ft (580 meters). Legend has it that the lake is bottomless, and certainly few feel the urge to swim in the strangely still water.

A **Visitors' Center** has information on the surrounding flora and fauna, and there are well-marked hiking trails which take from 15 minutes to 3 hours to complete. It is wet, sweaty, and sometimes slippery high in the mountains, but walkers will be rewarded with panoramic views and sightings of orchids, hawks, and even opossums (considered a delicacy locally).

On the way back to St George's it is worth making a half-mile detour to **Annandale Falls** ❾, where a stream drops 50ft (15 meters) into a pool used for swimming. The site attracts fair numbers of self-appointed "guides" as well as those eager to sell spices.

The southern tail of the island is comprised of a series of inlets, promontories, and beaches. The most celebrated of these is **Grand Anse** ❿, several miles of perfect white sand fringed with palm trees and hibiscus hedges. This is the tourist strip, with

*Annandale Falls.*

## SCULPTURE REEF

An unusual and very popular visitor attraction on Grenada is the **Underwater Sculpture Park** in Molinière Bay (www.grenadaunderwatersculpture.com), some 2 miles (3km) north of St George's. Started in 2006, it has grown to include some 100 sculptures, influenced by the island's history, folklore, and culture. In mid-2015 a new sculpture of the Nutmeg Princess, based on Grenada's fairytale and designed by Lene Kilde, was added to the park. Created predominantly from reinforced concrete, the sculptures act as an artificial reef, to be enjoyed by snorkelers and scuba divers, and more will be added. Boat tours are offered (about a 10-minute ride from St George's), or you can get there by land (south from Dragon Bay). There is a beach at one end of the bay.

*The well-tended gardens of The Calabash hotel.*

hotels bordering the beach and a road of restaurants and shops running parallel. Smaller and more secluded is **Morne Rouge**, lying in a protected cove farther round, and then there are smaller, emptier beaches delighting in the evocative names of **Portici**, **Magazine**, and **Pink Gin Beach**. East of **Maurice Bishop** airport (claimed by the US, in the Cold War days of 1983, to have been built by Cuba as part of its expansionist designs in the Caribbean) on the south coast are **Prickly Bay**, with the popular **Spice Island Marina**, and **True Blue Bay**, also with yachting facilities and water sports. The Lance aux Épines peninsula has many luxury homes alongside smart hotels such as **The Calabash**, whose lawns sweep down to the beach. In Woodlands Valley is the award-winning **Clarks Court Rum Distillery** (tel: 473-444 5363; www.clarkescourtrum.com; tours Mon–Fri 8am–4pm), the largest on the island. The 15-minute tour explains the production process and includes old steam engines from the 19th century, finishing with a tasting session.

*An old hut near the Caribbean Lagoon.*

Numerous paths wind around the headlands and inlets of the southern coast, leading to some interesting bays and isolated bathing spots, all the way to La Sagesse.

## Yachting hideaways

Grenada's two even smaller island dependencies, **Carriacou** ⑪ and **Petit Martinique**, a 3–4-hour boat ride off the northeastern coast, are a haven for those who want to get away from it all. You can fly, but taking the ferry up the coast of Grenada and into Carriacou's natural harbor is an experience to be savored. Carriacou is famous for wooden boat-building, the African-influenced Big Drum dance, and (some say) smuggling; tiny, volcanic Petit Martinique also has a reputation for illicit supplies of whisky.

The main town on Carriacou is **Hillsborough** (pop. 1,000) on the west side of the island. It was first used by the British as a launch pad for Admiral Ralph Abercrombie and his fleet of 150 ships on their way to take Trinidad in 1796. Today's sailors still come in search of safe harbor, either in Hillsborough

or in Tyrrel Bay in the west. The **Carriacou Museum** (Paterson Street, tel: 473-443 8288; www.carriacoumuseum.org; call for hours), housed in a restored cotton gin mill, contains exhibits from Amerindian settlements, British and French occupation of the islands, and an African section.

On the northeast coast, **Windward** has a Scottish heritage and used to be the center for boat building. You can still see some activity, although many of the craftsmen have moved to Tyrrel Bay. The techniques haven't changed since a boat builder from Glasgow first started making boats from local white cedar without the use of power tools, but the timber is now imported. The sturdy schooners and fishing boats can be seen racing in the **Carriacou Regatta** (www.ccouregattafestival.com) in August, over Emancipation weekend. Started in 1965 for local boats, it has developed into a major Caribbean event and attracts competition from other islands' working boats. Big Drum dances, lots of other activities, and competitions are organized, and a party atmosphere reigns. Petit Martinique also has a **Whitsuntide Regatta**, for sailors and boat builders, with onshore competitions and festivities such as tug-of-war, beer drinking, and the greasy pole. Boat building and fishing (or working at the Petit St Vincent resort across the narrow channel) are the main occupations of Petit Martinicans, who are descended from French fishermen, Glaswegian boat builders, pirates, and slaves.

The other major event on Carriacou is the 3-day **Maroon and Regional String Band Festival**, at the end of April (www.carriacoumaroon.com). Designed to keep local musical traditions alive, string bands from other islands, from Tortola to Tobago, take part as well. String bands are popular on the island and can be heard at most social functions and at the Parang Festival at Christmas. The African origins of Maroon culture are depicted through drumming, singing, eating of smoked food, and other rituals. Local food and drinks are an integral part of the accompanying entertainment.

**FACT**

Maroon culture, as celebrated in the Maroon and Regional String Band Festival, is about giving thanks to the source of all life, emphasizing community and sharing.

*Carriacou Regatta, held annually over Emancipation weekend.*

# BARBADOS

A coral island set apart from the rest of the Eastern Caribbean chain, this "singular" island has a character and landscape of its own, with an emphasis on beauty, fun, and friendliness.

Caribbean Sea

Barbados

**B**arbados has some of the most varied terrain in the Caribbean. The north is the least populated section, its shores punctuated by dramatic cliffs and crashing waves. Equally unspoiled is the scenic east, with miles of windswept beaches along the Atlantic coast fringing the hilly "Scotland District." As the Atlantic Ocean rushes wildly along the south coast westward toward the Caribbean Sea, the sand becomes whiter, hidden away in rocky coves edged by palm trees, washed by the breakers that are finally lulled into submission on the narrow but pretty beaches of the west coast, also known as the Platinum Coast for the luxury hotels here. The center of the island is covered with gently rolling cane fields, rural villages, and lush tropical vegetation. The southwest is the most heavily populated region, containing the capital, Bridgetown, and its suburbs.

Although some of the hills are very steep, Barbados is considered a flat island. Coral rather than volcanic, its highest point, Mount Hillaby, is just 1,115ft (340 meters) above sea level. Off the beaten track, 100 miles (160km) east of the rest of the Lesser Antilles, Barbados is often referred to as "the singular island." During the days of sailing conquerors and Caribbean settlement, this isolation provided Barbados with an unwitting

*A pannist (steel pan musician) in action.*

defense: it is difficult to sail here from the other islands because of the prevailing easterly winds.

Densely populated – about 277,000 people live in a space just 14 miles (22km) wide and 21 miles (33km) long – Barbadians, or Bajans, as they are generally known, have one of the highest incomes per head in the West Indies and a literacy rate of over 98 percent.

## The first Bajans

Amerindians came in canoes from Venezuela in around 1600 BC. Different

**Main Attractions**

Garrison Historical Area
Codrington College
Bathsheba
Andromeda Botanic Garden
Orchid World
Harrison's Cave
Holetown
St Nicholas Abbey

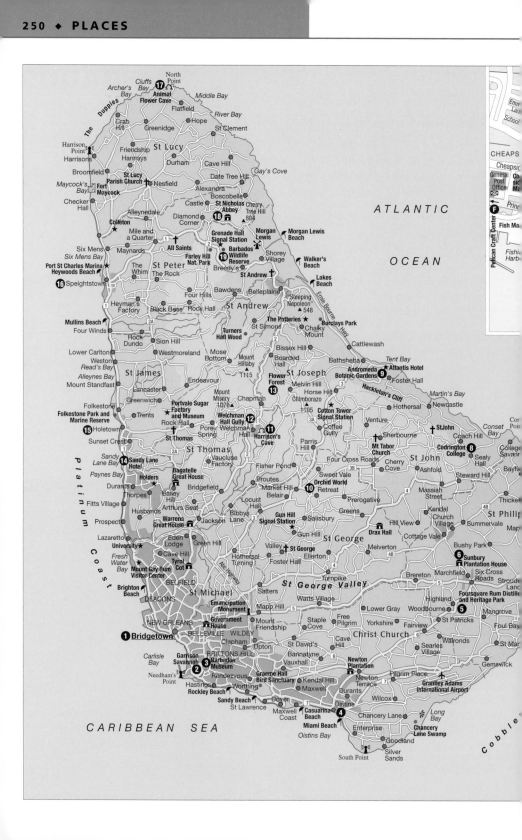

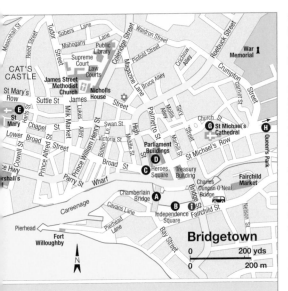

Bridgetown

| | |
|---|---|
| 0 | 200 yds |
| 0 | 200 m |

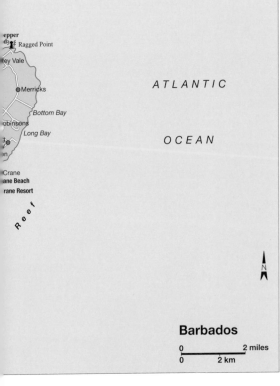

ATLANTIC

OCEAN

Barbados

| | |
|---|---|
| 0 | 2 miles |
| 0 | 2 km |

tribes came and went, with the Tainos remaining most evident, but these gentle fishermen and farmers are believed to have been captured by the Spanish at the beginning of the 16th century and taken as slaves to Hispaniola – no archeological evidence has been found that Caribs ever lived here. When the English arrived in 1625, all they found was a population of wild hogs left by Portuguese explorers who had anchored briefly in 1536.

In 1627, on February 17, 80 English settlers and 10 African slaves landed on the west coast. Barbados became the first English possession to cultivate sugar on a large scale. By the 1650s, it had a booming economy based solely on sugar cane, and became known as "the Brightest Jewel in the English Crowne." As the sugar plantation system evolved, the institution of slavery (see page 36) became firmly entrenched, but not without some notable uprisings – in 1675, 1695, and 1702 – cruelly quashed by the planters. The final 5,000-strong rebellion came in 1816 when the abolition of the slave trade had failed to give the slaves the freedom they mistakenly thought they were due. That didn't come until 1834–8.

## New challenges

Between 1850 and 1914, after abolition and the decline of the sugar industry, around 20,000 laborers desperate for work left for Panama to help build the canal. The lucky ones returned, their pockets stuffed with US currency, with which they bought land, educated their children, and increased their standard of living. However, there were few opportunities for black Bajans afterward and most returned to the plantations as laborers. The poor conditions there and a lack of political power sparked a half century of intense political and social change.

Perhaps the most noteworthy figure to challenge the ruling white planter class was Grantley Adams, the acknowledged leader of the Barbados Progressive League, the island's first mass-movement political party, formed in 1938, which over the course of 30 years and eventually under the title of the Barbados Labour Party (BLP) helped attain fair labor laws and universal voting rights.

Political independence from Britain finally came in 1966, with Errol Barrow of the Democratic Labour Party (DLP) at the helm. Remaining in the British Commonwealth, the island has continued with a Westminster-style parliament consisting of a Senate and a democratically elected House of Assembly, and now the government swings between the BLP and DLP.

## A city of contrasts

Bridgetown ❶, the capital of Barbados, features Unesco World Heritage sites (historical Bridgetown and its Garrison were inscribed on the list in 2011) and a city of contrasts. While duty-free shops sell luxury items like cameras, crystal, and cashmere, a Rastaman peddles coconuts from a wooden cart outside and country women, or hucksters, sit by their stalls of fresh fruit and vegetables picked from their gardens. Old ramshackle colonial buildings stand next to multimillion-dollar office blocks, and the strains of calypso emanate from juke boxes in back-alley cafés.

Early British colonists established a settlement here in what was no more than a swamp, where they found a bridge left by the Amerindians

*The Parliament Buildings in Bridgetown.*

– hence the name. The first harbor was built in the outer basin, called the Careenage, where the boats were "careened" or keeled over so that their hulls could be repaired and cleaned.

Now there are two bridges across the river, which in fact is just an inlet of sea: the wider Charles Duncan O'Neal Bridge and **Chamberlain Bridge** ❹, the gateway to Bridgetown, which used to swing back to allow boats to pass through, and is now closed to traffic. Down on the south bank, as part of a major renovation program, the old warehouses are being converted into shops and cafés, such as the **Waterfront Café** where you can relax and watch the water world and city life unfold in front of you. At night the tempo rises with a jazz band. In the Careenage, where the island's trading center once was, large catamarans offer sightseeing trips along the coast, and sportfishing boats are all set to hunt down the big wahoo and marlin.

## A controversial monument

Between the two bridges sprawls **Independence Square** ❺, a city park

## CRICKET, LOVELY CRICKET

Cricket is much more than a game in Barbados; it is a national religion, inspiring the islanders with a fierce passion, particularly when the West Indies meets England, their old colonial masters, in a Test match.

For 5 days, the **Kensington Oval**, the island's cricketing headquarters and national shrine, takes on a carnival atmosphere as supporters of both teams (Barbados almost sinks under the weight of the English fans who fly out for the event) pack the stands. With a "We must win but if we don't, then we must still have a good time" attitude, the West Indians welcome their visitors, encouraging them to join in the fun and share their picnics and "liquid sunshine."

The game of cricket has been described as "like abstract art – you only understand it when you have watched it for a long time." Introduced to the island almost 200 years ago by the British as a character builder, cricket now has no class boundaries, and Barbados has produced many heroes: the "Three Ws" – Clyde Walcott, Frank Worrell, and Everton Weekes – were knighted in the 1960s; Gordon Greenidge and Desmond Haynes, one of the world's best opening pairs; several fast bowlers; and the man often said to be greatest cricketer of all time, Garfield "Gary" Sobers, who was knighted in 1975, having scored 8,032 runs, taken 235 wickets, and held 110 catches.

dominated by a statue of the first prime minister and national hero, Errol Barrow. Walking over Chamberlain Bridge past the stalls of colorful fruit and vegetables, visitors come face to face with a bronze statue of Nelson located in what was known as Trafalgar Square, renamed **National Heroes Square** ⓒ. Seen as a symbol of colonialism, the monument to Nelson, erected in 1813 (17 years before Nelson's Column in London's Trafalgar Square) was controversial as early as 1833. Many local people want a Barbadian hero in its place.

The island's 10 National Heroes can be seen immortalized in stone in the **Museum of Parliament** and the **National Heroes Gallery** (tel: 246-310 5400; www.barbadosparliament.com; Mon, Wed–Fri 10am–4pm, Sat 10am–3pm) in the **Parliament Buildings** ⓓ, opened to commemorate 40 years of independence. These buildings were constructed in the 1870s to accommodate the Houses of Parliament, which were founded in 1639, making them the third-oldest parliamentary body in the Commonwealth after Bermuda and Britain.

**Broad Street** is the main shopping area, with several large duty-free stores; many of the buildings retain their old colonial grandeur. At the far end is the Georgian **St Mary's Church** ⓔ (daily; donations), which also serves as a hurricane shelter, surrounded by beautiful gardens. Opposite, the concrete facade of **Cheapside Market** fronts a typically colorful Caribbean scene on Saturday morning.

Westward along the seafront is **Pelican Craft Center** ⓕ (Mon–Fri 9am–5pm, Sat 9am–2pm) in a renovated purpose-built center where Barbadian artists and craftspeople can be seen at work, and where you can buy their wares – a handy spot for the passengers of the cruise ships that dock in the **Deep Water Harbor** at the end of the Princess Alice Highway. Some 665,000 people visit on cruise ships each year, compared with 532,000 who stay on the island.

From National Heroes Square, take the road east to **St Michael's Cathedral** ⓖ (daily; donations welcome). Dating from 1665, the original building was destroyed by a hurricane in

*Baxter's Road, in Bridgetown, is called The Street That Never Sleeps.*

*All aboard for an island safari.*

*St Michael's Cathedral was built from coral limestone in Greek Classical style.*

1780. However, it was rebuilt in solid limestone coral 9 years later, with the help of lottery money, ironically lending a church blessing to gambling. Inside is a single-hand clock. A few blocks farther to the east lies the tranquil oasis of **Queen's Park** with the magnificent **Queen's Park House** (1780) as its centerpiece. This fine Georgian building, with an impressive wooden balcony, houses a small theatre that puts on plays with a Caribbean flavor, and an art gallery exhibiting the work of local artists.

## The Garrison Historical Area

Leaving Bridgetown via Charles Duncan O'Neal Bridge, you pass the bus terminal for the south and **Fairchild Street Market**, and continue along Bay Street to the **Garrison Historical Area**, where the **Garrison Savannah** ❷, once a parade ground for the British West Indian forces, is now a busy racecourse and sports venue. Nearby is **George Washington House** (tel: 246-228 5461; Mon–Fri 9am–4.30pm), the restored Barbadian residence where the first American president stayed for

*Cannons at Garrison Savannah.*

2 months in 1751, aged 19. He never went abroad again.

East of the Garrison is the **Barbados Museum** ❸ (tel: 246-427 0201; www.barbmuse.org.bb; Mon–Sat 9am–5pm, Sun 2pm–6pm), housed in an early 19th-century British military prison. Beautifully presented in the old preserved prison cells, this portrayal of island history with an art gallery and children's hands-on gallery is one of the best in the Caribbean. There is also a café in the shady courtyard and a well-stocked museum shop.

## Southern hotspots

The road hugging the south coast leads through a built-up area of hotels, shops, and restaurants punctuated with glorious white beaches which offer plenty of fun and water sports. This part of Barbados is "jumping" after dark with islanders and visitors, all after some nocturnal action, from **Harbour Lights** and **The Boatyard** on Bay Street, open-air nightclubs on the beach outside Bridgetown, to the cluster of bars and restaurants at **St Lawrence Gap**, 3 miles (5 km) away

off Highway 7. Each nightspot has its own ambience and following, but they all rock with the sounds of soca, calypso, reggae, soul, or jazz.

**Oistins 4**, farther on, the fishing capital of Barbados, is another hot spot to try out on Friday night, but of a different kind. Here, the **Oistins Fish Fry** – fish cooked outside in enormous pans over burning coals – is held in an area of bars and stalls adjacent to the fish market on Friday and Saturday. Rum and beer are sold by the bottle and the music is turned up loud for dancing. You can still find a good fish supper here on other, quieter nights. On weekdays, the fishermen take their catch of dolphin (dorado or mahi mahi), snapper, king fish, tuna, and the national delicacy, flying fish, to the market, where women deftly gut and fillet them for sale.

Oistins also has an historical tale to tell: in 1652 the Royalist islanders had been besieged for weeks by Cromwell's Roundheads. The contretemps was finally settled in the Charter of Barbados, which pledged the islanders to obedience to the hated Cromwell and his Commonwealth Parliament in exchange for the right to religious freedom and consultation over taxation.

## Foursquare to Crane Resort

Heading inland from Oistins into the parish of St Philip, you reach **The Foursquare Rum Distillery and Heritage Park 5** (tel: 246-420 1977; www.rumsixtysix.com/foursquare-rum-distillery; Mon–Fri 9am–5pm, Sat 10am–9pm, Sun noon–6pm) at Foursquare off Highway 6, where you can a tour a modern, computerized rum distillery. In the adjoining Heritage Park is an amphitheater, an art gallery, and several craft shops. Farther north off Highway 5 is **Sunbury Plantation House 6** (tel: 246-423 6270; www.barbadosgreathouse.com; daily 9am–5pm), a beautifully restored 300-year-old plantation house, full of colonial antiques, which gives a real feel of what it must have been like to be a wealthy plantation

owner. You can stop for lunch here in the café at the back and return for a typical lavish evening banquet.

Back across Six Cross Roads to the southeast coast where two beaches and an old hotel are worth spending some time; all three are notable for their beauty and stunning location. Head south toward the first beach, **Harrismith**, where narrow steps lead down to a secluded cove lined with tall palms. Farther along the coast a left turn leads to **Bottom Bay**, a fine stretch of wide sandy beach that is perfect for picnics. It is here that the Atlantic meets the Caribbean and the waves build up some force, ideal for body surfing.

The waves are especially good around **Crane Resort 7** (daily; charge for non-guests, redeemable in the bar or restaurant). Opened in 1887, it was the island's first exclusive hotel, patronized by the wealthy. Before that the bay contained a small port where boats arrived with goods from Bridgetown. A crane at the top of the cliff unloaded the boats, giving the area its name. The resort, with its beautiful cliff-top view, has undergone

Map on page 250

**FACT**

Tyrol Cot, the former home of the first premier of Barbados, Sir Grantley Adams, and his son Tom, the second prime minister, is part of a Heritage Village (Mon–Fri 8am–4.30pm) northwest of Bridgetown.

*Found all across Barbados, the brownish-grey, yellow-speckled fur of the green monkey can appear green in some light.*

rapid expansion. Several five-story blocks of time-share apartments have been built alongside the original hotel and a glass lift takes people down to the pink-sand beach.

Sam Lord's Castle stands farther along this craggy coastline. Now closed, the 18th-century house was a hotel for many years, but before that it was the home of Sam Lord, a notorious planter and pirate and one of the most colorful characters in Bajan folklore.

## The wild and rugged east

The scenery changes dramatically along the East Coast Road compared with the flat pastureland of the south, and as it cuts through tropical woodland, the impressive entrance of **Codrington College ❽** (tel: 246-423 1140; www. codrington.org; daily dawn to dusk; free, donations appreciated in the chapel), with a drive lined with majestic royal palms, hoves into view. Founded in 1702 by Christopher Codrington, the Barbados-born governor-general of the Leeward Islands and de facto owner of Barbuda (see page 178), the theological college has a fascinating nature trail in

the grounds, leading through primeval forest. The adventurer and travel writer Patrick Leigh Fermor described it in the late 1940s: "in a hollow beyond a spinney of tall mahogany, south of the township of Bathsheba, a beautiful Palladian building, reclining dreamily on the shores of a lake among lawns and balustrades and great shady trees, suddenly appeared, its columns and pediments conjuring up, in the afternoon sunlight, some enormous country seat in the Dukeries." And it has barely changed.

## Bathsheba

Continuing north on the East Coast Road, the undulating sugar-cane fields change to steep hillsides of banana plantations that drop to the sea. A right turn plunges down to **Bathsheba** and the **Andromeda Botanic Gardens ❾** (daily 9am–5pm), with one of the finest displays of tropical flowers and shrubs in the Caribbean, currently containing more than 600 species. Created in 1954 on a rocky hillside by amateur horticulturist Iris Bannochie, who died in 1988, the garden is intelligently designed and harbors exotic plants she collected on

*Treat your tastebuds at the Fish Fry in Oistins.*

her travels around the world. There is a splendid example of a bearded fig tree alongside collections of orchids and bromeliads. A stream cuts through the 6-acre (2-hectare) profusion of tropical flora, now owned by the Barbados National Trust.

At Bathsheba is the wind-battered **Atlantis Hotel**, where Barbados's most famous author, George Lamming, sometimes stays when he returns. It is one of the oldest hotels on the island, and serves local dishes. Surfers flock to Bathsheba for the Soup Bowl, where the waves are a challenge. The beach here is distinguished by rows of giant boulders marching out to the white, surf-churned sea. There are pleasant rock pools you can cool off in, but swimming is dangerous. Better to sit on the beach and watch the daredevils riding the waves with their boards.

At Cattlewash, north of Bathsheba, the road runs beside a long golden beach washed by Atlantic rollers. Usually deserted during the week, the sea is dangerous for swimmers.

## The Scotland District hills

Homesick British colonists likened the lush landscapes of Barbados to England, and the rolling hills and bizarre rock formations to the Scottish Highlands, earning the nicknames Little England and the Scotland District. An excursion into the island's interior will take you through open countryside, past acres of cane fields and small hamlets of chattel houses, each with a rum shop-cum-store. Leaving the ABC Highway in Bridgetown on Highway 3, follow the signposts to **Gun Hill Signal Station**, where there is a small museum (daily) and a white stone lion. Just over a mile farther on you reach **Orchid World** ❿ (tel: 246-433 0306; daily 9am–5pm). Around 20,000 orchids of all sizes and species flourish here. The landscaped paths take you past a waterfall and through a coral grotto, offering views of the surrounding countryside.

Farther north, **Harrison's Cave** ⓫ (tel: 246-417 3700; www.harrisonscave. com; daily, tours 8.45am–3.45pm) is a geological feast for the eyes, a crystallized limestone underworld of gorges, grottoes, streams, and waterfalls encrusted with spectacular stalactites and stalagmites at which you can marvel from an electric tram, then on foot.

## Botanical beauty

For tranquil, natural beauty above ground, walk through the luxuriant jungle greenery of **Welchman Hall Gully** ⓬ (tel: 246-438 6671; www. welchmanhallgullybarbados.com; daily 9am–4pm) nearby. The half-mile (1km)-long ravine was once part of a series of caves connected with Harrison's Cave, whose roofs fell in. Now owned by the Barbados National Trust, there are some 150 species of plants, flowers, and trees, plus large families of green monkeys who snap up the fruit.

Another botanical delight is the **Flower Forest** ⓭ (tel: 246-433 8152; www.flowerforestbarbados.com; daily 8am–4pm) a little farther north, where

*Cherry Tree Hill, St Andrews, Barbados.*

**TIP**

The Morgan Lewis Sugar Mill in the northeast is the largest working windmill in the Caribbean. Restored and run by the National Trust, the mill can be seen in action on certain days. Call 246-426 2421 for more information.

you can touch and smell the wonderful array of tropical flowers and plants in 50 acres (20 hectares) of lawns and woodland set against magnificent views downhill to the east coast. In the center is a young baobab tree, traditionally grown in the middle of African villages.

## The Platinum Coast

The west coast of Barbados is lapped by the deep azure blue of the tranquil Caribbean Sea, with pinky-white coral sand beaches edged with casuarina trees and palms, living up to the tropical island dream. Earning the tag Platinum Coast, this is where the smart hotels jostle for the best sea view, each in its own landscaped paradise and sporting such tantalizing names as Glitter Bay, Coral Reef, and Tamarind Cove. As no one can own a beach in Barbados, it is possible to walk for miles along the water's edge, stopping at the beach bars for a rum punch and trying out the wide variety of water sports on offer.

The world-renowned **Sandy Lane Hotel ⓮**, refuge of the rich and

*Harrison's Cave, Barbados.*

famous, is tucked away in Sandy Lane Bay just south of Holetown (about 3 miles/5km north of Bridgetown on Highway 1). Built in 1961, the original hotel was demolished and the site redeveloped into a large, luxurious resort, which has a spa and three spectacular golf courses.

Captain Henry Powell accidentally landed in **Holetown ⓯** in May 1625 on his way to somewhere else. He took a fancy to what he saw as a nice piece of real estate and, as any true Englishman would have done in those days, he stuck his country's flag in the ground and claimed it on behalf of the king. In February 1627 an expedition to settle the island arrived and, today, the Holetown Festival celebrates the anniversary with parades and street parties.

## Speightstown and the spectacular north

**Speightstown ⓰**, the island's second town, was once an important port for transporting sugar to Bristol in England, earning it the name of Little Bristol. Its story is imaginatively told in the restored three-story,

## CREATION OF A NEW CULTURE

After more than 40 years as an independent nation, Barbados has come into its own culturally. There is an appreciation of things Bajan, and a movement to preserve aspects of the folk culture that had been dying out. With Britain as the sole colonial master, there is no French, Spanish, or Dutch influence in the language. There was no mass immigration from India or China after the abolition of slavery to add spice to the cuisine. So Bajans turned to their African roots for their cultural heritage rather than endure the pejorative name of "Little England." In the 1970s, the Black Power and Rastafari movements had a profound impact on island identity.

The enthusiasm the revived annual Crop Over Festival in July and August generates is one sign of the new cultural pride, and calypsonians are a major force in Bajan society. The 5-week-long festival celebrates the end of the sugar-cane harvest and is the highlight of an annual calendar of events.

Another powerful influence on Bajan culture in the past four decades has been US television and music. One of the island's most famous calypsonians, the Mighty Gabby, has sung about the negative effect of commercial programs on society, advocating more worthy Barbadian subjects instead.

18th-century balconied **Arlington House** (tel: 246-422 4064; Mon–Sat 9am–5pm), an interesting museum with interactive exhibits on sugar, slavery and trade. The town has a good selection of restaurants, bars, beaches, a boardwalk, and the largest art gallery on the island. Walking tours of the town and up into Whim Gully on the **Arbib Nature and Heritage Trail** (tel: 246-234 9010 for advance reservations; tours Wed, Thur, Sat 9am–2pm) to see bearded fig trees and coral boulders, are rewarding.

Highway 1 continues through the pretty fishing village of **Six Men's Bay** and into the rugged, sparsely populated northernmost parish of St Lucy. At the very northern tip of the island is the **Animal Flower Cave** ⓱ (www.animal flowercave.com; daily), named for the few tiny sea anemones that may be seen in the pools. The view of the sea from the cave is tremendous but it has to be closed in rough weather. The ocean's relentless pounding has created steep, jagged cliffs and rocky, barren land that resembles a moonscape. A restaurant operates daily between 11am and 3pm.

From here the road cuts inland to the Jacobean plantation house, the privately owned **St Nicholas Abbey** ⓲ (tel: 246-422 5357; www.stnicholas abbey.com; Sun–Fri 10am–3.30pm). Thought to be the oldest original building on the island, dating from 1660, it has never been a religious institution, despite the name, and is full of fascinating features (note the chimney) and antiques. Allow a few hours to see the house, the gardens and grounds, the rum distillery and rum and sugar museum, to watch the home movie, and visit adjacent Cherry Tree Hill. There is a café here and you can, of course, buy the rum, made by traditional methods.

Farther south you reach the main road back to the west coast and **Barbados Wildlife Reserve** ⓳ (daily). Here the only caged creatures are pythons and boas – the green monkeys, tortoises, sprocket deer, iguana, and other animals roam freely alongside the visitors in a mahogany woodland. The entrance ticket includes admission to Grenade Hall Forest and Signal Station.

*Animal Flower Cave, Barbados.*

The scarlet ibis.

# TRINIDAD

Geologically part of South America and politically the stronger half of a twin-island republic, this exhilarating, cosmopolitan, tropical island is also a land of natural beauty.

Pulsating with life, Trinidad is a vibrant island, much noisier than Tobago, its more tranquil partner, 21 miles (33km) away, in the republic of Trinidad and Tobago. It reaches a crescendo at Carnival time when the capital, Port of Spain, the birthplace of steel pan and capital of calypso, throbs to the rhythms of the bands and the dancing in the streets. Local people and visitors alike are welcome to join the flamboyant costumed parades and have a ball in the "greatest street party on earth" (see page 266).

The oil booms of the 1970s and early 2000s have created an economic climate comfortable enough for Trinidad not to encourage tourism. In the mountain rainforests of the north, the coastal swamps, and the flat palm-fringed beaches of the east, it is easy to escape the west coast's modern hubbub of industrialized life. Many of its stunning beaches are deserted and inaccessible except by boat or on foot. Nonetheless, outside the hurricane belt, the sheltered bays of the north-west have become a haven for yachties and there are numerous marinas.

## Multiracial, multicultural

It would be wrong to eulogize the beautiful blue waters that surround Trinidad, because on all but the northern coastline, they are distinctly brown. The southernmost and largest

island in the Eastern Caribbean chain (1,864 sq miles/4,660 sq km), it is washed by the waters of the Orinoco delta just 7 miles (11km) away in Venezuela, but the sea is still mostly warm, clear, and pleasant to swim in. Sailing or flying across to Tobago, halfway you can see the color of the water dramatically change to blue.

Amerindians had canoed across from the Orinoco region and settled these shores long before Columbus sighted the island on July 31, 1498. The Spanish colonizers failed to find

**Main Attractions**

Gasparee Caves
Maracas Waterfall
Asa Wright Nature Centre
Las Cuevas
Toco
Devil's Woodyard
Caroni Bird Sanctuary

*Trinidad's Carnival, unrivalled in the Caribbean.*

*The purple honey-creeper weighs less than half an ounce (14g).*

the gold of El Dorado here, but they did use the island for tobacco plantations. To cultivate them they enslaved the local Amerindians, who practically died out within a century as a result.

English sailors, Spanish farmers, French planters and their families, adventurers, thousands of African slaves, and, from the 19th century onward after the abolition of slavery, numerous Asian, Portuguese, and Chinese laborers, plus a small minority of Syrian and Lebanese merchants, have formed the basis of today's multicultural society of just over a million people. Here you can find Anglican, Roman Catholic, and Methodist churches, a Benedictine monastery, Hindu temples, and Islamic mosques, and any number of other places of worship.

## Rich resources

As oil replaced sugar as king, a multiracial middle class in the industrial centers of the west coast administered the profits from wells near La Brea. Manufactured products for export to the whole of the Caribbean grew sharply through the post-war years and onward, and the discovery of further rich oil and gas reserves in the 1970s nourished the island's hopes of a future free from economic worries. The new prosperity also helped ensure Trinidad's rise to having one of the highest literacy rates in the Americas.

Politically, Trinidad and Tobago were governed by Britain between 1888 and 1962. In the 1950s local politics flourished under the leadership of the brilliant historian Dr Eric Williams, who

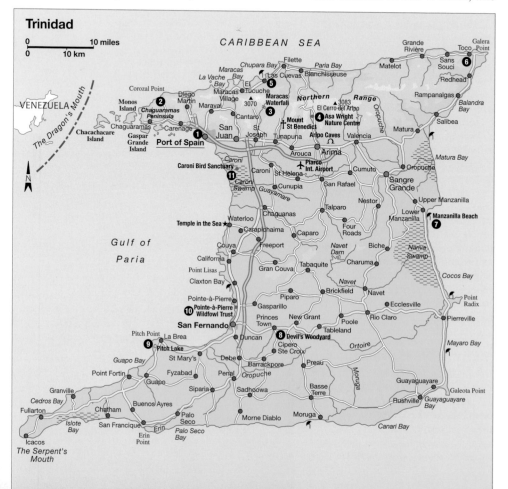

founded the People's National Movement (PNM) and became the first prime minister after independence in 1962. The republic was created in 1976. Power then alternated between the PNM and the largely East Indian United National Congress (UNC). However, in 2010 an unprecedented coalition agreement was reached by five parties, known as the People's Partnership, to defeat the PNM, which had been in government since 2002. Following the September 2015 general election, the PNM returned to power, with its leader Keith Rowley becoming prime minister.

## Port of Spain

Port of Spain ❶, the capital, was founded in 1754 by the Spanish at the foot of the Northern Range. Today modern skyscrapers, such as the 300ft (92-meter) Twin Towers, and elegant shopping centers contrast sharply with dilapidated gingerbread-style villas, wooden huts, and rusty fences. A daytime stroll through Independence Square and Queen's Park Savannah is not too strenuous. In the evening, walking downtown should be avoided, and the eastern suburbs only visited if accompanied by a local person.

**Independence Square** is bordered to the east by the neo-Gothic Cathedral of the **Immaculate Conception**. Extending westward toward the cruise terminal on both sides of this long square are shopping centers, banks, a statue of Columbus, and the Twin Towers, containing government offices. The attractive promenade along the center is named for Brian Lara, who has done much to make Trinidad famous as a cricket-playing nation.

**Frederick Street**, lined with street traders, leads to the park on **Woodford Square**. This is where dissatisfied citizens keep the Speakers' Corner tradition alive by loudly criticizing various decisions made in the imposing **Red House**, the seat of parliament, at the western end of the square. The Anglican Cathedral of the Holy Trinity, the Supreme Court, the Town Hall,

and police headquarters surround the park and its magnificent old trees. At the southwest corner, on Hart and Abercromby, rises the striking modern National Library, located next to a historic landmark – the Old Fire Brigade Station – which has been restored and incorporated into the new complex.

To the north, a 15-minute walk away, Frederick Street ends at Port of Spain's giant park, the **Queen's Park Savannah**. Nearby, in the **National Museum and Art Gallery** (corner of Frederick and Keate streets; tel: 868-623 5941; www.nmag.gov.tt; Tue–Sat 10am–6pm; free), you can see documents dating from the colonial era and also a collection of glitzy Carnival costumes.

West of the Savannah, the **Magnificent Seven** – a line of very fine (if partly dilapidated) colonial buildings dating from the turn of the 20th century – give Maraval Road flair and elegance. In the early morning, the sun shows them at their best. To the north are the beautiful **Royal Botanic Gardens** (daily 6am–6pm; free) and the President's House.

A good introduction to the national instrument, the steelpan, is a visit to a

*King's Wharf, Port of Spain.*

*Kamla Persad-Bissessar, leader of the People's Partnership, was the country's first female prime minister.*

*Manzanilla Beach.*

panyard, where steel bands rehearse: Amoco Renegades at the top of Charlotte Street, Witco Desperadoes up Laventille Hill, or Phase II on Hamilton Street, in the western suburb of Woodbrook, where there are excellent restaurants on Ariapita Avenue. Also in Woodbrook is the **Queen's Park Oval** cricket ground, the oldest ground in the Caribbean, where international test matches are played. West of Woodbrook is St James, lively with bars and clubs.

## To the northern rainforest

The rugged coast of the **Chaguaramas Peninsula ❷**, a former US naval base (1945–64) to the northwest of Port of Spain, is a popular sailing area. On the island of **Gaspar Grande**, a 20-minute boat ride from Chaguaramas town, guided tours of the **Gasparee** limestone caverns are available (tel: 868-225 4232 for advance booking; www.chagdev.com).

The mountainous hinterland of the Northern Range arrives quite suddenly when leaving the urban sprawl north and east of Port of Spain. The Eastern Main Road passes through several towns including Trinidad's first capital

under Spanish rule, **St Joseph**. Continuing north, the Royal Road meanders through rainforest and close to the 320ft (100-meter) **Maracas Waterfall ❸**, 20 minutes' walk from the road, which is especially impressive after rainfall.

Back on the main road, some good Chinese and East Indian roti restaurants mark your arrival in **Tunapuna**. High on the hill above lies **Mount St Benedict**, the oldest Benedictine monastery in the region (founded 1912), and 8 miles (13km) further east, you reach **Arima**, the island's third-largest town. From here the road north twists and turns through orchards and rainforest to the **Asa Wright Nature Centre ❹** (tel: 868-667 4655; www.asawright. org; daily 9am–5pm; accommodation and guided tours available, advance reservations required). This 182-acre (74-hectare) site contains a vast amount of fascinating tropical flora and fauna. More than 100 different species of birds, including several rare hummingbirds, can be observed here.

The wildly romantic coastline near **Blanchisseuse** on the northern coast is reached via 23 miles (37km) of hairpin bends with stunning views and dangerous potholes. The glorious sands and waterfall at **Paria Bay** lie a 2-hour hike from here, while more easily accessible is the half-moon-shaped sandy bay at the fishing village of **Las Cuevas ❺** to the west. **Maracas Bay** is the busier beach, but equally attractive.

## Palm-fringed bays

At the northeastern tip of the island are the dramatic cliffs of **Toco ❻**, a 3-hour drive from the capital via the Eastern Main Road and a rather bumpy route through some mountain rainforest. Leatherback turtles lay their eggs on the secluded beaches here between April and June.

The East Coast Road leads back down to **Matura** from where three sandy bays sweep southwards for 40 miles (60km). Edged by dense coconut plantations, **Manzanilla Beach ❼** in the middle has some public amenities,

and **Mayaro** at the southern end has houses to rent. However, swimming here is dangerous, due to a strong undertow and high waves. Behind the palm trees is the mangrove swamp of **Nariva**, and young boys can often be seen driving their water buffalo out into the fields. The rural south of Trinidad is mainly inhabited by East Indian farming families and oil workers.

## Where the earth bubbles

At **Devil's Woodyard** ❽, about 8 miles (13km) east of Trinidad's second-largest city, San Fernando, on the southwest coast, gas bubbles can be seen inside the mud holes of one of the island's 18 mud volcanoes. This is a holy site for Hindus, who leave sacrificial offerings here such as flowers and coconut oil. The **Pitch Lake** ❾ (tel: 868-675 7034; daily 9am–5pm), at La Brea, 13 miles (20km) southwest of San Fernando, is the largest natural asphalt lake in the world and up to 320ft (100 meters) deep in places. It was a spiritual site for Amerindians before being found in 1595 by the English captain Sir Walter Raleigh, who used the sticky substance to help keep his ship waterproof. You can walk on parts of the surface of the lake, but don't explore it without an experienced guide.

Just to the north of San Fernando, some rare wildfowl have found refuge right at the center of a crude oil refinery. The **Pointe-à-Pierre Wildfowl Trust** ❿ (tel: 868-658 4200 ext. 2512; www.pap wildfowltrust.org; daily by appointment) devotes itself to breeding threatened species and preserving natural habitats.

Heading north to Port of Spain, **Carapichaima** is famous for its 85ft (26-meter) statue of the Hindu monkey god, Hanuman, its impressive Waterloo Temple-in-the-Sea – joined to the mainland by a causeway – as well as the **Maha Sabha Museum** (tel: 868-675 7007; Wed–Sun 10am–5pm; free), documenting the East Indian Caribbean experience since the 1830s.

The national bird of Trinidad is the scarlet ibis, and every evening flocks of these elegant creatures return from their feeding grounds in Venezuela to roost in the mangrove swamp at **Caroni Bird Sanctuary** ⓫ (tel: 868-469 4076; daily 7am–8pm).

*Enjoying the view at the Asa Wright Nature Centre.*

# THE GREATEST STREET PARTY ON EARTH

**Carnival in the Lesser Antilles is alive and well and getting bigger every year as the islands fill up with revelers from all over the world.**

Neither age nor profession, nor money nor skin color matter when, every February, thousands of Trinidadians and visitors seem to drown in a sea of colors, feathers, rhythm, and rum. From Jouvay, the wild street party that takes place from dawn on the Monday before Ash Wednesday, until King Momo's death by fire in the last hours of Shrove Tuesday, Port of Spain is one big anarchic Carnival party. The heroes are soca stars and ingenious costume designers highly revered by a hip-swinging crowd dizzy with the beat and pulsating rhythm of the steel pans.

## New Carnivals

Trinidad hosts the biggest Caribbean Carnival, which originated out of the Christian tradition of having a last big feast before fasting during Lent. In Guadeloupe and Martinique people dress in black and white on Ash Wednesday and bury King Vaval. On St-Barthélemy King Moui Moui is burned, and on St Kitts Christmas and the New Year are the best times to enjoy parades and street festivals. Other so-called Carnivals in the summer months have developed from the harvest festivals after the sugar cane had been cut, such as Crop Over in Barbados, which includes the ceremonial delivery of the last canes. Some islands have only recently established Carnivals for tourism's sake – any excuse for an extended street party…

*When the slaves started creating their costumes, the mythology of their African ancestors inspired them to figures of good and evil.*

*Carnival is the most lavish party on earth, with spectacular costumes and extravagant jewelry all contributing to create a riot of color.*

*Junkanoo in the Bahamas is held on 26 December and 1 January from 2am to 8am, with colorful street parades and wild dancing to the beat of goat skin drums and cow bells.*

*Feathery mask at Carnival.*

## PLAYING MAS IN TRINIDAD

As soon as one Carnival ends the designers' imaginations are hard at work on the next one. Great Carnival designers such as Trinidadian Peter Minshall – whose renowned costumes led him to design the costumes for the opening of the Olympic Games in 1992 and 1996 – set up Mas Camps (workshops) where vast numbers of costumes are made on a theme for their bands. Each band has a Carnival King and Queen who wear the masterpieces, which are judged on Dimanche Gras, the night before Carnival officially begins.

The Mas tradition started in the late 18th century with French plantation owners organizing masquerades (*mas*) and balls before enduring the fasting of Lent. Slaves copied and lampooned their masters, and once set free from forced labor, their frustrations found a platform in clever calypso lyrics mocking their former masters, and then their political leaders. Calypsonians can trace their origins back to the late 18th century and the first "shantwell," Gros Jean. With African, French, British, Spanish, and East Indian influences, it has developed into today's keenly fought competition for the Calypso Monarch's crown.

*As the effigy of Vaval – a papier-mâché figure embodying Carnival – is consumed by flames, dancing in Martinique's carnival celebrations reaches its climax on Ash Wednesday.*

*Many of the island carnivals have a special day set aside for the children just before the official start. Their costumes are often made in the Mas camps of Trinidad.*

*All the fun of the fair – a thrilling display of pyrotechnics adds to the sheer energy of the carnival party in Trinidad.*

*Parlatuvier Bay, Tobago.*

# TOBAGO

Only a 20-minute flight away from frenetic Port of
Spain, Tobago is an oasis of calm in a bright blue sea
of tranquility, offering copious white beaches,
sheltered coves, and a wild forest interior.

Caribbean
Sea

Tobago

**T**rinidad's other half in the Republic of Trinidad and Tobago, this
small tropical island, 21 miles
(34km) to the northeast, provides a
complete contrast to its twin's cosmopolitan bustle, industrialization,
and magnitude. Rural tranquility and
Caribbean enjoyment of life go hand
in hand in Tobago, and the magnificent beaches and colorful coral landscape just offshore are an effective
means of dispelling stress.

At only 26 miles (42km) long and
7 miles (11km) wide, Tobago is a con-
tinual feast for the eyes: picturesque,
bumpy roads wind around the coast
past unspoiled bays of white sand and
bright blue sea, and climb up across
the mountainous backbone through
high stands of creaking bamboo and
dense rainforest, alive with colorful
birdlife, before plunging into panoramic views on the other side. No
wonder Columbus named it Bella-
forma (Beautiful Shape) in 1498.

Tobago does not share the cultural
mix that enriches Trinidad, despite
having changed colonial hands 29
times in 160 years; the population of
around 62,000 are mainly descendents of African slaves and make a
living from tourism and agriculture.
Despite the steadily increasing flow
of visitors to their island, Tobagonians
are friendly and development remains
notably low-key.

## Tobago's colonial past

Hope, Courland, Shirvan, Les Coteaux
– the place names are all reminders of
Tobago's colonial past. In the early 17th
century, the first Dutch and English
settlers arrived, only to be wiped out
or chased off by the Caribs. Eventually,
80 families from Latvia succeeded in
settling on Courland Bay in 1654 and
planted sugar cane, tobacco, pepper, and
cotton. Adventurers, smallholders, and
pirates from all over Europe followed
in their footsteps; many were killed by
tropical diseases or by Carib arrows.

**Main Attractions**

Hillsborough Reservoir
Argyll Waterfalls
Tobago Cocoa Estate
Little Tobago
Charlotteville
Tobago Forest Reserve
Englishman's Bay

*Tropical idyll at Pigeon Point.*

**TIP**

Delicious soursop ice cream and many other homemade specialties can be bought from the market women in the niches at the large round market building in Scarborough. Fresh coconut water, and ice cream coated in syrup are just two of the many delightful ways to refresh yourself around here.

Slaves were set to work on the first sugar-cane and cotton plantations 100 years later. In 1793, when the English had managed to seize control of Tobago yet again, the island was inhabited by 14,170 blacks, 850 whites, and five Amerindians. Numerous slave rebellions were dealt with ruthlessly by plantation owners – Tobago became one of the most profitable colonies by area, with around 80 estates.

After full Emancipation in 1838, most of the plantations went broke as freed slaves left to begin subsistence farming. French planters in particular took the opportunity to buy up land very cheaply and started several coconut plantations – later settling very comfortably on Trinidad.

To save money, the British decided from 1888 onward to treat their two southernmost islands in the Caribbean as a collective administrative unit. In 1962, the twin-island state was given independence, and since 1987 Tobago has had internal autonomy separate from Trinidad, although it is still heavily dependent on subsidies from Port of Spain.

## A village capital

The little town of **Scarborough** ❶ (pop. 25,000) on Rockly Bay is Tobago's main harbor as well as the island's center of trade and administration. It was founded by Dutch settlers (who named the site Lampsinburg) in 1654, and has been the island capital since 1769. A dusty, commercial place, the center consists of two road junctions and concrete structures housing the post office, the market, the ferry and cruise ship harbor, Scarborough Mall, and the bus station. On market days half of Tobago meets here to go shopping.

An oasis of calm behind the mall is the **Botanic Gardens** (free), where native trees, bushes, and flowers can be found in graceful and shady arrangements. From the harbor, Carnett Street leads up steeply past several tradesmen's stands to **James Park**; at the top end is the imposing-looking, Georgian-style **Court House** (built 1821–25).

Follow Fort Street uphill past the hospital and prison, and a few steep curves later you reach the impressive **Fort King George**, built in the

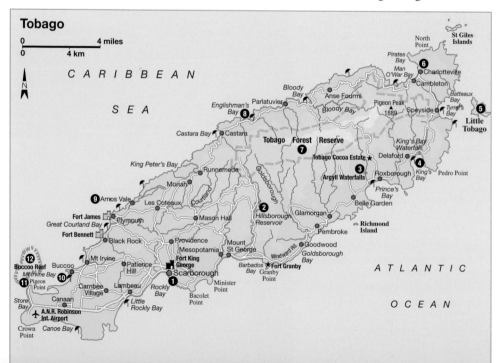

late 18th century 490ft (150 meters) above Rockly Bay. Severely damaged by a whirlwind in 1847, the fort was rebuilt according to old plans. Today, the complex contains the excellent **Tobago Museum** (Mon–Fri 9am–4.30pm) in the Barrack Guard House, holding Amerindian artifacts, military relics, and documents; the Officers' Mess is now a craft shop and the former Military Hospital contains the **National Fine Arts Center**.

## Along the rugged coast

**Windward Road** winds its way along the southeast coast of Tobago in steep curves. Spectacular views of the Atlantic, potholes that are often knee-deep, and idyllic roadside villages make this an unforgettable experience. Leave Scarborough via Bacolet Street and **Gun Bridge**, named after the two old cannon there. The only reminder that **Mount St George**, 4 miles (6km) along the road, was once the British seat of government is the renovated court building dating from 1788. A left turn shortly afterward leads inland for 2 miles (3km) to the **Hillsborough**

Reservoir ❷, an artificial lake providing drinking water and also the natural habitat of many rare species of bird; the dragonflies are very colorful, and you may even see a cayman (alligator).

Back on Windward Road, a weathered gravestone is all that remains of **Fort Granby**. During the 18th century this once-proud structure, looking across Barbados Bay, was home to the English 62nd Regiment; now it makes a perfect picnic spot. The road winds along the coast, between the dark fringes of the rainforest and the spray of the Atlantic, passing through picturesque villages like **Pembroke** and **Belle Garden**. Outside village bars, at road junctions, and in mini-markets, Tobagonians enjoy their spare time "liming" – the local word for hanging out.

## Seasonal waterfalls

Standing among the tropical greenery high above the rocky coast (just before you reach Belle Garden) is **Richmond Great House**, a renovated manor house dating from 1766. Just before Roxborough, 3 miles (5km) on, the road branches left to

*At the spot where Fort Granby used to stand.*

*Fort King George.*

**TIP**

When driving in Tobago remember that the locals are familiar with every pothole and hairpin bend and are prone to overtaking at dangerous places. To avoid stress, slow down and, when it's safe to do so, cheerfully wave past any traffic behind you.

*Goat racing in Buccoo village.*

**Argyll Waterfalls ❸** (9am–5pm; charge), the highest on the island at 177ft (54 metres), which pour out of the mountainside in two separate cascades during the rainy season. Even though they're reduced to trickles at other times of year, there's still enough water for a refreshing shower after the muddy 15-minute walk to get there.

Also in the area, you can tour **Tobago Cocoa Estate** (Cameron Canal Road; tel: 868-788 3971; www.tobagococoa.com; tours Fri 11 am), learn about the chocolate-making process, buy their single-estate fine chocolate, and try other local culinary delights. Longer tours with meals are available.

Another 3 miles (5km) past **Roxborough**, the largest settlement on the southeast coast – black workers led the Belmanna Uprising in 1876 – is **King's Bay ❹**, a picturesque coconut plantation and waterfall with a cool, wild beach nestled beneath.

In the village of **Speyside**, 3 miles (5km) away, in a beautiful broad blue bay, excursions are offered to the bird sanctuary on **Little Tobago ❺** just offshore. There are 58 species of birds on this tiny island, including a large nesting colony of redbilled tropic birds. Tours are best in the morning and usually include a snorkeling stop. Marine life here is truly spectacular with most species of hard and soft corals and even an enormous brain coral, thought to be one of the largest in the world. Glass-bottomed boats (plenty to choose from) are the most comfortable way on calm days to admire the underwater world. For experienced divers there is exciting drift diving and you can see manta rays feeding in the Guyana current. There are several small hotels, restaurants, and dive shops in Speyside and Batteaux Bay, the next bay along the coast.

## The picturesque northeast

Windward Road leaves the coast at Speyside and winds up a steep incline to a viewpoint over the northeastern tip of the island. The houses of **Charlotteville ❻** on the other side cling to the steep slope above **Man O'War Bay**. The 600 or so inhabitants live

mainly from fishing and tourism, and visitors appreciate the tranquility, although the introduction of a proposed small cruise ship terminal may change that. A flight of 68 steps leads down to **Pirates Bay**, where local women spread their washing on the rocks to dry. Just offshore is a reef teeming with life, and elegant yachts moor in the bay.

## Tobago Forest Reserve

From Charlotteville, a winding stretch of road navigates the northern Caribbean coast to Bloody Bay, from where another route cuts back across the island through the **Tobago Forest Reserve ❼**. This thick jungle in myriad shades of green spreads along the Main Ridge between Hillsborough and Charlotteville and is the oldest section of protected, unaltered rainforest in the world; the British declared it a nature reserve on April 8, 1776. The road and several hiking routes only allow visitors to cover a very small proportion of the area; the green thickets contain black-and-yellow weavers, green parrots, and dazzling hummingbirds, and the tropical vegetation is fascinating. Yellow poui and red flame trees stand out against the forested hillsides. The paths are sometimes steep and muddy, so it's best to go with an experienced guide.

At Bloody Bay, the road follows the coastline west for 2 miles (3km) to **Englishman's Bay ❽**, a magnificent beach where the forest comes down to the edge, coconut palms wave in the breeze, and the waves lap against the (usually) deserted beach. Almost as enchanting are the sands at pretty **Castara**, which also has a smattering of guesthouses and holds the **Fisherman's Fete** in August. A track branches off at Runnemede, 2 miles (3km) down the coast, to stunning panoramic views over **King Peter's Bay**.

Several more small bays are tucked away at the end of **Arnos Vale ❾**,

down a small road farther west, which offer excellent snorkeling and birdwatching.

## An endangered reef

Black Rock marks the beginning of the southwest side of Tobago. There are several expensive hotels as well as rooms for rent around the broad beaches, including **Mount Irvine Bay ❿**, where there is a championship golf course and good surfing waves. Locals and tourists meet up in **Buccoo** every Sunday evening for the "Sunday School" open-air disco – especially lively at Easter when the **goat races** are held.

At idyllic **Pigeon Point ⓫**, one of the most-photographed beaches in the Caribbean, glass-bottomed boats take snorkelers to the largely destroyed coral gardens at the now-protected **Buccoo Reef ⓬**. Boats offer trips that include a barbecue and a wallow in the shallow turquoise waters of the **Nylon Pool**. However, this is one place where it is obvious that tourism hasn't always been in the best interests of Tobago.

**FACT**

The cocrico is the national bird of Tobago and tends to descend on gardens in enormous flocks. When the pheasant-like bird starts squawking loudly it is considered a sure sign that rain is on the way.

*A windsurfer shows off his skills.*

*Flamencos on the beach.*

*Antique cannon.*

# CURAÇAO

A cosmopolitan kaleidoscope of people with a distinctive heritage live on this dry island, but with sheltered bays, turquoise water, and coral reefs it offers a world of discovery for divers.

own in the south of the Caribbean off the coast of Venezuela, Curaçao is dry, with a hilly and scrubby terrain, where acacia and cactus predominate. Some 38 miles (60km) long by just over 7 miles (11km) wide, the northwest coast of this long, thin island is rugged but the southeast has some sheltered bays for swimming and snorkeling. Underwater, however, Curaçao makes up for any scenic deficiencies on land, with colorful reefs and fish, coral, sponges, and other marine life, protected by an underwater park.

Long before the arrival of Spaniard Alonso de Ojeda, the first European to set foot on this rocky island off the north coast of South America in 1499, the land was settled by Amerindians from the Caiquetío tribe. Its Spanish conquerors exported these inhabitants to other islands as slaves, and limited colonization of the island to a few cattle farms. In the 17th century, the Dutch built a military base at Schottegat, a natural harbor with a deep-water entrance, and it soon became an important trading center.

Since agriculture on the dry soil was exhausting and unprofitable, the settlers, who included numerous Jewish families from Amsterdam and northeastern Brazil, switched to trading in indigo, cotton, tobacco, and slaves. After suffering the rigors and

inhuman conditions of their transatlantic voyage, hundreds of thousands of Africans were "freshened up" in the camps around Willemstad, and then sold like cattle at the slave market – a practice that continued well into the late 18th century. A bloody slave uprising in 1795 did nothing to alter the situation: after a month of fighting the leaders of the rebellion were executed. It was only in 1863 that the Netherlands finally abolished slavery but a form of neo-slavery lasted into the 20th century.

*An underwater wreck.*

*Hitting the shops in Curaçao.*

## Economic and political independence

It was the discovery of oil in the Maracaibo Basin in 1914 that changed workers' fortunes. The island experienced an economic upswing through the opening of a massive oil refinery on the flat isola in the Schottegat, where Venezuelan crude oil was refined. However, since the 1980s, petrodollar income has fallen. Tourism has become another important earner here, alongside lucrative finance business, international services, and a flourishing harbor with ultra-modern docks.

As a result of this mixed economy, Curaçao is home to around 152,000 people from more than 60 nations. The main languages spoken are papiamentu (see page 59), Dutch, Spanish, and English. Many people speak all four, and papiamentu is spoken by 85 percent of the population.

Curaçao was granted full self-government in 1954 as an island territory of the Netherlands Antilles, but independence gradually became a burning issue. By the early 21st century it was clear that the Netherlands

Antilles itself was no longer viable and after referenda on all the constituent islands, the bloc was broken up. On October 10, 2010, Curaçao became a country within the Kingdom of the Netherlands, independent in everything but defense and foreign policy.

## A tropical mini-Amsterdam

With Unesco World Heritage status, **Willemstad ❶**, the busy capital of Curaçao (pop. 150,000), is like a small tropical Amsterdam – a fascinating mixture of the Caribbean and attractive Dutch-style colonial architecture. It impresses visitors most with its candy-colored colonial buildings dating from the 16th to the 19th centuries. Magnificent merchants' houses with steep, red-tiled roofs, town houses with beautiful stucco facades, three well-preserved forts, picturesque little streets, and large airy churches all stand as reminders of the prosperity of the first European settlers.

The town is one huge sprawling development around the **Schottegat**, a large, deep inlet of water creating a perfect hidden harbor, with **Sint Annabaai** as the narrow entrance. The

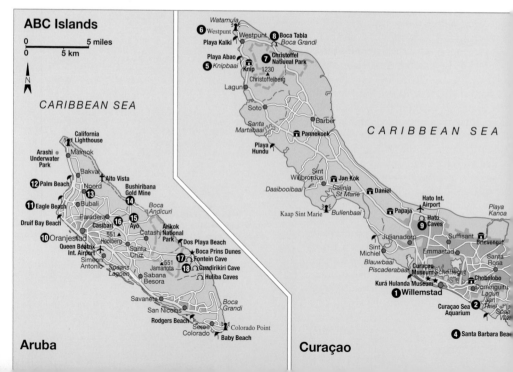

streets in the historic center of **Punda** (Point) and in **Otrobanda** (Other Side) on either side of Sint Annabaai are mainly pedestrianized, and lined with attractive cafés and snack bars.

## Sacred treasures

Sephardic settlers from Amsterdam and northern Brazil founded the community of Mikveh Israel (Hope of Israel) in the mid-17th century, and the **Mikveh Israel Emanuel Synagogue** has been in continuous use since it first opened at the Passover Festival in 1732. The three-aisled prayer room of the synagogue has enormous brass chandeliers from Amsterdam and the fine sand on the floor is a reminder of the Israelites' march through the Sinai Desert. In the central courtyard is the 200-year-old ritual bath, or mikvah, and along the walls you can see copies of ancient gravestones from the Jewish cemetery of Beth Chaim on the outskirts of town, across the Schottegat, where the originals have been severely eroded by sulfurous vapors from the nearby oil refinery.

The **Jewish Cultural Historical Museum** (Hanchi di Snoa 29, Punda; tel: 5999-461 1633; www.snoa.com; Mon–Fri 9am–4.30pm, closed Jewish and public hols) alongside the synagogue has an interesting display of valuable torah rolls, seven-branched candlesticks, and numerous ancestral objects belonging to the influential Luckmann and Maduro families.

## Renovated magnificence

Around the **Waaigat** are several colorful markets. The circular concrete structure houses the main market where the female traders are almost completely concealed from view behind mountains of fresh fruit and vegetables. At the **Marsh Biev**, by the post office, is the old market hall where cooks serve enormous helpings of stew (*stoba*) and other delicacies for the lunchtime crowd. Visitors can also buy fresh fish from the Venezuelan coast boats at the **Floating Market** (Sha Caprileskade).

Next to the main market, the **Queen Wilhelmina Drawbridge** leads across to the old Jewish quarter of **Scharloo**. Take a walk along **Scharlooweg**, where there are some magnificent renovated

**TIP**

Architect Anko van de Woude, art historian Gerda Gehlen, and monuments expert Michael A. Newton give regular tours of the old part of Willemstad. Tel: 5999-461 3554, 5999-510 6978 or 5999-668 8579 or check www.otrobanda-pundatour.com for details.

*Iguana in Christoffel National Park.*

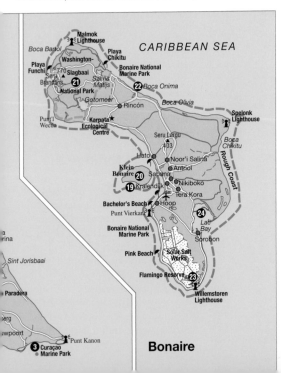

*A tall ship in port recalls the romance of a bygone age.*

*The gabled roofs of Handelskade, Willemstad.*

villas, now largely occupied by banks, legal practices, and administrative offices. Stars of David on some of the garden fences here serve as reminders of the buildings' former owners. Impressive examples of the elaborate architecture typical of the 19th century include the yellow-and-white Kranshi, the registry office, and the "Wedding Cake" or *Bolo di Bruid*, as the decorative green-and-white building at number 77 is referred to in papiamentu. Today it is home to the **National Archive**.

The gently swaying **Queen Emma Bridge**, with the colorful facade of the **Handelskade** in the background, is the most photographed scene in the whole town. This pontoon bridge has connected the business center of Punda with the picturesque old residential quarter of Otrobanda since 1888. Whenever a freighter or cruise ship needs to enter or leave the harbor through the Sint Annabaai, a powerful motor pulls the bridge aside; at the same time, a bell rings to warn pedestrians. Two ferries transport passengers across the bay, while cars roar across the spectacular 175ft (55-meter) arch of the **Queen**

**Juliana Bridge** (1974) to the north, flying high above the massive ships below.

Enormous forts are situated on either side of the harbor entrance. Iron rings were set into their walls to fasten a heavy chain or metal net that would prevent access to the harbor. The **Riffort** in Otrobanda today provides an atmospheric backdrop for eating in the pleasant Bistro Le Clochard. In contrast, on the opposite bank, a large and rather ugly hotel building towers above the walls of the Waterfort. Beside it is yellow **Fort Amsterdam**, built in 1641 and now the seat of the island's government. The inner courtyard houses the Protestant church, **Fortkerk** (1769), and a small **museum** (tel: 5999-461 1139; Mon–Fri guided tours between 10am and noon) with religious artifacts. A cannonball is still lodged in the masonry here: in 1804, during a 26-day long siege of Willemstad, the notorious English Captain Bligh's men fired on the fort.

The stylish shop windows along **Heerenstraat** and **Breedestraat** contain expensive cameras, watches, and cosmetics; designer clothes, perfumes, and elegant household items are sold duty-free in the local boutiques. The gables above, like many facades in this area, have been renovated. Pay special attention to the magnificent yellow-ochre **Penha Building** in Punda, which dates from 1708, next to the pontoon bridge. Initially the gallery on the upper story was left open so that air could circulate freely through the house.

## Stroll back through the centuries

The winding streets of Otrobanda were the site of the most remarkable renovation, however, which led to Willemstad joining the Unesco global cultural heritage list in 1997. Previously a run-down area, the Brionplein was the site of riots in May 1969, when a mob of unemployed refinery and harbor workers gave vent to their frustration at social injustice. With burned-out buildings remaining until the late 1990s, it is

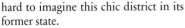
hard to imagine this chic district in its former state.

The owner and architect of the **Kurá Hulanda Hotel** off Klipstraat deserve much credit for the area's rejuvenation; the city's most luxurious accommodations option features a restored 18th-century Dutch village, with narrow cobbled streets separated by leafy courtyards, with high-end dining, a casino, and spa. Perhaps of even greater significance is the addition of the **Kurá Hulanda Museum** (Klipstraat 9; tel: 5999-434 7700; www.kurahulanda.com/en/museumx; Mon–Sat 9.30am–4.30pm), the Caribbean's largest permanent exhibition on the transatlantic slave trade and African civilizations, built around a courtyard used for slave auctions centuries ago. The impressive and moving collection includes a life-size model of the hold of a slave ship, alongside photographs and documents pertaining to the Dutch- and Portuguese-managed trade.

During the day a stroll along **De Rouvilleweg** and busy **Breedestraat**, past the attractive Haus Sebastopol and the picturesque buildings on Nanniestraat as far as the elaborately renovated Haus Belvedere, takes you back through two centuries of history. At night, visit some of the numerous bars and terraces at the **Koral Agostini** or the **Keizershof**.

Just outside Otrobanda, inside the former Dutch military hospital on Van Leeuwenhoekstraat, is the **Curaçao Museum** (tel: 5999-462 3873; www.thecuracaomuseum.com; Tue–Fri 8.30am–4.30pm, Sat 10am–4pm) with an unusual and eclectic collection of antique furniture, old kitchen equipment, and modern art.

## From Bolívar to beer

**Pietermaai**, the district to the southeast of Punda, has undergone a similar development to Otrobanda. Expensively renovated office buildings and the attractive **Avila Beach Hotel**, once the governor's residence, are certainly worth inspecting. The South American freedom fighter Simón Bolívar is commemorated in a small museum in the **Octagon** (tel: 5999-461 4377; Tue, Wed, Fri, Sun 10am noon or by appointment); he took refuge here with his two sisters for a while in the early 19th century.

*Make purchases from the Floating Market.*

## NATURAL REMEDIES

If you are interested in medicinal herbs, visit schoolteacher Dinah Veeris and her beautiful garden, **Den Paradera** (Seru Grandi 105A, Weg Naar Fuik; tel: 5999-767 5608). The name comes from the Paraguiri Indians who once had a large garden on the island. Veeris has been researching healing herbs and folk traditions since 1981, largely by interviewing older people to preserve their knowledge before it was lost. In 1991 she started her garden and now has 300 species of plants, all with medicinal properties, many of them saved before their wild habitats were destroyed by urbanization. Now known as a healer, or *curioso* in papiamentu, she has written books, including *Green Remedies and Golden Customs of our Ancestors*, and has won awards for her preservation work.

In the Landhuis Chobolobo in the Salinja quarter, the Senior family has been distilling the world-famous **Curaçao Blue** liqueur for more than 110 years (tel: 5999-461 3526; www.curacaoliqueur.com; Mon–Fri 8am–noon, 1–5pm); and in the modern Amstel Brewery on the Schottegat the island's delicious beer is produced, using desalinated sea water and imported ingredients. Many international hotels are located on the Piscaderabaai or the Jan Thielbaai, west and east of town respectively.

The latter is famous for the **Curaçao Sea Aquarium ❷** (Bapor Kibra z/n; tel: 5999-461 6666; www.curacao-sea-aquarium.com; daily 8am–5pm; charge) where rare and exotic tropical fish, turtles, and crustaceans can be seen from a boardwalk. In the Animal Encounter section, divers and snorkelers can feed sharks from behind a plexiglass screen while having their photograph taken.

Curaçao has several spectacular diving grounds for the experienced diver. The **Curaçao Marine Park ❸** extends from the Oostpunt and along the southwest coast as far as Jan Thielbaai. Most of the diving areas can be reached

*Dolphin show at the Sea Aquarium.*

directly from the shore, and the clear water is also excellent for snorkeling, with colorful coral reefs, massive sponges, and tropical fish. Anyone eager to discover the underwater world in all its magnificence and also visit the wreck of a Dutch steamer without getting their feet wet, should board *Seaworld Explorer*, the glass-bottomed, semi-submarine operated by Atlantis Adventures (tel: 5999-461 0011; www. curacao-atlantisadventures.com).

## Kunuku – wild and beautiful hinterland

**Banda Riba**, the southeastern part of Curaçao, has numerous attractions including broad, flat, and sandy **Santa Barbara Beach ❹**, where children can splash about and play quite safely in the clear warm water; and also the hidden bay of **Playa Kanoa**, where courageous surfers brave the waves and local bands congregate for dancing parties at weekends. Many beaches on Curaçao are privately owned and you have to pay to use them.

During any trip through the hinterland, or *kunuku*, to Westpunt you

will notice several magnificent, mostly yellow-ochre plantation houses, many of which have been converted into restaurants, small hotels, and museums. **Landhuis Jan Kok** (tel: 5999-738 2377; www.jankokcuracao.com), for instance, has a fine art gallery; **Landhuis Groot Sint Martha** (tel: 5999-864 1323) contains workshops for the disabled; the **Landhuis Daniel** (tel: 5999-864 8400; www.landhuisdaniel.com) is a gourmet restaurant. The other majestic buildings along the road are either privately owned or the property of official institutions. Back on the eastern side of the Schottegat is the **Landhuis Groot Davelaar**, an interesting colonial house built circa 1865 with a mixture of Curaçao style and Renaissance influences.

## Rough wilderness

With a bit of luck, on a tour through the **Banda Abao** – the western part of the island – you may see some of the shy flamingos that live on the **Salinja St Marie**, or sea turtles on the **Knip-baai ❺**. Here the sandy beaches, the best on the island, are surrounded by rocks, making an attractive setting for a rest stop. The majestic **Landhuis Knip** (tel: 5999-864 0244; Tue–Fri), once at the center of the wealthiest plantation on Curaçao, now holds a fascinating museum, and hosts cultural events on a regular basis.

Pelicans are the only creatures courageous enough to brave the waves off the **Westpunt ❻**, where the sea crashes down with unbelievable force onto the rocky shoreline off Watamula. Just a few miles to the east of the sleepy fishing village of Westpunt, a fence on either side of the road marks the **Christoffel National Park ❼** (tel: 5999-864 0363; Mon–Sat 7.30am–4pm, Sun 6am–3pm). This large nature reserve was opened in 1978 on land formerly occupied by three vast plantations; it can be explored by jeep, mountain bike, or on foot. Guided tours led by expert rangers introduce visitors to the typical local flora and fauna. Keep an eye out for the green parrots native to the island: they usually fly in pairs and seem to enjoy landing on the enormous cacti.

A short but exhausting climb leads to the top of the 1,230ft (375-meter) high **Christoffelberg**, where the view extends as far as Bonaire. Further attractions in the park include Amerindian rock drawings, some spectacular stretches of coastline on the Boca Grandi, and numerous rare palm trees and fragrant orchids in the wilderness of Zevenbergen.

To the northeast, the Christoffel National Park is bordered by the Die Shete Boka, a beautifully atmospheric piece of coast with the hidden grotto of **Boca Tabla ❽** and breathtaking scenery whenever the powerful breakers smash down on the cliffs. It was breakers similar to these that created the original cave system of **Hato ❾** (Rooseveltweg; tel: 5999-868 0379; daily 9am–4pm, guided tours every hour), not far from the airport. These limestone caves have a mirror-smooth underground lake, stalagmites, stalactites, bats, and Caiquetío rock drawings that are believed to date back more than 1,000 years.

*The liqueur, usually blue, that bears the island's name.*

*Aruba's windblown divi-divi tree.*

# ARUBA

Explore an underwater shipwreck and natural reefs, laze
on miles of white sandy beach, windsurf, kitesurf,
gamble in the casinos, and shop in modern malls.

Caribbean
Sea
Aruba

**A**ruba, the smallest and richest of the ABC Islands, has cosmopolitan shopping centers, elegant restaurants, and a refreshingly deserted hinterland, which all contribute to providing highly attractive alternatives to lazing away happily under the palms all day long on the island's 7 miles (11km) of white sand lapped by gentle turquoise and dark-blue waters.

For more than 50 years, the massive Lago oil refinery at San Nicolas was Aruba's main source of foreign revenue and not only as the biggest employer on the tiny island. Lago financed schools, doctors, houses, streets, and even a golf course for its workforce. When the refinery was unexpectedly closed down in early 1985 it came as a great shock not just to Arubans but also to the numerous workers from all over the Caribbean. On an island with a population of around 100,000 people, unemployment rose dramatically and affected thousands. The refinery reopened in the early 1990s, but by then the island had changed.

The closure caused potentially devastating economic problems, which struck just as Aruba officially assumed special autonomous status within the Kingdom of the Netherlands. Tourism was seen as a way of attracting much-needed foreign currency and this gamble has paid off. Today, visitors arrive from all over the world but especially

from the US and Venezuela. High-rise hotels appeared above the palm trees on Eagle Beach and Palm Beach, and the small town of Oranjestad developed a colorful shopping center. Cunning entrepreneurs created a holiday industry that catered to every taste, whether on water or land: undersea diving along the natural reef, with spectacular underwater scenery around wrecked ships and airplanes; romantic candlelit dinners on board sailing ships; tours on party buses; and Las Vegas-style shows on the stage of the

**Main Attractions**

National Archeological
    Museum Aruba
Eagle Beach
Arikok National Park
Fontein and Guadirikiri
    caves
Charlie's Bar

*Baby natural bridge.*

**FACT**

Paardenbaai (Horses' Bay) off Oranjestad got its name from the colonial merchants who used to unload horses from the boats by tying one to the beach and then shoving the rest overboard. They swam straight to their companion on the shore.

*The Netherlands meet the tropics in Wilheminastraat, Oranjestad.*

Alhambra – plus casinos where visitors can try their luck at roulette tables.

## A holiday bonanza

Around 800,000 vacationers spend a few pleasant days each year at Eagle Beach and Palm Beach, and that figure doesn't include the 600,000 or so passengers from cruise ships who visit the bars and boutiques in Oranjestad, eager to take advantage of the bounty of duty-free goods and impressed by the relaxed and polite service. But shopping can be an expensive business, especially when you're after European goods such as English and German porcelain, Belgian chocolates, or Swiss watches.

The horrors of the colonial era largely passed Aruba by, because the island was only inhabited by a handful of settlers, soldiers, and Caiquetío Amerindians. Agriculture, animal husbandry, the cultivation of aloe, and the export of tree bark containing tannin enabled the islanders to lead a largely self-sufficient existence. Papiamentu, the local creole language, sounds far more Spanish here than elsewhere and is also very melodious.

## Spruced-up Oranjestad

A handful of shopping streets, administrative buildings, churches, a harbor with three cruise ship terminals, and some magnificent hotels complete with shopping malls and casinos make up the center of **Oranjestad** ❿. Stroll past the colorful, Dutch-style facades and visit the few sights Aruba's capital has to offer, or soak up some local atmosphere and the sunshine in the numerous cafés and bars round the yachting harbor. The streets around the busy main street – **Caya G.F. (Betico) Croes** (formerly Nassaustraat) – are where local people do most of their shopping. There are still a few traditional Aruban houses with typically steep and flat torto roofs.

The most noticeable relic of colonial times here is the small **Fort Zoutman** and **Willem III Tower**, the oldest surviving structure on the island. The fort was built right beside the **Paardenbaai** in 1796, and since then land reclamation at the harbor has stranded it around 300ft (100 meters) inland. Its ancient walls contain the **Aruba Historical Museum** (tel: 297-582 6099; Mon–Fri

8.30am–4pm), where exhibits include sea shells, sections of coral, 19th-century household items, and a still working mechanical barrel organ from Italy. From the clock tower there's a fine view across the island, which is only 22 miles (30km) long and 4 miles (9km) across at its widest point. At 6.30pm every Tuesday the well-organised **Bonbini Festival** is held in the fort, where you can sample local culinary and liquid specialties and dance the energetic Latin American *tumba* and *merengue*.

The **National Archeological Museum Aruba** (Schelpstraat 42; tel: 297-582 8979; www.namaruba.org; Tue–Fri 10am–5pm, Sat–Sun 10am–2pm) is housed in the renovated historic Ecury complex, a beautiful family home dating back to 1870, transformed into a modern museum. Documenting the largely unresearched culture of the Caiquetíos and other pre-Columbian peoples who settled the ABC Islands long before the Europeans arrived, the collection contains some 10,000 artifacts spanning the pre-ceramic, ceramic, and historic cultural periods. There are interactive exhibits for children, reconstructions, video, and temporary exhibitions.

## Stunning beaches

**Eagle Beach** ⑪, 380ft (120 meters) wide in some places, is lined by so-called low-rise hotels, which blend harmoniously with the landscape despite their colorful mix of styles. Powdery white **Palm Beach** ⑫ is just as beautiful, but high-rises predominate here. Both beaches are signposted from the multi-lane highway that runs north from Oranjestad: most hotels here provide total luxury and excellent entertainment, and anyone who tires of the beach can enjoy air-conditioned boutiques, restaurants, and casinos.

Farther north the sea becomes rougher, but that is welcomed by the windsurfers and kitesurfers off **Malmok**, and doesn't affect the divers down at the wreck of the German warship *Antilla* either (see page 153). It was surrounded by the Dutch Navy on May 10, 1940, during World War II, and rather than hoist the white flag, the captain set the ship alight and sank it. The crew were interned in the Caribbean for the rest of the war, and at the end several of them were allowed to settle on the ABC Islands for good.

## Rocky attractions

The 100ft (32-meter)-high **California Lighthouse** towers above the craggy Noordpunt and the sand dunes around it. Built between 1914 and 1916, it stands close to the bright green **Tierra del Sol** golf course, set in the midst of the reddish-brown scrubland. A dusty track, which should only be attempted in a four-wheel-drive jeep, leads along the east coast, passing the **Alto Vista Pilgrimage Chapel** and a section of rocky landscape. The divi-divi trees here, bent by the northeasterly trade winds, are like natural signposts, always pointing southwest. The northeast coast of Aruba, with rough landscape, hidden sand dunes, large limestone caverns, and thorny scrubland, is a striking contrast to the tourist regions of the west coast.

*Cacti are a common sight in the arid countryside.*

*California Lighthouse, Aruba.*

Art and architecture lovers should take a detour to the unpretentious little church of **Sint Annakerk in Noord** . It contains a neo-Gothic altar of carved oak by Hendrik van der Geld (1870) from Antwerp, as well as stained-glass windows from the Wilhelm Heinrich workshop in Kevelaer. The ruins of the **Bushiribana Gold Mine** are another popular and photogenic destination. They stand in memory of the gold rush that took began in 1820 when a boy found some nuggets in the dry valleys on the northeast coast.

The romantic spot that was formerly the site of a natural bridge at **Boca Andicuri** is still worth a visit for its seclusion and raging surf – though the bridge itself collapsed in 2007.

Diorite boulders – a geological rarity – can be seen up close in **Ayo** and **Casibari**: enormous, cushion-like rocks with large sections gouged out of them, some of them decorated with Amerindian rock drawings. The 551ft (168-meter) high **Hooiberg** provides a fine view of the **Arikok National Park**, with a fascinatingly desolate wilderness of cactus fields. Near a small renovated farmhouse called **Kunuku Arikok** you can see wooden troughs in which the green juice of the aloe vera plant was collected and boiled. The juice from this plant is believed to purify the blood and regenerate the skin, and is highly treasured worldwide as an ingredient for health foods, skin creams, and balms for sunburn.

## Mysterious spirals

The cave systems of **Fontein** and **Guadirikiri** contain several strange and largely inexplicable Amerindian symbols such as spirals, circles, and lines of dots; in addition there are rare bats, bizarre rock formations, and the odd piece of graffiti left behind by ignorant visitors. The cave walls and roof have been cleaned by experts, and guards and grilles are now in position to ensure no further damage is done.

While surfers balance on the high waves out at Colorado Point, a good place to relax from a tour of southern Aruba is in the shallow waters at **Baby Beach**, where there is also good, secluded diving and snorkeling. Alternatively, visit **Charlie's Bar** (tel: 297-584

*Fontein Cave, Arikok National Park.*

5086), which is right beside the refinery at **San Nicolas** on Main Street. Over the past 50 years or so, guests from all over the world have lined the walls and ceiling with a scurrilous collection of personal mementoes. Local thespians, artists, and musicians, as well as tourists enjoy coming here for a drink and a chat with the owner.

Aruba made its giant leap from small island to international industrial nation in 1924, when the Lago Oil and Transport Company from the US built a massive refinery at Seroe Colorado in the southwest. Oil companies chose Aruba and also Curaçao as safe and easily accessible locations due to political instability in nearby Venezuela. After the oil crisis of the 1980s, parts of the refinery were shut down, and operations have occasionally stopped since. In July 2009 the refinery was shut down for 18 months because of the uncertain tax and economic climate but, after negotiations with the government of Aruba, it reopened in 2011. The 235,000-barrel-a-day refinery employed more than 650 people full-time, and represented more than 12 percent of Aruba's gross domestic product. However, the facility was once again idled in 2012 and has since been used as an oil storage terminal. Things may be about to improve, though – in September 2015, the Government of Aruba signed a deal with Citgo Petroleum to explore reactivating the refinery.

## Italian inspiration

On the other side of the main road between Oranjestad and the island's former capital of Savaneta, a turn-off leads to the ruins of the **Balashi gold mine**, and through the narrow path known as **Frenchman's Pass**, where legend claims that French soldiers surrounded and shot a group of Amerindian warriors. The village of **Sabana Besora** still contains some typical small houses, such as the Cas di Figura and Cas di Flor, with decorative patterned strips. Italian construction workers probably scratched the attractive ornamentation into the plaster around the turn of the 20th century. Colorfully painted flowers, stars, and other decorations can also be seen in the church of St Francis of Assisi in Oranjestad.

*Aruba's northeastern coastline.*

*Bonaire Desert.*

# BONAIRE

The waters around this island are a diver's paradise, with spectacular views of a magical underwater world, a stark contrast to its cacti-strewn desert and national park.

Parts of the tiny boomerang-shaped desert island of Bonaire lie just a few feet above the seemingly endless blue of the Caribbean. Most of its delights are found under the sea, in the diving grounds of the Bonaire National Marine Park. But there is also life on land: there's picturesque Kralendijk (pronounced "kral-en-dike"); the cactus-filled wilderness of Washington-Slagbaai National Park, the endless channels in the mangroves of Lac Bay, hiking and biking trails in the thorny back country, and the sight of more than 10,000 pink flamingos in the salt pans of the Pekelmeer.

Bonaire takes ecotourism and environmental issues seriously (the environment is a required subject in primary schools). The surrounding sea to a depth of 200ft (60 meters) is protected as a marine park, and about 40 percent of the total land area is preserved as national or private parkland.

In 1634 the Dutch established a small military base on a coral dike, the *kralendijk*, on the west coast. Bonaire was only interesting to the colonizers because of its dyewood and grazing land for livestock. The slaughtered animals were loaded on to ships at Slagbaai (Slaughter Bay) in the north, to be sold in Curaçao. During the 17th century the Dutch West India Company discovered a way of evaporating seawater in shallow basins to produce salt, which was much in demand to preserve fish and meat. The arduous labor was carried out under the scorching sun by so-called "government slaves."

Today, salt remains a major export for the chemical industry, but tourism has become the most important foreign-currency earner. Since the island is thinly populated (17,400 inhabitants in 111 sq miles/288 sq km) and has no other industry to speak of, nature is still largely intact.

After the dissolution of the Netherlands Antilles on October 10, 2010,

## Main Attractions

Bonaire National Marine Park
Klein Bonaire
Washington-Slagbaai National Park
Boca Onima
Flamingo Reserve
Lac Bay

*Colorful fish in the waters off Bonaire.*

*Iguanas of all sizes love the arid conditions.*

*Windsurfers at Lac Bay.*

Bonaire became a "public body" or "special municipality" within the Kingdom of the Netherlands, the same status as that of Saba and Sint Eustatius.

## A colorful capital

**Kralendijk** , the island's picturesque capital, is compact and easy to tour on foot. Many of the public buildings and restaurants are located along two streets on or behind the waterfront. On **Kaya Grandi** colorfully painted facades and coral mosaics shaped like flamingos create a tropical atmosphere, and the 1-mile (1.5km) long harbor promenade is a pleasant place to stroll. Bonaire has a cosmopolitan mix of 42 nationalities; Dutch is the official language but most people speak papiamentu and/or English and Spanish.

**Fort Oranje** – built in the 17th century – guards the cruise ship pier. The small lighthouse (1932) is the Harbor Office, while other restored fort buildings house the courthouse. **Plaza Reina Wilhelmina**, in the center, contains a Protestant church (1847) and the **Pasangrahan**, an attractive neoclassical

colonial-era building that was once the residence of the governor. In the funky pseudo-Greek market pavilion on the waterfront, traders from Venezuela sell tropical fruit and vegetables. The best views of Kralendijk can be had either from **Karel's Beach Bar** or from the terrace restaurants at the harborside. It is only when a cruise ship docks that things get busy. On the edge of town the **Museo Boneriano** (Kaya J.C. van de Ree; Mon–Fri) has an amazing collection of colonial furniture, pictures, and household items.

## Underwater magic

The sea around Bonaire is part of the **Bonaire National Marine Park**, and since 1979 has been strictly protected. The entire west coast is lined by coral reefs and provides some of the best diving in the Caribbean, mostly situated where the reefs slope down into the deep. Snorkelers swimming close to shore will find themselves above magnificent elkhorn, staghorn, or brain coral and colorful fish. The adjacent island of **Klein Bonaire** ⑳, a quarter mile offshore, is a wilderness

preserve also managed by the marine park. Spear-fishing is forbidden here, and it is illegal to touch the coral.

## Thorns, salt, and pink

Unspoiled nature begins a few miles beyond the former slave settlement of **Rincón**, a collection of yellowish-brown houses among the flat hills. With rocky volcanic upthrusts in the north, swamps in the center, and salt pans in the south, Bonaire's landscape is varied.

The **Washington-Slagbaai National Park ㉑** (tel: 599-788 9015; www.washingtonparkbonaire.org; daily 8am–5pm, no entry after noon for cyclists and hikers or after 2.45pm for cars) was established on the site of two former plantations in 1979. It takes up the entire northern part of the island, and its brackish salt flats are an important stopover for birds migrating between North and South America. Depending on the season you may see wild geese or ospreys, and the conures, parrots, and pelicans native to the island can be observed the whole year round. The idyllic beach of **Playa Chikitu** is an excellent place to relax – swimming is discouraged because of the dangerous currents. Two routes for car drivers and cyclists and several hiking paths lead through the park and around the base of 770ft (241-meter) **Seru Brandaris**, the highest point on the island.

A short, slightly bumpy road leads to **Boca Onima ㉒**. Beneath a rocky outcrop in the limestone terrace along the north coast are partially fenced-off Amerindian drawings. Reddish in color, they include spirals, circles, and stylized birds. No one is certain of their precise origin, but it is believed that, centuries ago, Amerindians prayed here to the goddess Onima for calm seas before rowing across to Venezuela.

In the flat, southern part of the island, the scenery is dominated by conical white mounds of salt and flocks of pink flamingos. A popular viewing spot is the **salt works** which extracts salt from seawater. Nearby are a number of peaked-roof buildings the size of dog kennels, where enslaved salt workers slept and stored their gear.

## Flamingo Reserve

The southern quarter of the island is taken up by the **Flamingo Reserve ㉓**, one of only four nesting grounds for pink flamingos in the Caribbean. The birds are disturbed by noisy visitors, and may only be observed from afar. During the morning many of these elegant creatures fly to Venezuela or Curaçao to feed on algae, shrimps, and other crustaceans (which give the older flamingos their striking pink hue), so get there early with a good pair of binoculars.

**Lac Bay ㉔**, on the east coast, bordered by mangroves, is popular with kitesurfers, windsurfers, and kayakers. The conditions are ideal, with strong winds throughout the year. The mangroves and seagrass beds are breeding grounds for many reef and pelagic fish as well as the endangered Queen conch. Conch shells can be found lying at the entrance to the bay at **Cai** (a good beach for families), but the shells are protected and must not be removed.

*Flamingo.*

*These tiny dwellings each slept six slaves.*

West End, St Thomas, Virgin Islands.

# TRAVEL TIPS
# CARIBBEAN

# TRANSPORTATION

# GETTING THERE AND GETTING AROUND

## GETTING THERE

### By Air

As far as accessibility goes, the islands fall fairly neatly into two groups: those that can be reached by direct flights from North America, South America, and Europe, and those that cannot. Islands that can be reached by direct flight are as follows:

Antigua
Aruba
Barbados
Curaçao
Grenada
Guadeloupe
Martinique
St Kitts
St Lucia
St Martin
Trinidad
Tobago
US Virgin Islands

All other destinations must be reached by inter-island airline from the nearest direct-flight island. All the islands, including those listed, can be reached from various points in the Caribbean via numerous carriers, on a tangled web of routes (see Inter-Island Carriers, page 297). If you want to know which islands can be reached from a particular island, see the listing for that island. Note that inter-island schedules and itineraries are liable to change. Once you have decided on all the places you want to visit, talk to a travel agent, your tourist board representative, or airline company to determine the most efficient way to get to your destinations.

A good travel agent will help you plan your trip and find the flights that best suit your pocket and your timetable. Fare prices can vary according to the season and special offers from airlines, so shop around. Many scheduled services are supplemented by charter flights, but even so, flights become heavily booked during high season. Budget fares to Martinique and Guadeloupe are available if you fly with Air France from an international airport in France.

### Cruise Lines

A large proportion of visitors to the Caribbean arrive by cruise ship, the combination of staying in a luxurious floating hotel and making short visits to different exotic locations being increasingly popular. The days on which cruise ships call see thousands of passengers flooding into usually low-key ports, and in many places shopping complexes, such as Heritage Quay in St John's, Antigua, have sprung up to accommodate them.

The Lesser Antilles are on the itineraries of several cruise lines, though frequency of service to the different islands in the group varies widely – from hundreds of port visits each year to the US Virgin Islands, to no stops at all at certain other smaller islands. Itineraries change constantly. The best way to plan your trip is to decide first where you would like to go, then visit the web, or contact a cruise operator or travel agent to see if there is a current itinerary that covers all or most of your destinations.

The following cruise ship companies have ships that call at islands in the Lesser Antilles:

**Azamara Club Cruises**, tel: 877-999 9553 (US); tel: 0844-493 4016 (UK); www.azamaraclubcruises.com.

**Carnival Cruise Lines**, tel: 800-764 7419 (US); www.carnival.com; tel: 0843-374 2272 (UK); www.carnival cruise.co.uk.
**Celebrity Cruises**, tel: 800-647 2251 (US); tel: 0844-493 6011 (UK); www.celebritycruises.com.
**Costa Cruises**, tel: 800-462 6782 (US); www.costacruise.com; tel: 0800-389 0622 (UK); www.costacruises. co.uk.
**Cunard Line**, tel: 0843-374 2224 (UK); www.cunard.co.uk.
**Disney Cruise Line**, tel: 0800-951 3532 (US); https:// disneycruise. disney.go.com.

## Airline Numbers

Contact details of major airlines serving the Lesser Antilles.
**American:** 800-433 7300 (US); www.aa.com
**Air Canada:** 1-888-247 2262 (Canada); www.aircanada.com
**Air France:** 36 54 (France); www.air france.fr
**British Airways:** 0844-493 0787 (UK); www.britishairways.com
**Caribbean Airlines:** 800-920 4225 (US); www.caribbean-airlines. com
**Delta:** 800-241 4141 (US, Canada); www.delta.com
**Jet Blue:** 800-538 2583 (US); www.jetblue.com
**klm:** 31(0)20-474 7747 (Netherlands); www.klm.com
**Lufthansa:** 49(0)1805-805 805 (Germany); www.lufthansa.com
**United Airlines:** 800-864 8331 (US, Canada); www.united.com
**Virgin Atlantic:** 0344-209 7777 (UK); www.virgin-atlantic.com
**WestJet:** 1-888-937 8538 (Canada); www.westjet.com

TRANSPORTATION

**Holland America Line**, tel: 206-286 3900 (US); tel: 0843-374 2300 (UK); www.hollandamerica.com.
**Fred. Olsen Cruise Lines**, tel: 44(0)20-7931 8888 (UK); www.fred olsen.co.uk.
**msc Cruises**, tel: 877-665-4655 (US); www.msccruises.com; tel: 0203-426 3010 (UK); www.msccruises.co.uk.
**Norwegian Cruise Line**, tel: 0845-201 8900 (UK); www.ncl.co.uk.
**Oceania Cruises**, tel: 305-514-2300 (US); www.oceaniacruises.com; tel: 44 345-505 1920 (UK); www.oceania cruises.co.uk.
**P & O Cruises**, tel: 0843-374 0111 (UK); www.pocruises.com.
**Princess Cruises**, tel: 1-800-PRINCESS (UK); www.princess. com.
**Regent Seven Seas Cruises**, tel: 1-954-776 6123 (US); tel: 02380-682 140 (UK); www.rssc.com.
**Royal Caribbean International**, tel: 866-562 7625 (US); www.royalcaribbean.com; tel: 0844-493 4005 (UK); www.royalcaribbean. co.uk.
**Seabourn**, tel: 206-626 9179 (US); 0845-070 0500 (UK); www.seabourn. com.
**SeaDream Yacht Club**, tel: 800-707 4911 (US); tel: 0800-783 1373 (UK); www.seadream.com.
**Silversea Cruises**, tel: 800-722 9955 (US); tel: 0844-251 0837 (UK); www.silversea.com.
**Star Clippers**, tel: 0845-200 6145 (UK); www.starclippers.co.uk.
**Windstar Cruises**, tel: 800-258 7245 (US); www.windstarcruises. com; tel: 020-399 7669 (UK); www. cruiseportfolio.co.uk.

### Cargo Ships

For the traveler in search of something out of the ordinary, a cargo ship offers a different type of cruise: comfortable cabins for only a handful of passengers (evening meals are generally taken with the officers) on a working cargo ship. Geest "banana boats," for example, leave Portsmouth on a round trip lasting approximately 25 days, calling in at some of the following ports: Antigua, Barbados, Dominica, Grenada, Guadeloupe, Martinique, St Kitts, St Lucia, St Vincent, and Trinidad. Note that, although ships depart weekly, not all vessels allow passengers on board. Horn Linie "banana boats," taking 12 passengers, depart weekly from Dover and sail to Martinique, Guadeloupe, Cartagena in Venezuela, and Costa Rica.

Enquiries should be made to the following travel agents:

#### UK
**The Cruise People**, tel: 020-7723 2450; www.cruisepeople.co.uk.

#### USA
**Maris Freighter Cruise and Travel Club**, tel: 1-800-99-Maris; www.freightercruises.com.

### GETTING AROUND

#### By Car

The islands are well stocked with rental agencies. International car-rental firms have offices at the airport as well as in many hotels. Travel by car allows great freedom and flexibility to explore the nooks and crannies of the islands, but there are a few things the driver should be aware of. Many of the islands are mountainous, and on all of them roads are narrower than most US and European drivers will be familiar with. Driving may thus be a little more harrowing than at home – not for the faint-hearted. Also, in some areas yearly rainfall is quite light and this allows a film of oil to build up on road surfaces. When it does rain on these roads, they become especially slick, requiring extra caution. All in all, drivers should prepare to drive defensively and with caution, perhaps following the advice of one of the islands' tourist agencies to "sound the horn frequently," especially when approaching bends. Regulations on driver's licenses vary from island to island – see under listings for individual islands.

#### By Taxi

Perhaps the most common means of transportation for visitors to the islands is the taxi. Taxis are available for hire at the airport, cruise terminals, and other central locations. Not only are taxis convenient, and relatively inexpensive, but taking a taxi also gives you access to the resources of the driver. Where else could you chat with an island expert for the price of a cab ride? Most taxi drivers will gladly help you find things you are looking for, or that you aren't looking for but may be delighted to find. It is usually possible to find a taxi driver who is willing to give you a tour of his or her island and, in some places, drivers are specially trained to do this.

### Inter-Island Carriers

Air Antilles Express, www.airantilles. com
Airawak, www.airawak.com
Air Caraïbes, www.aircaraibes.com
Air Sunshine, www.airsunshine.com
American Airlines/American Eagle, www.aa.com
Cape Air, www.flycapeair.com
Caribbean Airlines, www.caribbean-airlines.com
Fly Montserrat, www.flymontserrat. com
LIAT, www.liatairline.com
Seaborne Airlines, www.seaborne airlines.com
Surinam Airways, www.slm.firm.sr
SVG Air, www.svgair.com
Winair, www.fly-winair.com

Another positive feature of taxi travel for island visitors is that rates are generally fixed and published. Often, printed sheets with detailed rates are available from points of entry, drivers, and tourist offices. If you plan to travel much by taxi, one of the first things to do upon arrival is to familiarize yourself with the rates to different destinations and at different times of day. You can often negotiate for longer excursions out of town.
Taxi drivers are usually friendly and extremely helpful. If you receive good service, return the favor with a good tip – say, 15–20 percent.

### By Bus

Most of the islands have local bus services that many residents use to get around. Though they are not as flexible as taxis and rental cars, buses are quite inexpensive and have the advantage of allowing travelers to get a small taste of how local residents live. Your hotel, a tourist office, the bus station, or a police station should be able to supply information on schedules, and fellow passengers and drivers are friendly and helpful in making sure that bewildered visitors get off at the right stop. Some countries also have "route taxis," usually with a local name, which have fixed routes, like a bus, but they travel more frequently, have no fixed stops, and cost a bit more.
Tour buses (both mini and full-sized) are available on all the islands for taking groups sightseeing.

### Inter-Island Links

As you might expect in this region of islands cut off from one another by the sea, the options for getting around between islands are legion.

### By Air

For the traveler desiring quick transfers (and perhaps the novelty of a ride in a seaplane), there are a number of airline companies operating inter-island routes. LIAT is probably the largest and best-known of these carriers.

For a short list of inter-island air carriers, see Getting There, page 296.

### By Sea

Inter-island ferries are varied but sea transport is not as common as might be expected and most island-hopping is done by air. Some ferries are the old steel-and-smokestack variety, but there are also catamarans, hydrofoils, schooners, and other types of sailing vessel plying the waters. International ferries come and go; the only longstanding multi-island ferry is Express des Iles (see box). Most other ferries are shuttles between neighboring islands, such as Antigua–Montserrat, Sint Maarten–St-Barths, St-Martin–Anguilla or USVI–BVI. Countries made up of two or more islands also have ferries, eg Antigua–Barbuda, St Kitts–Nevis, St Vincent–the Grenadines, Grenada–Carriacou, Trinidad–Tobago. It is often possible for travelers to bargain with fishermen and other small-boat owners to arrange rides out to the many small islands which lie off the shores of the major islands. Anyone

### International ferry

**Express des Iles**, tel: 825-35 9000, www.express-des-iles.com, is an international ferry with daily services connecting Guadeloupe, Les Saintes, Marie Galante, Dominica, Martinique, and St Lucia, and occasional services to Antigua. Departure taxes must be paid and immigration and customs formalities complied with.
**Guadeloupe:** Gare Maritime, Bergevin, 97110 Pointe-à-Pitre, commercialguadeloupe@express-des-iles.com.
**Dominica:** H.H.V. Whitchurch & Co Ltd, Roseau, tel: 767-255 1125.
**Martinique:** Terminal Inter Iles, Quai Ouest, 97200 Fort-de-France, commercialmartinique@express-des-iles.com.
**St Lucia:** Cox and Co Ltd, tel: 758-456 5000 and at ferry terminal, tel: 758-456 5022.

wishing to travel the entire arc of the Lesser Antilles without flying would have to resort to a private yacht for some sections.

### Sailing

#### Chartering a Yacht

One of the most exciting ways to explore the Caribbean is on a private yacht, either with your own crew to sail the boat for you or bareboat – just the boat – for experienced sailors. Popular destinations are the Grenadines and the Virgin Islands as the islands are close together and easily explored in a week or two. A 3-week trip might take you, for example, from Antigua to the Virgin Islands or Antigua to Grenada, making leisurely calls at the islands along the way. Short charters of just a few days can also be arranged, and for those who prefer to sleep on dry land, most islands have day-sail operators too. Whatever your itinerary, if you are at home on a boat, this is a wonderful way to see the islands.

If you want to rent a crewed yacht, make sure you are happy with your choice – that the yacht is safe, comfortable, and well-equipped and the crew congenial enough to share close quarters. Organize the trip with a reputable agency, which will match you with the right boat and crew. One long-established agency is:
**Nicholson Yacht Charters & Services**, tel: 268-460 1530 (Antigua); www.nicholsoncharters.com.

An exhaustive list of companies offering bareboat Caribbean charters is published in the March issue of *Sail* magazine, while the August issue covers crewed yachts. *Sail* is available in many libraries, and back (or current) issues can also be ordered from the magazine's publisher. Contact: *Sail* **Magazine**, www.sailmag.com.

### ANGUILLA

#### By Car

Cars drive on the left, British-style, but are usually left-hand drive. The speed limit is 30mph (48kph). To purchase a temporary Anguillan driver's license, which is good for up to 3 months, present a valid driver's license from your country of origin, with a small fee, to the police station in The Valley. The ports of entry can also perform this service although usually the car-

rental agency organizes it. Bicycles are a good way of getting around this small island, available at some hotels and bike-rental agencies.

Car-rental companies include:
**Apex/Avis Car Rental**, tel: 264-497 2642; www.avisanguilla.com.
**Island Car Rental**, tel: 264-497 2723; www.islandcar.ai.
**Thrifty Car Rental**, tel: 264-497 2656; www.thrifty.com.

#### By Taxi/Bus

Taxis are available at all points of entry including Clayton J. Lloyd Airport, which is more or less at the center of Anguilla, and at the ferry terminal, west at Blowing Point. Taxis are not metered, but there are fixed charges for taxi rides; confirm the price before you start. There are no buses.

#### Inter-Island Links

From Clayton J. Lloyd Airport you can fly to Sint Maarten, St Kitts, St Thomas, bvi, Antigua, and Puerto Rico with a number of small charter companies. There are scheduled services to Puerto Rico with Cape Air and to Antigua with LIAT.
**Cape Air**, tel: 866-227 3247; www.flycapeair.com.
**LIAT**, tel: 264-497 5000; www.liatairline.com.

Marigot in St-Martin is a 25-minute ferry ride away from Anguilla and makes a good day-trip. Ferries leave Blowing Point every half hour, 7.30am–6.15pm. Don't forget your passport and immigration card. There is a departure tax. Ferries from Marigot to Blowing Point depart every half hour, 8am–7pm.

Ferry services and charters are also available between Blowing Point and Princess Juliana International Airport in Sint Maarten.
Link Ferries, tel: 264-497 2231; www.link.ai.
GB Ferries, tel: 264-235 6205; www.gbferries.com.
Funtime Charters, tel: 866-334 0047; www.funtime-charters.com.

### ANTIGUA AND BARBUDA

#### By Car

Driving is on the left, British-style. Finding your way around is not easy as there are few road signs. Drivers should present their regular license, along with a small fee at a police station or car-rental office in order to be issued with a local driving permit. Vehicles can be picked up at the airport, or delivered to your hotel. Agencies include: **Dollar Rent-a-Car**, tel: 268-462 0362; www.dollarantigua.com. **Hertz**, tel: 268-481 4440; www.hertz.com.

On Barbuda, jeeps are available from **Lynton Thomas**, tel: 268-721 2796.

### By Taxi/Bus

There are plenty of taxis to meet flights at V.C. Bird International Airport, and jeeps at Barbuda's Codrington Airport. Taxis also wait at the cruise terminal. Fares are pre-set (a list is posted in Arrivals at the airport, at the cruise terminal, at the tourist office, and in hotels). Confirm the price before you start. Many Antiguan taxi drivers are also qualified tour guides. Buses and minivans run from the bus terminal in St John's to most of the island, but not north of the capital, nor to the airport, so you have to take a taxi.

### Inter-Island Links

Barbuda is just 10 minutes away from Antigua by air, or 90 minutes by ferry from St John's. For links with Montserrat by boat, plane and helicopter, see page 297. Antigua has frequent links with most Caribbean islands, mostly with LIAT, tel: 268-480 5601; www.liatairline.com.

## ARUBA

### By Car

Driving is on the right. To rent a car you must be 21 years of age and in possession of a valid national driving license. Rent a four-wheel-drive vehicle if you want to explore the interior. Bicycles, scooters, and motorbikes are also available for hire. Rental companies include: **Ace Car Rental**, tel: 297-583 0840, www.acearuba.com; **More 4 Less Jeep & Car Rental**, tel: 297-588 7255, www.more4less-aruba.com.

### By Taxi/Bus

Taxis are plentiful and have set fares, not meters, but always check before beginning a journey. Buses run from Oranjestad to the resort areas in the north and to San Nicolas in the south and are inexpensive. In addition, taxis called "jitney cars," following fixed routes, cost slightly more than buses. Buses and jitneys to San Nicolas will drop you at the airport.

### Inter-Island Links

**Insel Air**, www.fly-inselair.com; and **Tiara Air**, www.tiara-air.com run scheduled flights between Aruba, Bonaire, and Curaçao several times a day. **Divi Divi Air**, www.flydivi.com flies from Curaçao to Bonaire several times daily and offers charter service to Aruba. There are no ferries.

## BARBADOS

### By Car

Driving is on the left, and by Caribbean standards the roads are good, although driving at night can be difficult on narrow unlit country roads, so leave plenty of time to reach your destination. The maximum speed limit outside urban areas is 50mph (80kph). Bajan rush hour is 7.30–8.30am and 4.30–5.30pm.

Visitors' drivers' licenses are available from the airport, many car-rental companies, and most police stations. To obtain one you must present your own license and a small payment.

The following car-rental companies offer a wide choice of cars, including mini-mokes (beach buggy-style vehicles), free pick-up and delivery to and from your accommodations, and free road maps. **Courtesy Rent-a-Car**, tel: 246-431 4160, www.courtesyrentacar.com; **Top Class Car Rentals**, tel: 246-228 7368, www.topclassrentals.com; **Stoutes Car Rental**, tel: 246-416 4456, www.stoutescar.com.

### By Taxi/Bus

Taxis are always in plentiful supply at the international airport, cruise ship terminal, hotels, and in town. Make sure you agree the fare before beginning your journey. Enquire at the airport or hotel reception for the official rates.

Buses radiate out from Bridgetown and are a good and cheap way of getting around the island. The large buses are state owned while the small minibuses and route taxis are private. Buses from the airport go to Bridgetown direct or via the hotel district on the south coast. There is a flat fare for each leg of your journey, so if you have to change buses you pay twice.

### Yachting Information

For yachtsmen and women who want to stay put for a while, there are community anchorages in Sint Maarten, Bequia (Grenadines), Grenada, and Trinidad. There are marinas with slips of different types and facilities for provisioning and repairs. Several of the larger ones have dry-dock facilities for boat storage.

### Inter-Island Links

There are frequent flights to nearly all the Caribbean islands with **LIAT**, tel: 246-428 8888, www.liat-airline.com. Other regional airlines include **Caribbean Airlines**, www.caribbean-airlines.com and **SVG Air**, tel: 246-247 3712, www.svgair.com. There are no ferries.

## BONAIRE

### By Car

Those wishing to rent a car must be 21 years of age and in possession of a valid national driver's license. The speed limit is 25mph (40kph) and you should watch out for goats and donkeys on the road. Some companies forbid the use of anything other than a four-wheel-drive on unmade roads and the Washington-Slagbaai National Park. Pick-up trucks are popular rental vehicles as they can carry dive gear. Motorcycles, quad bikes, bicycles, and scooters can be rented. Car-rental companies include: **Budget**, tel: 599-717 4700; www.bonaire-budgetcar.com. **Bonaire Motorcycle Shop**, tel: 599-717 7790; www.motorcycleshopbonaire.com.

### By Taxi/Bus

Taxis and water-taxis are available. There is a list of official rates, including touring and waiting time. Taxis wait at the airport but there is no taxi stand in town and you will have to call for one elsewhere. Buses, autobuses, run around town and will take you where you want, but there is no scheduled service. Some hotels have a shuttle service to town and to the airport.

### Inter-Island Links

**Insel Air**, www.fly-inselair.com; and **Tiara Air**, www.tiara-air.com run scheduled flights between Aruba, Bonaire, and Curaçao several times a day. **Divi Divi Air**, www.flydivi.com flies from Curaçao to Bonaire several times daily and offers charter service to Aruba. There are no ferries.

## BRITISH VIRGIN ISLANDS

### By Car

Driving is on the left, but many cars have the steering wheel on the left. The speed limit is 40mph (64kph), or 20mph (32kph) in residential areas. To drive here, a temporary bvi driver's license is required. It can be obtained through the rental agency on presentation of your valid driver's license. Advance reservation is recommended in peak season. Car rental firms include: **Avis**, tel: 284-494 3322; **Courtesy Car Rentals**, tel: 284-494 6443; **International Car Rentals**, tel: 284-494 2516; **D.W. Jeep Rentals**, Anegada, tel: 284-495 9677/8018; **Mahogany Car Rentals**, Virgin Gorda, tel: 284-495 5469. Bicycles can also be hired.

### By Taxi/Bus

Taxis are easy to find on the BVI. They stop if hailed on the road, and can be found waiting at the airports, cruise ship terminal, and ferry docks. On Virgin Gorda small converted lorries with benches run a shuttle service between the main tourist points at a reasonable price. Taxis have fixed prices, but it is always best to establish the fare before you start out on a journey.

There is a private bus service on Tortola, but it has no fixed timetable and goes to few tourist spots. Only taxis go to the Terrance B. Lettsome Airport on Beef Island.

### Inter-Island Links

#### By Air

Small planes fly from Tortola to Virgin Gorda and Anegada. Day-trips are possible with charter companies such as **Air Sunshine**, tel: 284-495 8900, www.airsunshine.com; **Caribbean Wings**, www.bvi-airlines.com; **Fly BVI**, tel: 284-495 1747, www.bviaircharters.com. There are

good connecting flights from the international airports on St-Martin, Puerto Rico, and the US Virgin Islands as well as other islands in the region with **American Airlines/American Eagle**, tel: 284-495 2559, www.aa.com; **Cape Air**, tel: 284-495 2100; **LIAT**, tel: 284-495 1693; vi **Airlink**, tel: 284-499 2938, www.viairlink.com.

#### By Ferry

Timetables are available in hotels, at the tourist board (www.bvitourism.com), and in the *Welcome* magazine (www.bviwelcome.com).

There are regular services:
from Road Town, Tortola to Spanish Town, Virgin Gorda and Peter Island.
from West End, Tortola to Jost Van Dyke.
from Beef Island, Tortola to North Sound and Spanish Town, Virgin Gorda (North Sound Express).
from Road Town, Tortola and West End to St Thomas and St John (both USVI).
from Virgin Gorda to St Thomas (USVI).

There is also a free ferry from Beef Island, Tortola to Marina Cay (Pusser's).

## CURAÇAO

### By Car

Those wishing to rent a car must be 21 years of age and in possession of a valid national driver's license. Cars, vans, four-wheel-drive vehicles, and pick-up trucks are all available, as are bicycles and motorbikes. Car-rental companies include:
**Avis**, tel: 5999-461 1255, www.aviscuracao.com; and **Budget**, tel: 5999-868-3466, www.curacao-budgetcar.com.

### By Taxi/Bus

There are taxi stands at the airport, at hotels, and in town. Always agree the fare before beginning a taxi journey. There are bus terminals in Punda and Otrobanda with services within town and to either end of the island. Big yellow or blue buses, called *konvooi*, cover most of the island and are the cheapest. Smaller buses, collective cars or vans, called *bus*, go more often but have no schedule and they cost a little more. Buses go to the airport but you must allow extra time.

### Inter-Island Links

**Insel Air**, www.fly-inselair.com; and **Tiara Air**, www.tiara-air.com run

scheduled flights between Aruba, Bonaire, and Curaçao several times a day. **Divi Divi Air**, www.flydivi.com flies from Curaçao to Bonaire several times daily and offers charter service to Aruba. There are no ferries.

## DOMINICA

### By Car

Driving is on the left-hand side, British-style. The speed limit in built-up areas is 20mph (32kph). Elsewhere there is no limit. Roads in Dominica are characteristically twisting and narrow, with steep gradients, but the surface is generally very good.

There are various car-rental companies in and around Roseau. Cars can be picked up at and returned to the airport. You need a national or international driver's license and a local visitor's permit. The latter can be obtained from your car-rental company. Hire companies: **Courtesy**, tel: 767-448 7763; **Island Car Rentals**, tel: 767-255 6844, www.islandcar.dm.

### By Taxi/Bus

Dominica's main airport, **Douglas–Charles**, is located near Marigot, on the island's northeast coast. Taxis are available there to take travelers on the long but scenic 36-mile (58km) drive to Roseau, where many hotels and guesthouses are located.

There are numerous taxi services. On fixed routes the fares are set by the government. Otherwise, settle on a price before you start your journey. Taxis do not cruise the streets and are sometimes difficult to find at night. Ask your hotel or restaurant to order one.

Minibuses are the local form of public transportation, from early in the morning to nightfall. They run mainly to and from Roseau. There are no fixed schedules; buses leave when they are full (in Roseau there are various departure points depending on the destination). There are frequent services to villages around Roseau, but making a round trip in one day from Roseau to more remote communities can be a problem. Coming into Roseau in the early morning from towns such as Plymouth or Marigot, and returning at lunch time or in the afternoon is easier. Buses do run

*Grenada forest tour.*

on the road past the airport, but infrequently.

### Inter-Island Links

Connections with Dominica are made with regional airlines, including **LIAT**, from neighboring Caribbean islands, including Antigua, Guadeloupe, and Martinique. **American Airlines/ American Eagle** flies daily from San Juan, Puerto Rico (with connections to North America). The main airport is Douglas–Charles Airport. LIAT and air taxi services also use the smaller Canefield Airport, close to Roseau. **American Airlines/American Eagle**, tel: 767-448 0628. **LIAT**, tel: 767-448 3980. **Winair**, tel: 767-448 2181 If you prefer to travel by ferry, **Express des Iles** connects Dominica with Guadeloupe (to the north) and Martinique and St Lucia (to the south). Ferries depart from Roseau almost daily; see page 298.

## GRENADA

### By Car

Driving is on the left. Roads are sometimes in poor condition, especially in the mountains. Drivers must be over 21 although most rental companies now stipulate that you must be over 25, and have a valid license as well as a local permit (available from the central police station). There is a good choice of rental firms, but cars are sometimes difficult to obtain,

particularly in high season and during Carnival. Rental companies include: **Maitlands**, tel: 473-444 4022, www.maitlandsrentals.com; and **McIntyre Bros Ltd**, tel: 473-444 3944/1550, www.caribbean horizons.com.

#### In Carriacou

**Sunkey's**, tel: 473-443 8382. Bicycles can be rented from **Ride Grenada**, tel: 473-444 1157. The island's mountainous terrain, tropical climate, and sometimes erratic road conditions should be borne in mind if you plan to tour the island on two wheels.

### By Taxi/Bus

Taxis are available at the airport, the Carenage, the cruise ship dock, and outside most hotels. They are not metered and there are no fixed charges, so try to establish the fare with the driver before setting off. Taxi drivers can normally be hired by the hour or day for sightseeing tours of the island. Allow a day for a tour of Grenada. Water taxis run from the Carenage and the Esplanade to Grand Anse beach. Grenada has an inexpensive and comprehensive bus network, but buses are normally crowded and have loud music. Buses or minivans leave from the bus station on the Esplanade in St George's for all parts of the island, Mon–Sat 7am–7pm, although in practice it can be difficult to find one after mid-afternoon. Fares are set according to distance. Only taxis go to the airport.

### Inter-Island Links

LIAT and SVG Air connect Grenada with Carriacou. LIAT also has services to all eastern Caribbean destinations. **LIAT**, tel: 473-440 2796/5428; **SVG Air**, tel: 473-457 5124.
The **Osprey Ferry** (www.osprey lines.com) connects Grenada with Carriacou and Petit Martinique daily (2 hours). Carriacou can also be reached by schooners, most of which depart in the morning from the Carenage, returning the following day. The journey takes about 4 hours, with loud music and refreshments.

## GUADELOUPE

### By Car

Drive on the right. To rent a car for 20 days or less, your current valid license is all you will need. For longer periods, Guadeloupe requires an international driver's permit. Visiting drivers need to be over 21 and should have at least one year's driving experience. The Pointe-à-Pitre/Pôle Caraïbes airport has car-rental agencies. Mopeds, scooters, motorbikes, and bicycles are also available for hire. Traffic is appalling around Pointe-à-Pitre. Rental agencies include **Avis**, tel: 590-590-836 900, www.avis-antilles. fr; **Budget**, tel: 590-590-211 349, www.budget-guadeloupe.com; and **Europcar**, tel: 590-590-915 822, www.europcar-guadeloupe.com.

### By Taxi/Bus

At all points of entry – air and sea – taxis are available. All taxis have meters, which are useful for short trips, but for longer excursions, negotiate a tariff. Some drivers speak English, but most speak only French. There are three main bus terminals in Pointe-à-Pitre, covering different areas of the country. Buses run to all towns and villages and are relatively cheap. During the week they run 5.30am–7pm, every 15 minutes or when full, but on Saturday afternoon and on Sunday there are very few buses anywhere. Buses do not run to the Pôle Caraïbes airport; the nearest bus stop is at Millenis, about 1km (0.6 mile) from the airport.

### Inter-Island Links

The Pôle Caraïbes airport at Les Abymes has two terminals: the

International Terminal and the Regional Terminal. There are also airports on Marie Galante, Terre-de-Haut, La Désirade, at St-François, and Baillif airport on the southern tip of Basse-Terre. **LIAT**, 590-590-211 140, www.liatairline.com; **Air Caraïbes**, tel: 590-590-824 747, www.aircaraibes. com; **Air Antilles Express**, tel: 0890-648 648, www.airantilles.com fly to neighboring Caribbean islands. There are a number of ferries linking Guadeloupe with La Désirade (**La Somade Le Colibri**, tel: 590-690-357 947), with Marie Galante (**Brudey Frères**, tel: 590-590-900 448; **Express des Iles**, www.express-des-iles.com), and Les Saintes (**Brudey Frères; Express des Iles**). **Express des Iles** connects Guadeloupe, Les Saintes, and Marie Galante with Martinique, Dominica, and St Lucia several times a week; see page 298.

## MARTINIQUE

### By Car

To rent a car, your current valid license is all you need. Drivers should have at least one year's driving experience. Traffic is heavy, so avoid the main roads at rush hour. There are lots of rental agencies at the airport, including **Europcar**, tel: 596-596-424 242, www.europcar-martinique.com; **Budget**, tel: 596-596-511 202, www.budget-martinique.com; **Euradom**, tel: 596-596-601 093, www.euradom.sup.fr.

### By Taxi/Bus

There are taxis at the airport and the cruise terminal. All taxis are fitted with meters, which makes it easier for short journeys, but expensive for longer trips. It is advisable to negotiate a fixed rate for excursions. Some, but not all, drivers speak English. There are bus stops along Boulevard Général de Gaulle for both urban and long-distance buses. Alternatively you can try the *taxicos*, shared taxis that leave from the terminal at Pointe Simon and run from early morning to 6pm all over the island, an inexpensive means of getting about. There are no buses to the airport although buses to Sainte-Anne pass fairly close by.

### Inter-Island Links

Airlines connecting Martinique to Antigua, Barbados, Dominica, Grenada, Guadeloupe, Puerto Rico, St Lucia, Sint Maarten, St Vincent, and Trinidad include: **Air Caraïbes**, tel: 590-590-824 747 (Guadeloupe HQ), www.aircaraibes.com; and **LIAT**, tel: 596-596-421 611, www.liatairline.com. **American Airlines/American Eagle** operates a nonstop service between San Juan, Puerto Rico and Fort-de-France. **Air Antilles**, tel: 596-596-421 671, www.airantilles.com, shuttles between Martinique, Guadeloupe, St-Martin, and St-Barthélemy and also flies to Santo Domingo. **Airawak**, tel: 596-596-516 688, www.airawak.com, flies between Martinique and Canefield airport in Dominica and both airports in St Lucia.

Ferries link Martinique to Dominica, Guadeloupe, and St Lucia: **L'Express Des Iles**; see page 298.

*The runway at Aimé Césaire airport, Martinique.*

## MONTSERRAT

### By Car

Drive on the left, British-style. A local driver's license can be obtained from the police. Island-wide road improvements are ongoing. The island has car, jeep, bicycle, and scooter rental services. **Gage's Car Rental**, tel: 664-493 5821, www.gagescarrental.com **Tip Top Enterprise**, tel: 664-496 1842, www.tiptopcarrentals.com

### By Taxi/Bus

Taxis and buses are available; they both have green license plates beginning with H and can be hailed on the street. There are no official stops and no scheduled times for buses. The Tourist Board can supply visitors with taxi contact details for island tours.

### Inter-Island Links

Scheduled and charter flights on nine-seater aircraft are offered between Antigua and Montserrat by **Fly Montserrat**, tel: 664-491 3434, www.flymontserrat.com and **SVG Airline/ABM Air**, tel: 664-491 4200, www.svgair.com. SVG Airline can be chartered for flights to neighboring islands and to St Vincent.

**Caribbean Helicopters**, in Antigua, tel: 268-460 5900, www.caribbeanhelicopters.net, offer a charter helicopter service to Montserrat.

There is a ferry service 4 days a week from St John's, Antigua, and Little Bay, tel: 664-496 9912 in Montserrat, and tel: 268-778 9786 in Antigua. An Antiguan-based company, **Ondeck**, provides a racing yacht crossing on demand for day trips, 4 hours to Montserrat, 5 hours return, tel: 268-562 6696, www.ondeck oceanracing.com/antigua/montserrat-adventure.htm.

## SABA AND ST EUSTATIUS

### By Car

All valid foreign drivers' licenses are accepted. Driving is on the right. Limited car hire is available: **Morgan Car Rental**, Saba, tel: 599-416 2881. **ARC**, Statia, tel: 599-318 2595. Watch out for animals on the road in Statia.

## By Taxi/Bus

Taxis are available on both islands for pick-ups at airports and ferry ports, and for island tours. Rates are fixed, but agree the price in advance. There are no buses.

## Inter-Island Links

**Saba**: **Winair**, www.fly-winair.com, flies at least five times a day from Sint Maarten. Saba's J. E. Irausquin airport has the shortest commercial runway in the world, 1,312ft (400 meters), and suffers from turbulence, with a mountain on one side and the sea on the other (and at the end). Only small planes can fly in and flights are cancelled if it is too windy. On landing, the runway looks so short it appears almost square. On takeoff the pilot puts on the brakes, then pushes the engines to full throttle until the plane vibrates, before releasing the brakes and taking off as quickly as possible. See page 297 for ferry details.

**Sint Eustatius**: **Winair** has five 20-minute flights a day from Sint Maarten. There is no ferry.

## ST-BARTHÉLEMY

## By Car

Drive on the right. French laws apply. Car rental should be organized in advance at busy times of the year. Minimum age for car rental is 23 and you must have been licensed for 2 years. Many companies have offices at the airport. Roads are narrow and twisting in the hills and the smaller the car the better. Open-topped cars are popular. There is a chronic lack of parking space.
**Budget**, tel: 590-590-276 630, www.st-barths.com/budget; **Europcar**, tel: 590-590-277 434, www.st-barths.com/europcar; and **Hertz**, tel: 590-590-277 114, www.hertzstbarth.com.

## By Taxi/Bus

Taxis are available at the airport and ferry port, and for tours. They will do island tours or take you to a beach and pick you up later. Rates are fixed, but agree the price in advance. There are no buses.

## Inter-Island Links

The main gateway to St-Barths is through Sint Maarten. From Sint Maarten, **Winair**, www.fly-winair.com; **Air Caraïbes**, www.aircaraibes.

com; and **St Barth Commuter**, www.stbarthcommuter.com make the 10-minute shuttle flights to St-Barths (SBH). From Guadeloupe, Air Caraïbes offers a few direct flights (45 minutes). The airstrip in St-Barths is short, 2,170ft (660 meters), and plagued by turbulence. Pilots have to negotiate a mountain, then drop sharply to land before they hit the sea at the end of the runway. Special training is required to land. For many passengers, the landing, especially on a windy day, is an adventure in itself.

**St-Barths** is served by catamarans and ferries; see page 297 for details.

## ST KITTS AND NEVIS

## By Car

Drive on the left, British-style. Visitors who wish to drive while on the islands must present a valid national or international license at the Traffic Department or through the rental company, along with a small fee.

Saloon cars, jeeps, and mini-mokes (like a beach buggy) are available for rental but should be booked well in advance, especially in high season.

For more details contact:
**Avis**, St Kitts, tel: 869-465 6507;
**Avis**, Nevis, tel: 869-469 5199;
**Caines**, St Kitts, tel: 869-465 2366;
**Nevis Car Rental**, Newcastle, Nevis, tel: 869-469 9837.

It is possible to split the rental between the two islands for the same price as renting a car on only one island.

## By Taxi/Bus

Taxis wait at the airports and at the harbors of both islands. Tariffs are fixed, but be sure to confirm the total price of your journey before starting out. Small minibuses are reliable and cheap. They do not run to Frigate Bay and the southeast peninsula but you can get a bus from Basseterre up the coastal road to Old Road and on to Brimstone Hill Fortress. On Nevis, minibuses run on the road round the island all day. Stand on the side of the road and hail one in whichever direction you are going.

## Inter-Island Links

St Kitts is linked by air with many islands including Puerto Rico, Antigua, Barbados, St Maarten, St Thomas, Anguilla, St-Barths, Saba, St Eustatius, BVI, Grenada, and St Lucia.

Nevis is linked with Puerto Rico, Antigua, and St Maarten.

Airlines serving the routes to and from St Kitts and Nevis include: **Winair**, tel: 869-469 5302 and **LIAT**, tel: 869-465 5491/469 5238.

An air taxi and a ferry run daily between Basseterre, St Kitts and Charlestown, Nevis. Journey time is 30–45 minutes. Tickets can be purchased at the ferry terminal.

## ST LUCIA

## By Car

Drive on the left. Visiting drivers must obtain a temporary driving permit, valid for 3 months, available from Castries police station or all car-rental companies. Cars and four-wheel-drive vehicles are available to rent at the port; a four-wheel-drive is best for places off the beaten track. Contact:
**Alexo Car/Avis**, tel: 758-452 2700, www.avisstlucia.com; **Cool Breeze Jeep-Car Rental**, tel: 758-459 7729, www.coolbreezecarrental.com; **Hertz**, tel: 758-452 0679, www.hertz.com; **West Coast Jeeps and Taxi Service**, tel: 758-459 5457, www.westcoastjeeps.com.

## By Taxi/Bus

Taxis are available at Hewanorra international airport in the south, the George F.L. Charles airport, near Castries, and at the cruise ship terminals. Most larger hotels lie in the northwest of the island; so if you land at Hewanorra, you are likely to have a long and expensive, albeit picturesque, journey to your destination. The prices are fixed for set routes, but check the current rates at the tourist office. Always agree the fare before starting your journey.

Public buses in St Lucia operate from early morning until early evening. The frequency tends to tail off after the end of the working day. Castries and Vieux Fort have the best services, while the more remote rural areas aren't always as well served. If you go to Soufrière by bus, it is usually quicker and easier to return via Vieux Fort, where there are better connections.

## Inter-Island Links

**Air Caraïbes**, **LIAT**, **Winair** and **SVG Air** fly from neighbouring islands while **American Airlines/American Eagle** flies from Puerto Rico for connections with us cities. Local flights usually go from George F.L. Charles airport, just outside the centre of Castries. **Express des Iles** has a high-speed catamaran car ferry service linking St Lucia with Dominica and the French islands of Martinique, Guadeloupe, Les Saintes, and Marie Galante.

## ST-MARTIN/SINT MAARTEN

### By Car

Driving is on the right. Foreign licenses are accepted. Rental companies operating on the island include:
**Dutch side: Paradise Car Rental**, Airport Boulevard 38, Simpson Bay, tel: 599-545 3737, www.paradisecarrentalsxm.com.
**French side: Alizés Car Rental**, Baie Nettlé, tel: 590-590-872 059, www.alizes-car-rental.com.

### By Taxi/Bus

Taxis are available at the island's ports of entry and in the centers of both towns. Wait either at the pier or where the tenders drop off. There are no meters, but there are fixed charges, so check the price before you start. A taxi tour is a good way of seeing the island.

Buses regularly travel between Marigot and Philipsburg, 6am–midnight, passing the airport, as well as on other principal routes. Ask at the tourist office about island tours by minibus.

### Inter-Island Links

Juliana airport is one of the busiest in the region and, in addition to a large number of long-haul flights, there are good connections with all the other Caribbean islands from the Dominican Republic down the chain to Trinidad and Tobago. Inter-island airlines include: **Winair**, tel: 599-545 4273, www.fly-winair.com and LIAT, tel: 599-545 2403, www.liatairline.com. There is a small airport on the French side too, L'Espérance, at Grand Case. Small aircraft use this airport and there are flights to the Dominican Republic, Puerto Rico, St-Barthélemy, Martinique, and Guadeloupe.

There are frequent ferries linking the island with its immediate neighbors: Anguilla, St-Barthélemy, and Saba. Ferries from Blowing Point, Anguilla, cross to Marigot or Juliana airport. *Voyager I & II* cross regularly to Gustavia, St-Barths, from either

Marigot waterfront or Captain Oliver's Marina, Oyster Pond. Day trips are organized to Saba with lunch and tour if required. Contact **Voyager**, 9 rue Félix Eboué, Lot 5, Marigot; tel: 590-590-871 068, www.voy12.com/.
**The Edge** is another ferry crossing to St-Barths and Saba, also offering day trips and tours, from Pelican Marina, Sint Maarten, 5 days a week, journey time 45 minutes, tel: 599-544 2640.
**Great Bay Express** additionally has two to three crossings a day from Bobby's Marina, Philipsburg, to Gustavia, tel: 590-690 718 301, www.sbhferry.com. The Saba ferry, MV *Dawn II* crosses three times a week, leaving Fort Bay in the morning and returning from Dock Maarten in the evening, journey time 2 hours, tel: 599-416 2299, www.sabactransport.com.

## ST VINCENT AND THE GRENADINES

### By Car

Driving is on the left, British-style. You will need your national license and a local license, which can be arranged at the police station in Bay Street, Kingstown, or the Licensing Authority in Halifax Street. Car hire is available on St Vincent and Bequia. Cars have limited access to some areas; a jeep is the best bet. Car-rental companies on St Vincent include **Avis**, tel: 784-456 6861; **Ben's Auto Rentals**, tel: 784-456 2907, www.bensautorentals. com. On Bequia: **D&N (Noel's) Car Rental**, tel: 784-458 3064, www.bequiarentalcars.com; jeeps, bicycles, and scooters from **Handy Andy Rentals**, tel: 784-458 3722, http://handyandybequia.tripod.com.

### By Taxi/Bus

There are plenty of taxis at the airport to take you to your destination. Taxis and minibuses are also available on Bequia and Union Island. There are fixed tariffs for journeys, but check the price before you start.

Local buses on St Vincent and the Grenadines tend to be both busy and noisy, but they are also inexpensive and run reasonably frequently, Monday to Saturday, stopping on demand rather than at bus stops. Routes radiate out from the Little Tokyo Fish Market in Kingstown to all parts of St Vincent. There is a frequent service along the south coast to Villa, passing the airport. Buses may be a minibus or a pick-up truck with seats in the back.

### Inter-Island Links

St Vincent is linked by air with other Caribbean islands including Barbados, Trinidad, St Lucia, Martinique, and Grenada. Bequia, Canouan, Mustique, and Union Island have airports capable of taking small planes – expect to be weighed along with your luggage. Airlines operating local flights: **LIAT**, tel: 784-457 1821; **Mustique Airways**, tel: 784-458 4380; **SVG Air**, tel: 784-457 5124.

Inter-island ferries are cost-effective. Contact **Admiralty Transport**, Port Elizabeth, Bequia, tel: 784-458 3348, www.admiraltytransport.com or **Bequia Express**, tel: 784-457 3539, www.bequiaexpress.com. The M/V *Jaden Sun*, tel: 784-451 2192, www.jadeninc.com, is a high-speed ferry linking Kingstown, Bequia, Canouan, and Union Island with stops in Mayreau on request. M/V *Gem Star*, tel: 784-526 1158, links St Vincent with Canouan, Mayreau, and Union Island. M/V *Canouan Bay* sails between St Vincent and Canouan. The M/V *Endeavour* services Mustique. The M/V *Barracuda*, the mail boat, mainly cargo, runs twice a week from St Vincent down the chain of Grenadines.

## TRINIDAD AND TOBAGO

### By Car

Driving is on the left. Visitors wishing to rent a car must be at least 21 years old and have a valid driver's license.
**Southern Sales Group of Companies** on Trinidad, San Fernando, tel: 868-657 8541, www.southernsalestt.com; **Kalloo's**, Port of Spain, tel: 868-622 9073, www.kalloos.com; **Hertz**, tel: 868-631 8650; **Island Automotive and Transport**, tel: 868-291 5353, www.tobagorentalcar.com.

### By Taxi/Bus

Any form of public transport is referred to as a taxi. Taxis are available at the airports, ports, and town centers. Fares are fixed. Route taxis (minibuses) run along set routes and have fixed fares. Maxi taxis (shared taxis) travel greater distances than route taxis. All taxis are privately owned; buses are run by the state, PTSC, tel: 868-623 7872 (Trinidad), tel: 868-639 2293 (Tobago), www.ptsc.co.tt. The main bus station on Trinidad

TRANSPORTATION

is City Gate, South Quay, Port of Spain, and is the hub for transport all over the island. On Tobago the bus station is at Sangster's Hill, Scarborough. There are no buses from Piarco airport; you have to take a taxi or walk to the end of the approach road to the terminal, catch a route taxi to Arouca, then another from the junction into Port of Spain. On Tobago you can walk from the airport terminal to several hotels in the Store Bay area or get a taxi further afield.

## Inter-Island Links

Trinidad has good connections with the rest of the Caribbean and its South American neighbors, Venezuela, Guyana, and Suriname. Flights to Antigua, Barbados, Curaçao, Dominica, Grenada, Jamaica, St Lucia, St Vincent, and Sint Maarten are with **LIAT**, tel: 868-669 2982; **Caribbean Airlines**, tel: 868-625 7200 and **Surinam Airways**, tel: 868-627 0102. **LIAT** also flies from Tobago to Grenada and Barbados.

The **Port Authority of Trinidad and Tobago (**patt**)**, www.patnt.com, has two high-speed ferries, *T&T Express* and *T&T Spirit*, running a daily service between Port of Spain and Scarborough (2.5 hours), and a conventional ferry, *Warrior Spirit* (6 hours). **Caribbean Airlines** runs the air bridge between the two islands with about 12 daily flights from 6am (20 minutes). Flights get booked up on public holidays.

# US VIRGIN ISLANDS

## By Car

Cars drive on the left, British-style, in the US Virgin Islands, despite the fact that most steering wheels are on the left, American-style.

A us driver's license is valid in the USVI. If your license is from another country and you wish to drive here, contact the USVI Division of Tourism in your home country before you go, to see what arrangements need to be made. Vehicles available to rent range from a standard saloon to an open jeep.

In St Thomas and St Croix, rental cars may be picked up at the airport. In St John rental vehicles are available in the main town of Cruz Bay. There are a variety of rental companies to choose from, which include: **St Thomas**: **Budget**, tel: 340-776 5774, 800-626 4516; **Dependable Car Rental**, tel: 340-774 2253, toll-

*Riding through the surf.*

free: 800-522 3076, www.depend ablecar.com. **St Croix**: **Avis**, tel: 340-778 9365; **Olympic Rent-a-Car**, tel: 340-718 3000, www.olympicstcroix.com; **St John**: **St John Car Rental**, tel: 340-776 6103, www.stjohncarrental.com.

## By Taxi/Bus

Whether you arrive by plane, cruise ship, or ferry, you will find taxis waiting at your point of entry to take you to your hotel or wherever else you want to go. Taxi fares are published by the Virgin Islands Taxi Association, but you should verify rates before getting in.

If taking a day trip to St John, an open-air taxi tour of the island is recommended. Taxi companies include: **St Croix**: **St Croix Taxi Association**, tel: 868-778 1088, www.stcroixtaxi. com. **St Thomas**: vi **Taxi Association**, tel: 868-774 4550, www.vitaxi association.com. There are regular bus services on St Thomas, St John, and St Croix; look for the Vitran bus stop signs. On St Croix buses run every half hour between Christiansted and Frederiksted.

## Inter-Island Links

There are airports on St Thomas and St Croix. You can fly between the US Virgin Islands on **Cape Air**,

tel: 1-800 352 0714; www.flycapeair. com; or **Seaborne Airlines**, tel: 340-773 6442; www.seaborneairlines. com. Local airlines link the USVI with nearby islands: Puerto Rico, the BVI, Anguilla, and Sint Maarten. They include: Seaborne Airlines, Cape Air, **LIAT**, www.liatairline.com, and **American Airlines/American Eagle**, www.aa.com.

For the ferry from St Thomas (Charlotte Amalie) to St Croix, contact **Smith's Ferry**, tel: 340-775 7292, www.smithsferryservices. com. From St Thomas (Red Hook or Charlotte Amalie) to St John (Cruz Bay) **Transportation Services and Varlack Ventures**, tel: 340-776 6282, www.varlack-ventures.com. For the Water Island ferry from Crown Bay, St Thomas, tel: 340-690 4159. For the ferry from Charlotte Amalie to Frenchman's Reef Resort, tel: 340-774 2992.

There are regular ferry services from St Thomas and St John to Tortola, and Virgin Gorda in the BVI with **Road Town Fast Ferry**, tel: 340-777 2800, www.tortolafastferry.com; **Smith's Ferry**, tel: 340-775 7292; **Native Son Ferry**, tel: 340-774 8685, www.nativesonferry.com; **Speedy's Ferry Services**, tel: 284-495 5235, www.bviferries.com. A two-hour ferry service runs from St Thomas to Fajardo, Puerto Rico; contact **Transportation Services STT**, tel: 340-776 6282.

A – Z

# A – Z

# A HANDY SUMMARY OF PRACTICAL INFORMATION

## A

### Accommodations

The range of accommodations in the Caribbean is as varied as the islands themselves, going from basic guesthouses and bed and breakfasts to luxurious five-star hotels. Some islands, such as Anguilla and St-Barths, deliberately aim for the upper end of the market, and it can be hard to find somewhere cheap and cheerful, while those islands with good scuba diving, hiking, birdwatching, and remote forests usually have several low-budget dive resorts, hostels, and rustic places to stay.

Islands receiving direct transatlantic flights, and therefore mass tourism, are more likely to have plenty of mid-range accommodations, with apartments and villas complementing the hotel sector. Antigua, Barbados, and St Lucia all offer a varied choice. While several small islands are given over to a single hotel, such as Peter Island in the BVI, or Petit St Vincent in the Grenadines, there are no really enormous resorts in the Lesser Antilles, unless you include the floating hotels – mega cruise ships which offload thousands of people a day onto the streets of a harbor town.

All-inclusive resort hotels are a popular option; the appeal of not having to reach for your wallet every time you want a drink or a snack is strong, especially when you have children in tow. But there are two main disadvantages: you miss out on all the local food, drink, and color beyond the resort, and you do not put money back into the local community; most resort hotels are foreign-owned.

Self-catering apartments and villas are good value if you are traveling in a group or as a family; often you share the amenities such as a pool and restaurant with other visitors in the "village." A local cook can usually be arranged if you want a treat, although you may have to take her shopping for the ingredients first.

High season is mid-December to the end of April nearly everywhere, with rates peaking over Christmas and New Year, during Carnival, and at Easter. Prices can be considerably lower off-season (from May to mid-December), when it's worth negotiating for an upgrade or a price reduction. Bear in mind, however, that this is also hurricane season, so check the likelihood of your favored destination being affected. Most major resort chains and some holiday packages offer hurricane protection; check before you book.

The internet is a useful tool for accommodation-hunting; try www.caribbeantravel.com. Alternatively, try the tourist offices in your home country or their websites.

### Age Restrictions

The legal drinking age throughout the Caribbean is 18. Some car-rental agencies only rent cars to drivers over 25, although more usually you have to be 21 or over. As for scuba diving, children as young as 8 may participate at some resorts.

### The Arts

The Caribbean Islands are better known for their musical heritage than the visual arts, but nonetheless there are numerous small art galleries that exhibit and sell work by local artists.

The **Gallery of Caribbean Art** (www.artgallerycaribbean.com) on Barbados exhibits regional art and photography at the Northern Business Center in Speightstown and the Hilton Hotel on Needham's Point.

The **Reichhold Center for the Arts** (www.reichholdcenter.org) is an amphitheater in Brewer's Bay on St Thomas, which hosts performances of every kind, including music and drama. The center, part of the University of the Virgin Islands, attracts local artists and visiting international performers. For further information about what's on and when, tel: 340-693 1550, or the box office on 340-693 1559. On the eastern side of the island, the **Tillett Gardens Center for the Arts** (www.tillettgardens.com) hosts classical and contemporary concerts, as well as the tri-annual Arts Alive Festival.

On the island of Anguilla, the renowned **Mayoumba Folkloric**

### Hurricane Categories

Hurricanes are categorized from 1 to 5 according to the Saffir Simpson Scale, which measures wind speed:
**Category 1:** 74–95mph (119–153kph).
**Category 2:** 96–110mph (154–177kph).
**Category 3:** 111–130mph (178–209kph).
**Category 4:** 131–155mph (210–249kph).
**Category 5:** over 155mph (249kph).

## CLIMATE CHART
### Aruba

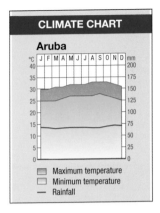

- Maximum temperature
- Minimum temperature
- Rainfall

## CLIMATE CHART
### Grenada

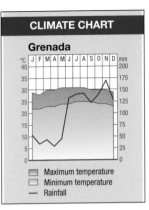

- Maximum temperature
- Minimum temperature
- Rainfall

## CLIMATE CHART
### Virgin Islands

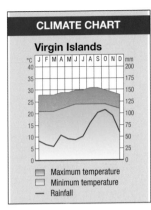

- Maximum temperature
- Minimum temperature
- Rainfall

TRANSPORTATION

N
A – Z

**Theater** perform at Anacaona Hotel in Meads Bay (www.anacaonahotel.com) on Thursday evenings. The group keep Anguillan traditions alive through music, dance, and the spoken word.

Two annual film festivals showcase Caribbean cinema – the Travelling Caribbean Film Showcase (www.artscayman.org/tcfs) on Barbados, and the **St-Barth Film Festival** (www.stbarthff.org) on St-Barthélemy.

## B

### Budgeting for Your Trip

Your costs will obviously depend on where you go; the cheapest destinations in the Lesser Antilles are Dominica and Trinidad and Tobago, while resorts in, for example, Anguilla or the Grenadines offer the ultimate in luxury and expense. Self-catering options are clearly more cost-effective than the all-inclusive resorts. Getting around by public transport and taxis is more economical than renting a car.

### Business Hours

The siesta, happily, is alive and well in much of the Caribbean, and throughout the region small stores may close for a couple of hours in the early afternoon, when the tropical sun is at its hottest. Stores open early, usually by 8am, certainly by 9am. They begin closing for siesta at noon or a little before, though in some areas, may stay open until 1pm. Business resumes about 2 hours later – 2pm in most places – with stores remaining open until 6pm. Again, there is some variation; on a few islands, closing time may be as early as

4pm (for example on Dominica). On Saturday, most stores are open in the morning, and many have full afternoon hours as well. Sunday is traditionally a day of rest, for church and family, although shops in cruise ship terminals will open if a ship is in port.

## C

### Children

The islands are a perfect vacation destination for a family. Many resorts now offer action-packed children's activity programs, and babysitting facilities. Do check with the hotel in advance, however, as during the high season, some hotels do not allow children under 12.

### Climate

The principal characteristic of the Caribbean's climate is the relative lack of temperature change from season to season. The islands' proximity to the equator means that seasonal temperature changes are limited to less than 10°F/6°C. Year-round, temperatures average around 80°F (27°C) throughout the region. An added bonus is the trade winds, which bring regular, cooling breezes to most of the islands. During the "winter" – which is peak season for tourists in the islands – night-time lows can reach about 60°F (16°C), with daytime highs reaching as much as 90°F (32°C).

Rainfall varies widely, ranging from around 20ins (50 cm) a year in Curaçao to up to 75ins (190 cm) a year in Grenada. Rainfall is generally heaviest during October and November, though June is wettest in Trinidad and Tobago. Hurricanes can

strike from June to November. The "dry" period, coinciding with the peak tourist season, is from December through April or May.

### Hurricanes

Hurricanes are one of the most damaging and dangerous phenomena affecting the Caribbean (see page 23 for a description of how a hurricane forms and develops). Recent devastating hurricanes in the region have included Irene in 2011, which passed over the Leewards, causing destruction and at least 56 confirmed deaths across the Caribbean, US and Canada, and Erika in 2015, which caused at least 30 deaths, and intensive flooding and landslides in Dominica.

Hurricanes usually occur between July and October, although visitations have been known in June and November, and the official "hurricane season" stretches from the beginning of June to the beginning of November, when some islands celebrate with a Hurricane Deliverance Day. The average lifespan of a hurricane is 8 to 10 days.

The risk of being hit by a hurricane varies from island to island; the southernmost islands – Aruba, Barbados, Curaçao, Bonaire, and Trinidad and Tobago – are rarely affected.

For more information on hurricanes, log onto www.nhc.noaa.gov.

### Crime and Safety

Crime and safety varies from island to island, with levels to a large extent dependent on such factors as standard of living, population density, and development. The disparity between the income of local people and the wealth of visitors can cause

## What to Do if a Hurricane Strikes

**During the storm.** Stay indoors once the hurricane begins buffeting your area. When the eye (the low-pressure area at the center of a hurricane) passes over, there will be a temporary lull in wind and rain for up to half an hour or more. This is not the end of the storm, which will in fact resume (possibly with even greater force) from the opposite direction. Wait for the all-clear from the authorities before starting to venture out of your shelter.

**If ordered to evacuate.** Stay tuned to local radio stations for up-to-date information and instructions. Follow designated routes as quickly as possible. Take with you blankets, a flashlight, extra clothing, and medications. Leave behind pets (which are not permitted inside public shelters).

**After the storm passes.** Drive with caution when ordered to return home. Debris in the roads can be a hazard. Roads near the coast may collapse if soil has been washed away from beneath them. Steer clear of fallen or dangling utility wires. Stay tuned to radio stations for news of emergency medical, food, housing, and other forms of assistance. If you have been staying in a rented home, re-enter the building with caution and make temporary repairs to correct hazards and minimize further damage. Open windows and doors to air and dry the house. Be particularly careful when dealing with matches or fires in case of gas leaks.

tensions. In some areas, such as Port-of-Spain in Trinidad, going out alone after dusk should be avoided.

The same precautions you take in any large town or city apply here: don't flaunt your wealth, keep your valuables close to you (avoid shoulder bags which can be pulled off easily), don't leave items in parked cars, use the hotel safe where possible, and never leave your possessions unattended anywhere, especially on beaches.

The high media profile given to violent crime against tourists does give a skewed impression; the incidence is actually very low (given its frequency and the number of visitors).

### Outdoor Hazards

**Manchineel trees:** these are usually indicated by red stripes painted on them and a warning notice. The apple-like fruit and the resin contain a poisonous substance (the Amerindians used it on their poison arrows) and when it rains they secrete an irritant that burns the skin – so never shelter underneath one. Don't handle the leaves or rub them, either.

**Fire coral:** never touch coral when snorkeling or diving as you will damage and maybe kill it. Fire coral fights back and will give you a nasty burn.

**Sea urchins:** when swimming over rocks be careful where you put your feet – stepping on one of these spiny balls is a very painful experience, as a spine may get stuck in your foot.

**Sea lice:** however tired you may be, don't hang on to a buoy or anything else covered in a fine green seaweed because the sea lice living in it can cause a very itchy, painful allergic skin reaction.

**Snakes:** the only dangerous snakes in the Eastern Caribbean are the fer de lance, found in Trinidad, St Lucia, and Martinique (if it bites it is not usually fatal but hospitalization will be necessary); and the bushmaster and two species of poisonous coral snake only found in Trinidad.

### Customs Regulations

Travelers arriving in the Antilles are generally allowed to bring in the following duty-free items:
personal effects.
a carton of cigarettes or cigars, or 0.5lb (225 grams) of tobacco.
one bottle (1liter) of an alcoholic drink (2 liters in some countries).
a "reasonable" amount of perfume.

### US Travelers

For US travelers returning to the United States from the USVI, there are a number of importation options. Each individual can bring back up to US$1,600 worth of purchases duty-free. Travelers may also mail home an unlimited number of packages valued at US$50 or less, provided not more than one such package is mailed to any one person in a single day. If you exceed your US$1,600 limit, upon returning to the States, the first US$1,000 worth of merchandise in excess is assessed at a flat duty rate of 1.5 percent.

### Jewelry and Art

US law allows the importation, duty-free, of original works of art. Because of concessions made to developing countries, jewelry made in the Antilles may qualify as original art, and thus be duty-free. If you purchase jewelry, be sure to obtain a certificate from the place of purchase stating that the jewelry was made in the islands. Contact the US Customs Service for further details.

## D

### Disabled Travelers

There are few special facilities such as ramps in public places. However, you will find them in new shopping centers, restaurants, and many modern resorts. Resort hotels may have a few specially adapted bedrooms or, at least, first-floor rooms and few steps to public rooms.

For more information, visit: www.access-able.com or www.makoa.org.

## E

### Eating out

#### ABC Islands

Varied and cosmopolitan, on all three islands you will find Indonesian, Chinese, French, Spanish, and Italian restaurants. On local menus you will see iguana soup (fish soup made with coconut), goat stew, Dutch-influenced dishes mixing meats with Gouda cheese, spices, and tomato, and a full range of fresh fish dishes. Cornmeal (funchi) is often served as a side dish, and snacks like pastechi and krokets are available at all hours.
**Beer:** Amstel (Curaçao), Balashi (Aruba).
**Liqueur:** Curaçao.

#### Anguilla

As you might expect on a boat-building, seafaring island, locally caught seafood is Anguilla's specialty: conch, lobster, whelks, and tropical fish, prepared in either Continental or the local creole style. Barbecues – of fish, chicken, or goat – are another distinctive aspect of local cuisine, often on the beach. The local word for meat is "relish," which can cause some confusion.
**Rum:** Pyrat.

## Antigua and Barbuda

There are some delicious local dishes worth trying, such as pepperpot, conch, shellfish (the local name for trunkfish), and the local staple of chicken, rice, and peas. Saltfish is traditionally eaten at breakfast in a tomato and onion sauce. Goat water is really a hot goat stew. Ducana is a mix of sweet potato, pumpkin, coconut, sugar, and spices, wrapped and boiled in a banana leaf. The local pineapple is called the Antigua black and is very sweet.
**Beer**: Wadadli.
**Rum**: Cavalier.

## Barbados

Barbados has restaurants featuring everything from traditional Bajan cuisine to Chinese, Italian, and American fast food. Flying fish cutters (breaded flying fish in a bun) are good for lunch. Other specialties are hot saltfish cakes, pickled breadfruit, and pepperpot, often accompanied by rice and peas, macaroni pie, plantain, sweet potato, or yam. Cou-cou is made from breadfruit or cornmeal, while pudding and souse is pickled breadfruit, black pudding, and pork. Try the non-alcoholic drinks: mauby is quite bitter, made from tree bark, and sorrel is made around Christmas from hibiscus petals and spices, making it bright red. Falernum is sweet, slightly alcoholic, and mixed with rum for a drink called corn and oil.
**Beer**: Banks.
**Rum**: Mount Gay, Cockspur, Malibu, Foursquare, St Nicholas Abbey.

## British Virgin Islands

The cuisine of the BVI includes touches of American and Continental cooking, in addition to such typically Caribbean creations as *funchi* (cornmeal pudding) and *roti* (curry

## Creole Cuisine

A few examples:
**Crabes farcis**: stuffed crabshell with a spicy crab-based stuffing.
**Blaff de poissons ou crustacées** (poached fish or shellfish): the ingredients are poached in water containing thyme, parsley, laurel, local chives, and pimento.
**Féroce**: a mixture made from crushed avocado, codfish, and cassava flour with a touch of hot pepper pimento.
Try a **Ti-Punch** aperitif before a meal and a dark rum afterwards.

wrapped in a thin chapati). Seafood and tropical fruits and vegetables are fresh and plentiful.
**Rum**: Pussers.

## Dominica

There are many little snack bars all over the island that may (or may not) produce some excellent meals. Fresh fruit juices (made with tamarind, guava, sorrel, grapefruit, and so on) are a delight, along with specialties such as mountain chicken (a large frog endemic to Dominica but endangered), crab backs, and *titiri* (fritters made of tiny fish). Other Dominican dishes include saltfish, couscous, ground provisions (dasheen, yam, sweet potato), and *callaloo* (young shoots of the dasheen) soup. Bakes, a fried dough patty filled with fish or meat, are a popular snack. Fruit and vegetables are plentiful: visit the market to see the wonderful range of produce.
**Beer**: Kubuli.
**Rum**: Macoucherie, Soca, Red Cap.

## Grenada

There are many local delicacies worth sampling. *Callaloo* soup (made from dasheen leaves, rather like spinach) is excellent, as are traditional pepperpot (a stew of almost every possible ingredient), and *lambi* (conch). Exotic game sometimes appears on menus, although it's better not to experiment with armadillo, iguana, or manicou, all of which are now endangered. The national dish is "oil down," a stew of saltfish or meat, breadfruit, onion, carrot, celery, dasheen, and dumplings, cooked slowly In coconut milk. Spices, especially nutmeg, are another favorite, delicious in rum punches and nutmeg jelly is good on your breakfast toast. For a non-alcoholic drink, try sea moss, a blend of algae, vanilla, and milk.
**Beer**: Carib.
**Rum**: Clark's Court, River Antoine, Westernall Plantation Rum.

## Guadeloupe

Guadeloupe is considered one of the true culinary capitals of the Caribbean and its cuisine mirrors its many cultures. Creole specialties combine the finesse of French cuisine, the spice of African cookery, and the exoticism of East Indian and Southeast Asian recipes. Fresh seafood appears on most menus. Other specialties are shellfish, smoked fish, stuffed land crabs, stewed conch, and a variety of curry dishes.

Rum is made from the juice of the cane, rhum agricole, rather than molasses. Ti-punch is rum mixed with a little cane or sugar syrup and a slice of lime, while planteur is rum with fruit juice.
**Beer**: Corsaire.
**Rum**: Damoiseau, Père Labat (from Marie Galante).

## Martinique

Martinicans love to eat well, and part of Martinique's French feeling is its celebration of good food. Familiar French dishes are given an unfamiliar twist by the use of tropical fruits, vegetables, and seafood. In addition to French-inspired cooking, there are plenty of spicy Caribbean specialties similar to those of Guadeloupe.
Several beaches have what look like snack bars serving a delicious set menu of local specialties, such as *accras* (deep-fried fishcakes), direct from a caravan or hut, with awnings over plastic tables and chairs.
**Beer**: Bière Lorraine.
**Rum**: Trois Rivières, Mauny, St-James, St-Clément.

## Montserrat

Most restaurants and snack bars (snackettes) are small, informal places. Some are only open for breakfast and lunch. Some only open in the evening with prior reservation. Others are no more than roadside stands serving excellent rice and peas, fish, chicken, and the like. Montserrat is famous for its goat water stew, which some believe has Irish origins.

## Saba and St Eustatius

Restaurants tend to offer international food like burgers and

pizzas as well as the catch of the day. Fruit and vegetables are grown on Saba but everything else is shipped in, so supplies can get short before the weekly supply boat comes in. Restaurants on Statia are few. If you are self-catering, you can get fresh fish from the fish processing plant at Lower Town on weekday mornings. Fresh bread time and bake sales are announced by the town crier.
**Rum**: Saba Spice.

### St-Barthélemy

The food is as cosmopolitan as the jet-setters it attracts; French-creole cuisine predominates but you will also find everything from pizza to sushi, with lots of fresh fish and lobster in season. Restaurants are expensive but there are lots of them, around 70 on this tiny island. There are some very good supermarkets and delis stocking French food at French prices. Wine and spirits are duty-free, so they are cheap.

### St Kitts and Nevis

St Kitts and Nevis have many restaurants specializing in Caribbean, creole, Italian, Indian, and Chinese fare. In addition to the Caribbean's ubiquitous fresh seafood, perhaps the most distinctive feature of St Kitts and Nevis cuisine is the abundance of fresh vegetables. Tropical produce such as breadfruit joins items such as eggplant (aubergine), sweet potatoes, and okra on island plates. Saturday is the day Kittitians eat out, choosing local favorites such as goat water, saltfish, black pudding, souse, and johnny cakes.
**Beer**: Carib, Stag.
**Rum**: Belmont, Brinley Gold (vanilla, mango, coffee).

### St Lucia

St Lucia's cuisine encompasses French creole dishes such as *bouillon* (meat or fish cooked in a peppery, broth-like tomato sauce); West Indian favorites like saltfish with ground provisions (dasheen, cassava); and even curries and *roti* wraps. Cassava bread comes in a range of flavors and makes a good, filling snack. Other highlights include pumpkin soup, flying fish, pepperpot (a rich and dark meat stew made with *cassareep* oil), conch, and *tablette* (a sweetmeat made of coconut) or *permi* (cornmeal and coconut wrapped in a banana leaf). Teas are made from many herbs, often for medicinal uses,

while cocoa tea (hot chocolate) is a breakfast staple.
**Beer**: Piton.
**Rum**: St Lucia Distillers' Bounty, Crystal, Chairman's Reserve, Admiral's, Denros (160° proof), and flavored rums.

### St Vincent and the Grenadines

Spicy Caribbean cuisine predominates with continental and American fare also available. A wide variety of exotic fruits and vegetables, along with an abundance of succulent lobster and other fresh seafood, enrich St Vincent's cooking. Snacks include salt cod rolls with hot pepper sauce, and grilled chicken with corn cobs, which you can pick up by the ferry boats or bus station in Kingstown.
**Beer**: Hairoun.
**Rum**: Sunset.

### St-Martin/Sint Maarten

Restaurants reflect the various cultures that have come together on the island. On both sides, traditional French cooking and spicy Caribbean cuisine are available. On the Dutch side, dining options include Dutch favorites such as pea soup and sausages. Look out for restaurants serving *rijstaffel*, an Indonesian meal with up to 30 dishes. There are many notable restaurants in St-Martin, particularly in Grand Case. Its "lolos" are snack bars by the pier serving good-value barbecue fish, chicken, ribs, and lobster.

### Trinidad and Tobago

In no other Caribbean country will you find such a colorful mix of origins. The culinary traditions of the African, Indian, Chinese, Middle Eastern, French, and Latin American settlers have all contributed to the wide variety of cuisine here. It is the home of the Caribbean-Indian filled *roti* wrap, a chapati pancake containing curried mango, potato, and pumpkin, with your choice of dal, meats, or seafood. Other specialties include *pelau* (caramelised meat cooked down with rice in coconut milk); bake and shark (succulent fried shark meat served in a sandwich with salads and tamarind sauce); South American *pasteles*; as well as fresh seafood. This is one of the best countries in the region for vegetarians: *saheena* are deep-fried patties of spinach, dasheen, split peas, and mango sauce; *pholouri* are fritters made with split peas; *doubles* are curried chickpeas between two

pieces of fried *barra* (mini pancakes), bought from roadside stalls and popular for breakfast. Non-alcoholic drinks include mauby, sorrel, and ginger beer.
**Beer**: Carib, Stag.
**Rum**: Angostura.

### US Virgin Islands

The multinational, multiethnic history of the USVI, combined with its tropical location and international reputation as a vacation spot, have contributed to a rich cuisine, using local fruits and vegetables and fresh seafood. Island cooks create anything from bullfoot soup (what it sounds like) and *funchi* (cornmeal pudding) to French, Italian, and Chinese food.
**Beer**: St John Brewers' Island Hoppin IPA.
**Rum**: Cruzan, Captain Morgan.

## Embassies and Consulates

### ABC Islands

The Netherlands handles consular matters.
**Canada:** Royal Netherlands Embassy, Constitution Square Building, 350 Albert Street, Suite 2020, Ottawa, ON K1R 1A4, tel: 1-877 388 2443, http://canada.nlembassy.org.
**UK:** Embassy of the Netherlands, 38 Hyde Park Gate, London SW7 5DP, tel: 020-7590 3200, www.netherlands-embassy.org.uk.
**US:** Netherlands Embassy, 4200 Linnean Avenue, Washington, DC 20008, tel: 877 388 2443, www.the-netherlands.org.

### Anguilla

The UK handles consular matters.
**Canada:** British High Commission, 80 Elgin Street, Ottawa, ON K1P 5K7, tel: 613-237 1530, www.ukincanada.fco.uk.
**UK:** Foreign and Commonwealth Office, King Charles Street, London SW1A 2AH, tel: 020-7008 1500, www.fco.gov.uk.
**US:** British Embassy, 3100 Massachusetts Ave NW, Washington, DC 20008, tel: 202-588 6500, www.ukinusa.fco.gov.uk.

### Antigua and Barbuda

**Canada:** Consulate of Antigua and Barbuda, 601–60 St Clair Avenue East, Toronto, Ontario, ON M4T 1N5, tel: 416-961 3085, www.antigua barbudaconsulate.ca.
**UK/Ireland:** High Commission for Antigua and Barbuda, 2nd floor, 45 Crawford Place, London W1H 4LP,

tel: 020-7258 0070, www.antigua-barbuda.com.
**US:** Embassy of Antigua and Barbuda, 3216 New Mexico Avenue NW, Washington, DC 20016, tel: 202-362 5122, www.state.gov/r/pa/ei/bgn/2336.htm.

### Barbados
**Canada:** High Commission for Barbados, 55 Metcalfe Street, Suite 470, Ottawa, ON K1P 6L5, tel: 613-236 9517, ottawa@foreign.gov.bb.
**UK and Ireland:** High Commission of Barbados, 1 Great Russell Street, London WC1B 3ND, tel: 020-7631 4975, london@foreign.gov.bb.
**US:** Embassy of Barbados, 2144 Wyoming Avenue NW, Washington, DC 20008, tel: 202-939 9200, washington@foreign.gov.bb.

### British Virgin Islands
(See Anguilla.)

### Dominica
**UK:** Dominican High Commission, 1 Collingham Gardens, London SW5 0HW, tel: 020-7370 5194, www.dominicahighcommission.co.uk.
**US:** Embassy of Dominica, 3216 New Mexico Ave NW, Washington, DC 20016, tel: 202-364 6781, www.state.gov/r/pa/ei/bgn/2295.htm.

### Grenada
**Canada:** Consulate General of Grenada, 90 Eglinton Avenue East, Suite 605, Toronto, ON M4P 2Y3, tel: 416-595 1343, www.grenada consulate.com.
**UK:** Grenada High Commission, The Chapel, Archel Road, London W14 9QH, tel: 020-7385 4415, email: office@grenada-highcommission.co.uk.
**US:** Embassy of Grenada, 1701 New Hampshire Ave NW, Washington, DC 20009, tel: 202-265 2561, www.grenadaembassyusa.org.

### Guadeloupe
France handles consular matters.
**Canada:** Consulate Général of France, 2 Bloor Street East, Suite 2200, Toronto, ON M4W 1A8, tel: 416-847 1900, www.consulfrance-toronto.org.
**UK:** Consulate General, 21 Cromwell Road, London SW7 2EN, tel: 020-7073 1200, www.ambafrance-uk.org.
**US:** Embassy of France, 4101 Reservoir Road NW Washington, DC 20007, tel: 202-944 6000, www.ambafrance-us.org.

### Martinique
(See Guadeloupe.)

### Saba
(See Aruba.)

### St-Barths
(See Guadeloupe.)

### St Eustatius
(See Aruba.)

### St Kitts and Nevis
**Canada:** High Commission of St Kitts and Nevis, 421 Besserer Street, Ottawa, ON K19 6B9, tel: 613-236 8952, email: echcc@travel-net.com.
**UK:** St Kitts and Nevis High Commission, 10A Kensington Court, London W8 5DL, tel: 020-7937 9718, www.stkittsnevisuk.com.
**US:** Embassy of St Kitts and Nevis, 3216 New Mexico Avenue NW, Washington, DC 20016, tel: 202-686 2636, www.embassy.gov.kn.

### St Lucia
**Canada:** Eastern Caribbean Liaison Service in Toronto, 200 Consumers Road, Suite 409, Ottawa, ON M2J 4R4, tel: 416-222 1988, www.oecs.org.
**UK:** St Lucia High Commission, 1 Collingham Gardens, Earls Court, London SW5 0HW; tel: 020-7370 7123, www.stluciahcuk.org.
**US:** Embassy of St Lucia, 3216 New Mexico Avenue NW, Washington, DC 20016, tel: 202-364 6792, eofsaintlu@aol.com.

### St Vincent and the Grenadines
**Canada:** Consulate of St Vincent and the Grenadines, 55 Town Centre Court, Suite 403, Toronto, ON M1P 4X4, tel: 416-394 4277, http://to.consulate.gov.vc.
**UK:** St Vincent and the Grenadines High Commission, 10 Kensington Court, London W8 5DL, tel: 020-7460 1256, www.svghighcom.co.uk.
**US:** Embassy of St Vincent and the Grenadines, 3216 New Mexico Avenue NW, Washington, DC 20016, tel: 202-364 6730, www.embsvg.com.

### Trinidad and Tobago
**Canada:** Trinidad and Tobago High Commission, 200 First Avenue, Ottawa, ON K1S 2G6, tel: 613-232 2418, www.ttmissions.com.
**UK:** Trinidad and Tobago High Commission, 42 Belgrave Square, London SW1X 8NT, tel: 020-7245 9351, www.tthighcommission.co.uk.
**US:** Embassy of Trinidad and Tobago, 1708 Massachusetts Avenue NW, Washington, DC 20036, tel: 202-467 6490, www.ttembassy.org.

### US Virgin Islands
**Canada:** Embassy of USA, 490 Sussex Drive, Ottawa, ON K1N 1G8, tel: 613-688 5335, http://canada.usembassy.gov.
**UK:** US Embassy, 24 Grosvenor Square, London W1A 1AE, tel: 020-7499 9000, www.usembassy.org.uk.
**US:** US Department of State, 2201 C Street NW, Washington, DC 20520, tel: 202-647 4000, www.state.gov.

## Entry Requirements

For travel in and around the islands a valid passport is required, even for US and Canadian citizens (re-entry to the US is impossible without a passport).

Visas are usually required only for visitors from Eastern Europe and Cuba. In addition to proper documents, all travelers must have a return or onward ticket, and adequate funds to support themselves for the duration of their stay.

# F

## Festivals

### Carnival and Events
Carnival is celebrated at different times on different islands, with the dates falling roughly into three main groups:

On Trinidad and Tobago, Dominica, St Thomas, Aruba, Bonaire, Curaçao, St Lucia, Martinique, Guadeloupe, St-Martin (French side), and St-Barthélemy, Carnival preserves an association with Easter, being celebrated (on all of these islands except St Thomas) in the period leading up to, and sometimes including, Ash Wednesday. On St Thomas, the celebration occurs after Easter.

On St Vincent, Anguilla, St John, Barbados, Grenada, the British Virgin Islands, Antigua, Saba, and St Eustatius, Carnival takes place in June, July, or early August. On these islands, Carnival is often held in association with the "August Monday" holiday, which marks the end of the sugar-cane harvest and the emancipation of slaves in the British islands around that time in 1834.

On St Kitts, Montserrat, and St Croix (in the US Virgin Islands), Carnival takes place in December and early January, in conjunction with the Christmas season.

On Sint Maarten (Dutch side), Carnival takes place in late April, coinciding with the Dutch queen's birthday celebrations on April 30.

### ABC Islands

### Aruba
**January–March:** Carnival. Grand Parade on last Sunday before Ash Wednesday.
**25 January:** festivities and sports for GF Betico Croes Day.
**18 March:** National Anthem and Flag Day.
**March/April:** Easter.
**30 April:** Queen's Birthday.
**End May:** Aruba Soul Beach Music Festival.
**June:** Aruba Food and Wine Festival; Aruba International Film Festival.

**24 June:** Dera Gai (St John's Day), Harvest Festival.
**June/July:** Aruba Hi-Winds windsurfing and kitesurfing competition.
**August:** Aruba International Regatta.
**September:** Aruba Piano Festival.
**October:** Caribbean Sea Jazz Festival.
**27 December:** Dande Festival.

### Bonaire
**January:** Mascarada Festival, Rincon.
**March/April:** Simadan Harvest Festival, Rincon.
**April:** Queen's Birthday; Rincon Day.
**June:** Bonaire Jazz Festival; PWA Windsurfing Competition; Bonaire Dive Into Summer (June–Sept); Feast of San Juan, San Pedro and San Pablo, Rincon.
**July:** Taste of Bonaire.

**September:** Bonaire Flag Day; local fishing tournament.
**December:** Bari Festival, Rincon; Sinterklass Birthday Celebration; End of Year Windsurf Race.

### Curaçao
**January–March:** Carnival, including Tumba Festival, Kite Festival and Grand Parade, Sunday before Ash Wednesday.
**April:** Curaçao Windsurfing Challenge.
**30 April:** Queen's Birthday.
**June:** Sunfish Championship.
**2 July:** Curaçao Flag Day.
**26 July:** Curaçao Day.
**September:** North Sea Jazz.
**5 October:** Banda Bou Day.
**November:** Heineken Regatta.
**December:** Hannukah, the Jewish Festival of Lights.

### Anguilla
**January 1:** New Year's Day; Boat Race.
**March:** Moonsplash Reggae Festival.
**Easter Monday:** Boat race.
**April:** Festival del Mar, boat races, fishing tournaments, seafood cooking competitions.
**May:** Anguilla Yacht Regatta; Anguilla Day boat race and athletics (May 30).
**July/August:** Anguilla Summer Festival/Carnival.
**November:** Tranquillity Jazz Festival.

### Antigua and Barbuda
**March/April:** Easter
**April:** Kite Festival; Antigua Sailing Week.
**June:** International cricket; Barbuda's Caribana.
**July/August:** Carnival; MangoFest celebrates the island's favorite fruit.
**October 31:** Heritage Day.
**November:** Antigua and Barbuda Literary Festival; Jolly Harbour Yacht Club Regatta.
**December:** Antigua Yacht Club – High Tide Series, Zoom 8 Championship, Nelson's Pursuit.

### Barbados
**January:** Windsurfing championships; Jazz Festival; the regional cricket series.
**February:** Holetown Festival.
**March:** Holders Season.
**April:** Oistins Fish Festival; Barbados Reggae Festival.
**May:** Gospelfest; Celtic Festival; Mount Gay Regatta.
**May/June:** Traveling Caribbean Film Showcase.
**June:** Harris Paints Sailing Regatta.

## Emergency Numbers

### ABC Islands
**Aruba:** Emergency 911
**Bonaire:** Emergency 911, Fire 191, Ambulance 114
**Curaçao:** Police and Fire 911, Ambulance 912

### Anguilla
**Emergency** 911
**Police** 911
**Dental clinic** 497 2343
**Hospital** 497 2551/2
**Pharmacy** 497 2366

### Antigua and Barbuda
**Emergency** 999/911

### Barbados
**Police** 211
**Fire** 311
**Ambulance** 511

### British Virgin Islands
**Police, Fire, Ambulance** 999/911

### Dominica
**Police, Fire, and Ambulance** 999

### Grenada
**Police, Fire** 911
**Coast Guard** 399
**Ambulance: St George's** 434; **St Andrew's** 724; **Carriacou** 774

### Guadeloupe
**Ambulance** 112
**Police** 17
**Fire and Ambulance** 18

### Martinique
**Ambulance** 112
**Police** 17
**Fire and Ambulance** 18

### Montserrat
**Emergency** 999/911
**Ambulance** 491 2552
**Police** 491 2555

### Saba
**Emergency** 112

### St-Barthélemy
**Emergency** 18

### St Eustatius
**Emergency** 111

### St Kitts and Nevis
**Emergency/Ambulance** 911
**Fire** 333
**Police** 911 **Police info** 707

### St Lucia
**Emergency** 999/911

### St-Martin/Sint Maarten
**Police** (French side) 17
(Dutch side) 111
**Fire** (French side) 18
(Dutch side) 120
**Ambulance** (French side) 29 04 04
(Dutch side) 130

### St Vincent and The Grenadines
**Police, Fire, Ambulance** 999/911
**Kingstown Hospital** 456 1185
**Bequia Hospital** 458 3294

### Trinidad and Tobago
**Police** 999
**Fire and Ambulance** 990

### US Virgin Islands
**St Thomas** and **St John:** 911
**St Croix:** Police and Fire 911, Ambulance 922

**July**: Crop Over festival begins; Sir Garfield Sobers International Schools Cricket Festival.
**August:** Kadooment Day.
**November:** Barbados Food and Wine and Rum.

### British Virgin Islands

**February/March:** Billabong BVI Kite Jam
**March:** Annual Dark and Stormy Regatta.
**March/April**: Easter Festival; Virgin Gorda Carnival; BVI Spring Regatta.
**May:** Annual Foxy's Wooden Boat Regatta; BVI Music Festival.
**June:** Swim the Sound and Water World.
**July:** Fisherman's Day.
**August:** Emancipation Festival.
**September**: Jost Van Dyke Festival.
**December**: Foxy's Old Year Party.

### Dominica

**February/March:** Carnival/Mas Domnik. Tewé Vaval (the ceremonial burial of the spirit of carnival) is traditional on Ash Wednesday in the Carib Territory and in Dublanc in the northwest.
**May/June:** Domfesta and Giraudel-Eggleston Flower Show.
**June:** Jazz 'n Creole, Fort Shirley, Portsmouth.
**June/July:** Dive Fest, annual water sports festival, Kubuli Carib Canoe Race finale.
**August:** Annual Nature Island Literary Festival and Book Fair Festival.
**October**: World Creole Music Festival: last weekend in month. Three-day vibrant music show.
**End Oct/early Nov:** Creole Day/ Independence Day festivities (national costume is worn).

### Grenada

**January:** Spice Island Fishing Tournament is held at the end of the month. Annual La Source Grenada Sailing Festival.
**Mardi Gras:** Shakespeare Mas; friendly festival on Carriacou.
**Late April:** Annual Carriacou Maroon and Regional String Band Festival.
**May:** Grenada Drum Festival.
**May/June:** Spice Jazz Festival.
**June:** Fisherman's Birthday in Gouyave at the end of the month.
**July:** Carriacou Regatta.
**August**: The second weekend is Carnival time in Grenada; Rainbow City cultural festival in Grenville.

### Guadeloupe

**February/March:** Carnival: the biggest festival on the island.

**April:** Crab Festival, Morne à l'Eau; Tour de Guadeloupe Regatta.
**May:** Fête de la Musique Traditionnelle in Sainte-Anne. Abolition of Slavery is celebrated on May 27.
**July:** Big Drum (Gwo-Ka) Festival, Sainte-Anne; Festival Guadeloupe.
**August:** Traditional Music Festival in Le Moule; Fête des Cuisinières, a festival of women cooks, in Pointe-à-Pitre; Patron Saints' Days and Fishermen's Days celebrated around the islands.
**November**: (first Saturday) Creole Music Festival, at Pointe-à-Pitre. All Saints and All Souls: the cemeteries come alive as family members clean tombs and picnic with their dead ancestors.
**December**: Chanté Noël: Christmas carols are sung at parties throughout the month. Pointe-à-Pitre Jazz Festival.

### Martinique

**February:** Vaval (Carnival) – four days of jubilation and dancing in the streets. A carnival queen is crowned at the end of the festivities.
**March**: International Sailing Week.
**April**: Aqua Festival (Festival of the Sea).
**May:** Le Mai de Saint Pierre – festivities in commemoration of the eruption of the Pelée Volcano; Abolition of Slavery festivities on and around May 27.
**June:** Jazz at Leyritz Plantation Estate.
**July**: Fort-de-France Cultural Festival; International Bicycle Race. Crayfish Festival in Ajoupa Bouillon; sugar-cane harvest festival.
**August:** Yole Race Around Martinique – traditional sailing vessels compete in the island's most popular event. Biguine Jazz Festival.
**October**: Journée Internationale du Créole; celebration of all things creole. International Fishing Tournament of Martinique.
**November**: Biennial International Jazz Festival or the International guitar festival (alternate years).
**December**: Rum Festival, Musée du Rhum, St James Distillery.

### Montserrat

**March:** St Patrick's Festival.
**April:** Local fishing tournament.
**June:** Queen's Birthday Parade.
**July:** Cudjoe Head Celebrations/ Calabash Festival.
**November:** Alliouagana Festival of the Word (Literary Festival).
**December:** Christmas Festival (Carnival – ArrowFest).

### Saba and St Eustatius

### Saba
**April:** Coronation Day and Queen's Birthday.
**August:** Carnival.
**December:** Saba Day and Weekend; Kingdom Day.

### Sint Eustatius
**July:** Carnival

### St-Barthélemy
**January:** St-Barths Music Festival.
**February/March:** Carnival.
**April:** St-Barths Film Festival; Les Voiles de St-Barth Regatta.
**May:** West Indies Regatta.
**July:** Anse des Cayes Festival; Bastille Day; Northern Neighborhoods Festival.
**August:** Fête du Vent in Lorient; Festival of Gustavia; the Feast of St Barthélemy (August 24); the Feast of St-Louis (August 25) in Corossol.
**December:** New Year's Eve Regatta on 31st.

### St Kitts and Nevis
**Easter Monday:** Horse racing, Nevis.
**Late June:** St Kitts Music Festival.
**July–August:** Culturama Carnival and arts festival, Nevis.
**September**: Independence celebrations.
**December/January:** National Carnival (mid-December to early January).

### St Lucia
**May**: St Lucia Jazz Festival.
**June:** Fishermen's Feast (Fête Peche).
**July**: Carnival; storytelling, traditional dancing, and soca music characterize the island's biggest event.
**August**: Emancipation Day (1st); Feast of St Rose de Lima, La Rose Flower Festival with songs, dance, and flowers at Micoud (30th).
**October**: Thanksgiving Day; Feast of La Marguerite (17th); Jounen Kwéyòl Entenasyonnal, Creole Day (25th).
**December**: Atlantic Rally for Cruisers; Festival of Lights (12th); National Day (13th).

### St-Martin/Sint Maarten

**French Side**
**February:** Lent: Carnival.
**Easter:** Easter Parade.
**May:** Black Heritage Week and Abolition Day.
**July 14:** Bastille Day: street celebrations and boat races.

TRANSPORTATION

A – Z

**July 21**: Schoelcher Day: street celebrations in Grand Case.
**November 11**: Discovery Day/ Armistice (celebrated by both sides of the island).

### Dutch Side

**April**: Carnival, three-week celebrations at Carnival Village, Philipsburg.

### St Vincent and the Grenadines

**February:** Mustique Blues Festival.
**Easter:** Bequia Regatta – boat races and festivities; Easterval, a weekend of music, culture, and boat races on Union Island.
**June:** Canouan Regatta.
**July:** Carnival/Vincy Mas: 12 days of calypso and steel pan music culminating in a costumed party.
**Late July/early August:** Canouan Carnival, Yacht Races and festivities.
**August:** Breadfruit festival.
**December 16–24**: Nine Mornings: parades and dances in the days leading up to Christmas.

### Trinidad and Tobago

**February/March:** Carnival in Trinidad and Tobago reaches a climax on the Monday and Tuesday before Ash Wednesday, and although not an official public holiday, everything is closed. The lead-up can be almost as frantic, with Panorama, the national steel pan competition, accompanied by nightly calypso performances.
**February/March:** Hosay, the Muslim festival with processions, music, and dance takes place.
**March:** Phagwa – Hindu "Holi" festival, celebrating the arrival of spring with participants covered in pink dye, is celebrated at the time of the March full moon.
**Easter:** On the Tuesday after Easter the Buccoo goat races are held, an important social occasion in Tobago.
**April:** Tobago Jazz Festival.
**July:** Tobago Heritage Festival.
**August:** Emancipation Day (1st), celebrates the end of slavery with a procession through Port-of-Spain.
**October/November**: Diwali, the Hindu Festival of Lights, is held in honor of the goddess Lakshmi. On this day, hundreds of tiny lights are lit by Hindus all over Trinidad and Tobago.
**Eid-ul-Fitr**, the Islamic New Year festival, also marks the end of Ramadan.

### US Virgin Islands

**6 January**: St Croix Christmas Festival.

**March:** St Thomas International Regatta.
**March 17:** St Patrick's Day Festival, St Croix.
**April:** St Croix Food and Wine Experience.
**April/May:** St Thomas Carnival.
**July:** (week of the 4th) St John's Carnival.
**October:** St Croix Jazz and Caribbean Music and Arts Festival.

## G

### Gay and Lesbian Travelers

Attitudes toward homosexuality vary from island to island but it's fair to say that the Caribbean is not renowned for its tolerance. Attitudes have improved since the late 1990s when several gay cruise ships were turned away from port, but public signs of affection are not commonplace and are generally disapproved of.

For more information, try: www.gaytravel.com, www.gay.com, or www.iglta.org.

## H

### Health and Medical Care

#### Health Hazards

The main (though small) health risk to travelers in the Caribbean is infectious hepatitis or hepatitis A. Although it is not a requirement, an injection of gamma globulin, administered as close as possible before departure, gives good protection against hepatitis A.

The most common illness amongst travellers is diarrhea, caused by a change in diet and unfamiliar bacteria. You can help avoid it by observing scrupulous personal hygiene, eating only washed and peeled fruit, and avoiding contaminated water (drink bottled water if you are unsure). Drink plenty of water to avoid dehydration.

The Caribbean has the highest incidence of HIV and Aids outside sub-Saharan Africa. Always take precautions.

#### Sun Protection

The sun in the tropics is much more direct than in temperate regions. Always use high-factor protection, especially on children, and be sure to reapply sunscreen after a dip in the pool or the sea. Bring a brimmed

hat, especially if you plan to do any extended hiking, walking, or playing in the midday sun. Drink plenty of water.

#### Drinking Water

In undeveloped areas away from resorts, it is best to avoid drinking tap water, especially after hurricanes, when water supplies can become contaminated. In these areas, stick to bottled water, and avoid ice in your drinks. Tap water in hotels and restaurants is safe to drink.

#### Insects

To combat mosquitoes, pack a plentiful supply of insect repellent. At night, a mosquito net over the bed provides the best protection, although plug-in repellents are also useful (check the voltage). Mosquitoes can carry dengue fever (causing fever, aching bones, and headache). Avoid aspirin if you suspect this disease.

#### Immunization

No immunizations are required for travelers to the Antilles, unless the traveler is coming from an infected or endemic area. However, it is a good idea to have a tetanus shot if you are not already covered, and possibly gamma globulin. Consult your government's travel health website for details.

#### Insurance

Comprehensive travel insurance to cover both yourself and your belongings is essential. Make sure you are covered for trip cancellation, baggage or document loss, emergency medical care, repatriation by air ambulance, and accidental death.

## I

### Internet

Most modern hotels in the Caribbean can provide guests with high-speed internet facilities, and there are also a number of independent internet cafés in town centers. Wi-Fi is becoming widespread. Ask your hotel for details.

## M

### Money

A range of currencies is used in the islands. Whatever the official currency, the US dollar is usually readily accepted throughout the islands. The Eastern Caribbean dollar (EC$) is used in the following islands:

*Unlike many islands, Barbados has its own currency.*

Anguilla, Antigua and Barbuda, Dominica, Grenada, Montserrat, St Kitts and Nevis, St Lucia, St Vincent and the Grenadines. On French islands, the euro is the preferred (and official) currency, although the US dollar is accepted. On Aruba, Curaçao, and Sint Maarten the Antilles florin or guilder is the preferred currency, but on Bonaire, Saba, and Sint Eustatius the US dollar is the official currency. The US dollar is also the official currency in the USVI and BVI.

Major credit cards and traveler's checks are welcome at the larger hotels, restaurants, and stores.

If you are bringing US dollars it is a good idea to check around before converting your currency, especially if you are on a limited budget. Try to get price quotes in both the local currency and the currency you are carrying, then check the applicable exchange rate. You may find you can save some money by making purchases in whichever currency gives you greater value.

### Banking Hours

Banks are normally open mornings, Monday through Friday from 8am or 8.30am until noon. Many banks also have afternoon opening hours, especially on a Friday. A few banks open on Saturday morning. You can use your credit and debit cards to withdraw cash from ATMs (cash machines). See under individual islands for specific banking hours.

### Tax

Two taxes which you might not expect will be levied on you during your travels in the Lesser Antilles. The first is a government room tax, charged on all hotel rooms, which generally averages 5–10 percent of the total cost. The second is the departure tax. This fee varies from island to island, and is usually payable at the airport upon departure (mostly in local currency). However, it can sometimes be included in the cost of your airline ticket or package holiday. Remember to check before you head off to the airport having spent all your holiday funds. The departure tax at ferry terminals is usually less than at airports.

### ABC Islands

The main currency on Aruba is the Aruban florin (Af), while Curaçao uses the Netherlands Antilles florin (NAf), also known as the Netherlands Antilles guilder, and Bonaire uses the US dollar.

### Anguilla

The currency is the East Caribbean (EC) dollar. Normal banking hours are Monday–Thursday 8am–3pm, Friday 8am–5pm.

### Antigua and Barbuda

The currency is the EC dollar. Banking hours are generally Monday–Thursday 8am–2pm, Friday 8am–4pm. On St John's, there are ATMs at Woods Shopping Center, Market Street, and High Street. There is a branch of Antigua Commercial Bank in Codrington, Barbuda.

### Barbados

The currency is the Barbados (BDS) dollar, which you are not allowed to export. Banks are open Monday–Thursday 8am–2pm, Friday 8am–1pm and 3–5pm.

Value-added tax at 17.5 percent is added to most goods and services, so check to see whether it's included. The rate is 8.75 percent on hotel accommodations.

Restaurants and hotels usually add a 10 percent service charge, but it is normal to add another 5 percent as a tip. It is also usual to tip porters BDS$1 per item of luggage and room maids BDS$2 per night of your stay.

### British Virgin Islands

The currency of the BVI is the US$. Banking hours are Monday–Friday 9am–2pm, although some banks are open until 3 or 4pm. There are banks in Road Town (Tortola) and Spanish Town (Virgin Gorda).

### Dominica

The currency is the EC dollar. Banking hours are usually Monday–Thursday 8am–2pm, Friday 8am–4pm. The National Bank of Dominica, the First Caribbean, the Royal Bank of Canada, and the Bank of Nova Scotia are the main commercial banks, all with branches in Roseau.

### Grenada

The currency is the East Caribbean (EC) dollar. Banks are open Monday–Thursday 8am–3pm, Friday 8am–5pm, but they close for lunch 1–2.30pm.

### Guadeloupe

The local currency is the euro (€), but US dollars (US$) are also accepted at some establishments. Most major credit cards are accepted and you can withdraw cash from ATMs.

### Martinique

The local currency on Martinique is the euro (€), but US dollars (US$) are also accepted at some tourist places. Most major credit cards are accepted throughout the island. There are also banks with ATMs.

### Montserrat

Montserrat's local currency is the EC (Eastern Caribbean) dollar; US dollars are acceptable in some places. The Royal Bank of Canada (with an ATM), is in Olveston, and the Bank of Montserrat is in Brades.

### St-Barthélemy

In St-Barths, the euro (€) is the official currency, but US dollars are widely accepted. There are several banks in Gustavia, some, such as Crédit Agricole, Rue Jeanne d'Arc, with ATMs.

### Saba and St Eustatius

In Saba and Statia, the US dollar is the official currency. Credit cards are rarely accepted outside hotels and dive stores.

### St Kitts and Nevis

The currency on both islands is the EC dollar; US dollars are also widely accepted. Banks are generally open Monday–Thursday 8am–2pm, Friday 8am–4pm. There are ATMs at several banks.

### St Lucia

The currency is the EC dollar, although US dollars are also acceptable in most places. There are foreign-exchange facilities in Castries and Rodney Bay. The National Commercial Bank (NCB) also has a branch at Hewanorra International Airport, open 12.30pm until the last flight leaves.

### St-Martin/Sint Maarten

The euro (€) and the florin or Antillean guilder are the official currencies, but US dollars are also universally accepted. Normal banking hours are Monday–Friday 8.30am–3pm. Several banks have ATMs.

### St Vincent and the Grenadines

The currency is the EC dollar. US dollars and major credit cards can be used in most places. There are banks in Kingstown, Bequia, Canouan, and Union Island.

### Trinidad and Tobago

The Trinidad and Tobago dollar (TT$) is the currency on both islands. Most hotels, restaurants, and stores accept major credit cards.

The First Citizens Bank has convenient foreign-exchange booths at Piarco airport and A.N.R. Robinson International Airport.

### US Virgin Islands

The currency is the US dollar (US$). Normal banking hours are Monday–Thursday 9am–3pm, Friday 9am–5pm. There are ATMs at the airport on St Thomas and in the Banco Popular, Sunny Isles Shopping Center in St Croix, among other places.

# O

## Outdoor Activities

### Birdwatching

A birdwatching tour to any of the following islands should offer plenty of chances to see some of the region's endemic and migratory birds: Guadeloupe, Martinique, Dominica, St Lucia, Grenada, St Vincent, Antigua and Barbuda, and Montserrat.

**Trinidad** and **Tobago** are noted for their birds. The Caroni Bird Sanctuary (tel: 868-645 1305), south of Port-of-Spain, is home to the national bird, the scarlet ibis, and the Asa Wright Nature Centre (tel: 868-667 4655; www.asawright.org) has over 100 different species of bird.

The island of **Bonaire** is a favorite with birdwatchers. It has 190 species of bird, mainly clustered around Goto Lake, Pekelmeer, Cai, and Dos Pos. Look out for the pink flamingo, Bonaire's national symbol.

Male frigate birds, with their distinctive red throats, inflated when attracting females, can be seen on both **Antigua** and **Barbuda**. There is a Frigate Bird Sanctuary on Barbuda, across the mangrove swamps of Codrington Lagoon. **St Lucia** also has thriving colonies of frigate birds at the Maria Islands Nature Reserve. Contact the National Trust, tel: 758-452 5005; www.slunatrust.org.

**Saba** is home to a very healthy population of tropical birds, frigate birds, and other sea birds. The topography provides a wide diversity of vegetation and, as a result, a wide diversity of forest songbirds. Contact the trail ranger (sabapark.trails@gmail.com) to arrange a guide or for more information.

In the US, Caribbean bird-watching tours are organized by:
**Field Guides Incorporated**, 9433 Bee Cave Road, Building 1, Suite 150, Austin TX 78733, tel: 512-263 7295, www.fieldguides.com.

### Hiking

Rainforests, mountains, waterfalls, and gorgeous views await you. Many islands have good-sized national parks with prime hiking opportunities (Dominica, Guadeloupe, Grenada, St Kitts, St Lucia, and St John in the US Virgin Islands, are particularly good), and St Lucia's Pitons offer experienced hikers a chance to test their skills. Guides are often available to lead excursions. Take water, sunscreen, and a hat and wear long trousers and sleeves if hiking in the forest. Below are details of the islands that offer interesting hikes.

### Cycling

The flat but rugged terrain of the the ABC Islands is ideal for cycling. It is

---

## Languages of the Antilles

The multiplicity of languages in the Antilles reflects the region's checkered colonial past. All of the islands use their own creole language, as well as a whole array of primary languages, which include:
**English:** Anguilla, Antigua and Barbuda, British Virgin Islands, Dominica, Grenada, Montserrat, St Kitts and Nevis, St Lucia, St Vincent and the Grenadines, Sint Maarten, Barbados, Trinidad and Tobago, and the US Virgin Islands.
**French:** Dominica, Guadeloupe, Martinique, St-Barthélemy, St Lucia, and St-Martin.
**Dutch:** Aruba, Bonaire, Curaçao, Saba, Sint Eustatius, Sint Maarten.
**Spanish:** Aruba, Bonaire, and Curaçao.

**Papiamentu** is the local language of Aruba, Bonaire, and Curaçao. It has evolved from a mixture of Spanish, Dutch, Portuguese, and English, as well as African and Caribbean languages.

In addition to the primary languages listed above, Chinese is among the languages spoken on Aruba. English (and, to a lesser extent, other European languages) are spoken in several areas throughout the islands that have a high concentration of foreign travelers, but don't expect everyone to understand you – especially in rural areas and smaller towns.

Any efforts to communicate with the islands' residents in their own languages are always appreciated.

*Hiking in St Lucia.*

a good way to discover the land and wildlife, and to reach some of the more secluded beaches. Bonaire is the site of a challenging triathlon in November. It includes a cycle route, a swim, and a run. For details of rentals and tours contact: **Pablito Bike Rental**, Oranjestad, tel: 297-587 8655 or **Outdoor Bonaire**, Kralendijk, tel: 599-785 6272, www.outdoor bonaire.com.

# N

## Nightlife

Nightlife on the islands ranges from relaxing over a leisurely dinner in a restaurant with a verandah onto the beach, to frittering your money away in a casino. In between these options are nightclubs, bars, and live music venues. The larger hotels provide much of the evening entertainment on the islands, including music and dancing, both during and after dinner, flashy floor shows, and "folkloric evenings" composed of elements of the music, dance, and drama of the Caribbean.

Travelers with an interest in the cultural lives of island residents may wish to venture beyond hotel walls in search of steel band, calypso, and reggae music, and bars and clubs frequented by local people. Nightclubs can be found both in and outside hotels.

The intensity of nightlife varies substantially from island to island. The islands that receive the most tourists may have several special entertainments every night of the week, while the quieter islands may sometimes have little more to offer than dinner to the accompaniment of recorded music, followed by a stroll along the beach.

In the latter category, things may pick up a little during the weekends; several establishments have discos that open only on Friday and Saturday nights. On all the islands, the peak tourist season – approximately December through April – is also the peak nightlife season; things are quite a lot slower during the rest of the year.

# P

## Public Holidays

Easter, May 1 (Labor Day), Christmas, and New Year are public holidays, when nearly all shops and offices are closed, but otherwise holidays vary from island to island.

### ABC Islands

January 1 New Year's Day
January 25 **G.F. Betico Croes Birthday**
March 18 **Aruba Day**
Easter **Good Friday, Easter Monday**
April 30 **Rincon Day; Queen's Day**

May 1 **Labor Day**
May (variable) **Ascension Day**
May/June (variable) **Whit Sunday/Monday**
July 2 **Curaçao Flag Day**
September 6 **Bonaire Day**
October 21 **Antillean Day**
December 15 **Kingdom Day**
December 25 **Christmas Day**
December 26 **Boxing Day**

### Anguilla

January 1 **New Year's Day**
March/April **Good Friday, Easter Monday**
May 1 **Labor Day**
May (variable) **Whit Monday**
May 30 Anguilla **Day**
June (2nd Sat) **Queen's Birthday**
August (1st Mon) **August Monday**
(1st Thur) **August Thursday**
(1st Fri) **Constitution Day**
December 19 **Separation Day**
December 25 **Christmas Day**
December 26 **Boxing Day**

### Antigua and Barbuda

January 1 **New Year's Day**
March/April **Good Friday, Easter Monday**
May (1st Mon) **Labor Day**
May/June (variable) **Whit Monday**
July (1st Mon) **Caricom Day**
August (1st Mon and Tue) **Carnival**
November 1 **Independence Day**
December 9 **National Heroes Day**
December 25 **Christmas Day**
December 26 **Boxing Day**

### Barbados

January 1 **New Year's Day**
January 21 **Errol Barrow Day**
March/April **Good Friday, Easter Monday**
April 28 **National Heroes Day**
May 1 **Labor Day**
May/June (variable) **Whit Monday**
August (1st Mon) **Emancipation Day**
(variable) **Kadooment Day**
November 30 **Independence Day**
December 25 **Christmas Day**
December 26 **Boxing Day**

### British Virgin Islands

January 1 **New Year's Day**
March **H. Lavity Stoutt's**
(1st Mon) **Birthday**
(2nd Mon) **Commonwealth Day**
March/April **Good Friday, Easter Monday**
May/June (variable) **Whit Monday**
June 14 **Queen's Birthday**
July 1 **Territory Day**
August (1st Mon/Tue) **Emancipation Festival**
October 21 **St Ursula's Day**
December 25 **Christmas Day**
December 26 **Boxing Day**

*Carnival time in Barbados.*

### Dominica

January 1 **New Year's Day**
March/April **Good Friday, Easter Monday**
May 1 **Labor Day**
May/June (variable) **Whit Monday**
August (1st Mon) **August Monday**
November 3 **Independence Day**
November 4 **Community Service Day**
December 25 **Christmas Day**
December 26 **Boxing Day**

### Grenada

January 1 **New Year's Day**
February 7 **Independence Day**
March/April **Good Friday, Easter Monday**
May 1 **Labor Day**
May/June **Whit Monday**
June **Corpus Christi**
August (1st Mon/Tue) **Emancipation Days**
August **Carnival**
October 25 **Thanksgiving**
December 25 **Christmas Day**
December 26 **Boxing Day**

### Guadeloupe

January 1 **New Year's Day**
February **Ash Wednesday/Carnival**
March **Mi-Carême (Mid-Lent)**
March/April **Good Friday, Easter Monday**
May 1 **Labor Day**
May 8 **VE Day**
May 27 **Abolition Day**
May (variable) **Ascension Day**
May/June (variable) **Whit Monday**
July 14 **Bastille Day**
July 21 **Schoelcher Day (Emancipation)**
August 15 **Assumption Day**

November 1 **All Saints' Day**
November 11 **Armistice Day**
December 25 **Christmas Day**

### Martinique

January 1 **New Year's Day**
February **Carnival**
March **Mi-Carême (Mid-Lent)**
March/April **Good Friday, Easter Monday**
May 1 **Labor Day**
May 8 **VE Day**
May (variable) **Whit Monday**
May 22 **Slavery Abolition Day**
July 14 **Bastille Day**
July 21 **Schoelcher Day**
August 15 **Assumption Day**
November 1 **All Saints' Day**
November 11 **Armistice Day**
December 25 **Christmas Day**

### Montserrat

January 1 **New Year's Day**
March 17 **St Patrick's Day**
March/April **Good Friday, Easter Monday**
May 1 **Labor Day**
May/June (variable) **Whit Monday**
June (2nd Sat) **Queen's Birthday**
August (1st Mon) **August Monday**
December 25 **Christmas Day**
December 26 **Boxing Day**
December 31 **Festival Day**

### St-Barthélemy, Saba, and St Eustatius

**St-Barths**: broadly the same as French St-Martin
**Saba and Statia**: broadly the same as Dutch Sint Maarten
November 16 **Statia/America Day**
First Fri in December **Saba Day**

### St Kitts and Nevis

January 1 **New Year's Day**
January 2 **Carnival Last Lap**
March/April **Good Friday, Easter Monday**
May (1st Mon) **Labor Day**
May/June (variable) **Whit Monday**
August (1st Mon) **Emancipation Day**
(2nd Mon) **Culturama Last Lap**
September 16 **National Heroes Day**
September 19 **Independence Day**
December 25 **Christmas Day**
December 26 **Boxing Day**

### St Lucia

January 1–2 **New Year's Celebrations**
February 22 **Independence Day**
March/April **Easter Good Friday**
May 1 **Labor Day**
May/June (variable) **Whitsun; Corpus Christi**
August 1 **Emancipation Day**
October 1 **Thanksgiving**
December 13 **National Day**
December 25 **Christmas Day**
December 26 **Boxing Day**

### St-Martin/Sint Maarten

#### Dutch Side

January 1 **New Year's Day**
March/April **Good Friday, Easter Sunday/Monday**
April 30 **Queen's Day**
May 1 **Labor Day**
May/June **Ascension Day**
May/June (variable) **Whit Monday**
October 21 **Antillean Day**
November 11 **Sint Maarten Day**
December 15 **Kingdom Day**
December 25 **Christmas Day**
December 26 **Boxing Day**

#### French Side

January 1 **New Year's Day**
March/April **Good Friday, Easter Monday**
May 1 **Labor Day**
May 8 **VE Day**
May/June **Ascension Day**
May/June (variable) **Whit Monday**
Late May **Slavery Abolition Day**
July 14 **Bastille Day/Fête Nationale**
July 21 **Schoelcher Day**
August 15 **Assumption Day**
November 1 **All Saints' Day**
November 11 **St-Martin Day/Armistice Day**
December 25 **Christmas Day**
December 26 **Second Day of Christmas**

### St Vincent and The Grenadines

January 1 **New Year's Day**
March 14 **National Heroes Day**
March/April **Good Friday, Easter Monday**

May/June **Whit Monday**
July 7 **Caricom Day**
July (early) **Carnival Monday/Tuesday**
August (1st Mon) **August Monday/Emancipation Day**
October 27 **Independence Day**
December 25 **Christmas Day**
December 26 **Boxing Day**

### Trinidad and Tobago

January 1 **New Year's Day**
February/March **Carnival**
March 30 **Spiritual Baptist Liberation Day**
March/April **Good Friday**
Easter **Easter Monday**
May 30 **Indian Arrival Day**
June 19 **Labor Day**
June (variable) **Corpus Christi**
August 1 **Emancipation Day**
August 31 **Independence Day**
August **Eid al Fitr (end of Ramadan)**
September 24 **Republic Day**
October/Nov (variable) **Divali**
December 25 **Christmas Day**
December 26 **Boxing Day**

### US Virgin Islands

January 1 **New Year's Day**
January 6 **Three Kings' Day**
January 16 **Martin Luther King Day**
February (3rd Mon) **President's Day**
March/April **Good Friday**, **Easter Monday**
May (last Mon) **Memorial Day**
June 20 **Organic Act Day**
July 3 **Emancipation Day**
July 4 **Independence Day**
July (4th Mon) **Supplication Day**
September (1st Mon) **Labor Day**
October (2nd Mon) **Columbus Day**
(3rd Mon) **Thanksgiving (local)**
November 1 **Liberty Day**
November 11 **Veterans' Day**
(last Thurs) **Thanksgiving (US)**
December 25 **Christmas Day**
December 26 **Boxing Day**

# R

## Religious Services

All the mainstream church denominations can be found on the islands, as well as little-known cults. Attending a local service, perhaps Baptist or Seventh Day Adventist, is a wonderful way to experience an important aspect of Caribbean life, and you will be assured of a warm welcome, as long as you dress smartly and act with decorum and respect. Local tourist offices and free tourist publications should be able to advise you of times of services.

# S

## Shopping

### ABC Islands

The ABC Islands have a range of tax-free shopping outlets. While Bonaire shopping is limited, Oranjestad in Aruba is a shoppers' paradise with designer wear, perfume, and local art, but it can be busy when a cruise ship docks. Sometimes stores are open 7 days a week here.

Curaçao offers great tax-free purchases, shopping malls, and interesting boutiques, all dotted around Punda in Willemstad.

### Anguilla

The most interesting shopping is in the studios of local artists.

### Antigua and Barbuda

In St John's, Heritage Quay and Redcliffe Quay attract cruise ship shoppers with a range of duty-free outlets and a street market.

### Barbados

Duty-free shopping is available at many stores throughout the island and at the cruise ship terminal. To make a duty-free purchase, you must present your immigration slip (given to you when you arrive), or your passport and ticket.

### British Virgin Islands

An assortment of stores, including duty-free, line Tortola's Main Street in Road Town. On Wickhams Cay I is a **Pusser's Company Store**, Waterfront Street, Road Town, tel: 284-494 2467; www.pussers.com. Apart from its own rum, it sells all things nautical, clothes, and antiques and has branches in Soper's Hole Wharf in the west and Leverick Bay in Virgin Gorda.

### Dominica

**The Craft Market** at the Old Market, Roseau, is a good place to get an idea of the crafts available on the island. Here and in other shops you can find local Bay Rum (aftershave and body rub), coconut soap, tea, coffee, jams and jellies, hand cream, shampoo, spices, chocolate, candies, and pepper sauce, all of which are made on the island.

Some of the best crafts in the Caribbean can be found in the **Carib/Kalinago Territory**, either at roadside stalls or in the model village, where there are several

artisans at work producing intricate and beautiful baskets from larouma reed, vetifer-grass mats, and calabash-gourd bowls. Craft stalls carrying a range of goods including necklaces and bracelets made from seeds or coconut, can also be found at Trafalgar Falls.

### Grenada

Local specialties include batik and screen-printed items, jewelry, and attractive spice baskets. Spices, cocoa sticks or balls, pepper sauce, nutmeg jelly, and nutmeg oil can be found in St George's Market, or, indeed, in the local supermarkets, where you can buy a lifetime's supply of cinnamon, cloves, nutmeg, mace, or vanilla. Locally grown, organic cocoa is made into delicious chocolate by the **Grenada Chocolate Factory** (www.grenadachocolate.com). Winners of a silver medal in 2011 from the London Academy of Chocolate for their 82 percent chocolate bar, the cooperative has a bonbon shop at Belmont Estate (see page 244). So pure, it will not melt in your luggage.

### Guadeloupe

Shoppers in Guadeloupe searching for quality local arts and crafts, perfume, and designer clothing, and all things French, will not be disappointed. There are modern shopping facilities at the cruise ship terminal in Pointe-à-Pitre. The largest commercial center with supermarkets is at **Destreland** in **Baie Mahault**.

The fashionable **Rue Frébault** in **Pointe-à-Pitre** has upscale, fashionable stores. Authentic purchases from Guadeloupe include music, jewelry, coffee, rum, fine embroidery from Vieux Fort, and clothing made from madras. Handicrafts include wood carvings, madras table linens and dolls, salakos (fishermen's broad-brimmed hats), and little baskets of spices, lined with madras cotton.

### Martinique

There are several modern shopping malls concentrated around the Fort-de-France area, while the **Village Créole** at Pointe du Bout has some original boutiques. Martinican rum is among the world's finest, and you can buy one of the various makes at distilleries or at local supermarkets. Chocolate made locally by Elot is good; most of the beans are imported from Africa nowadays, but their chocolate bars with lime or coconut are worth trying. Fresh flowers from one of the many tropical horticultural centers are packaged specially for airline transport.

Local artists whose work is worth acquiring include Claude Cauquil, Louis Laouchez, and Laurent Valère (one of his monumental sculptures is Manman Dio, underwater in the bay of St-Pierre). Manscour, whose atelier is situated in Trinité, specializes in glass sculptures.

### Montserrat

There are no big stores on Montserrat and shops are strung along the roads as there is no town center yet. You can find garments handwoven from locally grown Sea Island cotton, T-shirts, items made from volcanic ash and rocks, dolls and postcards of the volcano, preserves such as guava jelly and the ubiquitous hot pepper sauce; music and crafts incorporating the local madras green and yellow plaid cotton. Stores selling gifts and souvenirs are found in Brades, Woodlands, and Salem.

### Saba and St Eustatius

Saba lace, the drawn-thread work, is also known as Spanish work because it was learned by a Saban woman at a convent in Venezuela in the 19th century. It has been made for over 100 years here, and is on sale in stores and from private houses – any taxi driver should be able to take you to an outlet. The **Saba Artisan Foundation** in the Bottom sells locally designed and produced dolls, clothing, and silk-screened fabric. Statia has no handicrafts to speak of and shopping is unexciting.

Jo Bean's Hot Glass Studio, Windwardside, Saba, tel: 599-416 2490. Handmade colored glass fashioned into beads, frogs, lizards, and other fantastical creatures. Watch the craftspeople at work or do a course and make your own.

### St-Barthélemy

Gustavia and St-Jean are best for tax-free luxury goods such as designer wear, perfume, and quality local crafts. There are many chic designer shops in Gustavia where you can find designer labels such as Armani, Cartier, Hermès, Louis Vuitton, and Ralph Lauren, while in St-Jean there are the small shopping centers of La Savane, Les Galeries du Commerce, La Villa Créole, Le Pélican, Vaval, and Centre

*Fuel Station, Marina Cay, British Virgin Islands.*

Commercial de Neptune. Food shopping is also good, with many gourmet items brought from France, including good cheese and wine.

### St Kitts and Nevis

On St Kitts, Port Zante has duty-free stores and restaurants ideally located to catch the cruise ship market. In town there are several clothing stores and art galleries worth visiting. Look out for the local Caribelle Batik clothing and fabrics, local sea island cotton wear, cane and basket work.

### St Lucia

**Pointe Seraphine** (http://dfps. dutyfreepointeseraphine.com) and **La Place Carenage** (www.carenagemall. com) are duty-free shopping outlets either side of Castries harbour where cruise ships dock. **Castries Market** and the **Vendors' Arcade** are worth a look, if only to see the tropical fruit and vegetables and local handicrafts. These are good places to pick up T-shirts, spices, cocoa sticks, coffee beans, and hot pepper sauces. Rodney Bay is now the main area for general shopping since the construction of the Bay Walk Mall containing shops and a supermarket.

St Lucia is known for having a large number of world-class artists such as Llewellyn Xavier, Dunstan St Omer, Ron Savory, Sean Bonnett St Remy, Winston Branch, and many others.

### St-Martin/Sint Maarten

For duty-free goods head for Front Street in Philipsburg, Maho Beach, Mullet Bay and Blue Mall at

Cupecoy, or Rue de la République and Marina Porte la Royale in Marigot. Here you can find electrical goods, jewelry, watches, linens, and many consumer goods. Many artists have based themselves on the island and there are a dozen art galleries on both sides, so many that cruise ships offer art gallery and studio tours.

### St Vincent and the Grenadines

St Vincent has plenty of chandlers and food shops for yachties, but there is little in the way of tourist shopping. On Bequia you can find more souvenirs. For handicrafts from about 70 local artisans, try the **Artisans Art & Craft Center**, Bay Street, Kingstown, in the Bonadie Building. On Bequia, Sam McDowell is known for his scrimshaw, etchings, and carvings made on whalebone, traditionally used on knife handles.

### Trinidad and Tobago

Trinidad and Tobago are best for handicrafts, batik, rum, clothing, and duty-free goods. Main shopping areas are Frederick Street, Queen Street, Charlotte Street, and Henry Street, Grande Bazaar Mall on the Southern Highway, and Golf City Mall at San Fernando in the south. For a good selection of calypso and soca music try **Crosby's** at 54 Western Main Road in St James. Vendors on Frederick Street and Independence Square sell as hand-painted T-shirts, and crafts can be found at East Mall on Charlotte Street.

On Tobago, craft vendors are found everywhere; or try **Cotton House** on

Bacolet Street in Scarborough, for clothing, jewelry, and batik art.

### US Virgin Islands

The USVI enjoy duty- and sales tax-free status so most things are 20–50 percent cheaper than on the mainland. **St Thomas** has the widest choice of duty-free shopping, much of it in Charlotte Amalie; **Havensight Mall** by the cruise ship docks and **Red Hook** on the east coast are modern shopping malls selling jewelry, watches, cameras, liquor, and other duty-free goods. St Thomas also has a selection of handicraft outlets.

**St Croix**'s King's Alley Walk is a shopping area in Christiansted. In **St Croix Leap** in the west, there are some excellent woodcarvers.

**St John** has a variety of arts and crafts. The most popular shopping areas are **Mongoose Junction** and **Wharfside Village** in Cruz Bay.

## Sports

The climate and geography of the Antilles make the islands perfect for sports enthusiasts, and tourism has helped spark the development of a variety of sports facilities.

### Diving

The clear blue waters of the Caribbean are the setting for a marine landscape of breathtaking beauty, a hidden world – accessible only to divers and snorkelers – in which gloriously colored and patterned fish vie for attention with extraordinary coral formations.

All the islands offer equipment and excursion packages, including training courses. Addresses of well-reputed dive operators (always check on the reliability of operators and ask to see instructors' certificates) are listed below. The tourist offices provide informative brochures listing dive sites and schools.

### Fishing

Fishing is popular throughout the Caribbean. Most fishing boats can be chartered by the day or half-day, and can usually accommodate several passengers. Many quote rates that are all-inclusive of lunch, drinks, snacks, bait, equipment, and any other essential items you might need. Deep-sea fishing is usually for wahoo, dolphin (dorado), barracuda, tuna, and marlin, but there are seasonal variations. Fly fishing is more limited, but there

is some fishing for tarpon, snook, and bonefish in Aruba, Anegada, Guadeloupe, St-Barths, and the Virgin Islands.

### Tennis

Tennis is played on most islands. Courts are found primarily within the premises of hotels, but arrangements can be made for non-hotel guests to use them. Some islands also have private clubs that are open to visitors, and public courts that operate on a "first come, first served" basis. Many hotels have resident tennis pros to help you improve your game. Barbados even has a tennis resort.

### Water Sports

Windsurfing is available on most islands and all the necessary equipment may be rented. Kitesurfing is also popular.

A variety of rental options is available for sailing, from mini Sunfish to two-masted yachts and large motorboats. Equipment can be rented, and classes are conducted on almost every island.

If you are interested in chartering a yacht, either crewed or bare boat, for a day or a considerable period of time, see page 298.

Motorized water sports such as water-skiing and jet skiing are limited to resort areas, not in marine parks.

## T

## Telephones

Phone cards in several denominations are available on the islands. They are useful for avoiding the usually extremely high hotel charges on phone calls. Residents of the US and Canada can use AT&T USA Direct public phones with a charge card. Some public phones allow holders of a European charge card, such as a BT Chargecard, to access the home operator.

If you want to use you cellphone while abroad, check with your network to see if it will work there and what rates they charge. Sometimes, if you are likely to use your phone for a lot of local calls, the best thing to do is to buy a SIM card locally (from any LIME/Digicel outlet).

### Area Codes

**ABC Islands: Aruba** 297; **Bonaire** 599; **Curaçao** 5999.

Anguilla 264. Access codes: AT&T: 800-225 5288; MCI: 800-888 8000.
**Antigua and Barbuda** 268.
**Barbados** 246. Access codes: AT&T: 800-225 5288; MCI: 800-888 8000.
**British Virgin Islands** 284. Access codes: AT&T: 800-872 2881; MCI: 800-888 8000.
**Dominica** 767. Access codes: AT&T: 800-225 5288; MCI: 800-888 8000.
**Grenada** 473. Access codes: AT&T: 800-225 5288; MCI: 800-888 8000.
**Guadeloupe** 590 (must be dialed before dialing the Guadeloupe phone number, which is prefixed with 0590; drop first zero when dialing from abroad).
**Martinique** 596 (this is the country code, followed by the local number which is prefixed with 0596; drop first zero when dialing from abroad).
**Montserrat** 664.
**St-Barths** 590.
**Saba** 599.
**Statia** 5993.
**St Kitts and Nevis** 869. Access codes: AT&T: 800-225 5288; MCI: 800-888 8000.
**St Lucia** 758. Access codes: AT&T: 800-225 5288; MCI: 800-888 8000.
**St-Martin/Sint Maarten** The country code for the French side, St-Martin, is **590**, and the Dutch side is **599**. As in Guadeloupe and Martinique, the French local numbers are already prefixed with 0590, so to call St-Martin from abroad you must dial the country code +590 then the local number beginning with 0590 (but drop the first zero) so you have +590-590 and then the following six digits.
**St Vincent and the Grenadines** 784. Access codes: AT&T: 800-225 5288; MCI: 800-888 8000.

## Atlantis Adventures

**Atlantis Adventures** allows visitors a chance to explore the sea without getting their feet wet. The *Atlantis VI* submarine provides a view of the tropical underwater world of the Caribbean, usually only seen by divers. Alternatively, the *SeaWorld Explorer* is a semi-submersible trip that reveals the marine life below the surface, through a glass gallery, while the boat remains above the water. Atlantis Adventures (www.atlantis submarines.com) has four locations in the Lesser Antilles:
**Aruba**, tel: 297-588 6881;
**Curaçao**, tel: 5999-461 0011;
**Barbados**, tel: 246-436 8929; and
**St Maarten**, tel: 721-542 4078.

**Trinidad and Tobago** 868. Access codes: AT&T, 800-872 2881; MCI: 800-888 8000.
**US Virgin Islands** 340. Access code: MCI: 800-888 8000.

## Tipping

On most restaurant and hotel bills, a 10–15 percent service charge is added by the management. If this is the case, tipping is unnecessary, although a small gratuity given directly to an attentive waitress or bellman is always appreciated. When service is not included, a tip in the 15–20 percent range is appropriate. Taxi drivers should be tipped within this range as well.

## Tourist Information Offices

The general Caribbean Tourism Organization, www.onecaribbean.org, has the following overseas offices:
**UK:** 22 The Quadrant, Richmond, Surrey, TW9 1BP, tel: 020-8948 0057, email: ctolondon@caribtourism.com.
**US:** 80 Broad Street, Suite 3200, New York, NY 10004, tel: 212-635 9530, email: ctony@caribtourism.com.

### ABC Islands

**Aruba**
Aruba Tourism Authority, 8 L.G. Smith Boulevard, Oranjestad, tel: 297-582 3777, www.aruba.com.
**Europe:** Aruba Tourism Authority, Schimmelpenninckklaan 1, 2517 JN The Hague, The Netherlands, tel: 70-302 8040, email: ata.europe@aruba.com.
**UK:** Aruba Tourism Authority, The Saltmarsh Partnership, The Copperfields, 25 Copperfield Street, London SE1 0EN, tel: 020-7928 1600.
**US:** Aruba Tourism Authority, 1000 Harbor Boulevard, Weehawken, NJ 07087, tel: 201-330 0800, 800-TO-ARUBA, email: ata.newjersey@aruba.com.
Bonaire
Tourism Corporation Bonaire, Kaya Grandi 2, Kralendijk, tel: 599-717 8322, email: info@tourismbonaire.com, www.infobonaire.com.
**Europe:** Basis Communicatie B.V., Wagenweg 252, PO Box 472, NL-2000 AL Haarlem, The Netherlands, tel: 23-5430 705, email: europe@tourismbonaire.com
**US:** Adams Unlimited, 80 Broad Street, 32nd Floor, Suite 3202, New York, NY 10004, tel: 212-956 5900, email: usa@tourismbonaire.com.

### Curaçao
Curaçao Tourist Board, PO Box 3266, Pietermaai 19, Willemstad, tel: 5999-434 8200, www.curacao.com.
**Europe:** Curaçao Tourist Board Europe, Anna van Buerenplein 41, 2595 DA The Hague, The Netherlands, tel: 31-70-891 6600, www.curacaoinfo.nl.
**US:** Curaçao Tourism Corporation, 80 S.W. 8th Street, Suite 2000, Miami, FLA 33130, tel: 305-423 7156, email: northamerica@curacao.com

### Anguilla
Anguilla Tourist Board, Coronation Avenue, The Valley, tel: 264-497 2759, 1-800 553 4939 (toll-free), email: atbtour@anguillanet.com, www.anguilla-vacation.com.
**Canada:** SRM Marketing, 20-225 Dundas Street East, Suite 411, Waterdown, ON L0R 2H6, tel: 905-689 7697, email: dpusching@anguillacanada.ca.
**UK:** CSB Communications Ltd, Suite 11, Parsons Green House, 27–31 Parsons Green Lane, London SW6 4HH, tel: 020-7736 6030, email: info@anguilla-tourism.com.
**US:** 246 Central Avenue, White Plains, NY 10606, tel: 914-287 2400, email: mwturnstyle@aol.com.

### Antigua and Barbuda
Antigua & Barbuda Tourism Authority, ACB Financial Center, High Street, St John's, tel: 268-562 7600, www.antigua-barbuda.org.
**Canada:** 60 St Claire Avenue East, Suite 304, Toronto, ON M4T 1N5, tel: 416-961 3085, email: info@antigua-barbuda-ca.com.
**UK:** Victoria House, 4th floor, Victoria Road, Chelmsford, Essex CM1 1JR, tel: 01245-707 471.
**US:** 3 Dag Hammarskjold Plaza, 305 East 47th Street - 6A, New York, NY 10017, tel: 212-541 4117, email: info@antigua-barbuda.org.

### Barbados
The main tourist office is at Harbour Road, Bridgetown (tel: 246-427 2623). There are also offices at the airport (tel: 246-428 7101) and cruise terminal (tel: 246-426 1718). There is an information kiosk at the Cave Shepherd department store, Broad Street, Bridgetown, www.barbados.org.
**Canada:** 105 Adelaide Street West, Suite 1010, Toronto, ON M5H 1P9, tel: 800-268 9122, email: canada@barbados.org.

**UK:** 263 Tottenham Court Road, London W1T 7LA, tel: 020-7636 9448, email: btauk@barbados.org.
**US:** New York: 800 2nd Avenue, New York, NY 10017, tel: 212-986 6516/800-221 9831 (toll-free in US), email: btany@barbados.org.
Florida: 150 Alhambra Circle, Suite 1000, Coral Gables, FL 33134, tel: 305-442-7471, email: btamiami@barbados.org.

### British Virgin Islands

**Tortola**
British Virgin Islands Tourist Board, DeCastro Street, 2nd Floor, AKARA Building, Road Town, tel: 284-494 3134, www.bvitourism.com.

**Virgin Gorda**
Virgin Gorda Yacht Harbour, tel: 284-495 5181, www.bvitourism.com, www.bviwelcome.com.
**UK:** The BVI Tourist Board, 15 Upper Grosvenor Street, London W1K 7PJ, tel: 020-7355 9585, email: infouk@bvi.org.uk.
**US:** BVI Tourist Board, 1 West 34th Street, Suite 302, New York, NY 10001, tel: 212-563 3117, 800-835 8530 (toll-free in US), email: info@bvitourism.com.

### Dominica
Discover Dominica Authority, 1st Floor Financial Centre, Roseau, Commonwealth of Dominica. Tel: 767-448 2045. email: tourism@dominica.dm.
Old Market Square, Roseau (open Monday–Friday 8am–6pm), www.dominica.dm.
**UK:** Discover Dominica, tel: 020-7326 9880, email: sarah.emsat@brightergroup.com.
**US:** Discover Dominica, (toll-free) tel: 866-522 4057, email: dominicany@dominica.dm.

### Grenada
Grenada Tourism Authority: Burn's Point, PO Box 293, St George's, tel: 473-440 2279, email: gbt@spiceisle.com. www.grenadagrenadines.com.
**Canada:** Grenada Board of Tourism, 90 Eglington Avenue East, Suite 605, Toronto, ON M4P 2Y3, tel: 416-995 1581, email: canada@puregrenada.com.
**UK:** Grenada Tourism Authority, 1 Lyric Square, London W6 0NB, tel: 020-8328 0640, email: grenada@eyes2market.co.uk.
**US:** Grenada Board of Tourism, PO Box 1668, Lake Worth, FL 33460, tel: 561-588-8176, email: gta@eyes2market.co.uk.

*Blue Waters Resort wedding gazebo.*

## Guadeloupe

**Office du Tourisme de la Guadeloupe**, 5 Square de la Banque, BP 555, 97166 Pointe-à-Pitre, tel: 590-590-820 930, www.lesilesdeguadeloupe.com.
Office Municipal de Tourisme Terre de Haut-Les Saintes, rue Jean Calot, BP 10 97137 Terre-de-Haut, tel: 590-590-995 860, www.omtlessaintes.fr. All towns have local tourism bureaux.
**France**: 8–10, rue Buffault, 75009 Paris, tel: 33 1 40 62 99 07, email: infoeurope@lesilesdeguadeloupe.com

## Martinique

Comité Martiniquais du Tourisme, Immeuble Le Beaupré-Pointe de Jaham, 97233 Schoelcher, tel: 596-596 616 177, www.martinique.org. Tourist Office of Fort-de-France, 76 rue Lazare Carnot, 97200 Fort-de-France,
tel: 596-596-027 73, www.tourismefdf.com.
**Canada**: Comité Martiniquais de Tourisme, 4000 rue Saint Ambroise, Bureau 265, Montréal, Québec H4C 2C7, tel: 514-844 8566.
**US**: Martinique Promotion Bureau, 825 Third Avenue, 29th Floor, New York, NY 10022, tel: 212-838 6887, email: info@martinique.org.

## Montserrat

**Montserrat Tourist Board**, 7 Farara Plaza, Buildings B and C, PO Box 7, Brades, tel: 644-491 2230/8730, www.visitmontserrat.com.
**UK**: The Copperfields, 25D Copperfield Street, London SE1 0EN, tel: 020-7928 1600.

**US**: Cheryl Andrews Marketing Inc., 2655 Le Jeune Road, Suite 805, Coral Gables, FL 33134, tel: 305-444 4033, email: montserrat@cherylandrewsmarketing.com.

## Saba and St Eustatius

**Saba**: Windwardside, tel: 599-416 2231, www.sabatourism.com.
**Statia**: Fort Oranjestad, tel: 599-318 2433, www.statiatourism.com.

## St-Barthélemy

**St-Barths**: 1 Quai Général de Gaulle, Gustavia, tel: 590-590-278 727, www.st-barths.com.
**UK**: Lincoln House, 300 High Holborn, London WC1V 7JH, tel: 0906-824 4123 (premium rate)
**US**: 825 Third Avenue, 29th floor (entrance on 50th street), New York, NY 10022, tel: 00 1 514 288 1904

## St Kitts and Nevis

**St Kitts**: St Kitts Tourism Authority, Pelican Mall, Bay Road, PO Box 132, Basseterre, tel: 869-465 4040, www.stkittstourism.kn.
**Nevis**: Main Street, Charlestown, tel: 869-469 7550, www.nevisisland.com.
**Canada**: 133 Richmond St West, Suite 311, Toronto, ON M5H 2L3, tel: 416-368 6707, email: carolyn.james@stkittstourism.kn.
**UK**: 10 Kensington Court, London W8 5DL, tel: 020-7376 0881, email: jennifer.hensley@stkittstourism.kn.
**US**: 414 East 75th Street, Suite 5, New York, NY 10021, tel: 212-535 1234 (toll-free) 800-582 6208, email: newyork@stkittstourism.kn

## St Lucia

PO Box 221, Sureline Building, Vide Bouteille, Castries, tel: 758-452 4094, www.saintluciauk.org.
**Canada**: 60 St. Clair Avenue East, Suite 909, Toronto, ON M4T 1N5, tel: 416-392 4242, email: sltbcanada@aol.com.
**UK**: St Lucia Tourist Board, 1 Collingham Gardens, London SW5 0HW, tel: 020-7341 7005, email: sltbinfo@stluciauk.org.
**US**: St Lucia Tourist Board, 800 Second Avenue, Suite 400J, 9th Floor, New York, NY 10017, tel: 212-867 2950, email: stluciatourism@aol.com.

## St-Martin/Sint Maarten

**French side**: Route de Sandy Ground, Marigot, 97150 Marigot, St-Martin, tel: 590-875 721, www.st-martin.org, www.iledesaintmartin.org.
**Dutch side**: Sint Maarten Tourist Bureau, Vineyard Office Park, W.G. Buncamper Road 33, Philipsburg,
Sint Maarten, tel: 599-542 2337, www.vacationstmaarten.com.
**France**: Office de Tourisme de St-Martin, 54 rue de Varenne, 75007 Paris, tel: 01 53 29 99 99.
**US**: St-Martin promotional office, 825 Third Avenue, 29th floor, New York, NY 10022-7519, tel: 212-745 0945. Sint Maarten Tourist Office, 675 Third Avenue, Suite 1806, New York, NY 10017, tel: 212-953 2084, (toll-free) 800-786 2278.

## St Vincent and The Grenadines

Ministry of Tourism, NIS Building, Upper Bay Street, Kingstown, St Vincent, tel: 784-457

1502, www.bequiasweet.com, www.discoversvg.com.
There are also information desks at the cruise ship terminal, tel: 784-457 1592 and E. T. Joshua Airport, tel: 784-458 4685.
**Canada:** 333 Wilson Avenue, Suite 601, Toronto, ON M3H 1T2, tel: 416-630 9292, email: svgtourismtoronto@rogers.com.
**UK:** 10 Kensington Court, London W8 5DL, tel: 020-7937 6570, email: svgtourismeurope@aol.com.
**US:** 801 Second Avenue, New York, NY 10017, tel 212-687 4981, (toll-free) 800 729 1726, email: svgtony@aol.com.

### Trinidad and Tobago

### Trinidad

TIDCO (Tourism Development Company of Trinidad and Tobago), PO Box 222,

Maritime Center, 29 Tenth Avenue, Barataria, tel: 868-675 7034, www.gotrinidadandtobago.com. Information office, Piarco International Airport, tel: 868-669 5196.

### Tobago

Tobago House of Assembly Division of Tourism and Transportation, 12 Sangster's Hill, Scarborough, tel: 868-639 2125.
Information office, A.N.R. Robinson International Airport, tel: 868-639 0509.
**UK:** Lion House, 111 Hare Lane, Claygate, Surrey KT10 0QY, tel: 01372 469818, email: trinbago@ihml.com
**US:** Marketing Challenges International Inc., 915 Broadway, Suite 600, New York, NY 10010, tel: 212-529 8484 (toll-free from US and Canada) 800-816 7541, email: t&t@mcintl.com

### US Virgin Islands

**St Thomas:** there are two visitors' bureaux:
1 Tolbod Gade, Charlotte Amalie, tel: 340-774 8784.
Welcome Center, Havensight Dock, www.usvi.net, www.usvi-on-line.com, www.visitusvi.com, www.vinow.com.
**St Croix:** 53A Company Street, Christiansted, tel: 340-773 0495, www.visitusvi.com.
**St John:** the tourism office is next to the post office in Cruz Bay, www.st-john.com.
**Canada:** 3300 Bloor Street West, Suite 3120, Centre Tower, Toronto, on M8X 2X3, tel: 416-622 7600.
**UK:** Destination Marketing, Power Road Studios, 114 Power Road, London W4 5PY, tel: 020-8994 0978.
**US:** Chicago: 500 N. Michigan Avenue, Suite 2030, Chicago, IL 60611, tel: 312-670 8784.
**Los Angeles:** 3460 Wilshire Boulevard, Suite 412, Los Angeles, CA 90010, tel: 213-739 0138, email: usvi@destination-marketing.co.uk
**Miami:** 2655 Le Jeune Road, Suite 907, Miami, FL 33134, tel: 305-442 7200.
**New York:** 1270 Avenue of the Americas, Suite 2108, New York, NY 10020, tel: 212-332 2222.

## Weddings in the Caribbean

There are those who still prefer a traditional wedding at home, followed by a honeymoon away, but others – in increasing numbers – decide to combine the two, and bring family and friends along as well. A Caribbean island makes the perfect destination. Choose a hotel that employs a full-time wedding organizer, or, through your travel agent, choose one of the tour operators who now offer all-in wedding packages. Here are some points to note:
Rules vary from island to island (contact tourist offices for information), but in most cases it is required that couples be over 18, and for the wedding to be conducted after three working days on the island. Hotels prefer you to be resident there for 7 days.
You will need valid passports, birth certificates, and any relevant divorce or death certificates. Allow approximately half a day to complete administration prior to the ceremony (paperwork can be done only during government business hours, so check that public holidays don't intervene). On English islands, non-English documents must be translated by an officially recognized translator. The marriage may be carried out by a marriage officer or a clergyman. In the latter case, it may be necessary for your home minister to liaise with the island minister; this is always the case for Catholic services. The marriage is legally binding.

The bride and bridegroom can usually choose their own music. Wedding outfits (remember the heat and the relaxed setting when planning yours) can usually be pressed before the ceremony; major airlines all have arrangements for transporting them, either boxed or hanging in garment sleeves. Wedding photographs and videos can be provided, but the quality may not be the same as in the US and Europe.
Apart from the cost of staying in the hotel, couples pay an extra fee for the wedding ceremony. Prices vary considerably, depending on the standard of hotel and what extras are offered (these might include anything from a souvenir T-shirt to a sunset cruise). Some of the larger hotels employ a wedding planner.

### Weddings in Barbados

To get married in Barbados, apply for a marriage license at the Ministry of Home Affairs in the General Post Office Building, Cheapside, Bridgetown (tel: 246-228 8950). You need to show a valid passport and original or certified copies of your birth certificate, and proof of divorce (decree absolute) if you have been married before. You also need to show return air tickets. The license costs BDS$200 plus BDS$25 stamp fee. Many larger hotels will plan formalities and arrange the wedding as part of a package.

## W

## What to Wear

"Casual" is the word in the Antilles. Cool cotton clothes should make up the majority of your wardrobe. Air conditioning can be set too low when it's hot and the breezes are cooler at night during the winter, so it's a good idea to bring a light jacket or cotton sweater, just in case. Men should bring a jacket and tie if they plan to visit any casinos – most of them (and some of the fancier restaurants and hotels) require at least a jacket for the evening. A pair of sturdy walking shoes is obviously essential for those planning walks in the mountains and rainforests.
It is not appropriate to wear swimsuits and other beach attire around town. When you venture from beach or poolside into town, cover up – a simple T-shirt and a pair of shorts should do the trick. By following this rule, you will show respect for the standards of many island residents.
Nude or topless (for women) bathing is prohibited everywhere except for Guadeloupe, Martinique, St-Martin, St-Barthélemy, and Bonaire. Guadeloupe, St-Martin, and Bonaire have at least one designated nudist beach.

# FURTHER READING

## HISTORY AND SOCIETY

**Traveller's History of the Caribbean**, by James Ferguson.
**A Short History of the West Indies,** by J.H. Parry, Philip Sherlock, and Anthony Maingot.
**A Brief History of the Caribbean: From the Arawak and Carib to the Present**, by Jan Rogonzinski.
**The Slave Trade**, by Hugh Thomas.
**Last Resorts, The Cost of Tourism in the Caribbean**, by Polly Pattullo.

## NATURAL HISTORY

**A Field Guide to Reefs of the Caribbean and Florida**, by Eugene H. Kaplan.
**Birds of the West Indies**, by Herbert Raffaele et al.
**Caribbean Wild Plants and Their Uses**, by Penelope N. Honychurch.
**The Gardens of Dominica**, by Polly Pattullo and Anne Jno Baptiste.

## SPORT

**The Complete Diving Guide, Caribbean Volume I**, by Colleen Ryan and Brian Savage.
**Complete Guide to Diving and Snorkelling Aruba, Bonaire and Curacao**, by Jack Jackson.
**Caribbean Afoot!: A Walking and Hiking Guide to Twenty-Nine of the Caribbean's Best Islands**, by M. Timothy O'Keefe.
**75 Years of West Indies Cricket, 1928–2003**, by Ray Goble and Keith A.P. Sandiford.
**An Illustrated History of Caribbean Football**, by James Ferguson.

## FICTION

**A House for Mr Biswas**, by V.S. Naipaul. Classic, bittersweet account of a Trinidadian man's search for security.
**The Lonely Londoners**, by Samuel Selvon. Comic masterpiece of a Trinidadian immigrant's life in 1950s London.
**The Wide Sargasso Sea**, by Jean Rhys. An atmospheric prequel to Charlotte Brontë's classic novel *Jane Eyre*, partly set on the island of Dominica.
**The Orchid House**, by Phyllis Shand Allfrey. Acclaimed novel of family tensions and colonial decline in Dominica.
**In the Castle of My Skin**, by George Lamming. Growing up in a 1930s Barbadian village during the demise of colonialism. A novel of adolescence and political awakening.
**A State of Independence**, by Caryl Phillips. A wry study of small-island politics and an exile's return to his homeland.
**Omeros**, by Derek Walcott. Contemporary working of Homeric epic by St Lucian Nobel Prize-winning poet.
**The Dragon Can't Dance**, by Earl Lovelace. A story of life in a shanty town on Trinidad which captures all the exuberance of the island's Carnival.
**The Penguin Book of Caribbean Verse in English**, ed. Paula Burnett. The best available collection of verse from English-speaking Caribbean poets.
**Tree of Life**, by Maryse Condé. A tale of several generations of a Guadeloupean family.
**Tide Running**, by Oonya Kempadoo. Two young men growing up on Tobago find their lives and desires confused by the arrival of a well-to-do family, and have to confront relationships, wealth and responsibility.
**The White Woman on a Green Bicycle**, by Monique Roffey. British newly-weds arrive in Trinidad in the 1950s. He relishes the ex-pat life but she has difficulty adjusting.

## BIOGRAPHY

**Learie Constantine**, by Peter Mason. An overwhelmingly popular and talented Trinidadian cricketer, Learie Constantine (1901–71) paved the way for a new generation of black cricketers in a game dominated by whites. He went on to become a barrister, the Trinidadian High Commissioner in London, a cabinet minister, broadcaster, author, journalist and the first black man to enter the House of Lords, tirelessly campaigning for racial equality and West Indian self-government.

## MUSIC

**Awakening Spaces: French Caribbean Popular Songs, Music and Culture**, by Brenda Berrian. The development of the diverse music scene in the French islands is traced through zouk, the beguine, jazz, ballads and reggae. Through interviews and analysis of lyrics Berrian explores the musicians' feelings on exile, desire, identity and subversion.
**Carnival, Canboulay and Calypso: Traditions in the Making**, by John Cowley. An historical analysis of the rise of Carnival during the time of slavery, and the emergence of calypso as the popular music of Trinidad's Carnival up to 1920.

## Send Us Your Thoughts

We do our best to ensure the information in our books is as accurate and up-to-date as possible. The books are updated on a regular basis using local contacts, who painstakingly add, amend and correct as required. However, some details (such as telephone numbers and opening times) are liable to change, and we are ultimately reliant on our readers to put us in the picture.

We welcome your feedback, especially your experience of using the book "on the road". Maybe we recommended a hotel that you liked (or another that you didn't), or you came across a great bar or new attraction we missed.

We will acknowledge all contributions, and we'll offer an Insight Guide to the best letters received.

Please write to us at:
**Insight Guides**
**PO Box 7910**
**London SE1 1WE**
Or email us at:
**hello@insightguides.com**

# CREDITS

*Photo Credits*

akg images 40
Alamy 7ML, 112, 159B
Anguilla Tourist Boad 19T, 52, 126, 127
Anse Chastanet Resort 226
Antigua & Barbuda Tourist Office 100/101, 171, 173, 177, 178
Aruba/fotoseeker.com 284
AWL Images 88BL, 161, 266BR
Balenbouche Estate House 227T
Barbados Museum & Historical Society 46
Barbados Tourism Authority 6BL, 58, 124BR, 124BL, 248, 249, 253B, 255, 258
Bert Nienhuis 72
Blount Small Ship Adventures 125ML
Blue Waters Resort 323
Brenda S and R Duncan Kirby/ Fotoseeker 152/153T, 153BL, 157, 159T, 181T
BVI Tourist Board 122T
Calabash Hotel 246T
Callaloo Villas 237B
Cayman Islands Department Of Tourism 97T, 152BR
Chris Caldicott/St. Vincent & the Grenadines Tourist Office 231, 233, 234
Chris Huxley 224B
Comité du tourisme de Saint Barthélemy/Laurent Benoît 145, 147
Control Arms 264T
Corbis 7TL, 70, 74, 75, 76L, 80, 215
Corrie Wingate/Apa Publications 200T, 206BR, 206BL, 207ML, 224T, 238/239T
Courtesy Llewellyn Xavier 81
Curaçao Tourist Board 152BL, 153TR, 277, 278, 279, 280T, 280B 282, 296
David MacGillivary/Montserrat Tourist Board 77, 181B, 182, 302
Discover Dominica Authority 53, 196, 197, 199, 202, 203T, 203B, 204T
Elizabeth Saft, Courtesy of New York Public Library 38L, 44
FLPA 228B
Fond Doux Holiday Plantation, St.

Lucia 227B
Fotolia 67, 148, 149T, 151, 207BR, 245, 260, 263, 273
Fotoseeker 305
Geoff Howes/Antigua & Barbuda Tourist Office 56
Getty Images 6M, 7BR, 12/13, 14/15, 16/17, 18, 20, 21, 22, 28, 31, 32, 33, 34, 36, 37, 39, 42/43, 45, 47, 49, 51, 54/55, 63, 64/65T, 64BR, 64BL, 65BL, 65TR, 66, 73, 82, 83, 87, 89BR, 90/91, 92/93, 94/95, 96, 102, 109B, 116, 124/125T, 125BR, 125TR, 132, 133, 135, 136, 153BR, 163, 165, 174, 179T, 186, 201, 204B, 205, 214, 222, 235B, 257, 265, 266/267T, 267BL, 288, 291
Glyn Genin/Apa Publications 170
Grenada Board of Tourism 240, 301
Grenada Cocolate Company 244
Hans Hillewaert 235T
Horizon Yacht Charters 247
iStock 1, 4/5, 7BL, 7MR, 7TR, 8T, 9BR, 10T, 11T, 19B, 24, 26/27, 29, 41, 60, 62, 69, 71, 79, 84, 85, 86, 88/89T, 88BR, 89TR, 97B, 105, 106T, 106B, 108B, 114, 115, 118, 119, 120, 121, 122B, 123, 128, 129, 131, 137, 138B, 139B, 141, 143, 146B, 149B, 150T, 150B, 160, 175, 179B, 190B, 191, 200B, 207TR, 212B, 218, 221, 223, 225, 228T, 229B, 236, 241, 246B, 252, 254T, 254B, 267TR, 268, 271B, 274/275, 276, 281, 283, 289, 290, 292T, 293T, 294, 315, 317, 318, 320, 325
Jamaica National Library 35, 38R
Jean-Marc Lecerf/The Guadeloupe Island Tourist Board 184/185, 194
Jim Bleak 264B
John Whitaker 271T
Jolly Beach Hotel & Spa/ fotoseeker.com 176T
Kevin Cummins/Apa Publications 89BL, 207BL
Library of Congress 156
Luc Olivier/Martinique Tourist Board 134T, 209, 213, 216B, 217
Martin Rosefeldt/Apa Publications 253T
Martinique Tourist Board 208,

211, 212T
Monserrat Volcano Observatory 6BR
Montserrat Volcano Observatory 180
Mustique D.A.M. 237T
Nevis Tourism Authority 164, 169
Philippe Giraud/The Guadeloupe Island Tourist Board 187, 190T, 192, 193B, 195
Pictures Colour Library 7ML, 259, 266BL
Press Association Images 23, 65BR
Public domain 30, 117, 183T, 183B, 193T, 216T, 220
Rawlins Plantation Inn 166T
Robert Harding 57, 59
Saint Lucia Tourist Board 125BL, 219, 229T
Scott Lowden/Aruba Tourism Authority 285
Shutterstock 9TL, 9BL, 10B, 11B, 25, 50, 103, 107, 108T, 130, 138T, 139T, 146T, 155, 158B, 168, 176B, 267ML, 286, 287T, 287B, 292B, 293B
SKNweb 167
Spice Mill 166B
St Eustatius Tourist Board/Nicole Esteban 158T
St Maarten Tourist Bureau 134B, 140
St Maarten Tourist Bureau/Claude Cavalera 61
St Vincent & the Grenadines Tourist Office 230
St Vincent & the Grenadines Tourist Office/Chris Caldicot 238BL
SuperStock 142, 154, 238BR, 239BL, 239BR, 256
Sylvaine Poitau/Apa Publications 206/207T, 243
TopFoto 48
Tourism Corporation Bonaire 153ML
Trinidad & Tobago Tourism Development Company 8B, 68, 239TR, 261, 262, 267BR, 269, 272, 306
U.S. Virgin Islands Department of Tourism 109T, 110, 111, 113
Werner Forman Archive 78

*Cover Credits*

**Front cover:** Tropical beach *iStock*
**Back cover:** Marina Cay, BVI *iStock*
**Front flap:** (from top) Flamingos in Aruba *iStock*; reef in St. Lucia *Saint Lucia Tourist Board*; Carnival in Barbados *iStock*; Ti punch *Shutterstock*
**Back flap:** St. Thomas *iStock*

## Insight Guide Credits

**Distribution**
**UK, Ireland and Europe**
Apa Publications (UK) Ltd;
sales@insightguides.com
**United States and Canada**
Ingram Publisher Services;
ips@ingramcontent.com
**Australia and New Zealand**
Woodslane; info@woodslane.com.au
**Southeast Asia**
Apa Publications (SN) Pte;
singaporeoffice@insightguides.com
**Hong Kong, Taiwan and China**
Apa Publications (HK) Ltd;
hongkongoffice@insightguides.com
**Worldwide**
Apa Publications (UK) Ltd;
sales@insightguides.com
**Special Sales, Content Licensing and CoPublishing**
Insight Guides can be purchased in bulk quantities at discounted prices. We can create special editions, personalised jackets and corporate imprints tailored to your needs.
sales@insightguides.com
www.insightguides.biz

**Printed in China by CTPS**

All Rights Reserved
© 2016 Apa Digital (CH) AG and Apa Publications (UK) Ltd

First Edition 1992
Seventh Editon 2016

Every effort has been made to provide accurate information in this publication, but changes are inevitable. The publisher cannot be responsible for any resulting loss, inconvenience or injury. We would appreciate it if readers would call our attention to any errors or outdated information. We also welcome your suggestions; please contact us at:
hello@insightguides.com
**www.insightguides.com**

**Editor:** Sarah Clark
**Author:** Sarah Cameron, Magdalena Helsztynska
**Head of Production:** Rebeka Davies
**Update Production:** AM Services
**Picture Editor:** Tom Smyth
**Cartography:** original cartography Apa Cartography Department, updated by Carte

## Legend

### City maps

| | |
|---|---|
| | Freeway/Highway/Motorway |
| | Divided Highway |
| | Main Roads |
| | Minor Roads |
| | Pedestrian Roads |
| | Steps |
| | Footpath |
| | Railway |
| | Funicular Railway |
| | Cable Car |
| | Tunnel |
| | City Wall |
| | Important Building |
| | Built Up Area |
| | Other Land |
| | Transport Hub |
| | Park |
| | Pedestrian Area |
| | Bus Station |
| | Tourist Information |
| | Main Post Office |
| | Cathedral/Church |
| | Mosque |
| | Synagogue |
| | Statue/Monument |
| | Beach |
| | Airport |

## Contributors

This new edition of **Insight Guide: Caribbean** was updated by travel writer Magdalena Helsztynska and commissioned by Insight Guides editor Sarah Clark. This book builds on the work of Caribbean specialist Sarah Cameron, who has traveled and written on the Americas both as an economist for a British bank and as an author of guide books, as well the original produced by David Schwab.

### Regional maps

| | |
|---|---|
| | Freeway/Highway/Motorway (with junction) |
| | Freeway/Highway/Motorway (under construction) |
| | Divided Highway |
| | Main Road |
| | Secondary Road |
| | Minor Road |
| | Track |
| | Footpath |
| | International Boundary |
| | State/Province Boundary |
| | National Park/Reserve |
| | Marine Park |
| | Ferry Route |
| | Marshland/Swamp |
| | Glacier / Salt Lake |
| | Airport/Airfield |
| | Ancient Site |
| | Border Control |
| | Cable Car |
| | Castle/Castle Ruins |
| | Cave |
| | Chateau/Stately Home |
| | Church/Church Ruins |
| | Crater |
| | Lighthouse |
| | Mountain Peak |
| | Place of Interest |
| | Viewpoint |

## About Insight Guides

**Insight Guides** have more than 45 years' experience of publishing high-quality, visual travel guides. We produce 400 full-colour titles, in both print and digital form, covering more than 200 destinations across the globe, in a variety of formats to meet your different needs.
  **Insight Guides** are written by local authors, whose expertise is evident in the extensive historical and cultural background features.

Each destination is carefully researched by regional experts to ensure our guides provide the very latest information. All the reviews in **Insight Guides** are independent; we strive to maintain an impartial view. Our reviews are carefully selected to guide you to the best places to eat, go out and shop, so you can be confident that when we say a place is special, we really mean it.

# INDEX

*Main references are in bold type*

# INSIGHT GUIDES
TRAVEL MADE EASY. ASK LOCAL EXPERTS.

# UNIQUE HOLIDAYS, CHOSEN BY YOU
## Dream it. Find it. Book it.

**COLLECT YOUR VOUCHER**
insightguides.com/2016
code: BOOKS2016

# MORE THAN 30 DESTINATIONS

 PLANNING MADE EASY

 LOCAL EXPERTS

 TAILOR-MADE

 BOOK SECURELY

**10%**
DISCOUNT
OFF YOUR NEXT BOOKING

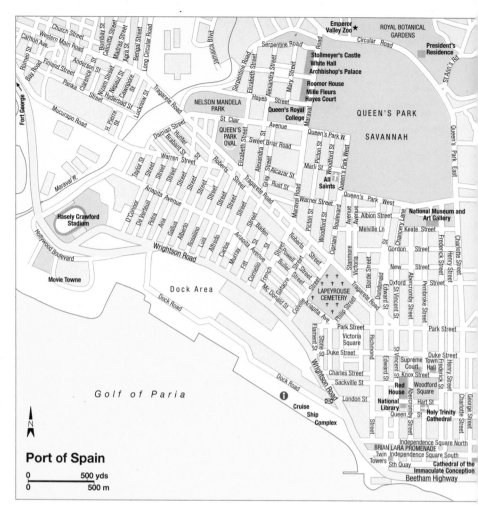